ADVENTURES IN CONSERVATION WITH FRANKLIN D. ROOSEVELT

ADVENTURES IN CONSERVATION

WITH

FRANKLIN D. ROOSEVELT

by IRVING BRANT

Foreword by STEWART UDALL

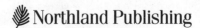 Northland Publishing

Frontispiece : *Irving Brant in his office, winter 1936-37
(photograph courtesy Ruth Brant Davis).*

The publisher wishes to gratefully acknowledge the cooperation of the Brant family members, including Marc Gaede, the author's grandson; the Franklin D. Roosevelt Library, Hyde Park; and the Trustees of the Ansel Adams Publishing Rights Trust in securing photographs to illustrate this volume. All photographs by Ansel Adams and Marc Gaede are copyrighted by the photographers, and the balance are also protected. No reproduction of these images is permitted without express permission by the copyright holder and/or the publishing company.

Also by *Irving Brant*

Dollars and Sense	The Bill of Rights
Storm Over the Constitution	James Madison and American Nationalism
James Madison: The Virginia Revolutionist	The Fourth President
James Madison: The Nationalist	Impeachment
James Madison: Father of the Constitution	
James Madison: Secretary of State	
James Madison: The President	*Fiction*
James Madison: Commander in Chief	Friendly Cove
Road to Peace and Freedom	The Cave of Kingarew
The New Poland	The Youngest Argonaut

ISBN 0-87358-474-0
Library of Congress Catalog Card Number 88-60919
Composed and printed in the United States of America

Library of Congress Cataloging-in-Publication Data

Brant, Irving, 1885–1976
Adventures in conservation with Franklin D. Roosevelt.

Bibliography: p.
Includes index.
1. Roosevelt, Franklin D. (Franklin Delano),
1882–1945—Views on conservation. 2. Environmental
protection—United States—History—20th century. 3. National
parks and reserves—United States—History—20th century.
4. Conservation of natural resources—United States—
History—20th century. 5. United States—History—1933-1945.
6. Brant, Irving, 1885–1976. I. Title.
E807.B74 1988   973.917   88-60919
ISBN 0-87358-474-0

Designed by Lisa Dunning Maps by Robin Brant Lodewick
Typeset in Galliard by Arrow Graphics & Typography, Missoula, Montana

CONTENTS

FOREWORD

In many ways, Irving Brant was a representative American of the first half of the twentieth century. Reared in the small Iowa town of Walker—later in Clinton—by parents who were covered-wagon immigrants, he was nurtured in an area where he could savor the grandeur of the Middle West's relatively unsullied environment at the turn of the century. As a young newspaper reporter on the *Iowa City Republican*, Brant fell under the influence of Henry George's brand of progressivism; then, still in his twenties, he was named editor of the *Clinton Herald*. At thirty-three he was in Missouri as assistant editor (later editor) of the editorial page of the *St. Louis Star*.

A young man with a creative mind, Irving had a near-successful fling as a playwright before he immersed himself in the conservation issues that would occupy much of his life. This transition came in 1925 on a family auto excursion that started in the snows of Yosemite and ended in his outrage at the desecration he witnessed at the Petrified Forest National Monument.

In his initial venture into the thicket of conservation controversies, Brant dashed off an angry article for the *Saturday Evening Post* that read: "Day by day and month by month, the Petrified Forest of Arizona is being looted and smashed to pieces by the motoring public of America . . . [and] the government of the United States is virtually on the side of the looters." Fortunately for posterity, Irving Brant's baptism at the Petrified Forest converted him

". . . into a conservationist for life," and put him on a crusader's path that eventually brought him into Franklin D. Roosevelt's inner circle as a trusted advisor on resource issues.

Although he was a major figure in the conservation movement for over thirty years (and performed some of his final, sterling work for the Interior Department during my tenure) the main focus of this book is on policy disputes that were dominant in the New Deal years. As the self-appointed point man in many of these controversies, Brant wrote speeches and strategy papers for FDR and for Secretary of the Interior Harold Ickes. What enlivens the pages of this volume are the vividly written, blow-by-blow accounts of the big fights that made history during those years.

What also makes this volume exciting reading for every person interested in our conservation history is that Irving Brant was a keen-eyed historian who preserved all of his papers and used a trenchant pen to recount what he remembered about the great years under FDR. Another factor that adds historical resonance to every page of this book is that even while Brant was collaborating with Roosevelt, he was simultaneously working in the Library of Congress on his multi-volume biography of President James Madison. This coincidence gave the author extra insights into the character, personality, and presidential working habits of President Franklin D. Roosevelt.

Brant's text describes a chief executive who was also a committed conservationist. The picture is of a model president who was always mentally fresh, always interested in the crucial details—and always ready to pick up the telephone and issue orders to his subordinates. Brant studied "his" president with a photographic mind, and one of the poignant passages in this work is his description of Roosevelt's shocking physical deterioration on the eve of the 1944 election. Brant, ever the authentic reporter, wrote these sorrowful words: "He answered questions slowly, carefully, and with full command of his line of thought. But the old fire was gone, the exuberance had disappeared: he looked tired and wan. The sense of his being in command had vanished."

Conservationists owe a great debt to Irving Brant's daughters, Ruth and Robin, for having the love and tenacity to bring to publication this splendid book that their father completed in the last year of his life.

Stewart L. Udall

PREFACE

I rving Brant was always, until now, the overseer of his manuscripts. The writing of the conservation book occupied the last three years of his life, but when he finished the final chapter in May 1976, his failing eyesight interfered with revision. Therefore the text finally had four editors, the first being Brant's daughters, Robin Lodewick and Ruth Davis. Lodewick checked sources in the Irving Brant Papers at the Library of Congress and the Presidential Papers at the Franklin D. Roosevelt Library, while Davis did general editing in consultation with Lodewick, who had firsthand knowledge of the subject matter. Harold K. Steen and Alice Ingerson, both of the Forest History Society, then undertook to reduce the overlong text by one fourth. As a last step, Davis and Lodewick reedited. Surprisingly, they were often able to restore Brant's wording when it had been lost through paraphrase. After all the winnowing, especially of quoted material, the present text is more Brant's than was the original.

A number of people helped by their strong belief that the book must be published: foremost among them, Holway Jones, Harvey Manning, David Brower, and Harold K. Steen. Thanks for their assistance are due also to the University of Oregon library staff, and to Peter Edge (for permission to quote from the letters of Rosalie Edge), Virginia Bruckart Pagter, Carsten Lien, and Sylvia Sloan. Susan McDonald of Northland Publishing has brought enthusiasm and knowledge to presenting the story of Roosevelt's and Brant's conservation efforts.

We wish Brant had known that Ansel Adams played a role in the creation of Kings Canyon National Park. With that purpose, he visited Washington in 1936 with a portfolio of photographs to show to congressmen. Adams's 1938 book, *The Sierra Nevada and the John Muir Trail*, also served to promote the park. When Harold Ickes showed his own copy to FDR, the president, in Adams's word, "commandeered" it for the White House. Marc Gaede, the other photographer for Brant's book, has worked as Adams's assistant. He is Brant's grandson. Our thanks and Gaede's go to Virginia Adams and the Ansel Adams Foundation for allowing the use of Adams's photographs.

ROBIN BRANT LODEWICK
RUTH BRANT DAVIS

Main road in Petrified Forest, 1925. Photo by Irving Brant.

CHAPTER ONE

CRISES IN CONSERVATION:
BEFORE FDR

Although I had enjoyed the out-of-doors and wildlife since childhood, my active participation in the conservation movement had its start on a transcontinental motor trip with my wife and two young daughters in 1925. After visiting Yosemite National Park (the first car to get through the snow on the Wawona Road), we swung south to Los Angeles, thence eastward across the Mohave Desert at five miles an hour, driving in ruts that were ten inches deep after a downpour of rain. At the Grand Canyon I hiked to the bottom (round trip fourteen miles) with a husky young basketball player who kept urging me to speed up going down and to slow down going back up. Our route took us next to the Petrified Forest National Monument. It was a scene of vandalized desolation—chunks of agatized wood hammered to pieces on varicolored tree-trunk boulders whose flat tops were reduced to a powdery gray. One look at the awful scene turned me into a conservationist for life.

"Day by day and month by month," I wrote in an article in the *Saturday Evening Post* of June 26, 1926, "the Petrified Forest of Arizona is being looted and smashed to pieces by the motoring public of America . . . the Government of the United States [is] virtually on the side of the looters." Superintendent William Nelson's small staff could not possibly patrol the monument's forty thousand acres effectively. Nelson had told me that visitors carried off petrified wood at the rate of a ton a day. Perhaps my article helped;

1

adequate protection was furnished soon thereafter and the monument ultimately became a national park.

BELEAGUERED WATERFOWL

Publication of the *SEP* article led to larger contacts. Returning to New York in 1926, I first called on George D. Pratt, Standard Oil vice-president and conservationist, who (Superintendent Nelson had told me) was concerned about the monument. Pratt suggested that I write a Sunday-newspaper article in support of legislation, pending in Congress for three years, to establish a national system of waterfowl refuges to implement the Migratory Bird Treaty with Canada. The person to see was John Burnham, president of the American Game Protective Association.

Waterfowl numbers were sinking toward the vanishing point in the 1920s, under the combined pressures of overshooting, land drainage, and frequent droughts. The decline would continue into the 1930s. Combining the plausible guesses of the past with the breeding grounds censuses that were just being instituted, the story of population decline pointed and would continue to point straight toward extinction of all species of ducks: 1870—1 billion; 1930—100 million; 1934—20 million. With seven million hunters holding licenses, the killing of three ducks in 1934 by every licensed hunter would have left not one of these waterfowl alive on the North American continent. Yet in 1929, each hunter was legally entitled to kill twenty-five hundred ducks.

The bill currently before Congress in 1926 provided for a one-dollar-a-year federal waterfowl hunting license, the money to be used to buy land for federal refuges, with a changeable 40 percent of each refuge set aside for public shooting grounds. Burnham filled me in on the arguments for the bill, emphasizing that the shooting grounds were for the "one-gallus" hunter who could not afford membership in a private duck club. He listed a number of supporters and said that virtually the only opponents were Dr. William T. Hornaday, the lately retired curator of the New York Zoological Garden, and Dr. William A. Bruette, publisher of the magazine *Forest and Stream*. When I spoke of going to see them, Burnham said it would be a waste of time to do so—their views were so visionary that they ought to be disregarded. The advice was echoed by a visitor in Burnham's office, the secretary of President Coolidge's National Conference on Outdoor Recreation.

These comments, disparaging the foremost American naturalist-writer and champion of wildlife, and the publisher of an outdoor magazine devoted to conservation, produced their logical effect. Before calling on Dr. Hornaday at his Stamford home, I talked with Bruette. From him I learned that the American Game Protective Association, headed by Burnham, was established, financed, and controlled by the gun and ammunition makers of the United States. Bruette himself was in a difficult situation, caught between his dependence on gun-company advertising and dislike of the trade's policy.

Dr. W. L. Hornaday, curator of the New York Zoological Garden during the 1920s, was considered by many in the American conservation movement to hold "visionary" views (photograph courtesy Department Library Services, American Museum of Natural History, neg. #312378).

The only effective moral support of public shooting grounds in wildlife refuges, Bruette said, was derived from the backing of it by Dr. T. Gilbert Pearson, president of the National Association of Audubon Societies.

My thoughts flashed back to George D. Pratt, to whom I had said that I favored reduction of the twenty-five-per-day limit on ducks. For answer, he had handed me a copy of the Audubon Association's Bulletin No. 6, remarking that it supported the existing bag limits. Pratt's manner seemed to say, "Coming from Audubon, this settles it." So great was my faith then in the Audubon Association, whose magazine *Bird-Lore* had been my boyhood guide, that I postponed a reading.

Taking up this bulletin after my talk with Bruette, I was appalled. Anonymous, it bore an approving foreword by Pearson. Not only did it oppose a bag-limit reduction, but it declared that the number of birds to be killed in a day was an ethical question which "each sportsman must decide . . . for himself." The individual states (most of them notoriously subservient to wealthy gunners) might intervene if a majority of the people so decided, but "the federal government, never." What was going on inside the association that had taken feathers off women's hats? I stored up that question for a future answer.

A partial answer came when Dr. Hornaday, early in our talk at Stamford, pulled out his scrapbooks and showed me one for 1911. It contained reams of New York City newspaper clippings—articles, editorials, and letters to the editor—detailing a fight over a contribution of $125,000 from the gun and ammunition makers, offered to and accepted by the Audubon Association. This sum, to be paid in five annual installments of $25,000, was offered with "no strings attached"—except that executive director T. Gilbert Pearson was to have sole management of the fund and his salary was to be doubled, half of it coming from the gun companies.

At the time this offer was made and accepted, William Dutcher, founder and president of the Audubon Association, lay helpless at his home, permanently paralyzed and unable to speak. After Dutcher's stroke, Pearson, a subordinate, had taken over, later becoming president. Announcement of the gift's offer and acceptance produced a sensation. The *New York Times* cried "scandalous." Floods of protesting letters echoed the cry. On June 16, 1911, the Audubon directors reconvened and revoked their acceptance of the $125,000, which the gunmakers then devoted to establishment of the American Game Protective Association.

Dr. Hornaday described what he called the "shooting-grounds bill," favored by the AGPA, as a device to turn waterfowl refuges into nighttime resting places for ducks and geese, which would fly off in the morning to be shot over natural feeding grounds in the public shooting area, or over "baited" (corn-sprinkled) waters of nearby private duck clubs. His own plan, formulated in the Norbeck-Andresen bill then before Congress, provided for a system of inviolate wildfowl sanctuaries across the nation.

I decided to go ahead with the refuge article, shaping it into an account of the warfare between rival conservation factions, making a full and impartial presentation of the arguments on both sides. In it, no hint was given of my own position until this final "suggestion": "That bird sanctuaries should be permanent and inviolate and that the law creating them should forbid shooting over baited waters in the neighborhood of such refuges."

I was in Florida when the *New York Herald Tribune* published the article on December 5, 1926. Burnham wrote to me in high anger. Conceding that I had respected what he told me in confidence about possible amendments to the bill (I did not tell Hornaday about them, either), he accused me of doublecrossing him and Pratt about the nature of the article. Every favorable argument was accompanied by a rebuttal, he said. I replied that the converse was equally true: every unfavorable argument was rebutted, and I was not responsible if one set of arguments outweighed the other. My own opinion of their relative weight, I said, was governed entirely by what I had learned during the investigation.

From Florida we went to Victoria, British Columbia, where, in April 1928, Dr. Hornaday wrote me about the "triumphant passage" by the Senate of Senator Norbeck's bill to create a nationwide system of inviolate waterfowl refuges—no public shooting grounds. "The old gang"—Nelson, chief of the Biological Survey; Burnham; Pearson—exulted Hornaday, "have been completely unhorsed."

As part of my research for a historical novel, the Canadian government allowed me to spend six weeks as a low-paying guest on the lighthouse tender *Estevan*, during a working cruise around Vancouver Island. This put me in touch with isolated Indian settlements along the roadless west coast, with opportunity for exploration. A ten-mile hike between two lighthouses introduced me to the marvelous coastal rain forests of gigantic conifers rooted on decaying stumps and logs, festooned with moss, which extended from southern Oregon to Alaska.

I continued my historical research after the summer of 1928 at the University of California's Bancroft Library. When I wrote to Hornaday that we would probably spend the winter of 1929-30 in the East, I received an enthusiastic letter from him that concluded, "You are wanted, HERE!" If I would come and fight for congressional action on a bag-reduction bill, Hornaday's Permanent Wild Life Protection Fund would "pay $400 [actually $650] worth of your expenses in Washington next January and February." In a few months, after six years as a free-lance writer, I would return to the editorship of the *St. Louis Star*, but now I accepted Hornaday's offer.

Arriving in New York, I learned that Hornaday had been trying since early spring to induce Senator Charles L. McNary of Oregon to introduce the bag-limits bill. So I wrote the senator a letter which Hornaday, in his characteristic enthusiasm (when he wasn't in despair), termed "a masterstroke of initiative, logic and persuasion." McNary on September 18 wired this reply: "Enjoyed contents your letter thirteenth and have just notified Mr. Hornaday that I would sponsor in the Senate a bill reducing the bag limit on migratory birds. I should be glad to have your kind cooperation." Representative Gilbert N. Haugen of Iowa, chairman of the House Committee on Agriculture, soon made a similar commitment to Dr. Hornaday. Thus the way was opened for joint introduction of the McNary-Haugen bill, cutting bag limits on ducks from twenty-five to fifteen per day, and on geese from eight to four.

The forces opposing the bill were powerful. Wealthy sportsmen and commercial duck clubs fought with fanatical desperation to preserve bag limits and hunting methods that put the extermination of waterfowl only a few years ahead. Representing the rich shooters was their corporate amalgam, the American Wild Fowlers, organized in 1928 to work for high bag limits, also many powerful smaller groups. Lined up with them were the American Game Protective Association, propaganda organ of the gunmakers, and the National Association of Audubon Societies, once the most aggressive champion of wildlife in the country. State and local Audubon societies, two hundred in number, were still faithful to the principles of the founder, William Dutcher, but were almost totally ignorant of the national association's affairs.

Capping it all, the federal regulatory body—the Biological Survey—was completely obedient to these forces of destruction, and the secretary of agriculture leaned in the same direction. Adding solemnity to farce, the secretary had an advisory board on waterfowl regulations, permanently chaired since 1918 by John Burnham of the gunmakers' AGPA, who also informally selected the board's members. These included T. Gilbert Pearson of the Audubon Association, who regularly helped Burnham defeat resolutions for bag-limit reduction—until 1926, when the advisory board under western-state pressures generated by rank-and-file hunters astonished both sides by voting sixteen to two to reduce the limit. Pearson was ill and absent, but an Audubon director, Dr. George B. Grinnell, cast one of the two votes against reduction. The Biological Survey, which had previously treated advisory-board advice as binding, rejected it this time.

On December 2 and 3, 1929, I attended the annual American Game Conference in New York City as official representative (though not a member) of the conservation-minded Associated Sportsmen of California. There I teamed up with John P. Cuenin, sports columnist of the *San Francisco Examiner*. This conference was financed by the Sporting Arms and Ammunition Manufacturers Institute through the American Game Protective Association, with the principal officers of the Remington Arms Company and Western Cartridge Company as decision-making overseers of the meeting. Cuenin and I decided to push for a resolution to reduce bag limits. We put the matter up to Spencer T. Olin, secretary of Western Cartridge and son of its president. He affirmed that he personally favored reducing the limit, but admitted his company could not afford to support such reductions openly.

We could not find Marcellus H. Dodge, head of Remington Arms, but were told he felt the same way (a fact later confirmed by Dodge to Hornaday). John M. Phillips of Pittsburgh[1] then told Cuenin and me that if the resolutions committee refused to recommend bag-limit reduction he would submit a resolution himself and force a floor fight on it. We reported all this to conference chairman J. W. Titcomb, superintendent of the Connecticut State Board of Fisheries and Game, and Titcomb tried to consult Chief Paul Redington of the Biological Survey but could not locate him. Then word spread that Olin and Dodge regarded reduction as inevitable and wanted a resolution passed to avoid a floor fight harmful to industry interests.

The upshot was that without reaching Redington, J. W. Titcomb (whose state was "owned" by the gunmakers) brought a resolution out of the committee room and submitted it to Cuenin, Phillips, and me. It was written, he said, by Dr. Pearson of the Audubon Association (to make himself look good, we were told later). The resolution said not a word about bag limits; it provided only advice to reduce the kill and an appeal for more wardens. "Better have a weak resolution adopted," said Cuenin, "than a strong one beaten."

We approved it and unanimous adoption followed. Actually, the wording was immaterial. The whole bag-limit battle was won when Western Cartridge and Remington Arms decided to prevent a fight. The gun-and-ammunition industry had changed fronts, and thereby changed government policy without a word to or by the official regulators.

The Biological Survey got the message. The advisory board hastily advised a reduction and on December 31 the Survey cut the bag limit on ducks from twenty-five to fifteen per day and on geese from eight to four. This of course killed the McNary-Haugen bill as it then stood. Dr. Hornaday, to prevent a future reversal by the Survey, still wanted to press for the bill's passage, and I wanted a hearing held in order to make it a forum for abolition of shooting over baited waters.

Reaching Washington early in the first week of 1930, I called at once on chairman Haugen and found him thoroughly committed to his bag-limits bill but inclined on account of his age to let others on the agricultural committee take the lead. The driving force for conservation, I quickly found, lay in August H. Andresen of Minnesota (co-creator of waterfowl sanctuaries), John C. Ketcham of Michigan, Thomas Hall of North Dakota, and David H. Kincheloe of Kentucky—all from states where duck baiting had not taken hold. All of them showed eagerness to go beyond the McNary-Haugen bill by shortening seasons and prohibiting baiting and the use of live decoys. Indeed, Kincheloe bawled me out for not bringing up these subjects at the outset of our talk. "The trouble with you fellows," he said, "is that you don't have nerve enough to ask for what you want." It was good to hear that untruth from a congressional committee member. Congressman Andresen had two reasons for being emphatically opposed to baiting. In addition to being destructive it was monopolistic: when he went out onto the open waters of the Potomac to hunt, he failed to get a single shot—all the birds had been

7

decoyed onto baited preserves.

Probing the lower levels of the Biological Survey—the technicians—I learned that the most severe pressures upon the bureau came from a game-hog minority in Congress, and most heavily from Senator Lawrence C. Phipps of Colorado, who seemingly had been sent to the Senate to represent the Bear River Duck Club of Utah, the most prestigious collection of millionaire sportsmen west of the Mississippi. Biologist Dr. W. B. Bell told me that, just before Survey chief E. W. Nelson resigned in 1927, he had seen "Senator Phipps seize Dr. Nelson by the neck and shake him . . . as a terrier shakes a rat."

Thus fortified I made an appointment, as Hornaday's representative, to call on Paul G. Redington, chief of the Biological Survey since 1928. Almost at my first technical question Redington called in Associate Chief W. L. Henderson, and the three of us talked for two hours. After the pattern of conversation developed, I remarked that Henderson appeared to be running the bureau. Redington, a transferee from the Forest Service, admitted that he had heard—but said he did not believe—that the American Game Protective Association was founded and financed by the gun companies. Such ignorance seemed incredible. He also did not know that George A. Lawyer, as chief U.S. game warden but de facto as head of the bureau, had represented the gunmakers' interests. Henderson insisted that Lawyer and any undue influence were both gone from the bureau. I then pointed out that, whatever his motives, Henderson had consistently acted to delay new measures for protecting waterfowl. For example, at hearings on a bill to ban use of the automatic shotgun he had said twice as much in favor of the shotgun as he had against it. Although we all agreed that insufficient funds made it difficult to enforce hunting regulations, I suggested that baiting would be abolished within the next five years, and that Congress was more likely to appropriate money for a truly effective program of protection than for small-scale changes.

Henderson responded that abolishing baiting would reduce property values and might therefore be illegal. So, baiting was to be continued, under their concept of due process of law, to preserve the value of million-dollar marsh properties whose value would automatically sink back to two dollars an acre as soon as baiting wiped out the waterfowl. On that same day (January 7, 1930) I typed a nine-page, single-spaced questions-and-answers reproduction of the interview as nearly as I could remember it. I sent this account at once to Dr. Hornaday, with surprising results.

My letter arrived, he wrote on January 9, during a strategy meeting in his Stamford office with Dr. Bruette and Edmond Seymour, Wall Street broker and chairman of the Committee of One Hundred on game protection (which consisted largely of himself). Hornaday wrote to me that my letter had broken a strategic "impasse" and inspired them to set their sights high. The course it inspired coincided exactly with the desires of the agricultural committee progressives as I described them in a letter which crossed this one from

Hornaday. These men, I said, were "intelligent, sincere, friendly to wild life, and ready to do something." As a guest at a Potomac River club, Andresen had been sickened by the sight of shooting over bait. Quoting Kincheloe's remark about our "lack of nerve," I said that although incorrect it did represent a truth: "We will get nowhere without a program big enough to impress Congress." All of these legislators and chairman Haugen, I said, had displayed keen interest in the tie-up between Biological Survey policy makers and wealthy sportsmen.

"I believe," I wrote to Hornaday, "that we can knock the Biological Survey higher than a kite. A man like Redington will go down before Kincheloe like a piece of cheese. But it cannot be done by talking about bag limits."

My talk with Redington and Henderson quickly produced repercussions. I was told that Nash Buckingham, lobbyist for American Wild Fowlers, wrote to the Remington Arms Company that Henderson had called me "a very dangerous man." The telephone must have been taken off the hook rather quickly after my departure.

Chairman Haugen ordered public hearings on his bill to be held on January 27, 28, and 29, 1930. This sent the American Wild Fowlers into action with a telegram to all state game departments, national protective associations, and outdoor magazines. After first describing the bill, Wild Fowlers president John C. Phillips went on to warn that the "fanatical sentimentalists" who supported the bill "apparently favor little or no shooting" at all. One of the telegram's recipients, Harry McGuire, editor of *Outdoor Life*, furnished us with the Phillips telegram and his own telegram in reply, in which he charged that "U.S. Biol Survey as at present administered has opened itself to charge of being puppet of a wealthy clique of sportsmen of which you are one. . . . Outdoor Life strongly urges congressional investigation of present Survey administration."

The millionaire sportsmen heard the call and descended on Washington for the hearing, swamping the conservationists in number of spectators. The hearing opened with a letter from the secretary of agriculture opposing any legislation on bag limits as harmful in principle and needless in practice. Several southern congressmen then dutifully supported their states in behalf of the duck clubs and their paid guides.

Dr. Hornaday opened the case for the bill, citing principally the danger of a return to the twenty-five-a-day limit unless Congress in response set a lower maximum. Senator Harry Hawes of Missouri then defended the automatic shotgun. Given that no one at the hearing had said anything about that weapon, I supposed that someone had reported to Hawes my remarks to Henderson. The Campfire Club of America then characterized the bill as nothing except an attack on the Biological Survey.

The hearing really got onto track next day when Redington was given a going-over by committee members—particularly Kincheloe of Kentucky. The Survey, Redington said, based all its regulations on factual investigation of the waterfowl situation. That had caused it, in the past, to abolish spring shooting and the commercial marketing of ducks and geese. Questioned, he put the estimated waterfowl population at 80 to 100 million, and still diminishing. A closed season would cut off too much state revenue; all he could suggest, in that direction, was complete protection of the most-endangered species until they built up in numbers. The hearing then turned to a subject I was waiting for. Andresen of Minnesota asked, "What is your personal opinion as to doing away with shooting over baited waters?"

Redington answered that there were "two angles to this question." In rare cases baiting was harmful, where food was scarce and water area limited. Otherwise, baiting helped the birds survive; they had more to eat and might be spread out away from the hunters. Redington admitted under questioning that hunters used the bait to draw ducks to their guns. Kincheloe then asked whether baiting was a conservation measure. Redington's replies were that it was not "doing the damage it is alleged to do" and that there were "certainly two sides to the proposition."

After listening to that "two sides" statement four times, Kincheloe asked, "Which side are you in favor of?" This drew the answer "I am in favor of con-servation, by eliminating baiting when it is shown to be unduly detrimental to the ducks." Joined to his other testimony, that seemed to make baiting a conservation measure when detrimental, if not unduly so.

I followed Redington to the stand, appearing as representative of the Associated Sportsmen of California (a large group of occasional shooters) and Dr. Hornaday's Permanent Wild Life Protection Fund. During the preceding evening, Dr. Bruette and I had agreed that it was necessary to expose the inac-tivity and harmful lies of the Audubon Association. In that connection I had searched the files of *Bird-Lore* and found, as expected, complete silence about shooting over baited waters. This led me to ask a California friend to make an inquiry of Audubon president Pearson: What did he think of the rumored congressional attack on baiting? Pearson wired him that the hearing was of no importance, had poor sponsorship, and would get nowhere. The wording was noncommittal, but the pro-baiting bias was unmistakable. Should I use the telegram in my testimony? "Do so," Bruette advised.

I opened by presenting the strongly protectionist views of the California Associated Sportsmen, then, turning to Audubon, made the mistake of jumping into accusation, in the manner of a newspaper editorial campaign. With Pearson sitting right in front of me, I read his telegram, telling how it was obtained. Congressman John D. Clarke of New York stopped me. The committee was there, he said, to consider a bill, not to pass on disagreements among conservation organizations. When I tried to bring up the $125,000 gift to Audubon by the gun and ammunition makers, the opposition in-creased to an uproar. Clarke moved that all remarks on the subject be stricken from the record. No vote was taken on that, and I went on with testimony against baiting and for lower bag limits.

I learned next day how a controversy of this type should be handled. Dr. Bruette of *Forest and Stream* took the stand *as an opponent* of the bag-reduction bill, thus (incidentally) getting his time charged to the opposition. He made no opening statement but offered to answer questions. These led him to express the opinion, based largely on reader reaction to his magazine, that "90 percent of the sportsmen of this country favor . . . reduction of this bag limit"; the waterfowl crisis, he predicted, would produce a call for greater reductions. Gradually the questioning turned to the Biological Survey, whose staff he praised highly for competence and good intentions—but it acted too slowly. Bruette then remarked that this was partly out of fear that Congress would reduce the agency's appropriations, but that "there was another side to that, if you want to bring it out." The committee certainly did. This gave Bruette his chance to suggest that organizations favoring the current bag limits, including the Audubon Association, had been closely affiliated with the Biological Survey.

Questioned further by Kincheloe of Kentucky, Bruette said that the secretary of agriculture's advisory board, the American Game Protective Association, and Audubon were "closely interlocked." Kincheloe thought that this pointed toward action by Congress. When Bruette's time expired, the chairman said he was not sure to which side his testimony was to be charged. The record then shows that I offered to give Bruette our remaining time, if his time to that point was charged to the opposition.

So Dr. Bruette went on, the committee pursuing further his comment about interlocking directorates. Remarking that Dr. T. S. Palmer of the Biological Survey was vice-president of the Audubon Association, Bruette said there was no finer or more competent official in the government. "But," he continued, "I do not like affiliation with an organization collecting money from the public . . . an organization that gets on both sides of every question connected with conservation. They are on both sides, and they collect money from both sides, and the man at the head of the organization gets a percentage of what is collected."

This was more devastating than anything I had said or planned to say about T. Gilbert Pearson, but, being a part of criticism of a government bureau, it did not provoke a peep of censure. Indeed, one congressman remarked in an unrecorded aside that Bruette was a "square shooter." So he was, and he could hit a target located around the corner.

Dr. Pearson, following Bruette to the stand, denied that the Audubon Association had ever accepted contributions "from any source that might be questionable—gun makers, ammunition manufacturers, or anything else of that sort." (In his lexicon, apparently, public acceptance of $125,000 from gun and ammunition makers, followed by revocation amid public outcries, did not constitute acceptance.) The givers of money were "simply doctors and lawyers, bird lovers, and the public generally throughout the country."

Pearson took up Bruette's reference to the Audubon organization "speaking out against [reduction of] bag limits." What really happened, said Pearson, was that when reports came in of the "enormous increase in ducks because of stopping of spring shooting and stopping of sale," Charles Sheldon, "a man of very great erudition in game matters," prepared an analysis of the bag-limit laws and concluded that the average legal kill of ducks was fifteen per day.

This was misleading. Dr. Pearson neglected to mention three facts: (1) when Audubon published and endorsed Sheldon's anonymous pamphlet, in May 1926, the "enormous increase" that followed reforms of the 1910-20 decade had long since changed into calamitous declines; (2) the main thrust of the Sheldon pamphlet was that all federal waterfowl regulations should be abandoned as unconstitutional and the subject left to the states (where protection was poorest where it was most needed); (3) Charles Sheldon, the "man of very great erudition in game matters," whose authorship of the Audubon bulletin was thus revealed by Pearson, was the first chairman of the executive committee of American Wild Fowlers, the propaganda arm of the duck hunters' clubs of America.

Late in his testimony Pearson was asked by Congressman Andresen whether he desired to say anything "in connection with the attack made upon you yesterday, to the effect that the Audubon Society was not in favor of conservation, or that you were not a conservationist yourself." Pearson replied that he would stand on his and the association's thirty-year record, "which is pretty well known." Asked why the attack was made, he replied, "From that source it has been coming for a great many years." That put the assessed blame on Dr. Hornaday and carried the issue back to Pearson's 1911 acceptance and forced relinquishment of the gunmakers' money.

At the request of Dr. Pearson, chairman Haugen followed the waterfowl hearing with a next-day hearing on a Pearson-sponsored bill for protection of the bald eagle as the national emblem. The obvious purpose of the bill and hearing was to counter a pamphlet attack on Pearson by three Audubon members for his seven-year failure to join the battle against the Alaska eagle bounty which had led to the destruction of seventy thousand eagles. Facetious comments by the committee members turned the hearing into a disaster for both Pearson and the bald eagle. Alaska delegate Dan Sutherland completed the rout when he read aloud a magazine article declaring the bald eagle unworthy to be the national emblem. The article had appeared in *Bird-Lore*; its publisher—T. Gilbert Pearson.

By this time I had discovered that the agricultural committee members, individually, were much friendlier to me than they had been collectively. John Clarke, who had led the bombardment of me in the hearing, told me that I was "lucky to get out of the room alive with that bunch of duck-club men around." Several members of the committee, I reported to Hornaday, had later "volunteered their opinion that the [waterfowl] hearing uncovered something that ought to be uncovered."

Ten days after the bald-eagle hearing, chairman Haugen appointed a sub-committee of three to decide what to do about my testimony attacking Pearson. Its chairman, Ketcham of Michigan, was friendly to me. He told me that the members desired to smooth out the record without depriving it of substance, which, as I commented, the controversy had obscured. We agreed that I should recast my testimony, replacing the eliminated material with a description of the pressure exerted on the Biological Survey by the American Wild Fowlers. This would shift the heaviest blame for the breakdown of the regulatory system from a weak government bureau to its powerful mis-guiders. Ketcham closed a second conversation with this astonishing remark: "The members of the committee are more anxious to eliminate the remarks of its members than to get your stuff out." This meant that those who had defended Pearson wanted no public record of their defense; and it meant that the record of the hearing would be printed, regardless of whether or not the Haugen bill was reported for passage. Ketcham already had indicated this by saying, "There will be plenty in the record to show the situation surrounding the Biological Survey without any personal criticisms."

Besides my criticisms of Pearson, the committee struck out a personal at-tack on Dr. Hornaday by Marshall McLean of the Campfire Club and one sentence spoken by Senator Harry Hawes of Missouri. This first-term senator, after defending the automatic shotgun from a non-existent attack, had devoted seven words of his testimony to the bag-limit bill. "Its only sup-porters," he said—and here he looked straight at Hornaday and me—"are two old grannies." That remark was left out of the printed record, along with my concealed grin. Dr. Bruette, long intimate with Hawes, later told me enough about him to show that the Missouri senator was a paid agent of the gun companies for influence on the drafting of the Smoot-Hawley tariff. Hornaday confirmed this information. Thus it came as no surprise when Hawes's next job, when his Senate term ended, was as a paid Washington lob-byist for the gunmakers.

THE EMERGENCY CONSERVATION COMMITTEE

One of the by-products of the 1930 conflicts over waterfowl was organization of the Emergency Conservation Committee of New York City. Preliminary to this, in June 1929, a striking manifesto entitled *A Crisis in Conservation* had been published by Dr. W. DeWitt Miller of the American Museum of Natural History (also vice-president of the New Jersey Audubon Society); Dr. Willard G. Van Name, a biologist at the same museum; and Davis Quinn, a youth of no renown. Sounding a well-documented alarm over the threatened immi-nent extinction of nine varieties of birds and danger to twenty-six more, these men accused the National Association of Audubon Societies of chronic inac-tion and gave a clarion call to conservation organizations to wake up.

The American Museum, whose high officers included secretary Frank M. Chapman and treasurer Robert Cushman Murphy of the Audubon Associa-

Willard G. Van Name, respected biologist at the American Museum of Natural History, was considered the "spiritual godfather and non-wealthy financial backer" of the Emergency Conservation Committee (photograph courtesy Department Library Services, American Museum of Natural History, neg. #125302).

tion, reacted at once. Dr. Van Name was forbidden to publish anything under his own name without the museum's prior approval. Dr. Miller had just been killed in an automobile collision—a terrible loss to the nation. A month after his death George H. Sherwood, director of the museum, put out a statement "in regard to a pamphlet entitled *A Crisis in Conservation*." Eulogizing the Audubon Association, praising federal game-law enforcement, Sherwood declared that not a single member of the staff, qualified to speak by experience and information, agreed with Miller and Van Name. "The Museum is, therefore, of the opinion that the alleged 'Crisis in Conservation' exists largely in the minds of the authors of this pamphlet."

Dr. Bruette was specifically requested to publish a statement in *Forest and Stream*. He did so in November 1929, embedding it in a two-page editorial which I wrote. The editorial expressed regret that the partisan-toned comments about Dr. Miller were not made before his death instead of so soon after that tragic event. I presented the Audubon record on conservation and described so extensive an interlock between that body and the museum that (I said) the "defense of the Audubon Society by the American Museum turns out to be a defense of the Audubon Society by the Audubon Society."

This article led to a telephone call from Rosalie (Mrs. Charles N.) Edge, who wanted Dr. Bruette to publish an account of what had happened when she tried to bring up *A Crisis in Conservation* at the annual Audubon meeting. At Bruette's suggestion I called on Mrs. Edge and was impressed by her keen mind, fighting spirit, and devotion to conservation. In February I wrote to her that I was "very much inclined to write a detailed history of Pearson's record." She replied, "Our need is a small committee to sponsor such pamphlets. . . . Would you like to be a member of such a committee?"

So was born the Emergency Conservation Committee, with Mrs. Edge chairman, Davis Quinn secretary, and myself treasurer without financial duties. Mrs. Edge was the real treasurer, while I acted as general adviser and occasional pamphlet writer. The committee fully deserved the charge leveled against it by provoked critics, that it was a small, self-appointed body without a parent. Quinn dropped out after a time, the changing membership never exceeded five, and Mrs. Edge and I were the only ones continuously in it during the thirty-two years of its existence.

However, the ECC started off with a spiritual godfather and nonwealthy financial backer in Dr. Van Name, whose standing as a biologist prevented the museum from firing him. A monastic bachelor, he devoted most of his salary and all income from a modest inheritance to protection of wildlife and preservation of scenic forests. Mrs. Edge described him as a man who "lives literally with the poverty of St. Francis and gives all he has."

Brilliantly endowed with insight and foresight, Van Name had been the first to call public attention to virtually every assault on natural resources in the 1920s. He was correspondingly unpopular among the exploiters and the short-visioned. Experience bred a touch of bitterness in him, along with a

15

Mrs. Rosalie Edge at entrance to Hawk Mountain Sanctuary, Pennsylvania (ca. 1940), one of the several conservation efforts to which she devoted her life (photograph courtesy Peter Edge).

tendency to mistake blindness and self-interest for malevolence, but his instincts were right and his conservation policies were invariably sound.

Apart from the personality of Mrs. Edge, the small size of the Emergency Conservation Committee was its greatest asset. It could strike hard on any issue without being toned down by the conflicting interests of a large board of directors or a diverse membership. That was particularly valuable at a time when almost every nationally organized conservation body was in the paralyzing grip of wealthy sportsmen, gun companies, or lumbermen who were devastating whole states with their "cut and run" methods of operation. Usually there was a potential or actual conflict in such organizations between a deluded or dissatisfied membership and subversive directorates. Some avoided controversies to preserve income-tax exemptions.

Mrs. Edge started out with the extensive mailing lists built up by Hornaday and Van Name. Responses to every pamphlet were tremendous. Small donations multiplied and grew. Mailing lists doubled and redoubled. Ultimately she had fourteen thousand names on her list, including more than a thousand "regulars"—many high in political and social position—who would respond to every call for letters or telegrams. Subject matter expanded from wildlife protection to include forest preservation.

Thus my connection with the Emergency Conservation Committee, as adviser and pamphlet writer, projected me into virtually every nationwide conservation fight for more than thirty years, on virtually every subject that arose, except one. Mrs. Edge took complete charge of the campaign against disruption of the balance of nature by an ill-judged strategy of extermination directed against predatory animals or birds of prey. The time came when even a member of the president's cabinet would say to me, on one subject or another, "Can you get Mrs. Edge to put out a pamphlet on this?" Sports columnists derided or denounced her, as did some members of Congress, but in a battle of wits before a congressional committee the effective punches came from her. She was old and bent of frame when her death put an end to the committee, but her spirit never bowed.

The first aim of the Emergency Conservation Committee was to restore the National Association of Audubon Societies to the place it had originally won by its triumph over the feather trade. This had given it a pre-eminence which persisted in the public mind for years after the right to its reputation vanished. Audubon president T. Gilbert Pearson won the first round of this conflict when he raised his automatic shotgun (he had defended that weapon in 1923) and brought down a swan—silencing a major voice for conservation. During the waterfowl hearing in January 1930, Dr. Bruette told me that unidentifiable persons had been trying to purchase *Forest and Stream*, of which he was editor but not owner, for the purpose of ousting him. He said he frustrated the move by securing pledges of funds to buy the magazine himself. But in May came the startling word that *Forest and Stream* had been purchased and suppressed by its rival *Field and Stream*, which in that day was backward on con-

17

servation. Bruette wrote to me that he thought "Audubon put up the money," with the backing of commercial fishermen who were fighting conservationist demands to abolish salmon traps and reduce excessive river netting.

My first ECC pamphlet, *Compromised Conservation: Can the Audubon Society Explain?*, was published early in October 1930, timed to appear seven weeks before the annual meeting of that body. It traced the course of the Audubon Association under Pearson's control, from its 1911 acceptance of the gun-and-ammunition money to its current tie-up with American Wild Fowlers, the gunmakers' American Game Protective Association, the Biological Survey, and the millionaire sportsmen's clubs.

I challenged the Audubon membership to appoint an investigating committee to determine the truth or falsity of Dr. Bruette's statement to a congressional committee that the society stood on both sides of every conservation question and that Pearson's salary was linked to contribution levels. The Audubon annual reports, I asserted, "do not even show what President Pearson receives. . . . They do not show whether Dr. Pearson receives a percentage on gifts, and inquiries receive evasive answers." What, I asked, caused "Administrative Expense," which included his remuneration, to jump five thousand dollars in 1922—the year in which Audubon received a lump-sum gift of two hundred thousand dollars—and drop by almost the same amount in 1923? That was at the heart of the whole question. "For ten years," I wrote, "the aims and ideals and militant spirit of the Audubon Society have been subordinated to the raising of money." Its motto had become "Tread softly, lest an enemy be made."

Knowing that the Audubon–American Museum interlocked directors would blame Dr. Hornaday for the pamphlet, I had not given him even a hint about it. His enthusiasm was conveyed by telegram: "Your Compromised Conservation manifesto is a great piece of constructive conservation. It is scholarly judicial just and devastating to the treachery and chicanery that for seven[teen] long years has ruled the fortunes and misfortunes of the abused and mishandled National Audubon Society. I hope it marks the end of Benedict Arnoldism in that organization."

In a later telegram Hornaday asked for my photograph, to illustrate an article to be published in his conservation periodical *Plain Truth*. My refusal said that anything written about or quoted from me "would sound more authoritative if not accompanied by a visual likeness. I have the kind of physiognomy—be it confessed with humiliation—that causes a policeman to say instinctively, 'Hey, kid, get off the grass.'"

President Pearson had the Audubon annual meeting well under control for the planned counterattack. Aiding him was the Honorable Frederic C. Walcott, gun-and-ammunition senator from Connecticut and chairman of a newly established Senate Select Committee on (pigeonholing) Wild-life Resources (legislation). On Walcott's motion, the membership voted to create a "disinterested" committee of three (who were named in the motion) to investigate the charges made in *Compromised Conservation* and *A Crisis in Conservation*.

Those so chosen were Dr. Alexander G. Ruthven, president of the University of Michigan, a genuinely disinterested man; Dr. Thomas Barbour, curator of the Harvard zoological museum; and Chauncey Hamlin, a lawyer and longtime president of the Buffalo Society of Natural Sciences. Dr. Ruthven took the advice of his friend, ornithologist T. C. Stephens of Morningside College, and declined to serve. Stephens wrote to me that Ruthven was appointed without his (Ruthven's) knowledge, at the instance of Barbour.

That left Barbour and Hamlin as the "disinterested committee." As for the former, Senator Bingham of Connecticut had told a Senate committee on January 25, 1927, that he appeared at the request of Barbour, who had declared to him that a bill to reduce duck bag limits, then under consideration, was "opposed by every responsible naturalist in the country."

The other member, Chauncey Hamlin, was executive director of the president's National Conference on Outdoor Recreation. In that capacity he had called together its excellent game-protection committee and declared it dissolved. By setting up a new committee, he had been able to transfer the chairmanship from John M. Phillips of Pittsburgh, one of the finest conservationists in the country, to Charles M. Sheldon, first executive secretary of American Wild Fowlers and anonymous author of the Audubon Association's Bulletin No. 6, challenging the power of Congress to regulate waterfowl hunting.

Three weeks after this Barbour–Hamlin committee was appointed, I received an inquiry from Dr. E. F. Bigelow, publisher of a bird-study leaflet which, I had heard from Dr. Hornaday, was kept alive by Audubon grants. Bigelow asked me to tell him the motive and history of my "attack upon the Audubon Association," which seemed to him to be "remarkably efficient and well managed." Knowing that I was writing for Pearson's eyes, I replied that my motive was "to help restore the Audubon Society to the place it held and the principles it adhered to in the days of Dutcher and Wilcox. . . . Frankly, the deterioration of the organization seems to be the result of ceaseless thoughts about money. There is only one influence that will sap mental integrity more subtly than the successful solicitation of money, and that is the hope of getting more. When men yield to that influence, they are doomed."

By this time (late November 1930) state and local Audubon societies, and other groups and individuals, were asking for copies of *Compromised Conservation* in such numbers that we ordered a new printing of eight thousand. The next step, I wrote to Mrs. Edge, affirming her own suggestion, should be to obtain the membership list of the national organization and circularize it. If the association persisted in refusing to furnish it to her (she was an Audubon member), "a court action would either force them to do so, or would give them some unpleasant publicity." Denied the list, Mrs. Edge brought suit in the New York courts.

By its own statement, the Barbour–Hamlin "disinterested committee" held just one meeting—"at Dr. Pearson's office, June 24"—and in September it printed a twelve-page report completely clearing Pearson and the association of all charges. The pamphlet *A Crisis in Conservation* was disposed of in a few words: joint-author Miller was dead; Quinn was "completely unknown to fame"; and Van Name was overruled by museum director Sherwood's opinion that "the alleged 'Crisis in Conservation' exists largely in the minds of the authors" of the pamphlet.

The investigating committee then turned to *Compromised Conservation*, a pamphlet "purporting to be written by Irving Brant and distributed by the 'Emergency Conservation Committee.'" The "so-called" committee was "simply a small, self-appointed group representing nothing but certain personal interests." And there was "little point in attempting to analyze the motives of the persons hostile to the Association, who have used this method of attack."

"Certain personal interests" meant Dr. Hornaday, the Audubon treasurer told me. They dared not name him because of his high standing. On the subject of the gunmakers' $125,000 contribution, the committee omitted the amount and presented two short paragraphs with these highlights:

"The first charge concerns the alleged taking of 'Gunmaker's Money.' . . . The Committee cannot agree that there is any moral turpitude involved in being a gunmaker. . . . Not a cent of this money was ever received. . . . At one meeting the sentiment was in favor of acceptance, at the next meeting the offer was refused."

Presented as the result of investigation, the final two sentences quoted above were taken almost word for word from the account given by Pearson himself in the July 1911 issue of *Bird-Lore*. Had Messrs. Barbour and Hamlin gone to the *New York Times* and other newspapers of that period, they would have found that the gun and ammunition companies offered the Audubon Association twenty-five thousand dollars a year for five years in early May, 1911; that the Audubon directors voted six to three in favor of the offer on June 2; that from June 3 to June 5 the New York papers announced—and denounced—the offer; and that the directors rescinded their acceptance on June 16.

The committee made no mention of Audubon "Bulletin No. 6" opposing duck bag reduction, but disposed of the general subject by quoting Governor Al Smith against fixing bag limits by legislative action. It then devoted five thousand words—seven pages out of the nine dealing with my pamphlet—to the trivial question of whether T. Gilbert Pearson's name was printed with or without his approval on the advisory-board list of E. A. McIlhenny's projected four-thousand-member shooting preserve, to be destructively set up between the great Russell Sage and Rockefeller bird sanctuaries on the Gulf Coast. On that subject I had written that Pearson's name was "withdrawn following criticism of his connection with [the project]."

The Barbour–Hamlin report was totally silent on my challenge that the

Audubon directorate admit or disprove Bruette's charge that the association collected money from both sides of every question and that Dr. Pearson "gets a percentage of what is collected."

By odd chance, I was drawn into extensive and friendly correspondence with Audubon treasurer Robert Cushman Murphy on Pearson's remuneration. In a letter whose recipient forwarded it to Murphy, I had written that "officers" of the association admitted a commission basis for his salary. Murphy denied making any such admission. I replied that the admission had been made by Audubon secretary Chapman, in his affidavit answering Mrs. Edge's lawsuit. Dr. Murphy stuck to his own denial, and finally sent me a tabulation of annual gifts to the association and of Pearson's annual remuneration, to show that one was not a percentage of the other.

That was true, but there was still an upturn when gifts went up and a downturn when they dropped. Finally, working by trial and error, I found that each year's presidential "take" was 6 percent of the gifts plus $6,000. Murphy then informed me that this had been changed. Pearson now received 6 percent on all contributions received prior to 1924, up to a total of $14,500. This meant, I replied, that in 1922 he had received 6 percent of the great educational "Wilcox Fund for Children" and was still receiving, each year, an amount equal to 40 percent of the income derived from that educational endowment.

In opening my correspondence with Murphy, I had said that the principal evil of the Pearson salary commission did not lie in the small proportion of gifts received from sportsmen. It lay in "the tendency to put the president under a mental subsidy from all possible givers." In closing the correspondence I wrote, "Has anybody ever made a graver charge of maladministration against the present management . . . than you, the treasurer, have made in your defense of it?" Robert Cushman Murphy, as he proved in later years, was a good conservationist who had been caught in a bad system.

Without waiting for her lawsuit to grind its way through the New York court, Mrs. Edge sent an appeal for proxies to all state and local Audubon societies and to the sizable ECC mailing list. Roger Baldwin, head of the American Civil Liberties Union, determined the format of the appeal. Don't make it a pamphlet, he advised. State your case in a letter "so simply and persuasively that there can be only one answer," all in two or three pages. I wrote the three-page letter, asking thirteen questions, each one a single "do you approve" sentence concerning damaging deviations from early Audubon principles. They centered on Pearson's commissions from sportsmen's organizations and his tie-up with the defenders of waterfowl baiting, coupled with revelation of similar ties for Barbour and Hamlin of the "disinterested" Audubon investigating committee.

The circular, mailed only twelve days before the association's annual meeting, brought Mrs. Edge an amazing 1,646 proxies. The administration, holding 2,806, easily controlled the meeting, but the handwriting was on the wall. I wrote to Mrs. Edge, "Let Pearson gloat, if he feels like it, over the meeting. His whole crowd is on the run."

Two weeks later George D. Pratt, my early consultant on the Petrified Forest, proposed to Roger Baldwin (now an ECC member) that a small group including anybody except Hornaday (this meant Baldwin and Mrs. Edge) should meet with a similar Audubon administration group and work out a set of reforms. The Audubon directorate was agreeable to anything, provided Dr. Pearson was left in office. On that issue the effort aborted. Such was the unsatisfactory situation at the beginning of 1932.

Not until October 1934 did the five-year campaign of the Emergency Conservation Committee to oust President Pearson of the Audubon Association come to a climax. In August of that year Mrs. Edge won a New York court decree requiring the association to give her the names and addresses of its eleven thousand individual members. Pearson gave notice of appeal. "I do not see how we can defend the case," Mrs. Edge wrote to me. Her lawyer's fee for contesting the appeal would be five hundred dollars, payable in advance. Dr. Van Name, financial mainstay of the committee, was unreachable in the Far West. She was suing her husband for the support of their two children, and "I am literally wiped out."

All of this was unknown to Dr. Pearson and his lawyer. To them, as to virtually all of the targets hit by the Emergency Conservation Committee, Mrs. Edge was a New York society woman of unlimited wealth who fed her vanity and her hot temper by dabbling in conservation. "A common scold," Pearson's lawyer called her in a legal paper. However, Pearson himself unwillingly united with Appellate Judge Sherman to break Mrs. Edge from financial stalemate. The judge agreed to hear the appeal, conditioned on postponement of the Audubon Association's annual meeting until two months after the appeal was finally decided. Pearson, envisioning the effect of eleven thousand letters to Audubon members, dropped his appeal. And on October 30 Mrs. Edge sent me a three-word telegram: "Pearson has resigned."

The reason was clear and simple: he could not face an informed membership. The National Association of Audubon Societies changed its name to National Audubon Society, made the presidency an honorary office to which Theodore Roosevelt's son Kermit was elected, and appointed John H. Baker executive director.

Slowly, painfully, still clogged with reactionary directors, the society fought its way back toward the high standards of its founders—standards which two hundred state and local Audubon societies and eleven thousand individual members had never abandoned. At last a miracle, physiologically impossible, was achieved in the field of morality: the National Audubon Society recovered its virginity.

Even while we were building a successful challenge to Pearson's wrongful management of Audubon, other conservation issues demanded attention. Just at the close of the waterfowl hearings in 1930, a controversy over the boundaries of Yellowstone National Park came to a climax. Two bills were involved. The first proposed to extend the park to the southeast, to include the principal habitat of moose and grizzly bears, and to the south, to take in the winter grazing ground of the southern Yellowstone elk herd and the range of the pronghorn antelope. The second bill renewed the perennial effort of private-power interests to take out Bechler Meadows, in the southwestern corner of the park, in order to flood it with a hydroelectric dam. The confident and aggressive Forest Service, strongly backed by the secretary of agriculture, opposed all park additions. On the other side, the politically weak National Park Service was so afraid of losing Bechler Meadows that it took no steps to promote the park's enlargement.

In our family travels, I had become so disgusted with the concessionaire system in the national parks that I had developed a strong bias in favor of the Forest Service's informal administration of the national forests. At the same time I recognized that the national parks provided the only mandatory and complete protection for the nation's scenic forests. I had written in the *New York Times* (on September 22, 1929) about the trend to reduce the national parks by adding to them "untimbered lands at high altitudes" and taking out larger areas of timberland at low elevations, making these available for logging.

In another article, this one in the December 1929 *Forest and Stream*, I criticized the concessionaire monopolies in the national parks. National Park Service director Horace Albright, talking with Dr. Bruette and me, acknowledged that I had my facts straight but denied that the parks were administered primarily for the profit of the concessionaires. Turning to the conflict over Yellowstone Park, Bruette and I both urged Albright to marshal public support for extension of the boundaries.

President Hoover had recently created a Yellowstone National Park Boundary Commission, chaired by Dr. Edward E. Brownell, a San Francisco physician. The commission held a public hearing in Washington, D.C., on February 1, 1930. My own part in the hearing turned into a dialogue with Governor Frank C. Emerson of Wyoming, top man for the opposition. He argued that moose and antelope would be best protected on lands outside the park, under state game and fish commission regulation. I replied that the Wyoming commission had revealed itself four months earlier by proclaiming a six-day open season on pronghorn antelope, previously hunted only by permit. I then read an editorial from the *New York Times* of October 26, 1929, headed "Massacring Antelope"; it called the six-day slaughter a disgrace. I testified that two local ranchers, Phelps and Belden, had told me that the total kill was 2,200 (73% of the herd) in contrast to the game commission's estimate of 1,000. Emerson insisted that neither those two men—on whose property the antelope had been slaughtered—nor the eastern newspapers knew what was really going on in Wyoming. The herd, he claimed, would quickly grow back to its original size. I parried this optimism with Phelps and Belden's observation that the remaining 800 were mostly does and immature bucks, meaning there would be no breeding for at least two years.

Leading the fight against enlarging the park was the Forest Service, which contended that lodgepole pine south of the park (currently unmarketable) must remain in the national forest as a timber reserve. Off the stand the Service was still more active. Before the hearing ended I reached a dismaying conclusion. Van Name and I were sentimental interlopers in a pro-hunting, pro-lumbering, pro-power, anti-park gathering stacked in advance and stage-managed by the Forest Service. At the hearing Ovid Butler, the supposedly impartial editor of *American Forests* and a former Forest Service employee, had led the opposition to enlargement. A former chief forester, William B. Greeley, had resigned in 1928 to become general manager of the West Coast Lumbermen's Association; its member companies, I learned, were the main source of funds for the American Forestry Association, publisher of Butler's *American Forests*. Lesser Forest Service officials had made similar shifts into the timber industry.

The tie-up between the Forest Service and the lumbermen had little direct bearing on the attempt to cut down Yellowstone Park for the benefit of private-power companies. It was, however, the paramount factor in the fight against its enlargement, and the alliance has been predominant in every controversy, from that day to this, involving conflict between conservation and commercial exploitation in the public-lands policy of the United States.

The National Conference on State Parks convened on May 31, 1930, in St. Louis, where I had returned to my old job as editor of the editorial page of the *Star*. The convention brought together a large number of people who were interested also in national parks. I took this occasion to suggest, in an editorial, the formation of a State and National Parks Association to promote both park systems and to differentiate them. I also reminded our readers of the need to expand the existing national parks, including Yellowstone, in order to "get ahead of the depletion of wild life and the ruin of scenic wonders by industry."

The cause of conservation had other enemies in government itself. That same year I ran into a conflict that placed the Army Corps of Engineers on one side and defenders of environment on the other. When General Edgar Jadwin retired as chief of the Corps of Engineers in August 1929, he left two dreams unfulfilled. He had not yet buried the Great Falls of the Potomac or the Cumberland Falls of Kentucky under the waters of power-company reservoirs. Luckily, the old Federal Power Commission under Secretary of the Interior Ray Lyman Wilbur had delayed the Kentucky project so that the state legislature had time to buy that property. On June 28, 1930, I sent to the White House a copy of an editorial favoring preservation of the Potomac's Great Falls. Three days later, however, President Hoover announced that he intended to nominate General Jadwin as chairman of the new, independent Federal Power Commission, putting the Potomac at his disposal. To the great benefit of the country, General Jadwin declined the appointment.

No such good fortune attended the beleaguered North American water-fowl. For them a new threat of extinction surfaced in August 1930, when Joseph P. Knapp, multimillionaire owner of *Collier's*, announced the incorporation of More Game Birds in America, A Foundation. Its policies were revealed in his magazine: (1) Repeal all game laws. (2) Exterminate all hawks. (3) Establish the English game-breeding system.

With the Biological Survey showing a disposition toward further bag-limit reduction and a shorter hunting season, Joe Knapp's wealth, publicity resources, and political clout made him the prospective successor of Colorado senator Lawrence Phipps as overlord of waterfowl "protection." His spoken motto was "breed more ducks in Canada," but he was far more active in the encouragement of killing than of breeding.

Organization of the Knapp foundation was followed by a startling announcement: its president was to be Senator Harry Hawes, at a salary of thirty-five thousand dollars a year. He was to take office at once, but his salary was not to begin until January 1933, at which time, he disclosed, he would retire from the Senate. The information that he would not run for a second term came as no surprise: he had conducted a thorough poll of Missouri Democratic political leaders and discovered that he had no chance whatever of winning a renomination. The complaint was that he had attended to everything except the interests of his state. The Missouri Democratic leaders, it is only fair to say, cared nothing about his morals: what they objected to was his lack of productivity.

Even bigger newspaper headlines came three months later (November 12, 1930) when the *New York Herald Tribune* announced: "SENATOR HAWES / QUITS POST WITH / BIRD FOUNDATION / Gives up $35,000 Position." The explanation Hawes gave was that Knapp had broken his promise to let Hawes do his work in Washington, and that the foundation's program was not broad enough to receive general approval.

There was no financial sacrifice in Hawes's resignation. As a Washington-based lobbyist he could (and later did) draw down far more than the lost thirty-five thousand dollars. His financial peccadilloes did not in the least diminish his popularity and influence during his remaining two years in the Senate. Aided by the gun-and-ammunition senator Walcott of Connecticut, he created and controlled the Senate Select Committee on Wild-life Resources: its business, pigeonholing protection bills.

Harry Hawes had his good points. He was a genial, friendly man whom even his strongest critics liked personally. A fisherman to the tips of his fly rods, he almost single-handedly created the American half of the great Quetico-Superior canoeing wilderness, at a cost to the taxpayers of only $128 for fishing tackle. Fond of dogs, he was particularly proud of his own pooch, which, he told guests, was housebroken to use only the *St. Louis Star*.

During 1931 I wrote two waterfowl pamphlets for the Emergency Conservation Committee: *Unsportsmanlike Sportsmen* and *Shotgun Conservation*. The first called for the abolition of shooting practices—artificial feeding and the use of live decoys—that were wiping out ducks and geese on every North American flyway. The second analyzed the miscalled conservation societies that were paralyzing the protective arm of government and thus drawing all waterfowl toward extinction.

Bag-limit reduction, I said in the first pamphlet, came ten years too late. The shorter season that was in prospect would also come too late. To save waterfowl from extermination the irreducible minimum of reform must be: Abolish shooting over baited waters. Abolish the use of live decoys. "This proposal," I wrote, "is profanation and sacrilege. It assaults the holy of holies of the wealthy club shooter. It will be met by a thousand twisting, squirming arguments." Not one of them, I said, would alter the fact that baiting meant extermination.

Shooting over baited waters, I continued, "will be defended to the last ditch by wealthy shooters whose influence is paramount in the official realm of federal bird protection, and whose unspoken motto is: 'To hell with the future. The birds are going and we'll get ours.'"

In congressional hearings, I pointed out, the defenders of baiting called it "feeding the ducks." The whole thing was pictured as "a philanthropic undertaking by which kind hearted men keep migratory wild fowl from starving on their way south, in return for which charity they bring down a few birds as they pass along."

In isolated cases this was true. I acknowledged that some people fed ducks to keep them away from the baited club-waters; but "typical baiting is feeding for the sake of killing the bag-limit." I told about Lake Merritt, in the business section of Oakland, California, on which wild mallards would alight, nervous and fearful from gunfire on the baited marshes of the Sacramento River. In four days' time they would be taking food from the fingers of children.

This quick taming by feeding, I said, was what made baiting so deadly. The duck clubs, as their members told Congress and the public, provided "rest days" each week to reduce the kill. That, I wrote, was hypocritical pretense: "Rest days give the ducks a chance to forget the guns and come back to the bait."

The universal practice in these clubs was for attendants to drive hundreds of ducks away from the baited waters before shooting began. They would return two or three or half a dozen at a time. Coming straight toward the guns, every one met death. Successive quartets of hunters would occupy the blinds, each man getting his limit; at commercial clubs this process would be kept up all day. It was "market hunting" on the wing or on the water, a sport (I said) "more barbarous than the trap-shooting of live pigeons."

The Biological Survey, I wrote, "has legal authority to abolish baiting. It will not do so." I predicted that the Survey's director would "abolish baiting in five minutes" if only "the wealthy and politically powerful game-hogs of the country would leave him alone." The purpose of that argument was to undermine Pearson's contention that the Audubon Association's silence on baiting was based on the wise leadership of the Biological Survey.

My second pamphlet, *Shotgun Conservation*, listed four organizations as major controllers of federal hunting regulations. One was the Audubon Association. The three others were all supported by the gun and ammunition makers: the American Game Association (which had dropped the word "protective" from its title), the American Game Conference (sponsored by the AGA), and the Sporting Arms and Ammunition Manufacturers' Institute. All of these organizations were displaying alarm over the disappearance of game, but were silent about excessive shooting and baiting. Also listed as active in defense of baiting were the National Committee on Wild-Life Legislation, the American Wild Fowlers, the Conservation Committee of the Campfire Club, and a powerful faction of the equally prestigious Boone and Crockett Club, in which there were enough true conservationists to produce a stalemate on official policy. Latest to arrive on the scene but taking swift leadership of the "baiting" forces was Joseph P. Knapp's misnamed More Game Birds in America Foundation, whose founder wielded a mighty wallop at the White House through his ownership of *Collier's*.

Against this powerful combination stood a growing number of alarmed western game commissioners lacking organization, a few small conservation groups, a number of state and local associations of small-time sportsmen, and numerous relatively helpless individuals. My effort, and that of the Emergency Conservation Committee, was to reach the vast number of Americans who felt concern but did not know what to do, especially farmers and other occasional hunters who tramped the marshes and riverbanks and got nothing; also the millions of nonhunters with outdoor interests. The pamphlet closed by calling for the country's "hundreds of thousands of nature lovers" to "put new life and leadership into the existing demoralized conservation societies."

Measured by the requests for copies, many of which came from Canada, and by the outraged cries of the targeted gentry, the pamphlets produced quite an effect. *Shotgun Conservation* brought me a three-page single-spaced letter from Joshua Clayton, a lawyer from Elkton, Maryland, who described the slaughter along the Eastern Shore in terms that made my account look pallid. "I have utter contempt," he wrote, "for the wealthy, so-called sportsmen." On their club grounds the shooting was done by concealed employees who wiped out feeding ducks. On the Susquehanna flats, too broad for baiting, wealthy sportsmen employed "bushwhackers" to shoot and bring in their kills at an agreed price, and "they go back to their homes with ducks killed in every quarter of the Flats." In contrast, he said, when J. Pierpont Morgan obtained control of the Spesustia Island Club he banned automatic shotguns, strictly enforced the bag limits, and put an end to shooting for pleasure only, by "sportsmen" who left dead birds to float away.

There were other signs of improvement. Frank Stick, president of the Atlantic Coast Sportsmen's Association, wrote to me that all baiting would have to be abolished because it was impossible to draw a distinction between what was good and what was bad. I sent this information to Survey chief Paul Redington, with the comment that "the baiting issue cannot be postponed much longer." I praised him for resisting the pressure of Missouri game hogs to turn the clock back on bag limits and seasons and suggested that "Lake Cooper" (the Mississippi from Burlington to Keokuk) be made a wildlife sanctuary as a "link in what should ultimately become a protected Mississippi River fly-way" from source to mouth.

Redington's attitude on waterfowl was improving but did not go much beyond words. Totally unalleviated was another Survey atrocity—decimation of mammals with an ill-considered and expanding program of predator control. At that year's convention of the American Ornithologists' Union, Redington said that he desired its counsel at all times. That society, however, was under heavy attack from its own members for inaction. Firing one shot at two targets, I wrote to *The Auk*, its official organ, suggesting that the ornithologists follow the example of the American Society of Mammalogists, whose members, when Redington made a similar request for advice, opened up in that very meeting and gave the Survey unshirted hell. I compared the Survey's poisoning program for predatory animals, opposed by the mammalogists but supported by sheep and cattle ranchers, with waterfowl baiting, and asked if "ornithologists care less for bird life than mammalogists do for mammalian life."

During the summer of 1931 a disastrous grasshopper plague hit the Middle West—fulfilling a prediction made eighteen months earlier by naturalists of the American Society of Mammalogists that such a plague would result from policies of the Biological Survey. Now the Survey proposed scattering poisoned bran in front of the advancing hordes. This, I wrote in a semi-facetious editorial headed "Grasshoppers," would round out that bureau's full policy, which was: "(1) Get money from Congress to poison the mammals that prey on rodents. (2) Get money from Congress to poison the rodents that increase when the [predatory] mammals are killed. (3) Get money from Congress to poison the insects that increase when the rodents are killed." I added, "While the bran is killing the grasshoppers, won't it kill everything else that eats bran? Or perhaps the Survey will put up a sign advising other animals not to eat the bran, like the signs put up around coyote poison baits in the West, warning dogs, badgers and skunks to leave them alone."

The *St. Louis Star*, by request, furnished the Emergency Conservation Committee with five thousand copies of the editorial, to be used as "envelope fillers" in correspondence. Dr. A. B. Howell, leader of the fight against the Survey, objected to the "levity" of the piece, but mammalogists from all over the country asked for batches of reprints. On the day the last of them was sent out (January 15, 1932), Mrs. Edge wrote that my editorial was "the leaven that made . . . possible" the vigorous stand of the American Society of Mammalogists against the Biological Survey's poison policy.

In 1931, with gun-company pressure subsiding, a new menace was steadily rising. This was the concentration of shooting-club influence upon President Hoover and Secretary of Agriculture Arthur M. Hyde. At the center of the effort were Joe Knapp and his More Game Birds Foundation. Outwardly devoted to restoration of the waterfowl population to nineteenth-century levels, it inwardly reflected Knapp's unyielding determination to "get his" by shooting practices that were leading straight toward obliteration of ducks and geese.

Knapp's first stroke in public policy was an attempt to have all protective game laws repealed in New Jersey, ostensibly (and perhaps actually) to open the way to effectual game breeding for shooting purposes. Failing in this effort, he turned to national affairs. On March 29, 1932, I wrote to Governor Gifford Pinchot of Pennsylvania that "the situation in the Washington departments is enough to make a person sick," and announced my intention to expose Knapp's influence in an editorial.

The editorial, "This Is Government," published April 2, 1932, opened with the statement that "there is now being witnessed in Washington the transfer of a government bureau, the Biological Survey, to private ownership." The movement had begun in the fall of 1931, stimulated by "the courageous and necessary step" of the Survey in cutting down the duck kill and shortening the season. The transfer of ownership, I said, was taking place in three stages: (1) the old advisory board to the secretary of agriculture had been dismissed because it was too heavily weighted toward "well-to-do hunters"; (2) a new advisory board even more biased in that direction, and including Knapp, had been appointed; (3) a provision, attached to a bill taxing shotgun ammunition to fund wildlife sanctuaries, would require the Biological Survey to obtain the new advisory board's approval before submitting any regulation protecting migratory wildfowl. Redington had told me, in reply to a query, that although his bureau had drafted the bill for funding the wildlife refuges, it was not to be taken as representing the views of the Survey. Recounting this, I wrote in the editorial: "Nevertheless, the Biological Survey put in, or left in, a clause stripping itself of authority to enforce an Act of Congress entrusted to its care, and turning that authority over to an Advisory Board dominated by the man who asked to have the bill drafted. No government bureau in the history of America ever did anything like that except under duress."

Knapp failed to get his bill through Congress. In the executive department, however, he would be the power behind the throne as long as Herbert Hoover occupied the White House.

Beset from both sides, the Biological Survey was completely on the defensive and struck out wildly. C. C. Woodward, Florida state game commissioner, wrote to Associate Chief Henderson about the latter's remark to me, quoted in *Shotgun Conservation*, that abolition of baiting involved destruction of property values in duck clubs and might on that account be unlawful. Woodward sent me the reply he received, not from Henderson, but from the acting chief, H. P. Sheldon, who said it was "a practical impossibility to check all such statements about the Bureau."

However, wrote Sheldon, "We are familiar with the statement made in the bulletin alleged to have been sent out by Mr. Irving Brant, and I know this to be a misquotation or a misinterpretation of Mr. Henderson's actual remarks made to Mr. Brant."

The phrase "alleged to have been sent out by Mr. Irving Brant" had the same significance as the Audubon investigation committee's reply to a pamphlet "purporting to be written by Irving Brant." The unknown person of that name was too ignorant of conservation matters to have written either pamphlet. (In other words, Hornaday wrote them.)

What Henderson said, wrote Sheldon, "was to this effect—that baiting would be a difficult matter to control, owing to the fact that it would be difficult to prevent a person from distributing grain or other food on his own property . . . there was nothing whatever in his statement with relation to the value of private property, but it rather referred to the property *rights* of an individual"—i.e., the rights that permitted him to do things on his own property that could be denied on public property. Witnesses were present, Sheldon said, who could verify this.

The only witness was Redington, who was too honest a man to verify the denial, nor did Henderson see fit to do so personally. I sent Commissioner Woodward a transcript of the entire conversation with Redington and Henderson, written on the day the meeting took place. He in return gave me a copy of his reply to Sheldon: that after investigation, he saw no reason to revoke the criticism he had made.

My last effort to influence public policy during the Hoover administration took the form of a series of editorials urging Congress to pass Congresswoman Ruth Bryan Owen's bill to establish the Everglades National Park. This cherished project was supported by the Florida legislature but bitterly opposed by corporate tomato growers. My final editorial was a plea to Congress to make this park "A Farewell Gift to Mrs. Owen." She thanked me for my support of the park with a handwritten note expressing the "urgent need to preserve oases of wild life which will inevitably be destroyed by the commercial developer, the homesteader and the careless tourist if no steps are taken by the government." Mrs. Owen eventually received her "farewell gift," but it was sent to her on May 30, 1934, by the Roosevelt Congress.

Franklin Delano Roosevelt had a life-long dedication to the management and conservation of the land. This photograph, taken in 1933 at his home in Hyde Park, New York, has in the background part of the forest that covered estate lands (photograph courtesy Franklin D. Roosevelt Library, Hyde Park).

CHAPTER TWO

PUTTING IT UP TO FDR

I had a casual exchange of letters with Franklin D. Roosevelt in the presidential campaign of 1920 and considerable correspondence with him during his last two years as governor of New York. Only one of his letters in the latter period had a bearing on conservation. Up to the last week of the pre-convention campaign the *St. Louis Star* was not committed to his support, but in editorials (which I sent him) and in correspondence I sought to draw him out on one subject after another. On March 20, 1932, Roosevelt thanked me for the clippings and enclosed in his letter "one or two pamphlets which show what I have tried to do in New York during the past three years." The principal enclosure, a leaflet entitled "What ROOSEVELT has done for THE FARMER," was indeed enlightening. I had been concerned that Roosevelt, as a big-city, big-state man, might neglect farming and conservation issues. The pamphlet, however, told of programs he had launched for electrification, health, and land use in the countryside. In addition, his program of forest conservation and reforestation, directed toward the Adirondack Forest Preserve, put Franklin Roosevelt and his state in sharp and praiseworthy contrast with the remainder of the nation.

This letter and its enclosures furnished a clincher as far as Roosevelt's candidacy was concerned, although in fact none was needed. My editorial calling upon the Democratic convention to nominate Roosevelt was carried on the United Press wire service, and Roosevelt's convention floor manager, James

A. Farley, telegraphed an order for an extra five hundred copies. The St. Louis half of the Missouri delegation (after holding a shouting match with Boss Pendergast in a hallway) shifted its vote to Roosevelt in the early balloting and started what later became a stampede.

Four days after Roosevelt's November victory, I urged him to choose Henry A. Wallace for secretary of agriculture. I had known Wallace when we were both members of a Des Moines, Iowa, discussion club from 1915 to 1918. One comment in my letter endorsing Wallace, on demoralization in government bureaus, brought this later note from Louis McHenry Howe, Roosevelt's secretary: "I know Mr. Roosevelt would very much like to receive your ideas on re-organization in the various bureaus you mention, and may I ask that you send them along?" So, addressing President Roosevelt on March 31 (four weeks after his accession), I said that the conclusion had been forced upon me "that to insure continuity of a sound national program there must be a new set-up in the conservation agencies," meaning the Biological Survey, the Forest Service, and the National Park Service. I told of the long dominance of the Survey by the gun and ammunition companies, adding that although Paul Redington, chief of the Survey, was "an honest, well-intentioned man . . . bewildered by his environment," Associate Director Henderson was "the real head of the bureau." Whatever his motives might be, I said, he "affiliates easily and naturally with reactionary agents, and not at all with others." The Forest Service, I continued, had an admirable field force and high morale but too much of a commercial point of view. "It thinks of all trees in terms of board feet" and "obstructs every effort to preserve scenic areas which contain merchantable trees." Finally, the National Park Service, in my view, was "so completely cowed by the Forest Service that it dares not call its soul its own" and therefore would not seek "a legitimate park expansion measure in one locality for fear of reprisals in another." In addition, the public saw the Park Service in an unfavorable light because of "a concessionaire system which . . . gives the appearance (probably unwarranted) of a compact between the N.P.S. and the concessionaires to bleed the public."

The Forest Service, I said, could not be entirely blamed for unwillingness to have lands in the national forests turned over to the administrative system of the national parks. Nevertheless, "The development of our national parks at the expense of the national forests is demanded by the more fundamental needs of our country—permanent preservation of magnificent primeval forests which cannot be replaced for centuries if once cut down as the Forest Service intends they shall be, and preservation of wild life through large, permanent sanctuaries."

A set of deductions followed. With Henry Wallace going into office as secretary of agriculture and conservationist Harold Ickes as secretary of the interior, conditions would improve without reorganization, but "a poor system works well only under exceptional circumstances." Two steps were necessary. The first was to group all the conservation agencies *in one department*, to reduce inter-bureau jealousies; the second, to make conservation the

Harold Ickes, secretary of the interior during the Roosevelt administrations, was deeply involved in FDR's conservation programs (photograph courtesy Time *magazine).*

primary work of that department. With most conservation agencies already in the Department of Agriculture, I told FDR, the natural impulse was to put them all there. Results would be good as long as Wallace was in charge, but the impulse was wrong. Conservation could never be the primary purpose of that department, and the relationship between agriculture and conservation, though close, was to a great extent a conflicting one. The Department of the Interior, I said, was the logical center for conservation activities, but it had a history of low morale. "Somebody always has to rescue it, as Pinchot did from Ballinger and you have done from Wilbur."

The best alternative was to take control of the Interior Department away from the public-land states, since "the most important duty of its head is to defend the national interest in the public land against local and state attack." I proposed that "all bureaus primarily devoted to conservation be placed in the Interior Department, that all others be eliminated from it, and that the name be changed by congressional enactment to Department of Conservation. The change in name may appear superficial, but it is not. It will wipe out the mortgage claimed by the public land states, establish a new principle, set a new standard, centralize responsibility for conservation, and focus public attention upon that responsibility." This memorandum embodied the most controversial features of Mr. Roosevelt's first attempt to reorganize the executive branch through a grant of discretionary power by Congress.

My personal acquaintance with President Roosevelt began on July 11, 1933, when I was in Washington to speed the final revision of my first book, *Dollars and Sense*. Jay N. Darling ("Ding"), cartoonist of the *Des Moines Register*, chanced to be there at the same time, and press secretary Stephen P. Early invited both of us to attend a White House press conference, to be followed by my introduction to the president.

I stood in great awe of the presidency at that time and was so thrilled at attending the conference that the questions and answers just left a blurred impression. But I did mark Mr. Roosevelt's evident enjoyment of the give-and-take and his mastery of the proceedings. At the close, while waiting for Early to take us back to the Oval Office, I remarked to a staffer that I wanted to meet top secretary Louis Howe. "Come with me," he said.

After a few minutes with Howe I became uneasy. Then the awful thought came that Darling might already be with the president. I excused myself and hastened down the hall. My fear was justified, but the two had been together for only a few seconds. So it was Darling instead of Early who introduced me. Darling was an extreme extrovert, awed by nobody, overflowing with self-confidence. I was almost tongue-tied while the two exchanged cordial nothings. Still, it was an introduction.

Besides being old friends and colleagues on the *Des Moines Register*, Jay Darling and I had a common interest in waterfowl conservation. A duck hunter himself, he loathed overshooting and believed, as I did, that baiting must be stopped to prevent the extermination of North American waterfowl. Both of us were friends of Secretary of Agriculture Henry Wallace, new overseer of the Biological Survey. Two weeks earlier, Wallace had appointed Darling to the still-reactionary advisory board on waterfowl protection, which had gathered to give advice on regulations for the 1933 hunting season.

At the board's public meeting its chairman, conservation-minded Judge Miles of Arkansas, called on me to speak first. My general survey of the waterfowl situation stirred up a trio of hard-boiled reactionaries, who, as I described the session to Dr. Hornaday, "began at once to ask what they thought would be embarrassing questions and a good time was had by all for about half an hour." At the request of Judge Miles, I submitted a set of proposals, all of which were presented in executive session by Darling and voted down. My old Audubon antagonist Dr. T. Gilbert Pearson, Darling told me, switched over and supported all of them vigorously.

The resolution to abolish baiting, Darling reported, lost by a single vote, ten to nine. It would have carried, he said, except that one member, a Mrs. Wilson, misunderstood the motion and voted wrong. She moved at once to reconsider the vote but her motion was postponed and ultimately blocked. Dr. T. S. Palmer of the Biological Survey gave me the reason: several among the nine who voted "aye" secretly favored baiting.

As Darling described the executive session to me, and as I relayed the story to Dr. Hornaday, whenever a member spoke in favor of stricter regulations, one of the reactionaries would call on Redington for aid and the poor fellow would "tremble and stutter and support the reactionaries." This, I wrote to Hornaday, "is probably the result of a movement by the Knapp bunch to get rid of Redington and put a worse man in his place." Keep all of this confidential, I urged Hornaday, the fighter. "There is still a chance to get something out of the situation, but only if the opposition assumes it is all over. . . . At the present moment there is no pressure on the Department of Agriculture. . . . But if there is even a hint that this [continuance of our effort] is the situation, Barney Baruch and Joseph Knapp will begin to belabor Roosevelt, and everything may be spoiled."

Jay Darling felt the same apprehension. We might get away with the abolition of baiting, he wrote on the day he returned to Des Moines, or shortening the sixty-day season to forty-five or reducing the bag limit to twelve per day, but not with ALL of these in one year. He worried that Bernard Baruch and his cronies would force the president to undermine any radically protective regulations by executive order. All of this ran directly counter to advice and assurances both of us had received from Undersecretary of Agriculture Rexford Guy Tugwell, a leading member of the Roosevelt "brain trust," who had told me "that we should 'write our ticket' and he would put it through."

During the few days we were both in Washington, Darling and I discussed a possible successor to Redington. The only person on the staff who might combine all qualifications, we agreed, was biologist Waldo L. McAtee, whom neither of us knew personally. The only other person who came to mind was Aldo Leopold, a conservation-minded scientist and writer whose eligibility was somewhat clouded by a recent short-lived connection with the educational work of the gun manufacturers. His post with them had lately been abolished because of failure to allot funds to it—a fact which involved no reflection upon him, perhaps the contrary.

A day or two after the meeting of the advisory board, just before returning to St. Louis, I talked with Biological Survey staffers who were willing to risk their jobs by confidentially describing conditions there. This information was relayed at once to Darling and to Wallace's personal assistant Paul Appleby, at whose suggestion the inquiries had been made. Trustworthy members of the staff, I wrote to Appleby, gave me the following picture:

"The Survey has been going from bad to worse. A meeting was held a few weeks ago at which various members of the staff urged Redington and Henderson to present a vigorous program of game-bird protection to the Advisory Board, but they refused. Henderson is a good administrator, but a poor conservationist. It would be unfortunate if he left the Survey, unfortunate also if he became chief. The Survey would have collapsed under Redington, except for Henderson's ability to deal with congressional committees, etc."

I added my impressions of McAtee and Leopold. The former was a good administrator and conservationist. He was opposed to baiting and to the predatory-animal campaign, and was in favor of controlling crop-destroying birds in California. He should be a competent head. Leopold had won praise at the Survey for ability, but drew some skepticism because of a former connection with the Sporting Arms and Ammunition Manufacturers Institute. He had urged Darling to work for a shorter shooting season. But owing to inadequate information and lack of personal acquaintance, I did not feel like expressing an opinion concerning him.

Redington's present course, I continued, "is probably due to the fact that he has been so thoroughly cowed by Knapp, Foran [Colonel Arthur Foran of New Jersey], Hawes, etc., in the past, and is so slow in his mental processes, that he is still acting as he would if [Secretary] Hyde were in office. He is a good bureau man for forestry, but I don't believe the Biological Survey can function while he is at the head of it."

Invited to do so by Appleby, I submitted on August 1 a set of suggestions for the 1933 waterfowl hunting regulations, presenting them "in descending order of importance": (1) abolition of shooting over baited grounds; (2) reduction of the bag limit on ducks to twelve per day and of the possession limit to twenty-four, with a closed season on birds threatened by the disappearance of eel grass, like the brant (I took considerable joshing as a member of that endangered species); and (3) shortening of the shooting season. The first of these, I wrote, was fundamental. Abolition of baiting was "the only reform that will prevent the ultimate disappearance of waterfowl." This step ought to be taken at once, but "If it is done, the Biological Survey should have a head who sympathizes with that action, and will support the conservation policies of the Department vigorously." The few wealthy and influential sportsmen who defended baiting were coming to see that it was doomed, Middle Western game commissioners had taken a public stand against it, and in addition, "If its defenders raise an uproar, there will be plenty of 'one-gallus' hunters to support the Department when they know what the issue is."

"Your letter to Appleby," Darling wrote on receipt of a copy, "meets with my entire approval. . . . All my desires support your contention that we should not postpone everything until next year." His only reservation was that too much zeal for immediate regulation could jeopardize the reorganization program in the department.

Two weeks later word came from Appleby that the season's regulations were in the works. Signed by Wallace, they bore the stamp of Tugwell's "write your ticket" advice. Baiting and live decoys were to be outlawed.

I barely had time to congratulate Jay Darling, quoting Appleby, when telegrams came from both of them asking me to attend a new conference in Washington on regulations. A letter from Darling followed. He suspected that some adviser of the president had seen the amended regulations as an affront to the "killer crowd." The regulations had been returned, unsigned, with a statement by the president that Wallace ought to hear the "forceful" arguments against them before going further.

A hearing had been set for August 28. The request for testimony from supporters of the regulations made it evident that both sides would be heard, and Darling had hopes of a safe conservationist majority in the new hearings. Appleby was optimistic and expected that the regulations would go through pretty much as written. I contributed my own ideas in writing, as representative of the Emergency Conservation Committee of New York City. My statement was devoted entirely to rebutting the stock arguments of wealthy gun-clubbers that "baiting" conserved the victims of it. I pointed out that the few cases where baiting involved "little shooting and much feeding" were far from typical: "The typical baited pond or waterfront is a shambles, with waterfowl shot down as fast as they come in to hover practically motionless above the sprinkled corn and the quacking decoys." Such shooting, I said, "satisfies only the killer's lust, but that lust exists, and it seems to blind its possessors to every consideration except the pleasure of indulging in wholesale slaughter."

All this talk about "feeding the ducks" and "rest days," I said, was Sunday-go-to-meeting language. What the Department of Agriculture really needed was a verbatim record of the clubhouse conversations that ensued when a member announced that one of their ignoramus guests had "burned out the flock"—that is, fired on a main flight of ducks lured to the baited ground. The "sporting" goal was to drive ducks away to ensure their coming back in twos, threes, or sixes, to be killed as fast as they came in. The three biggest swindles in waterfowl conservation were "feeding the ducks," "rest days," and "the duck-club sanctuary," the purpose of which was to hold ducks within reach for future shooting; these practices turned hunting into a monopoly for those few able to pay the price. The argument that abolition of baiting would be an unlawful invasion of private property rights made no sense because the "practicers of baiting are destroying their own property rights. They are speeding the day when they will have shooting clubs with nothing to shoot." But even if this were not the case, property rights should not be based on behavior abhorrent to public policy—especially not on the practice of "enticing" onto one's property game birds belonging to the entire nation.

At the August 28 hearing, the advocates of baiting made up in numbers, fervor, and financial standing what they lacked in logic, and they were met in kind on fervency. Appleby and I worked out our interpretation of the hearings in an exchange of letters. The heaviest pressure against the proposed regulations came from former senator Harry Hawes, now a professional lobbyist, with the American Game Association (of the gunmakers) as a leading client. However, Hawes identified himself at the hearing as representative of the prestigious Izaak Walton League. Hawes, I told Appleby (on August 31), had sought that position at the last annual convention of the league, but had been turned down on the ground that the league should not be tied up with the gun companies. "Apparently," I wrote, "the Izaak Walton League directors [by appointing him now] have repeated their ancient game of selling out the rank and file, something they have done regularly ever since Will Dilg was beaten for [re-election to] the presidency." Appleby replied that "we all regret the unsatisfactory result [of the hearings], but we are making plans to effect some improvement next year."

The 1933 hunting regulations were published on September 12. The duck bag limit was reduced to twelve per day—a good gain if total expectations had not been so much higher. Summing up the situation that day for Dr. Hornaday, I said it had become apparent by the end of the hearings that there was now no chance to act on baiting. It was my impression, I said—actually I knew—"that the seaboard crowd got to Roosevelt and demanded this hearing. That left Wallace in a position where he could not proceed, because he would have had to tell the President that he was acting without the approval of the advisory board, without the request of the Biological Survey, and against the violent protest of eastern sportsmen, many of whom are close to Roosevelt." Before baiting could be abolished, I said, there would have to be a reorganization of the Biological Survey. A single new face on the advisory board would produce a conservationist majority. All was not bad. "Think how the Knapp crowd would have howled about the bag-limit reduction if they hadn't been so scared about baiting!"

Hornaday in reply relayed new information that appeared to solve the mystery of Hawes's appointment as Izaak Walton League representative in defiance of the league's national convention. Said Hornaday: "A friend of mine . . . brought back from Washington the news that the gun and ammunition makers recently have placed $60,000 in the hands of Mr. Hawes, of which he was required to give $20,000 to the Izaak Walton League to pay off the debts of the Chicago headquarters, and give $18,000 toward the running expenses of the American Game Association. The remaining $22,000 Hawes was supposed to keep."

This information I sent to Paul Appleby. Such tactics of desperation, forecasting defeat of the baiters, reconciled me to the regulations, which I had regarded as an unavoidable compromise. The killer crowd had drawn first blood in the new administration, but (I took satisfaction in thinking) although the president stood *with* them, he was not *of* them, and our tactics had been wrong. Rex Tugwell had been too sure of his influence with Franklin Roosevelt.

As had become almost a habit, the new hunting regulations produced a request by Mrs. Edge for another pamphlet on waterfowl protection, to be published by the Emergency Conservation Committee. The resulting product was *A Last Plea for Waterfowl*, put out in January 1934. It could almost be called a joint product of my pen and that of Biological Survey technicians, who had been reporting the desperate plight of the game birds about which the bureau chiefs were so lacking in specific policy. Even the organizations that fought against effective protective measures testified statistically to the need for them. I quoted a warning sent by the Biological Survey to all state game commissioners shortly after the obstructive August 28 hearing on the rejected 1933 hunting regulations: "Present conditions tend surely toward extermination of our waterfowl and we must without delay take more effective steps to preserve these birds."

This warning, I pointed out, was being echoed by the same sportsmen's groups that were blocking effective remedial action: More Game Birds in America and the American Game Association. Both organizations had reported essentially the same set of facts: "A disastrous drouth, drying up the water areas of the prairie provinces and destroying feed, [has] wreaked terrible havoc among the waterfowl, and disease caused by low water levels [has] increased the destruction." (The disease was botulism.) But only the Biological Survey had been willing to face the inescapable conclusion that overshooting, not drought, was the primary cause of the shortage. The Survey, speaking through its associate chief W. C. Henderson, disclosed that over a vast northern area where food was plentiful and water conditions were good, only a sparse breeding population had been found. Clearly, the Survey report concluded, "over-shooting has not left sufficient stocks" to use the breeding space.

More Game Birds in America, dealing with the same admitted facts, reached a different conclusion. The absence of breeding stock where conditions were good indicated "that prairie nesting ducks preferred to breed in alkaline environments, but this is merely a conjecture." The conjecture reflected published rumors about a "lost legion" of waterfowl that had moved to "remote regions of northern Canada." The American Game Association, in the summer of 1933, had sent an observer by airplane and canoe to hunt for this legion. He reported food and water plentiful but had found "nothing like the number of missing ducks." This forced the American Game Association to agree with those who said flatly that the "missing" ducks were dead. Faced with such admitted conditions, what did these "protective" organizations do? Joe Knapp's group called for restoration of Canadian marsh vegetation and establishment of U.S. sanctuaries, and warned against "petty, unpopular and unenforceable shooting restrictions." (That is, don't abolish baiting.)

From these organizations my pamphlet turned to the representation of the Izaak Walton League by ex-senator Harry Hawes of Missouri, currently lobbyist for the gunmakers. I wrote that Hawes had been appointed legislative representative of the Izaak Walton League after being turned down for that position at the 1933 league convention. At that convention, the league had adopted a resolution that "whereas the baiting of ducks has come to be considered by many sportsmen as harmful to the true purposes of conservation [be it resolved] that the federal government conclude its investigations about the control of this practice and present same together with the proper remedies to the next session of the Advisory Board." This resolution was sent to Hawes to be presented at the August 28 hearing on baiting. With it went the further statement by the league's conservation director, S. B. Locke, that the Izaak Walton League "is opposed to the commercialized baiting of waterfowl and favors the limitation of all forms of feeding which do not show a net benefit to the birds." In the face of these declarations against baiting, I wrote, "Senator Hawes went before the Secretary of Agriculture, placed the official views of the league in the record, and then, in the name of the Izaak Walton League and the American Game Association, led the fight in defense of baiting." I reported that Hawes had asked during the hearing who had gotten the secretary of agriculture to ignore his "great Advisory Board" and that Hornaday had answered that question with a question about why "these enemies of wild life were put into that board" in the first place.

These remarks about Hawes stung the ex-senator. "It is not true," he wrote to me (January 17, 1934) that he "led the fight in defense of baiting." Nothing in the transcript, he said, "justifies such a conclusion. I have never on any occasion, privately or publicly, verbally or in writing, ever said—(1) That I favored baiting; or (2) that I was opposed to baiting. I am open to conviction." I replied that whether he did or did not lead the defense of baiting depended entirely on the definition of "defense." If a defense consisted of getting up and saying, "Baiting is a good practice. I believe in it. It should not be interfered with," then in truth he did not defend baiting. "But if following the course most likely to prevent interference with baiting is defending it, then you led the defense. . . . You and I both know that your appeal for 'study' of baiting is an exact analog to the demand for 'study' of bag-limit reduction after it was recommended by the Advisory Board in 1926. . . . You know, as well as any man in the United States, whether it [baiting] is defensible or indefensible, and your unwillingness to essay its open defense is one of the surest auguries of its disappearance."

My visual description of baiting in this pamphlet attracted a good deal of attention, with many calls from Canada for copies. Dr. Bruette (by this time connected with a publishing house), considered the pamphlet "the best thing by far that has come out" on baiting.

On the last day of February 1934, Appleby wrote that Paul Redington had resigned as chief of the Biological Survey and returned to the Forest Service—an escape, for him, from Purgatory back into Paradise. A week later came an astonishing announcement. Jay N. Darling, the Des Moines cartoonist and Iowa state game commissioner, had been invited to head the Survey, and had accepted. Late in May, Secretary Wallace and Appleby popped into my office in St. Louis and explained that Darling had refused a permanent appointment. He was to head the Biological Survey for six months—the legal limit without going under civil service. His chief purpose was to reorganize the Survey and reshape its policies as much as possible. I reported this news to Dr. Hornaday, along with my suspicion that either Leopold or McAtee, but not Henderson, would be the Survey's new permanent head. Hornaday, pessimistically, replied that he was "very sorry about the prospect of losing Darling" and suspected that Hawes and Knapp would dictate the choice of his successor.

Darling wrote me a month after the Wallace-Appleby visit. He explained that his hectic schedule during the preparation of recommendations to the advisory board had prevented him from writing until then, but "we have evolved a series of recommendations for this year's shooting which do not embody all the convictions nor all the restrictions that most of us would like to see incorporated into the code for this year, but we came as near to it as is humanly possible considering the extremes of sentiment which exist."

The proposed regulations, worked out in a mild tug of war between the Survey and the advisory board, disappointed me. They provided a thirty-day shooting season chosen by each state within an overall period of three and a half months between October 1 and January 15. Each state could establish rest days within its thirty days, thus lengthening the total season. Baiting was to be regulated by permits from the Biological Survey, with records kept of the ducks killed and the amount of bait used.

Commenting later on my critical *Star-Times* editorial on the subject,[1] Darling wrote that he could understand my anxiety over the shooting season, adding that he "had the same feeling about it too, but it was the best compromise we could make." At least, he said, the duck clubs would have rest days whether the state authorized them or not, and they did 85 percent of the killing. But on the other hand, Darling said he nearly fainted when the advisory board adopted unanimously his recommendation that a permit from the Biological Survey should be required for baiting.

"The only conclusion I can draw," I wrote in reply, ". . . is that, practically speaking, the hunting season will be lengthened instead of shortened by the proposed regulations." In 1933, I said, California clubs shot two days a week for two months, a total of eighteen days' shooting. Next fall "They will be able to shoot for two days a week for fifteen weeks"—a total of thirty days. Permits would not restrict baiting. It seemed to me that LeCompte and Adams (reactionary East Coast game commissioners) "have put over something on you."

No, Darling replied, they had not, and—"If there is any crime in what we have done I will have to take the blame myself." In fact the staggered thirty-day season had been adopted to defeat the demand of LeCompte and others for sixty straight days of shooting. By lengthening the overall season and limiting the days of shooting, Darling said, they hoped to put an end to unlawful killing in the South after the end of the official season. From Chesapeake Bay to the Florida coast, when duck-club members had left their blinds, "The guides and the local shooters [would keep up] a continuous and unrestricted kill as long as the ducks were present in their neighborhood." The Survey hoped to end this practice. Summing things up, Darling said he did not believe "that it would have been possible to have over-ridden the findings of the Advisory Board and gotten by the President anymore than we did last year."

Least controversial among the altered regulations was an extension of a system begun several years earlier—preferential protection given to the most-endangered species. The new season was totally closed on the ruddy duck and the bufflehead. In a bag limit of twelve ducks, not more than eight in all might consist of eider, canvasback, redhead, greater scaup, lesser scaup, ringneck, blue-winged teal, cinnamon teal, shoveler, and gadwall.

The crisis thus implied was spelled out in October 1934, in a Department of Agriculture publication (Miscellaneous No. 210) written by doctors W. B. Bell and E. A. Preble of the Biological Survey. It dealt with the great and growing discrepancy in surviving numbers among the twenty-five species of ducks found in North America. The two scientists said that "the Mallards, Pintails, and the Canada Geese, whose adaptability makes their breeding grounds practically unlimited, may be able to weather the present crisis." The black ducks might be put in the same class though depleted. The situation of all other species "calls for thoughtful consideration." This understatement swelled to its true proportions as they described conditions in Canada and prescribed the remedy: "It cannot be too strongly emphasized that in the great northern breeding grounds, immense areas of the finest waterfowl breeding grounds remain in virtually primitive condition and await only a sufficiency of breeding stock." That sufficiency could be produced only by sparing enough of the breeding stock from "the most powerful enemy the birds have ever known—millions of well-equipped hunters."

After my return from our 1934 vacation (canoeing on drought-stricken Ozark rivers), I asked Darling what the situation was regarding a permanent head of the Biological Survey. McAtee, I said, seemed to me the only man in the bureau who combined basic conservation principles with knowledge and administrative ability. "Henderson does well enough under existing circumstances, but he is like . . . a stretched rubber . . . ; let go, and he will spring back to his natural affiliations."

"As to brother McAtee," Darling replied, ". . . I thought of him as the logical successor to the top place." But McAtee's first assignment had produced a chaotic report. "It took all summer," said Darling, "to convince me that McAtee has absolutely no administrative capacity, has never been able to work with anyone." On waterfowl, Darling wrote (and I thought he was right) that there was no possibility of getting away with a closed season. FDR was a "sturdy soul," in Darling's judgment, but he had great difficulty saying no to the delegations, senators, personal friends, and "big shots" who wanted longer seasons and continued baiting. "I consider ourselves fortunate that the compromise we suggested was finally signed by him without alteration."

The waterfowl situation did not look promising as the shooting season opened. The staggered season caused a staggering problem in enforcement. By the time shooting ended in mid-January 1935, the hunting regulations had proved to be an unmitigated disaster. Almost every state worked the staggered thirty days of hunting to produce the maximum kill. The preferential protection of species was ridiculed even by the gunmakers' American Game Association, which heartily approved its objective. At the annual meeting of the AGA-sponsored American Game Conference, in January, skins of many varieties of ducks, mostly females, were held up before the assembled sportsmen, and they were asked to identify them. They could not. Speakers at the meeting described what happened in the blinds and in the field. Ducks were shot indiscriminately and those illegally killed were thrown away by hunters who kept on shooting until they reached the legal bag limit.

When the season results were checked up, it was found that the redhead was almost exterminated, the canvasback, greater scaup, and lesser scaup were alarmingly depleted, and the black duck was dropping further behind the mallard and pintail. All through the season, the wealthy clubbers and commercial clubs had easily shot the limit. In spite of these signals of calamity, the baiters clung to baiting, while hundreds of thousands of "one-gallus" hunters tramped marshes and riverbanks and did not even see a winging flock.

Several circumstances united to make me spend a week in Washington, D.C., in January 1935. The National Public Housing Conference asked me to address its second national conference, to be held there from the eighteenth to the twentieth; Rosalie Edge was coming down from New York immediately after she appeared at the American Game Conference,[2] and hoped to see me; and finally I wanted to talk to Roosevelt about the abolition of shooting over baited waters. My first contact in Washington was with Jay Darling, whose appointment as temporary chief of the Biological Survey was stretching out beyond the legally allowable six months without civil service status. I found him dissatisfied with his current situation; and his discontent centered impersonally upon FDR. As America's foremost political cartoonist he had had easy access to the White House. Now, as a bureaucrat, he had to go through channels to the president. In spite of the identical views held by Darling and Henry Wallace, this process took some of the heart and effectiveness out of his endeavors.

During an evening I spent with Darling and Mrs. Edge, they exchanged barbed but good-tempered comments on government waterfowl regulations. Always enjoying each other's company, they could not agree on policy. Darling complained that ECC circulars heaped his desk high with letters to the president, which overburdened the secretarial staff and did no good because the president never saw them. Mrs. Edge's occasional "blasts" at him showed that she did, as Darling once told her, "fear for his soul"—in conservation matters.

Darling was of course anxious that I should talk with Roosevelt about waterfowl, but he also gave me an extra assignment. Congress, with the president's backing, was about to set up a Division of Grazing in the Interior Department, and Darling wanted presidential support for the establishment of numerous big-game refuges on the public lands to be managed by the division. This involved both Interior and Agriculture. Darling believed that Interior secretary Ickes favored the project and suggested that I talk with Harry Slattery, Ickes' personal assistant on conservation. Slattery was tied up, so I walked from his office to the White House and asked press secretary Stephen Early for my first appointment with the president.

Instead of inquiring what I wanted to talk about, Early asked abruptly, "Are you telling him or is he telling you?" I hesitated for a moment. The word "temerity" came into my mind. Then I said, "I'm telling him." "All right," said Steve. "You can see him. But I'm not going to let him waste his time talking to callers."

The meeting, affirmed by Marvin McIntyre, appointments secretary, was to be off-the-record, after the close of the next morning's press conference. Well before the hour, I went to the office of Dr. Preble of the Biological Survey for a final talk—and maybe to brag a little about the coming interview. That, of course, took some time. When I looked at my watch I was horrified: the press conference was due to open—and the office doors to close—in five minutes.

I dashed out of the building, looked in vain for a taxi, and ran all the way to the west executive entrance to the White House. I was late—but so was the conference. At its close Early took me back into the Oval Office. A man sat with the president—somebody who had been at the press meeting. As we came in, the visitor walked to the back of the room and sat down.

I opened at once on baiting. Steve Early, a duck hunter, caught the subject and, to my surprise and delight, expressed hearty agreement with me before leaving. A few more remarks by me, and Roosevelt called out to the man at the back of the room:

"Here, Joe, come up here. I want you in on this."

As Joe came forward, smiling broadly, I had a double think about FDR's tactics: "He is saying to Joe," I thought, "'You are so important that I want you in on this.' He is saying to me, 'The subject is so important that I want Joe in on it.'"

Joe turned out to be Joseph Osborne, New York state game commissioner. Roosevelt repeated to him, almost verbatim, all that I had said to him, with what I took to be an approving intonation. Osborne's presence proved to be a continuing asset. Again and again, the president turned to him, repeating points I made, and the game commissioner, without taking part in the discussion, nodded assent. As I wrote to Dr. Preble the next day, the president's reaction to my warnings of impending extinction for the rarer duck species had been "satisfactory indeed and absolutely unequivocal." I had described to Roosevelt the conversion of wild ducks into virtual barnyard fowls by several days of feeding without shooting. This, I said, was particularly harmful to the disappearing species, for it took away—indeed reversed—the natural wariness that increases to preserve birds and animals as they diminish in numbers. Thus as numbers shrink, the ratio of gunners to the surviving birds increases, while all of the rarer species rush pell-mell toward extermination in the baited ponds.

I also wrote to Hornaday about the president's attitude. "He said (but don't repeat this to anybody) that he was against all baiting of any kind of game, ducks, doves, or anything." It did not necessarily mean, I said, that baiting would be abolished the following summer, but it began to look like it, especially if we demanded a closed season. I thought it inadvisable now to call for an end to baiting, even though "once it is done away with it is gone for good," whereas a closed season only replenished the supply of ducks for more baiting. I said that the repercussions would be unfortunate "if we spread word around that the President is ready to act against baiting."

Darling, I said, was ready to go as far as he was allowed to go. I had been told that although he accepted full responsibility for the last year's regulations, they were not at all his idea. But that statement, if published, "would put him on the spot frightfully."

In a later letter to Hornaday on strategy I was more specific about FDR's reaction to my argument. The president completely endorsed my theory that if regulations were based on the numbers of mallards, pintails, and black ducks, all others would be exterminated. So we should emphasize that argument before the public, to offset "the work of the game hogs." In my remarks to the president there had been no "game hogs"—just well-meaning people blind to reality.

During that same visit I spoke also about two other conservation issues:

establishing big-game refuges on the public domain and bringing sections of the nation's ocean shorelines under public ownership. I brought up big-game protection at the request of Jay Darling. The question was whether the Biological Survey in the Department of Agriculture or the Division of Grazing in the Interior Department should administer the wildlife refuges on the public domain, which had been authorized the year before by Congress.[3] The president seemed to be extremely interested in the need to protect game from grazing interests, and "took notes on all of it." Writing this to Harry Slattery the next day, I added that I was passing along to Steve Early for the president's eye a suggestion by Darling that the refuges be freed from interdepartmental strife by proclaiming them national monuments. The speed with which FDR acted became evident in a note from Darling dated January 31: "Yesterday I saw a memo from the White House (confidential) stating that the Secs of Ag and Interior should get together on the . . . public domain matter. So your little visit [with the president] evidently bore fruit."

I heard no more about the refuges, however, until November 30, 1935. On that day Darling, who had just resigned from the Biological Survey, wrote to me from Des Moines encouraging me to see the president about breaking the interdepartmental deadlock on the refuges. Reclamation and Grazing had stalled on signing the agreements. I wrote to Roosevelt on December 14, and he replied (in a letter drafted by Ickes) on January 7, 1936, that "the matter should be adjusted within a short time." But Darling told me that Congressman Taylor, author of the act setting up the Division of Grazing, was still holding up progress by his insistence that full control of the big-game refuges be given to that division.

Roosevelt himself finally provided the solution. When I talked with him on January 31, 1936, I described the deadlock over management of the refuges. He asked me to suggest a way to handle it. For four days I cudgeled my brain, but I went back to the White House without an idea in my head. I was about to confess my failure when FDR opened the conversation with these words: "How do you think it would work if the Biological Survey had power to say how many head of livestock should graze on the refuges and if the Division of Grazing had power to decide whose livestock should graze there?" "Perfect," I said. It was a simple, logical, fair arrangement. It took some time, however, to implement, because of a runaround in the Interior Department, reported by both the Biological Survey and Ickes. Ickes mentioned to me several times that he could neither control nor fire one unidentified official in the Division of Grazing because of protection given him by influential "livestock congressmen." Ickes proposed to fire him during the distraction of midterm elections. He may have done so. In any case the president's wishes were finally followed.

In January 1935, when I had my first conference with Roosevelt, I brought up a matter on which I had written occasionally for several years: the need for government ownership of a good part of the ocean front. "His response," I wrote to Slattery the next day, "was that the entire front on the Gulf of Mexico, from Avery Island 350 miles westerly, ought to be owned by the government." I had mentioned the support that would be given the general project by people living in the interior, I told Slattery, and concluded: "I don't know what the New Deal will do for the nation generally, but in conservation it is certainly time to apply the motto of the Indiana lady, 'While you're gittin, git a-plenty.'"

President Roosevelt's interest in conservation covered so much of the field, and was so spontaneous, that even when most immersed in affairs of state, he was ready to give part of his time and thoughts to environmental subjects. On March 17, 1935, at the suggestion of Mrs. Edge, I sent him a copy of the Emergency Conservation Committee's teaching unit for young people on the threatened extinction of the bald eagle, with a covering letter to Steve Early asking if the president might endorse the pamphlet. The resulting letter from Roosevelt, which filled the title page of future issues of the eagle unit, closed with this sentence: "The case made for the protection of the eagle, if indeed it were necessary to make a case for it, is convincing and persuasive, and I share with you the desire to see this bird adequately protected by law."

One predictable aftermath of the 1934-35 shooting regulations was a call by Mrs. Edge for another ECC waterfowl pamphlet. It lacked a few days of completion when, early in May, Secretary Wallace and Paul Appleby turned up in St. Louis for another unexpected visit, this time on their way to Louisiana. We spent the afternoon on a gravel bar along the Meramec River, in the Ozark foothills. Afterward I reported to Mrs. Edge that "present prospects are good for a tightening up of regulations—that is, for something real. But please don't be outwardly optimistic about it, for the present purpose seems to be to hand the game hogs a *fait accompli*, and nobody can tell what will happen if they start belaboring the White House."

A few days after the excursion with Wallace and Appleby, I was invited to be the Sunday speaker at what its sponsors predicted "will undoubtedly be the largest convention of the Minnesota Game Protective League ever to be held." Meeting jointly with this body for three days (June 15 to 17) would be the Minnesota Izaak Walton League. The invitation came from the Midwest Conservation Alliance, established in "Eight States Allied on the Only Expedient to Meet the Present Emergency." That expedient was "Close the Season on Migratory Waterfowl for One Year," and enforce the closure.

The list of eleven counselors was headed by Kermit Roosevelt, the new Audubon president, and included his predecessor, T. Gilbert Pearson; Dr. William T. Hornaday; Jack Miner and another Canadian; two Minnesotans; representatives from Michigan, Iowa, and Nebraska; and myself.

The meeting was to be held near Gaylord in a large state park on the shores of Lake Titlow, forty miles southwest of Minneapolis. The invitation extended by Cyril W. Plattes, head of the Midwest Conservation Alliance, was a vanity tickler: "Your wide knowledge of the waterfowl and general game conservation situation would contribute more than any other factor toward rounding out Sunday's program beyond reproach."

The convention may well have been the largest conservation gathering ever held in the United States. A Gaylord high school teacher took me out to the park, where approximately twenty thousand men, women, and children were assembled. The parkwide loudspeaker system—and I mean loud—carried my voice far beyond the thousands who were in sight, to the many more thousands hidden by the trees. What I said was substantially what I had told President Roosevelt in January; primarily it was an attack on baiting while overtly calling for a closed season. As I talked I became a bit worried: people were walking around, eating, talking to each other. Were they listening? Then I realized that with that loudspeaker system in operation they didn't need to listen in order to hear. There was no applause; but, to applaud, they would have had to hold a sandwich or chicken leg between the teeth.

Since the audience, I began to suspect, was divided about twenty thousand to zero on the controversy involved, it was a mystery why they felt the need to have any speaker at all. Educationally, I seemed to be the chief beneficiary of the meeting. Here one met the main body of American hunters—men who hunted for wholesome enjoyment of the outdoors and the game. Here one saw the reason why Minnesota stood at the top of the forty-eight states in number of hunters, in number of ducks killed, and in the movement for their protection—a blending of rural activities, position on the great Mississippi River flyway, and the character of the people. In sharp contrast, and absent, were such states as Missouri and Illinois, whose game departments were dominated by big-city bosses, wealthy club shooters, and commercial sellers of "ducks on the wing," states which competed for a footing on the lowest rung of the conservation ladder. In Minnesota the officially recorded duck kill had diminished from over 2 million in 1930 to 147,000 in 1934. In that state there was no baiting of waterfowl, no concentration of migrating birds on corn-sprinkled waters to give the illusion of undiminished numbers.

I soon learned, however, that my impression of unanimity of opinion was an illusion. No such thing originally prevailed in the eight-state Midwest Conservation Alliance which sponsored the Gaylord gathering. That was made clear in what Dr. Hornaday wrote to me on June 29, 1935: "Cyril Plattes says that your address was what turned a tide of opposition, and struck a keynote which made the whole occasion a glorious success."

I took a good deal of satisfaction in having my old adversary T. Gilbert Pearson as one of the sponsors of the Gaylord convention, but the participation of Audubon executive director John H. Baker signaled a real turning point in Audubon policies. I had received an earlier indication of this in January, when Baker sent me a strong statement on waterfowl policy. My reply, praising it, brought a reaffirmation from Baker a month later. "Rest assured," he wrote me in advance of the Gaylord convention, "that we are making every move that we know how to bring pressure on the President, on Secretary Wallace and on Darling with relation to the waterfowl hunting regulations in 1935."

Baker was authorized by the eight-state alliance to present the convention's request for a closed season to the president, and I was asked by Baker to arrange his personal presentation of the material to Mr. Roosevelt. My application to that end (through McIntyre) was followed by a reply to Baker that "the immediate pressure of official and legislative matters precludes arranging an appointment at this time." The president, McIntyre said, wished to see Baker "a little later on and discuss this and related matters." Two weeks later word came to Baker (in Washington) that he and Darling should "work it out between them" before he saw the president later at Hyde Park.

This put the matter on the best possible basis, since both Baker and Darling wanted baiting abolished. Presumably Baker ultimately met with Mr. Roosevelt, since the resolutions adopted at the eight-state conference are stapled in as part of the twenty-one-page documentation of the matter in the presidential papers.

My ECC pamphlet, put out in June, bore the self-explanatory title *The Collapse of Waterfowl Protection: Danger of Immediate Extinction of Various Species*. The pamphlet was in the main an expansion of my exposition to President Roosevelt five months earlier. It contained, however, one important factual addition. A Biological Survey winter count of waterfowl on their southern concentration grounds indicated that only eighteen to twenty million ducks were still alive in the United States, a shrinkage of eighty percent in four years.

The pamphlet, from beginning to end, was an attack on baiting as the assured exterminator of all waterfowl; but in accord with tactics worked out with Darling, the call was for a complete closing of the shooting season. In line with this strategy, I presented a five-point program, opening with two choices of action: either "immediate and complete closure of the season, with rapid restoration of a few species of waterfowl and slow restoration of others," or "complete closure after a few years, with slow restoration of a few species and no restoration whatever of the others." The pamphlet also called for an international system of sanctuaries, "from Canada to the Gulf," to protect wildfowl against loss of habitat. I used rough language about "the small, powerful clique of influential baiters whose sole thought is to give up no present privilege and let the future care for itself"; rough language also for their system of baiting: "Compared with real hunting, it is about as sportsmanlike as shooting a pig in a barrel." Some private preserves were true sanctuaries, I conceded, but when the vast majority of owners made their baited waters "an agency of monstrous destructiveness, the privilege of the few must be sacrificed to curb the abuse of the many." The thousands of more farsighted Americans who had given up hunting voluntarily were aligned with millions of nonhunters "who take joy in the outdoors and wish our waterfowl preserved for the benefit of all." These people had rights, too long ignored, which must come first when the choice was between extermination or perpetuation of wildlife. Subordinating all else to the lust of killing, the exterminators saw no wrong in destroying the Creator's handiwork. "The idea that the world exists in part for its non-human inhabitants is beyond their ken."

On August 1, 1935, President Roosevelt and Secretary of Agriculture Wallace signed regulations reducing bag limits, shortening the hunting season, prohibiting the use of live decoys, and abolishing the shooting of waterfowl over baited waters. Mrs. Edge and Hornaday congratulated me on the effects of my pamphlets. Nobody, it seems, thought to congratulate Franklin Roosevelt, who took time out from a herculean economic-recovery task to grasp and perform a job in conservation by action that antagonized most of his wealthiest friends and enemies.

The Mariposa Grove at Yosemite, 1925, with Brant's car in foreground; the threat-ened Carl Inn sugar pine grove adjoined the boundaries of Yosemite, and, unlike the Mariposa, was at the mercy of logging interests (photograph by Irving Brant, courtesy Robin Brant Lodewick).

CHAPTER THREE

THE CARL INN SUGAR PINES

During my talks with the president in January and February 1936, I brought up the conflict between the Interior and Agriculture departments in relation to the projected Olympic National Park, but dealt more especially with the immediate threat to the Carl Inn Grove of sugar pines, on the border of Yosemite National Park. This involved the preservation or destruction of ninety-six hundred privately owned acres of forest that had originally been included in the park, but were eliminated in the "Ballinger days" of 1912 on the false pretense that the land was chiefly suited for grazing. That was true only of a small cutover and scrubby area north of the Carl Inn Grove.

For about twenty years, the two-hundred-foot-tall sugar pines were protected by inaccessibility. Not even a dirt road ran near them. During 1928 the lumbermen reached and had begun to fell privately owned sugar pines near the Carl Inn Grove, but lying inside the national-park boundaries. Alerted by Dr. Willard Van Name and others, conservationists waged a successful campaign to preserve these trees. Congress appropriated $1 million and John D. Rockefeller, Jr., put up the same amount (which he had previously offered) as the required matching funds. The trees were saved.

The nationwide publicity given this successful campaign obscured the fact that still more magnificent sugar pines, part of the same forest, were in growing peril. Naturalist John Muir wrote about the trees of the Carl Inn Grove while they were still within Yosemite Park: "The sunbeams streaming through their feathery arches brighten the ground and you walk beneath the vaulted ceiling in devout, subdued mood as if you were in a grand cathedral."

The American public knew nothing about this majestic grove, domed and doomed, until the building of the Big Oak Flat Road from Yosemite Valley to the High Sierra put a paved highway along the park boundary, exactly between the Rockefeller purchase and the Carl Inn Grove. Motorists, winding between the great pines, did not dream that one side of the road was marked for destruction.

Spurred by Dr. Van Name, Mrs. Edge persuaded Senator Nye of North Dakota, chairman of the Senate Committee on Public Lands, to introduce a bill for acquisition of the forest and inclusion of it in Yosemite Park. Unfortunately his bill provided for acquisition by a trade of national-forest stumpage for the grove, thus ensuring the violent opposition of the Forest Service. In January 1932, I wrote an editorial strongly supporting the Nye bill and rejecting the contention of the Forest Service (accepted by the weak-kneed National Park Service) that the scenic quality of the Big Oak Flat Road would be adequately preserved by a carefully cut or non-cut roadside strip. That meant, I said, that anybody who walked two hundred yards off the highway would encounter utter devastation.

The Davey Tree Surgeons of Kent, Ohio, sent my editorial to Ovid Butler, executive secretary of the American Forestry Association, which was financed by West Coast lumber interests. Butler replied that all this agitation resulted from misinformation by "a certain man" (he meant Van Name) who was not to be trusted. Scenic interest, Butler assured Mr. Davey, was adequately protected by an agreement between the Forest Service and the National Park Service. For the next four years, with the Park Service thus tangled in knots it had helped to tie, the Nye bill lay in a pigeonhole; meanwhile the Carl Inn Grove was saved from immediate destruction by the Great Depression.

By 1936, with the new highway open and the lumber industry reviving, the situation had reached crisis proportions. I recounted this history to President Roosevelt on February 4 and warned him of a recent sharp increase in the danger to the grove. The Yosemite Lumber Company "had started cutting toward the Carl Inn Grove, which meant that a race was on to see how much could be saved before they cut to the park boundary." I wrote to Ickes what I had told the president, that "these sugar pines are hardly if at all inferior to the great sequoias, for they make up in beauty the little they lack in size, and it would be a crime if a grove which naturally belongs to Yosemite Park, and once was inside of it, should be destroyed." Concerning the Carl Inn bill and one recently introduced for an Olympic park, I said that if the administration would "get behind the two bills and tell the Forest Service people to keep their hands off, they would go through Congress without difficulty."

President Roosevelt left no doubt about his sympathetic attitude toward the preservation of the sugar pines, but he did not give a directive and a clash ensued between the departments involved. Four weeks after I wrote to Secretary Ickes, he sent a favorable report to the Senate lands committee on the Nye bill for acquisition of the grove. At about the same time (March 12) Secretary Wallace made an adverse report on the bill, principally because, by Forest Service estimate, the acquisition would cost $2 million in exchange stumpage, plus a probable seven hundred thousand dollars to Tuolumne County for reimbursement of future taxes and road and trail allocations. The Bureau of the Budget was rejecting such expenditures.

This adverse report, undoubtedly written by the Forest Service, was loaded with fallacious arguments. The timber valuation was grossly exaggerated and the county reimbursements were grotesque. Ickes not only was affirmative on conservation, he put his feelings into his thoughts. On April 4, he wrote to me:

"The Yosemite sugar pine situation is very bad indeed. I had word the other day that a big mill had been set up and that lumbering operations were about to begin. According to the present plans everything in the big privately owned grove will be cut during the next five years. I am tremendously interested in the situation but don't know where to turn. I have given instructions, however, to see whether we can't unloose some publicity that might arouse public interest in this atrocity."

Ten days after Ickes wrote this, an opening came for national publicity. Responding to an overture by me, editor Richard Westwood of *Nature Magazine* wired that he would publish a thousand-word article about the sugar pines in the June issue if it reached them by their deadline, April 25. That left eleven days in which to get the article into Westwood's hands—time enough, but none to spare. I sealed the envelope on it two days before the deadline. So that was that.

Or so I thought. One week later, burrowing for something else, I found that envelope on my desk. I put airmail postage on it—risky in that day—with an explanation and the comment "Is it too late? I hope not." It was too late for the planned display, but Westwood gave it two fore-pages with illustrations and carried the rest into the back of the magazine. In planning this article I had decided to play down the Nye bill and concentrate on an appeal for private gifts. I warned that the great trees were about to go "down beneath the axe and saw and overhead cables of the lumberman. When the crime is completed, the northern approach to Yosemite Park, now a source of awe and inspiration to all who pass through it, will be a sickening shambles—a scene of desolation familiar to all who have witnessed the destructive ferocity of high-rigging lumbering." In the past, I said, no one had realized that the virgin forests of the Far West were doomed to disappear as surely as the grizzly, except where preserved by state or nation. Sugar pines "were so numerous thirty years ago . . . that the thought of protecting them would have raised a laugh." But intensive lumbering was now eliminating all mature trees. Specimens would survive "as a widely scattered forest crop, lumbered before reaching maturity," but if the people of America were to know the pines as John Muir did, it must be within a sanctuary. There is bitter irony, I wrote, in the fact that the motorist on the new highway winding in and out of Yosemite "assumes that he is still in the Park when he passes through the finest and most inspiring portion of his route. Little does he dream . . . that this glory of the Yosemite region is doomed." In the high-rigging logging headed for the Carl Inn Grove, every tree would be cut, every sapling torn out by the roots, and the forest streams would soon dry up as the land dried, unshielded from the sun. The article closed with an appeal for action:

"For fourteen years this tragedy has been protested against, and the nation has done nothing to forestall it. Now it is at hand, and desperate speed is necessary, for the inexorable mills will never stop to argue. Can America produce a miracle, a second miracle indeed, rivaling in generosity and timeliness the great gift of John D. Rockefeller in 1928? Can some emergency organization spring into being and work with a rapidity never known before? Or shall this be written down as a day, dark in human annals, when man lives only to destroy the miracles of Nature?"

This article produced immediate repercussions. S. D. Platford of Los Angeles, president of the Joint Conservation Committee of Southern California, wrote on May 20, "I have just this minute finished reading your article 'California Sugar Pines' and the thought strikes me that if Mrs. Will Rogers was approached in the right manner and by the right people, the purchase of this property could be accomplished. There is a Will Rogers Memorial Fund already established for such a memorial you know."

I forwarded the suggestion to Secretary Ickes, who put the matter before the Will Rogers Memorial trustees. They decided that it was outside the purview of the foundation.

A woman in Santa Barbara, California, offered me a check for five dollars as part of the purchase price. "The March of Time," leading radio-news programmer of the day, dallied with the idea of a feature on the subject. A young man named William G. Schulz, living in Long Beach, wrote to me that he intensely desired to get into the business of writing on conservation and outdoor life. Could I give him any suggestions, especially in regard to saving the sugar pines and creating an Olympic national park?

I recommended him to "The March of Time" as a field worker in their project and advised him to try to plant feature stories in the California Sunday newspapers, "terrible as they are," and in the New York press. I suggested also that he write to Colonel Thomson, superintendent of Yosemite National Park, who had received orders from above to get into the fight to save the pines.

Schulz responded with an offer to work for almost nothing above expenses for any organization set up to preserve the grove. His expressed eagerness to get into the work without regard to money had a genuine ring. I rushed his letter to Mrs. Edge, saying that the offer "represents, apparently, the last chance to do anything effective to save the sugar pines. The young man has made a good impression on me by what he has written and done, and I think he is moved by more than a desire to earn a few dollars. Colonel Thomson evidently realizes that it is now or never. Can the E.C.C. do anything directly? . . . The place to start undoubtedly is California. If an agitation can be stirred up there, it will spread."

My uncertainty about the Emergency Conservation Committee reflected a crisis within that organization. Mrs. Edge and Dr. Van Name, both devoted to the same goals by the same methods, were high-strung individuals with conflicting personalities. Mrs. Edge had an element of spitefulness in her makeup and Dr. Van Name—invariably right on conservation issues—believed that everybody who disagreed with him had evil motives. Van Name had withdrawn from the committee in anger at Mrs. Edge for her having paid a visit to Colonel Thomson, back before Ickes discovered that Thomson was under NPS wraps and took them off. But Van Name still counted on the committee to go on working. Mrs. Edge now asked Thomson for an appraisal of Schulz, who had just visited Yosemite, and she received this telegram on August 19:

"Schulz interest apparently inspired by Brant. His background and ability unknown to us. Is young and unacquainted hereabouts but seems enthusiastic and resourceful. Has just secured temporary job Ahwahnee Hotel [in Yosemite]. After reviewing situation in field he proposed generalized plan of publicizing facts widely through such media as Christian Science Monitor conservation and civic clubs et cetera. Only barest possibility that Schulz or anyone else can produce results and am not even hopeful but present outlook hopeless and full time services of some individual in the field might prove fortunate move. Am informed this summers cut will exceed sixty million board feet."

Funds for Schulz could come only from Van Name; so it was up to me to break the impasse between him and Mrs. Edge. I told him about my correspondence with Schulz and said that Mrs. Edge was "rather hesitant about making arrangements with him," but finally agreed to put up $150 from the ECC toward $300 which would be necessary for a six weeks' campaign. "If he accepts the small salary of $25 [per week] and the same for expenses," I said, it will "prove that he is [acting] as a nature lover, and not for gain. That is the impression I formed of him."

I expressed hope that Van Name would put up the other $150, as this venture offered the last hope of doing anything for the pines "and there is a chance that it will lead to action in the White House next winter." I was sure that Roosevelt was interested, I said, "from what he said to me last winter." It was politically impossible for the president to do anything before election, and almost impossible for him to do anything afterward unless there was a *Pacific Coast* demand for action. If women's clubs and other organizations could be stirred up, "a campaign to raise money by public subscriptions can easily be converted into a movement to save the grove by appropriation." I hoped that Van Name would make this last speculative effort to bring the long campaign to a successful conclusion: "The odds are against it, of course, but they always have been. Every fight in conservation is made against odds, and many are won by a strategic thrust at the right moment, with whatever weapon lies at hand."

Dr. Van Name replied that he would "gladly give the $150 if there is still a possibility of saving anything." But he would like to know how much of the forest was left—"before I throw any more money after the thousands I have already thrown away." He would send the $150 at once if I would inform him of the present status of the logging and it did not look too hopeless.

I told him that the projected 1937 cut was sixty million board feet, which would denude one seventh of the Carl Inn Grove's ninety-six hundred acres. This left a year for salvation of the greater part of the grove. All of the grove could be saved, by a miracle, if purchased before snow melted in the spring.

Van Name sent the money and Schulz took up his hundred-dollar-a-month job as field agent of the Emergency Conservation Committee, reporting to Mrs. Edge and informally to me. He began by calling on John Ball, president of the Yosemite Lumber Company, who, he reported, went into elaborate detail concerning expanded equipment and the extension of logging railroads "with spurs pushing deep into the very choicest of the sugar pine"—spurs that Van Name said were "alarmingly close to the park boundary." Cutting was to start in mid-March or early April, depending on snow conditions. This left four months in which to check the devastation before it began. Schulz appraised Mr. Ball:

"As far as I could see, he . . . gave me the whole situation frankly from the company's point of view, thus enabling us to see exactly where we stand if we are to regain that timber area. . . . As Colonel Thomson has already said, Mr. Ball certainly is not bluffing, with an eye to Government purchase of his property; rather, it is purely a business venture with him and he is working it for all that he can realize out of it."

Schulz made a guess that $3 million would be needed to buy the grove. That figure obviously included payment for abandoned logging railroads, buildings, and other capital investments on which John Ball had laid emphasis—items which Congress would be certain to reject.

In November, at my request, Superintendent Thomson obtained a map showing the area marked for cutting in 1937. It revealed a drastic change of plans. Instead of continuing to cut outwards from the sawmill, the Yosemite Lumber Company was aiming straight into the heart of the forest. The next season's logging was scheduled to reach and follow the national-park boundary along the Big Oak Flat Road. I described the program to Harry Slattery and commented:

"This means that the last chance to save this magnificent grove is this winter, through congressional action . . . they are proceeding to strike with sole regard to maximum immediate financial returns, and that takes them into the finest regions first, with no regard whatever to any public considerations. . . . It seems strange that with the President interested and Secretary Ickes concerned about it, the thing runs along until it is almost too late to do anything."

Senator Nye's bill, I remarked, had been introduced as a "request" measure. Now we needed "something under administration auspices. Can you make any suggestions about sponsorship?"

Slattery's reply expressed concern, but said preservation of the sugar pines depended on stirring Congress to action by evidence that enough people throughout the country were interested. "If, however, such public sentiment is to be effective it must be supported by the people of California." That threw the burden of arousing sentiment onto the Emergency Conservation Committee and particularly onto Schulz.

A few days earlier, on November 25, 1936, Schulz had reported to Mrs. Edge on a lengthy meeting he had with L. A. Barrett, chairman of the conservation committee of the Commonwealth Club of San Francisco—an organization which, Schulz thought, could be as influential an ally as the Sierra Club. Barrett, regarded as California's foremost forest-conservation authority, had retired in April after thirty-odd years in the Forest Service, much of that time as regional forester. "Far from being our enemy," wrote Schulz, "[Barrett] is our friend. . . . He repeatedly said to me: 'I'm a freelancer now. I can say what I please.' " Barrett told Schulz he had opposed the Nye bill, but only because it took in lightly timbered lands north of the sugar pines, inclusion of which would stir up livestock grazers and hunters against the project. He was eager to save "the very best and finest-stand sugar pine," whose location he marked on a map.

Barrett had been highly critical of the way the 1928 Rockefeller purchase was carried out, with $300 per acre paid for sugar-pine and other timberland worth $120 to $150 at the high prices prevailing then. Eight years later the finest sugar pine was selling at $3 to $3.50 per thousand board feet, intermingled white fir and Douglas fir at $.50 to $1.50 per thousand. The entire area suited for the park, Barrett said, should cost about $1.5 million.

A few days later Mrs. Edge wrote to urge me to talk to the president and Ickes about the sugar pines (unneeded advice) during a planned January trip to Washington. "I ask this," she wrote, "not as a last desperate measure, but because the whole project is going perfectly splendidly in California under Mr. Schulz." He had the official endorsement of the Sierra Club and the Commonwealth Club, as well as lesser groups. The Hearst papers had come out for the pines, without antagonizing other newspapers. The DAR was going right into the fight. "Schulz is really magnificent."

Without having met him, I sensed that Schulz "had a way with women"—with women, that is, in garden clubs, church groups, sewing circles, and the DAR. He had a way, also, with businessmen, editors, scientists, legislators—and a way with opponents. Both Sacramento newspapers were won over in their news columns, with the *Bee* giving strong editorial support. He had asked the *Bee* to reprint an editorial of mine and was using it selectively with other newspapers and various organizations. "I have not gone after news publicity so much as yet," he wrote. "I have been waiting first to get some good, sound backing from reputable organizations, and with these names as justification for the news, to follow with news stories."

He said the California State Chamber of Commerce had turned down his proposal, but former regional forester Barrett had suggested changes in it that might win them over. Wherever he went, Schulz said, he had first had to act as conciliator and diplomat, "to meet hurt feelings and much misunderstanding on the part of those antagonized by previous efforts to save the Carl Inn area." That reflected Van Name's distrust of everybody who did not immediately agree with his ideas. People also were scared by the Yosemite Lumber Company's purchase estimate of $4 million or $5 million, given to the park people, but Barrett had helped greatly by scaling this down to $1.5 million, or $2 million at the most.

On January 4, 1937, I wrote to White House secretary Marvin McIntyre that I would arrive in Washington on Wednesday (the sixth) to give a radio broadcast on Congress and the Constitution, and would like to speak with the president. The appointment was made, and I briefed the president on the critical sugar-pine situation, stressing the need for a purchase agreement with the Yosemite Lumber Company before the end of March. Congressional action had to be completed within three months.

"How much will it cost?" Roosevelt asked.

Not wanting to state a definite maximum, I said, "You could go a long way on a million dollars." Roosevelt replied without hesitation: "Secretary Ickes has some leftover relief funds. Go to him and say that I want him to make an allocation for the sugar pines."

I bee-lined to the Interior Department and delivered the message. "Did he say how much?" Ickes asked. I told him of my remark about a million dollars going a long way. He thought a moment or two and said, "I think we'd better make it two million."

I returned to St. Louis on the following Monday (January 11) and on that day received a telephone call from Ickes which caused me to send the following telegram to the Emergency Conservation Committee: "Secretary Ickes telephoned today asking me [to] return Washington to secure congressional support bill enlarging Yosemite. Go next Tuesday. Ickes wants California supporters and others to write president and himself and senators and congressmen calling for action. Have them send Ickes copies of all letters. Haste needed."

I wrote to Ickes that I would arrive in Washington on January 19. On the sugar-pines project, as Ickes had requested, I put in virtually all my time at the Capitol. Senator Nye's bill was out of date by reason of the shift from timber exchange to relief-fund allocation. Although, under the arrangement proposed by President Roosevelt, the money was on hand, Congress had to authorize the appropriation of it to this use. A new bill had to be introduced and I hoped that Californians would sponsor it.

I put the proposition up to Senator William G. McAdoo. He "took about one minute," I wrote to Mrs. Edge, "to say he was for the bill and will introduce it if the Interior Department wants him to." Considerably more work, I found, needed to be done among California congressmen. Representative Harry Lane Englebright, in whose district the Carl Inn Grove was located, spoke favorably about preservation of the trees but made a remark that showed who, as well as what, would control his vote: "If the Yosemite Lumber Company sells this land to the government, I want them to get all they can for it."

Heads of the Senate and House public lands committees were both favorable. The House chairman, Rene De Rouen of Louisiana, seemed ready to do whatever the administration wanted, but said that speedy passage of the bill would depend on agreement between the Interior and Agriculture departments. I outlined the proposition to Senator Alva Adams of Colorado, conservative chairman of the Senate lands committee. He responded with a flashback of memory. After forty years, he said, he still grieved over the cutting down of a single cottonwood in eastern Colorado, and it governed his attitude on all questions involving trees.

Congressman Ed Eicher of Iowa, a personal friend, chairman of a group of forty Middle Western farmer representatives, said that he would line them up. Senator Charles McNary of Oregon, Republican floor leader, declared himself heartily for the bill. I had a talk with Ferdinand Silcox, head of the Forest Service, and wrote to Mrs. Edge that he declared himself "absolutely in favor of saving the pines and [ready to] help before the congressional committees." I made no effort to see President Roosevelt on this trip but wrote to him on January 24: "The sugar pine situation in Congress seems excellent. Senator McAdoo offers to introduce a bill. Congressman Englebright is favorable, but wants to take care of Tuolumne County (in his district) by a payment of future taxes from the timber. That seems a pretty strong demand to me, as the land will be worthless when the timber is cut and taxes will soon disappear. . . . Several other California congressmen are interested favorably and the chairmen of the Senate and House public lands committees have a co-operative attitude. I have told all of them, in response to inquiries, that the administration is favorable provided the demand for action comes from California. Public sentiment out there has developed greatly in the last two weeks, since I talked with you."

In reporting these developments to Mrs. Edge, I repeated my telegraphed request of January 12 that an appeal be made to Californians to write to the president and to their senators and representatives in support of an allocation of funds to buy the trees. This was essential, I said, because the president "has to have something to show if there is opposition or criticism. But of course don't say that this has been requested."

The last warning was needed because Mrs. Edge, in her enthusiasm, had overreacted to my telegram on that subject. She had sent out a circular letter, saying, "Secretary Ickes telegraphs us"—that he wanted letters sent to

Roosevelt, himself, and members of Congress; and she compounded the indiscretion with a postscript reading, "Secretary Ickes wants copies of all letters." Fortunately her circular went only to a selected list of supporters and was unlikely to reach opponents of the bill. One of the recipients, however, was Nathan Margold, solicitor of the Interior Department, who turned it over to Secretary Ickes. The result was that on the day after I sent my warning against a repetition of the indiscretion, Ickes wrote her a scathing letter of rebuke, combining pretended indignation and genuine alarm.

"I know," he wrote, "that you have at heart the cause in behalf of which this [circular] letter was written, but I also know of nothing better calculated to defeat that cause." Personally, he was in favor of saving those pines, but he did not know by what authority she had said the campaign to save them had the approval of himself, or of the president. He had never telegraphed her and never authorized anybody, at any time, to urge the sending of letters in support of the measure, and never had asked that copies of such letters be sent to him. He asked her "never to quote me again except with my prior consent," unless on the basis of an authentic public statement that he had made.

Mrs. Edge rushed a copy of this letter to me, with the comment that she was "surprised at his rudeness." I replied:

"Don't worry about Ickes's letter. That was defensive technique, to protect himself—and the sugar pine proposition—in case somebody attempted to use your circular letter to inspire prejudice against the bill in Congress. Of course his language was rough; but the rougher it is the more effective if the issue comes up, which is unlikely."

Should there be any necessity to explain it, I added, she could "say that Secretary Ickes told me [Brant] that he would like to see evidence of California support for the proposition," and that *my advice* to send him copies of letters was misinterpreted as a request *by him* that they be sent.

Before this soothing explanation reached Mrs. Edge, that hot-tempered lady had fired a reply to Ickes saying that if he denied telephoning to "an officer of this Committee," asking that letters be sent, "I must believe you." However, she had "believed that you did so telephone to our Treasurer, Mr. Irving Brant"— and she enclosed a photostat of my telegram on the subject. Ickes replied to her, "As I read Mr. Brant's telegram, he doesn't even authorize you to use my name, much less that of the President." He said that my telegram had simply expressed his wish to be kept informed of support for the project in California.

That misunderstanding laid to rest, I then wrote to Ickes that I feared a conflict with the Forest Service would develop over a request just received from Yosemite superintendent Thomson (who died a few weeks later) for inclusion of national-forest land north of the sugar pines for recreational development. This, I said, had induced me to write to Ferdinand Silcox, asking his opinion of the proposed boundaries and explaining that my concern was to avoid a disagreement between the two bureaus.

The chief forester replied on February 11 with a sweeping endorsement of government purchase of the Carl Inn Grove and an assurance that there would be no disagreement over boundaries. He and Assistant Chief Demaray of the National Park Service had spent the previous day studying maps and, he said, "I have written a letter for the Secretary's signature notifying the Department of the Interior that we are ready to agree on the boundaries Mr. Demaray and I went over yesterday." These would include "scattered areas of National Forest land that are within the purchase area."

Lying ahead was the all-important matter of an agreement on price with the Yosemite Lumber Company. On that subject Secretary Ickes had publicly announced the projected allocation of $2 million, while John Ball, president of the lumber company, was insisting that if any land was to be bought "it is all or nothing." "All" would probably cost about $4 million for fourteen thousand acres, half again the area of the Carl Inn Grove. However, the bill drafted for Senator McAdoo contained a provision for condemnation, which meant that any part of the company holdings could be acquired at a price fixed by the courts. On March 9 I wrote to Secretary Ickes that lumbering was set to begin in three weeks; would it be possible to push a bill through Congress in that time? I volunteered to write to Congressman Cochran of St. Louis, who headed the Committee on Expenditures in the Executive Department, urging his support.

Early in April Arno Cammerer, director of the NPS, sent me a summation of the sugar-pines situation, based on a field report by Interior Department forester W. H. Horning, who had dealt with the lumber people before and after the death of Colonel Thomson. The company was demanding that the government buy any of its acreage rendered inaccessible by purchase of the sugar pines. Aware that a partial purchase could be made by condemnation, it cited the threatened loss of a company payroll of half a million dollars or more, loss of local purchases, loss of business by the Yosemite Valley Railway, loss to other mining interests by collapse of the railroad, and tax loss to the counties.

The San Joaquin and Central Valley councils of the state chamber of commerce, opposing the purchase, offered a substitute program: acquisition of scenic roadside strips and careful selective cutting of the remaining area under Forest Service supervision, the timber reserved in the scenic strips to be paid for by the government, the company to be paid for the extra cost of selective cutting in lieu of high-rigging, and the counties to be given 25 percent of the annual revenues of Yosemite National Park. All of this was presented seriously!

Congress moved fast once the McAdoo bill was in the works. A House hearing was quickly set for April 20. Mrs. Edge, one of the witnesses, wrote me next day that Cammerer "put in a splendid report," which gave high credit to Van Name. Demaray also was at his best. Don Tressidor, of the Yosemite Park concessionaire company, "made a perfectly splendid witness."

Congressman Englebright, who had been presenting himself to me as a not-fully-convinced friend of the sugar pines, led the opposition. Mrs. Edge, who followed him on the stand, gave me a modest account of her testimony. Noted for her impromptu wit and rapier thrusts on cross-examination, she had no brief but had taken careful note of "all the things that Englebright had twisted falsely. I think that I got my points over; anyhow I got them all laughing at Englebright." Rene De Rouen, she commented, "is the fairest and most courteous chairman I have ever seen."

Mrs. Edge wrote on the same day to California congressman John S. McGroarty, who had introduced the sugar-pines bill in the House, giving him additional insight into Englebright's tactics. Early in the campaign, Schulz and Mrs. Codman, head of the DAR in California, had gone to Englebright, found him apparently enthusiastic for preservation of the Carl Inn Grove, and asked his permission to forward all supporting letters to him for presentation at the hearings. Englebright agreed to the plan. Now about two thousand individually written letters were in his custody. Those letters, Mrs. Edge wrote to McGroarty, "should be in your hands. I hope you will obtain them from Mr. Englebright. . . . [He] gave an entirely erroneous impression when he insinuated that the letters were form letters emanating from some central source."

I relayed word of Englebright's apparent duplicity to Secretary Ickes, who, after an inquiry, reported that Englebright did introduce the California letters as evidence and that they were likewise introduced in the Senate hearings, held on April 29. Ickes believed that they carried considerable weight. The House committee, Ickes said, had voted favorably on the bill. The Senate committee did the same two weeks later, and the bill sailed through the Senate without opposition. Its fate would be decided in the House and would depend on the relative pulling power of Englebright of California and Cochran of Missouri—Englebright by reason of his California constituency and Cochran as chairman of the committee on expenditures.

Wednesday, June 9, was calendar day for the House Committee on the Public Lands, and on Tuesday chairman De Rouen repeated a promise to Cochran that the sugar-pine bill would be the first one called up, ensuring action without delay. De Rouen kept his promise. In the debate Englebright did a complete flipflop on the issue of cost. He had told me that he wanted the Yosemite Lumber Company to get the highest possible price for the land. On the floor he denounced the purchase as an extravagant waste of public funds. He asked again and again: where did Secretary Ickes get that figure of $2 million? What was it based on and who set the amount? De Rouen or Cochran could have told him—that Ickes simply doubled the figure I had suggested to the president—but they said nothing. Cochran's reputation as a "watchdog of the Treasury" made his support vital. Later, sitting in his wheelchair (he was legless from bone cancer), Cochran told me he had helped to beat Englebright's amendment requiring that the government pay the counties for all property taxes lost by enlarging the park.

The House passed the bill, 184 to 127. Reporting this to me, Cochran said the fight was not over. A procedural snag had been struck. For some unexplained reason and without it being noticed, McGroarty, author of the House bill, had failed to move that the Senate bill be substituted for his own. So each house had passed its own bill. The bills were identical in wording, but were different entities. The effect was that neither bill had passed both houses. The Senate would now have to pass the House bill or there would be no legislation.

I wrote at once to Senator Adams, urging quick action to prevent the start of a logging railway. The Senate did more than act quickly. It amended the House bill to confer limited jurisdiction over private lands, then passed it. I expressed hope to Congressman Cochran that the House would agree to the Senate amendment, since it would be much easier to administer the park extension as a territorial unit. "All legitimate private rights," I said, "would be preserved on any territory which might be brought in without being purchased. If failure to purchase any given plot would automatically exclude it from the park, the government might be forced to buy at a disadvantage in order to prevent uncontrolled commercial development on a private tract completely surrounded by park lands." Also, under the Senate amendment, additional private tracts could be purchased later without passage of a new act of Congress.

The House accepted the Senate amendment and the bill went to the president, who promptly signed it. The Carl Inn Grove was saved. Or so it seemed.

Then, early in August, lightning struck out of a clear sky. The National Park Service put out a news release revealing that the president did not have power to make the $2 million allocation at the time he made it. The bill that passed Congress was valid, purchase of the sugar pines was authorized by law, but the money for them had vanished. There would be no purchase unless Congress made a regular appropriation. Congressman Cochran sent me an explanation which I relayed to Dr. Van Name just as he was about to leave for the Philippines on an American Museum assignment. I wrote:

"The trouble, I am told, has no connection with any opposition to the sugar pine bill, but results from a maneuver made last spring by Senators Glass, Byrd and other reactionaries . . . to cut down the discretionary powers of the President. They got a provision inserted into the relief bill that reappropriated balances from old emergency appropriations could only be used for relief. Nobody noticed this when the sugar pine bill came up, but it cut off the power of the President to use the residue of a 1933 appropriation for the pines, although the congressional debate showed plainly that the purpose of Congress was to have this fund used. The present intense hostility of the anti-Roosevelt forces makes it a pretty delicate matter to handle, but it ought to be merely a routine correction to make the money available."

Roosevelt's influence in Congress had just struck an all-time low in the rejection of his bill to enlarge the Supreme Court. Fortunately the sugar-pine bill had been treated as congressional, not administration, policy, and there had simply been an oversight in the Bureau of the Budget. The House Appropriations Committee promptly offered an amendment to a deficiency appropriations bill, but Congressman Englebright knocked it out on a point of order—that it was legislation in an appropriations bill. The point was evidently correct, I wrote to Van Name, for four other items were knocked out on similar grounds, including one for taking American refugees out of China.

The Senate had no such rule. When the House bill came over a couple of days later Senator McAdoo offered an amendment, which was promptly adopted, restoring the sugar-pine appropriation. This made its fate dependent on the conference committee and on House action if the committee retained it. On reading of this action, I informed Van Name, "I telegraphed to Majority Leader Rayburn and Congressman Cochran, who is one of the most influential men in the House on money matters, and asked them to urge the House conferees to follow the Senate. Cochran wired back that he had already done so and the conferees were in session."

Two days later (August 23, 1937) Sam Rayburn sent me this telegram: "House accepted Senate amendment Yosemite appropriation to third deficiency bill on Saturday." The Carl Inn Grove was purchased for $1.5 million, the exact valuation that had been placed on it by retired regional forester Barrett.

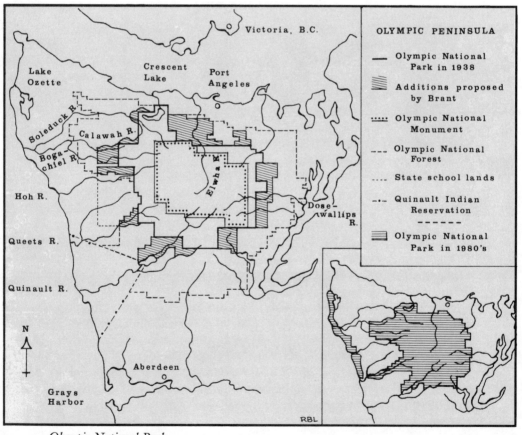

Olympic National Park

CHAPTER FOUR

AN OLYMPIC
NATIONAL PARK

On the Olympic Peninsula of the State of Washington, surrounding the Olympic Mountains, the people of the United States own the last great forest wilderness still standing in their country." The quotation is from the opening paragraph of a pamphlet, *The Olympic Forests for a National Park*, which I wrote in October 1937. Published some weeks later by the Emergency Conservation Committee and widely distributed, the pamphlet was printed in the *Congressional Record* of March 8, 1938, in the climactic period of the campaign to establish Olympic National Park. The pamphlet described a rain forest of three-hundred-foot-tall Douglas fir, spruce, red cedar, and hemlock that had no counterpart on earth. Beneath the towering evergreens spread moss-hung maples and alders; on the ground, ferns and moss enveloped huge decaying logs. The forest, extending between snow-capped peaks and seashore, home of the Roosevelt elk, was marked for destruction "unless the people protect their property."

The effort to save these gigantic trees and the matchless rain forest from total destruction began in the presidency of Theodore Roosevelt under the leadership of Congressman John F. Lacey of Iowa, a pioneer conservationist almost forgotten today but of great contemporary renown. Lacey sponsored three notable pieces of legislation: the Lacey Act, wiping out the commercial sale of bird plumage; the act setting aside the Olympic Range Elk Reserve; and the Antiquities Act of 1906, under which Theodore Roosevelt converted the elk preserve into the Mount Olympus National Monument.

In 1915 the Mount Olympus National Monument, then administered by the Forest Service, was subjected to a devastating attack by that bureau in alliance with private timber interests. The government was engaged in a crash program of military preparedness. The country was short of manganese, vital to the manufacture of steel. The Forest Service, reporting to President Woodrow Wilson that manganese deposits existed within the national monument, persuaded him to issue three successive executive orders which reduced the monument from six hundred thousand to three hundred thousand acres.

From that day to this, not an ounce of workable manganese ore (hausmannite) has been discovered within the original boundaries of that national monument. There was no warrant in law for the action taken by President Wilson. War excitement prevented a judicial challenge at the time the action was taken.

In choosing areas to be eliminated, the Forest Service ignored the report on manganese and stripped virtually all marketable timber out of the monument. It was a pure and simple grab of trees for future exploitation. During the campaign to establish the Olympic National Park I asked Dr. Willard Van Name, who was always factually accurate concerning lands and trees, to give me an appraisal, in that regard, of the areas taken out. His reply was based on blueprints of Forest Service timber cruises. The reduction had moved the western boundary of the monument six miles eastward. The area thus taken out included "the splendid stands of Douglas fir in the southern part" and small areas of big timber farther north; also most of the second-rate timber. He went on: "It is, therefore, not surprising that most of the timber still left in the Monument is small, scrubby high mountain stuff, worthless commercially. . . . The Forest Service took all the meat and left the bone for the public."

The cutdown monument was a snow-covered mountain massif, lacking every striking forest feature of adjoining government terrain. The part taken out, if brought into a national park, would constitute and perpetuate one of the wonders of the world.

I did not specifically cite the Olympic situation when on March 31, 1933, requested by President Roosevelt to criticize government bureaus, I wrote that development of national parks at the expense of national forests was necessary for "permanent preservation of magnificent primeval forests which cannot be replaced for centuries if once cut down as the Forest Service intends they shall be." But the greatest of all such conflicts was about to take shape on the Olympic Peninsula. Long smoldering, it burst into flame in October 1933, when 230 head of Roosevelt elk were slaughtered in the Olympic National Forest during a four-day open season.

Responding to appeals by Mrs. Edge of the Emergency Conservation Committee and Irving Clark of the Seattle Mountaineers, sharing the horror stirred by the elk slaughter, and aided by a National Park Service study team,

Congressman Monrad C. Wallgren introduced a bill in March 1935 to create a Mount Olympus national park. Lying almost entirely in Wallgren's district, the bill's 730,000 acres included the national monument (as reduced by President Wilson) and about 400,000 acres of the Olympic National Forest which surrounded the monument.

Two centers of violent opposition developed at once: the Forest Service and the Grays Harbor sawmill industry to the south of the proposed park. The lumbermen coveted the gigantic trees of the river valleys which ran westward within the projected park boundaries. The southernmost of these valleys were in the congressional district of Representative Martin Smith, who took up the fight in Congress against the Wallgren bill. Opposing it also, but a little less vociferously, was the Washington State Planning Council under anti-New Deal Democratic governor Clarence Martin. This official group sided in general with business interests hostile to conservation.

The Forest Service was the key factor. It administered the entire area in dispute, controlled the flow of information, had powerful ties with local business groups, and was fiercely devoted to its own policies and its own authority. Its officials were hostile to national parks and hated and despised the National Park Service, which in turn hated and (with good reason but cowardly spirit) feared the Forest Service. That bureau's methods confirmed the axiom that unlimited power corrupts its possessor.

My first recommendation to Franklin Roosevelt as president (submitted at his invitation during his first month in office) was that the warfare between these two bureaus be ended by placing both of them in a new Department of Conservation. Secretary of the Interior Ickes worked hard to that end. Knowing that this was in the works, the Forest Service used its enormous political clout to help defeat Roosevelt's bill giving him broad powers to reorganize the government. (A more limited bill passed, Congress retaining power to override reorganization orders.)

My view of the Forest Service was of course governed by conservation objectives; that of Ickes was touched in addition by a desire for power. But during the fight to preserve the Carl Inn Grove of sugar pines in California I received, from an unbiased congressional source, a strong suggestion of the Forest Service's power and methods. Congressman John J. Cochran of Missouri wrote to me in 1937, at the height of the bureau's fight against a transfer to the Interior Department, describing the agency's ability to safeguard its vested interests. "Those interested in the Forest Service," he said, "have a National Organization which I understand has about 7000 members and they are the greatest propagandists in the country. I hear from this Organization indirectly every day because of my position on the House Committee on Re-Organization. They have the Conservation division and Forestry division of every State in the Union sending in resolutions protesting against disturbing the Forest Service."

Cochran's own opinion was that if there were any two agencies that should be in the same department, "it is the National Park Service and the Forest Service." He had talked with the president about this and was sure that, if empowered by Congress, "he will place these two agencies together." There was a strong move in Congress—and he was against it—to pass a bill forbidding a transfer of the Forest Service. Senator McNary of Oregon had said at a closed committee hearing "that he would die on the Senate floor before they would ever pass any bill that would enable the President to disturb the Forest Service."

With Henry Wallace heading Agriculture there was an alternative. If the Forest Service could not be detached from that department, the secretary might be detached from Forest Service domination. I also tended to draw a distinction between that bureau and Chief Forester Ferdinand Silcox, who, after a few pre-war years as a forest ranger, had left the Forest Service but was later brought back to head it by President Roosevelt. Veteran Forest Service personnel looked upon him as an alien.

During a two weeks' stay in Washington in January and February of 1936, I spoke to Secretary Wallace about the unwillingness of the FS to sanction the transfer of national-forest lands to national parks. He suggested a three-way discussion, to be held at lunch with him and Silcox. We had the talk, and after its close I secured an appointment with President Roosevelt to tell him about it. I made no notes about that meeting with Roosevelt, but in leaving the Oval Office I had encountered Secretary Ickes waiting to go in. I told him the subject of my conversation with FDR and wrote to him in detail about it on my return to St. Louis.

I had told the president that at the luncheon with Wallace and Silcox I presented a factual statement about the area sought for an Olympic national park, basing it on a study made by Interior Department forester W. H. Horning, a thoroughly competent and reliable man. Horning's figures, I said, were derived entirely from the latest Forest Service Olympic timber survey. His study showed that the national-forest land covered by the Wallgren bill, and claimed to be essential to the lumber industry of Grays Harbor, contained only 5 billion board feet of timber marketable under current conditions. That would last only three to five years in the Grays Harbor sawmills at Aberdeen and Hoquiam, Washington.

Placed on a sustained-yield basis, the Horning-Forest Service study showed, the area sought for a national park would produce only 5 percent of the entire sustained yield of the area tributary to the Olympic Peninsula lumber interests. This meant, I told the president as I had Silcox, that trees four hundred to one thousand years old, irreplaceable and the last of their kind, would be sacrificed to keep the mills running five years and to postpone for that time the relocation or employment shift of 172 families, 5 percent of the population.

Silcox had replied (as I described the three-way talk to Ickes) that "the Forest Service could be trusted to guard these trees in perpetuity." I had responded that "in 1927 or thereabouts the Forest Service officials at Portland had told me they were going to make these forests into a wilderness area to be preserved forever, but now they were planning to run roads and railroads in and log them off."

Silcox said that if the facts were as I had stated them to him and Wallace, he would support a move to give permanent protection to additional areas of virgin timber in the Olympic National Forest. He did not say how large. But, he added—and these were his exact words—"I will not sanction the transfer of a single acre to the administrative methods of the Park Service."

Silcox then said he would be willing to see the Mount Olympus National Monument extended if administration of the added area were left to the Forest Service. I replied that in the light of President Wilson's action (cutting the monument to half its size) an act of Congress would be necessary to ensure its permanence. I raised no objection to divided jurisdiction because, in agreeing to monument status, Silcox was agreeing that the trees were to be protected. He thus abandoned the economic argument on which the Forest Service was opposing a national park. In reporting all this to FDR, I added that another need which would be met by park status was the provision of additional protected winter range for the (Theodore) Roosevelt elk.

In this talk with the president I put heavy emphasis on Silcox's personal basis of opposition, that although he favored permanent preservation of scenic forests, he would not willingly sanction the transfer of *a single acre* to the administrative methods of the Park Service. This in my opinion, I told FDR, put action up to the president.

Among photographs by Horning which I had brought to the White House were a number showing the higher areas that would be brought into the proposed park. Looking these over, the president said that he would like to get into that high mountain country and asked if a road was to be built. I told him that the National Park Service planned a highway into the high country "but wanted to leave most of the land in a wilderness condition." FDR, I wrote to Ickes, "took notes . . . and seemed decidedly interested."

Summing up to the secretary, I suggested, in relation to the Olympics and the Carl Inn sugar pines, that the "administration . . . tell the Forest Service people to keep their hands off." Back of this was the thought that only the president could do so because the Forest Service was too well-entrenched politically in the Pacific Northwest for Wallace, or even Wallace and Silcox, to control it effectually. For such presidential action, a necessary preliminary was total commitment by the president himself to preservation of these scenic forests. The prospect of that seemed implicit in Roosevelt's final remark to me. Running through the Olympic photographs once more, he declared positively that he was going to make a trip to the peninsula and look at those trees himself. "If you do," I replied, "and if you have the same experience Henry Wallace had out there, the Forest Service will throw a cordon around you and not let you see a single supporter of the park."

House hearings on the Wallgren bill began late in April 1936, and lasted eight days. Unable to be present, I wrote an editorial on the subject and sent prepublication proofs of it to congressmen Wallgren and Cochran, with the suggestion that they agree on the manner of use. I hoped, I said, that it would be read to the committee, rather than merely inserted in the record. Mrs. Edge, who testified for the Emergency Conservation Committee, sent me an account of the meeting. The high spots, as she described it, were furnished by Major Vollmer and Chris Morgenroth of Port Angeles, Washington, who, with several other park supporters, raised six hundred dollars for expenses, mainly from local women's clubs, and traveled across the continent by bus to testify. They "made perfectly grand witnesses"; their testimony made it clear that their community wanted the park established and they "confounded the villainy of the Gray's Harbor group."

Congressman Wallgren, Mrs. Edge wrote, "read your editorial in his opening speech, and it was a feature in his evidence." In this editorial I repeated the statement (made to FDR) that preservation of the marketable timber comprehended within the Wallgren bill would displace only 172 families (860 individuals) in the Grays Harbor area. Expecting this to be challenged, I had given Wallgren the basis of those figures in my letter of April 22. That estimate was made by taking the figures of W. H. Horning showing that the proposed park lands amounted to 5 percent of the area tributary to Grays Harbor under the sustained-yield system, and then taking 5 percent of the 17,200 population of that region.

In contrast, spokesmen for Grays Harbor labor unions declared that establishment of the park would throw thousands of workers out of their jobs. Forest Service witnesses likewise pictured the withdrawal of the park area from lumbering as unmitigated disaster. Routinely, Silcox would have been their principal witness, but he did not possess the expertise (and perhaps not the inclination) to do the kind of arguing that the opposition needed. Instead, the burden of FS argument was carried by Assistant Chief L. F. Kneipp, an oldtime hardliner, and by Assistant Regional Forester Plumb of the Portland office.

The effect of this arrangement was manifest in the testimony of the Forest Service officials. They kept harping on size and age of the trees as a reason for cutting them. A single tree, hostile witnesses correctly pointed out, might contain forty thousand board feet of lumber; so, they argued, cut it. Silcox, to judge by his talk with Wallace and me, would have said such trees ought to be preserved, but not by the National Park Service.

The Forest Service witnesses dwelt on sustained-yield timber practices, but in this hearing they were tactically allied with the Grays Harbor sawmill people, who had ruined the entire forty miles between the Hoquiam-Aberdeen sawmills and the Olympic National Forest, turning it into a waste of slash and brush that was still barren desert forty years after the lumbering. (That was why the sawmills were closing.)

Irving Clark of the Seattle Mountaineers and the Wilderness Society appeared as a witness, as did Mrs. Edge. They stressed the scenic and scientific values of a park and contended that, to the extent determined by Congress, commercial exploitation must give way to the superior claims of the nation. Landscape photographer Asahel Curtis, closely tied to business interests, offered his opinion, as an expert, that only the mountain tops came up to national-park standards. Secretary Ickes offered his no less expert opinion that entrusting preservation of scenic forests to the Forest Service would result in the same sort of "multiple use" that is applied to a pig in the stockyards—"All that is left is the squeal."

It developed that Secretary of Agriculture Wallace had been persuaded by the Forest Service to sign a letter to committee chairman Rene De Rouen, opposing the Wallgren bill, on May 22, 1935, only two months after the bill was introduced and eleven months before the hearings were held. The letter repeated the argument used to deceive President Wilson in 1915—the alleged presence of manganese ore in the park area. Wallace, being thus committed, was in no position to change his stand in public, although he had made it clear to me that he was restudying the matter. Secretary Ickes, of course, sent a report to the chairman strongly approving the bill. The committee reported the bill for passage.

Mrs. Edge wrote in June of her suspicions, formed since the hearings, that Wallgren had secretly agreed to a reduction of park acreage. She said he had failed to answer her direct inquiries about boundaries. Accordingly, I asked him the same question. He replied that the boundaries reported by the committee were the same as in his original bill. He had hoped that by this time (June 10, 1936) his bill would have been passed and sent to the Senate, "but the press of business has made action difficult." He still hoped for "favorable breaks" that would make a vote possible. Those breaks never came. The presidential campaign swept all controversial legislation into cold storage and the bill died with the passing of the old Congress.

In one of my early 1936 talks with President Roosevelt about preservation of scenic forests, he had spoken approvingly of the Black Forest of Germany, which had been maintained for centuries on a sustained-yield basis through selective cutting and replanting. Unfortunately, I failed to point out the great difference between those manicured trees and a primeval cycle of growth, decay, and natural reforestation spanning hundreds or even thousands of years. Late in 1936, FDR made some casual comment to a visitor about selective cutting in the Olympic area.

The consequences of this remark were reported to me by William Schulz, who had spent a year-end holiday in Seattle during his campaign to save the Yosemite sugar pines. When Congressman Martin Smith went home for Christmas, Schulz wrote, "He announced publicly that he is now *for* an Olympic park. His exact statement is that he supports the President's recommendation for a park wherein certain commercial development would be permitted." This, Schulz reminded me, was exactly what the Washington State Planning Council had unanimously voted for. Of course, Schulz commented, "the park they want isn't the park we want"; however, this development seemed to leave the Forest Service as the only body still opposed to any park at all.

Prior to Congressman Smith's shift, Schulz reported, local support of the park project had been steadily growing. During his two weeks in the state, he had placed favorable stories in twenty-eight Washington newspapers. National publicity also was increasing. In the current issue of the *North American Review*, Donald Culross Peattie was giving the Olympic park "a great boost" and Schulz had circulated several hundred copies of a fine article which he himself wrote for the *Christian Science Monitor*.

Two days later (January 10, 1937), Schulz wrote that he had talked the situation over with Irving Clark. Congressman Wallgren was to introduce a new Olympic bill and Clark feared that if the drafting of it were left to Wallgren and the Park Service there would be little chance of getting a large park. Secretary Ickes was strong for a big one, and Mrs. Edge had urged him to stiffen the position of the NPS. But would he have a hand in writing the bill? Schulz wrote: "Clark and I feel strongly that some one of us should, if possible, sit in on the conference when the bill is drawn, and we feel you are the man. This will assure us the largest possible boundaries, and also prevent any joker from being slipped in."

Washington senators Bone and Schwellenbach, Schulz reported, were still noncommittal about the park. The latter undoubtedly was for it, but Bone "refuses to say yes or no, or make any statement whatever." Clark thought this was because Bone would be up for re-election in 1938, and it was Clark's intention to put him on the spot by asking him to introduce a Senate companion to the Wallgren bill.

Unfortunately, both of Schulz's letters reached St. Louis while I was in the national capital. Consequently, I knew nothing about President Roosevelt's reported endorsement of selective cutting in an Olympic park and was unable to discuss it with him in our February conference about preservation of the Yosemite sugar pines.

On March 5, 1937, I received a welcome note from Jim LeCron, Secretary Wallace's personal assistant. "You promised Paul Appleby and me that you would send us a memorandum embodying your ideas about the Olympic National Park. It would be helpful to us just at this time if you could send the memo in." The words "just at this time" pointed to some new development about the park. Next day's mail clarified that. Congressman Wallgren sent me an outline of his new bill, H.R. 4724, and it was appalling. It cut the proposed park down by close to one hundred thousand acres. Worse than that, it eliminated the magnificent rain forests of the Hoh and Bogachiel river valleys—the finest scenic areas in the entire Olympic Peninsula, containing gigantic Sitka spruce and equally large old-growth Douglas fir. It was evident at a glance that the National Park Service had taken part in the drafting, but there was not a trace of the influence of Secretary Ickes or the president.

With the invitation from LeCron opening the way, with the second Wallgren bill supplying a text, and with the Forest Service as the target, I wrote to Secretary Wallace that Congressman Wallgren had just sent me a description of his revised bill to create a national park in the Olympic Peninsula. "It is a shocking retreat," I wrote; "It is possible, of course, that the change in boundaries represents a capitulation by Congressman Wallgren to the lumbering interests," but it might instead reflect renewed Forest Service opposition.

The proposed park boundaries, I told Wallace, "make a mockery of the movement to save the last primeval stand of Douglas fir and Sitka spruce on our Pacific Coast." Thirty years earlier Theodore Roosevelt "looked ahead and saw the time approaching when all these great trees would be gone forever. By proclamation, he converted these Olympic forest lands and mountains themselves into a national monument, to be held inviolate forever." During World War I, lumbering interests had induced President Wilson to cut the monument in two, eliminating all trees that had commercial value. Since then, "Nothing but the will of the Forest Service [has stood] between them and the lumbermen. That will has now failed."

I then assailed the idea that sustained-yield forestry could be practiced in Douglas fir through selective cutting instead of clear-cutting. The cost differential made that impossible, as I had been told time and again by Forest Service officials.

Turning to people and jobs, I went on to say that there was a "deeper fallacy" in the claim that logging these forests was necessary to the local economy. The total amount of timber in question could support local mills for only two and one-half years. "Is it for such an end that the United States must sacrifice its own property, and deny the people of the country, through all future generations, even this slight reminder of former magnificence?" I repeated the evidence that all that was involved was the relocation of a few hundred people, at a time when the Roosevelt administration was making such relocations by the hundred thousands. I ended the letter by stating that I could not believe that "the Department of Agriculture will become a partner in this wanton commercialism. . . . Knowing you as I do, I hope that you will not hold the pen that dooms [the trees] to destruction."

Five weeks passed before Secretary Wallace responded to the comments I had made at his (indirect) request. Then, to my surprise, he sent the unsigned draft of a reply prepared for his signature by the Forest Service and asked for my comments on it. The draft opened with a touch of flattery. The secretary had delayed replying until he could do so "in a manner as considerate and thoughtful as is deserved by your earnest and forceful presentation of the Olympic situation as you see it."

The secretary (with the Forest Service choosing his words) then assured me that "Silcox and I are just as determined as you are that adequate and representative portions of our remaining virgin forests, in the Northwest and elsewhere, shall be preserved for posterity." This determination was visible in the fact that "the present National Park system contains more than 2,500,000 acres which have been transferred from the National Forests with the concurrence of the Forest Service and this Department. Some of this acreage . . . includes forests comparable in their own way with the virgin Douglas fir and spruce of the Olympic peninsula."

The letter-draft then turned to the Olympic situation, with contents plainly indicating that it was the work of Assistant Chief Leon Kneipp or some equally talented Forest Service hardliner. Did I realize, the drafter asked, that in the present Olympic National Monument of 299,000 acres there were slightly more than 3 billion board feet of timber "in addition to that classed as non-merchantable"? (That was deliberate deception. This 3 billion feet of *impliedly* commercial timber was locked up forever on inaccessible mountain heights.) Was I aware "that many people—including Asahel Curtis whom I am sure you know—say this virgin timber includes, both in the commercial and non-commercial classes, bodies as representative and as impressive as any described either in the original Wallgren bill or in the one introduced in the present Congress"? (This same Asahel Curtis, a lumberman's ally, had testified in the 1936 House hearing that none of the forests sought for the park came up to national-park standards.)

From this overpraise of the national monument, the drafter of the Wallace letter swung to his main position, challenging the accuracy of my assertion (based on Forest Service data) that sustained-yield lumbering of the park area would support only 172 families (860 persons) in the Grays Harbor sawmill area. The Grays Harbor economy, he wrote in rebuttal, had taken "a very definite trend toward pulp production and types of remanufacture that afford much larger work-opportunities per timber unit than does lumber."

Forest Service figures of potential employment were eight times as high as mine. For direct and indirect workers and their dependents, based on sustained-yield possibilities, they showed that the present national monument would support 3,300 persons; the area covered by the present Wallgren bill would support 6,630.

In answering Wallace's request for comments on this draft, I could have said that the transition of Grays Harbor from sawtimber to wood pulp was limited by the near-exhaustion of clear-flowing water for the sulfite process. I could have assailed the absurdly high ratio of employment to timber acreage. I chose instead to apply that same ratio to larger areas.

According to the Forest Service ratio, the entire acreage of the original Wallgren bill would sustain 9,585 persons instead of 860. The entire Grays Harbor timber area would sustain a population of 191,700. And 10 percent of the Grays Harbor cutover lands, reforested on a sustained-yield basis, would support the entire existing Grays Harbor population of 17,000. The whole proposition was preposterous.

I turned next to the Forest Service claim, for which park-enemy Asahel Curtis was cited as authority, that the Mount Olympus National Monument contained more than 3 billion board feet of merchantable timber, including "scenic stands" comparable to those in the original Wallgren bill. Take a practical lumberman to see these trees, I said, and his comment would be "Yes, this stuff would make pulpwood if we could get it out." The remainder classified as merchantable was high-mountain scrub along with limited stands of small-growth Douglas fir. Anybody familiar with the Olympic forests knew that the three-hundred-foot-tall Douglas firs, Sitka spruces, western hemlocks, and giant cedars "grow to full height only at low altitudes. It is a botanical impossibility to restrict the Olympic National Park to the mountains and upper reaches of the river valleys, as is done in the revised Wallgren bill, without automatically excluding the very forests that give occasion for creating the park."

In conclusion I wrote: "I know, from our long friendship and your record in office, that the course outlined by the Forest Service is not one you will support if you have the facts before you. I do not believe that Mr. Silcox would tolerate the course he has approved if he were free from the myopic effects of the rivalry between the Forest Service and the National Park Service. . . . I hope you will have nothing to do with a deed which will be execrated by future generations, even if it passes unnoticed by this one, which is unlikely."

I returned the unsigned draft of Wallace's letter. It never came back to me. I then sent the entire Wallace correspondence to Secretary Ickes with additional comment on a related report about manganese, just sent to me by James LeCron (my long-time friend as well as Wallace's personal assistant). My note pointed to the "utter duplicity" on the part of the Forest Service. Since its sustained-yield theory had been "exploded," the agency could only fall back on a recommendation by the Geological Survey that an area containing low-grade ore should be excluded "unless . . . of particular value to the park."

By return mail Secretary Ickes sent me a copy of a letter to him from Margaret Thompson, head of the Northwest Conservation League. She had just returned, she wrote, from a monthly meeting of the Washington State Planning Council. At this meeting chairman Ben Kizer, Spokane attorney, had reported on "his recent trip to Washington, and the success (?) of his presentation before the House Public Lands Committee of the Mount Olympus National Park question." He stated that a special meeting of the committee was called for his especial benefit, and the members "were very frank in their approval" of the stand he took.

Two points, Mrs. Thompson said, were stressed by Kizer to the congressmen: "(1) That the controversy was simply a struggle between the Department of Interior and Department of Agriculture for territory, and that the Planning Council study was the only disinterested one which had been made. (2) That the present Monument contained a large stand of timber. (He said the Committee was amazed to learn this.)"

The timber map of the monument used by Kizer, Mrs. Thompson said, was on so small a scale that large and small Douglas fir were all lumped together, whereas the large-scale Forest Service map showed that nearly all the fir was small stuff. The planning council treated all of it as large old-growth Douglas fir. Mrs. Thompson wondered whether chairman Kizer's devotion of so much time and attention to this park matter could be due to the fact "which he disclosed at this meeting, that his law firm is handling the Northern Pacific land-claim cases in this state." This land-grant railway had enormous financial stakes in timberlands given to it by Congress and in public-land policies. During this meeting the planning council announced that it was preparing an amendment to the Wallgren bill, and Kizer stated that the House committee had promised to wait until this was offered before starting its hearings.

Early in September Mrs. Edge asked me to write a pamphlet on the Olympic situation, subject to her ability to raise money to pay for it. Being at outs with Van Name, she had to seek support by circularization. I agreed to write it and was rewarded with discountable flattery: "You are a sort of Rock of Gibraltar in human form."

The American Museum was sending Van Name on a lengthy scientific mission to the Philippine Islands, with a feeling, probably, of temporary relief from his aggressive conservationism. On his way to the West Coast he stopped for a visit in St. Louis, refused to put up a penny to send William G. Schulz to work for the Olympic park under ECC auspices, and wound up by giving me a check for six hundred dollars (with more in prospect) to set up a special bank account for Schulz to work under my direction.

That made a rift on the Olympic horizon, and then the sun burst through. Press dispatches announced that President Roosevelt was going to the Olympic Mountains to take a personal hand in getting and giving the answers to two questions: Should a national park be established there? If so, how large should it be?

FDR, while touring Olympic National Forest in October 1937, watched a logging demonstration as forest supervisor J. R. Bruckart explained some of the loggers' techniques to the president (photograph by Neil Mortiboy, courtesy Virginia Bruckart Pagter).

FDR TAKES UP THE CUDGEL

Presidential Roosevelt left for the Olympic Peninsula so soon after the newspapers announced the trip that there was no time to write to him at the White House. Therefore I sent him a letter in care of his daughter, Anna Boettiger, wife of the publisher of the *Seattle Post-Intelligencer*. She replied two days later, September 24, 1937, that she would turn it over to him "as soon as I see him." Along with my letter I sent a memorandum sheet of facts and figures about the forest industry of the Olympic area with particular bearing upon the impact of a national park on the predominant wood-pulp industry. The memorandum had been prepared by the Interior Department forester, W. H. Horning; every factual statement in it was drawn from a recent Forest Service survey of the timber resources of the Olympic area.

The newspaper story disclosed the president's intention to travel several hundred miles by automobile around the base of the Olympic Mountains from Seattle to Lake Quinault, encompassing all of the northern and western sides of the peninsula. This meant that almost the entire journey would be within the Olympic National Forest, consequently under Forest Service guidance. I decided to open my letter with a reminder: "You may possibly remember that last year, when you told me you wanted to visit the area, I made the remark that if you had the same experience Secretary Wallace did, local Forest Service officials would see to it that you saw nobody who wanted a real park. I hope your party will include Preston Macy, custodian of the Olympic National Monument, though I do not know his views."

The Olympic situation, I went on, was badly complicated by the fact that Congressman Mon Wallgren, who sponsored a good bill in 1936, abandoned it in 1937 in spite of approval by House and Senate committees. He had replaced it with a bill cutting down the boundaries so as to eliminate the great Douglas firs, Sitka spruces, and giant cedars that most needed preservation. Wallgren claimed, I wrote, that he was following the wishes of the Interior Department, "but the attitude of Secretary Ickes does not support that claim."

The second, cut-down Wallgren bill, I told FDR, was reported for passage under remarkable circumstances. Although it involved a transfer of public lands from Agriculture to Interior, neither Wallace nor Ickes had made a report on it to the chairman of the House Committee on the Public Lands. Ickes held back, I believed, because he hoped for a better bill, and Wallace because he felt that the Forest Service position was vulnerable.[1] I recounted the Forest Service's fallacious arguments about (non-existent) manganese and attacked its claim that there were large rain-forest trees in the reduced Wallgren area.

Announcing the trip at his September 21 press conference, the president had warned against any conjecture that the journey was motivated by politics. The *New York Times* quoted him as saying he wanted to "take the pulse of the country" on the objectives of the second New Deal. Thus forewarned, the reporters filled the nation's press with political speculation. The president was said to have routed his special train across Wyoming and Montana in order to knock the spots off senators O'Mahoney and Wheeler, who had defeated his Supreme Court reform plan. With this in prospect, twenty-one members of the press, instead of the seven who usually accompanied him, piled onto his train when it pulled out of Hyde Park late next day with the president, Mrs. Roosevelt, and the official party. The first programmed speech was to be at Cheyenne, Wyoming, where, commentators predicted, O'Mahoney would be skinned alive.

Senator O'Mahoney boarded the presidential train at Cheyenne, was ushered into Mr. Roosevelt's private car, and rode with him across the state as far as Casper, where the party toured a WPA-restored fort. Senator Burton K. Wheeler sent his regrets from California; the president omitted mentioning his name in speeches. Daughter Anna joined her parents at Yellowstone, with her husband John Boettiger, and remained on the train all the way to Seattle. The only discoverable politics on the journey was a powerful speech by Roosevelt on future public-power development delivered at the site of Columbia River's Bonneville Dam.

The Olympic National Park business was to begin after the president spent a night at the Boettiger home and the following day in Victoria, British Columbia. After a trip to and from that city on a destroyer, he would spend the night of September 30 at a lodge on Lake Crescent, within the hoped-for boundaries of the park. Next day he was to drive 217 miles around the peninsula, accompanied by Congressman Wallgren and Washington senators Bone and Schwellenbach. The Associated Press story on the sojourn at the lodge, where meetings crucial to the park were held, mentioned only the primitive and uncomfortable accommodations. Some of the party had begun calling themselves "Roosevelt's Rough Riders."

A *New York Times* report on the trip around the peninsula said that the presidential party was shown work done by the Forest Service and stopped to watch a top-rigger as he sawed and chopped off the crown of a two-hundred-foot-high Douglas fir. After this came the only reference to the national-park project that I was able to find in the eastern metropolitan press: "C. J. Buck, regional forester, accompanied the President and gave him arguments against making the area a national park, a thing Mr. Roosevelt had promised to the school children of Port Angeles yesterday."

Buck's apparent monopoly of presidential attention made it look bad for the park; the remark to the school children made it look better. Except for a few items devoted to lumbering and the Forest Service, this was the sum total of the news about Roosevelt's trip to the Olympics that came out of the Northwest. The next day gigantic headlines informed the public that Roosevelt had not heard the radio speech of Justice Hugo Black explaining his past membership in the Ku Klux Klan because the presidential limousine on the way to Tacoma did not have a radio.

In the newspaper accounts there was not a word about national-park personnel or other park supporters—nothing to indicate that the president had heeded my warning against being fenced in by the Forest Service. However, some days after FDR got back to Washington, I received letters from Schulz and Irving Clark of the Wilderness Society, telling of remarkable events that took place before and during the presidential stay, all undetected by reporters.[2]

The morning after the visit was announced, Preston Macy, superintendent of Mount Olympus National Monument, and Major O. A. Tomlinson, superintendent of Mount Rainier National Park, went together to the Seattle headquarters of the Forest Service. They asked to be included in the president's drive around the peninsula. They were flatly turned down. Reading that Mr. Roosevelt was to spend a night at the Lake Crescent lodge, they tried to reserve rooms there. They were told that the Forest Service had taken over the entire lodge for the night of the presidential visit.

Back to the Forest Service went Macy and Tomlinson and applied for rooms at the lodge. Again, an emphatic No. Then, on the morning after the president reached Seattle, the Forest Service telephoned to Macy and Tomlinson and gave each of them a terse message: "You will be in the president's party in the trip around the peninsula. Rooms are reserved for you tonight at the Lake Crescent Lodge."

It became evident that Anna Boettiger had taken my letter with her when she joined her father at Yellowstone. That began to unfold in Irving Clark's letter. The president had summoned Macy and Tomlinson to his cabin for a preliminary talk about the park, then held a joint session with the National Park and Forest Service people.[3]

At this joint meeting, Clark said, Regional Forester Buck led off with arguments against creation of a national park, giving detailed statistics to portray its devastating effect upon the timber economy of the Olympic Peninsula. The president listened without saying a word until Buck finished his recital. Then he said:

"Is that the situation? I thought it was this way."

The president then proceeded, Clark wrote, to refute every statement Buck had made about timber requirements and supply. At the conclusion he asked, "Isn't that correct?"

Buck admitted that it was correct. Then, wrote Clark, the regional forester started again on another tack, buttressing his argument against the park with more statistics about peninsular timber needs and supplies. Again the president listened in silence until Buck had finished. Again he said, "Is that the situation? I thought it was this way." Once more he set up opposing facts and figures that utterly demolished Buck's case. A second time he asked, "Isn't that correct?" and a second time Buck answered "Yes."

Clark did not explain Buck's division of his argument into two parts, but it was easy to surmise what had taken place. The issue of a national park's impact upon the peninsular economy had bearings on two distinct industrial centers—the wood-pulp industry of Port Angeles, north of the proposed park, and the sawmill industry of Grays Harbor, south of the mountains, which was treated statistically in the Forest Service survey as if converted to wood pulp. Buck would naturally divide his argument to fit Port Angeles and Grays Harbor. The statistical material I had sent to Mr. Roosevelt, drawn by Interior Department forester Horning from the Forest Service timber survey, had precisely that same division. Horning's figures, fixed in Roosevelt's photographic memory, were accurate; Buck's were manufactured to fit his argument.

The Horning material, thus employed by the president, threw a strange light both on the Portland office of the Forest Service and on the two industrial communities involved. Why was it that public sentiment for a national park was strong in Port Angeles, while Grays Harbor was the focal point of all the opposition that existed in the state? Because, although both communities had plenty of pulpwood, Grays Harbor was working desperately to postpone the shutdown of sawmills for which, in the absence of a national park, there was still a few years' supply of sawtimber in the national forest.

The Forest Service, in opposing the park, was not thinking of peninsular welfare. It was trying to preserve its own power to rule and dispose of the nation's forests. That compulsion, buttressed by the doctrine that the end justifies the means, was what lay behind Buck's systematic effort to mislead the president.

The next time I talked with FDR, which was not for several months, he remarked to me, "I told Henry Wallace to take that fellow [Buck] out of Portland." Wallace, I soon thereafter learned, did not remove him, but I said nothing about that to Mr. Roosevelt.

The president's trip furnished a great send-off for Schulz's work, about which I wrote to Secretary Ickes on October 4. During a short stay in Seattle that July, I said, Schulz had discovered that the pro-park people had been led to believe they had to choose between the reduced Wallgren area and nothing. They seemed to think that this was the view of the Park Service. Now Schulz would try to organize a group calling for a park equal to the one proposed in the original bill, and he would be greatly aided in getting this group together if he could say that "between the two Wallgren bills, you prefer the first." I explained my view that Interior must have withheld its report in hopes of a better bill. The need was to bring the supporters of the park together on a proposition worth fighting for. They had been confused and misled, I said, by a Washington State Planning Council dominated by the lumber interests. As long as the people around Puget Sound believed that Interior favored a smaller park, it would be difficult to upset the lumber company-Forest Service combination. Wallace now seemed to doubt Forest Service counsel, and the president's support for the park would help get a "real one."

The Ickes reaction to this came initially in a drastic change of mental attitude within the National Park Service, whose director, Arno Cammerer, possessed a streak of timidity. Associate Director Arthur Demaray wrote me on October 15, "We naturally prefer the larger area if the people of Washington and their Representative[s] in Congress will support the necessary legislation." In addition, he said, the Park Service would like to see the park further enlarged, for administrative convenience, by bringing in a strip ten miles long and three miles wide in the Queets River valley—an area which would otherwise be isolated from the main body of the national forest after the park was formed.

Schulz returned to Seattle on October 22 and reported to me next day on the incidents and aftermath of the president's visit. He found that John Boettiger had written several signed articles for his *Post-Intelligencer*. Unlike the eastern correspondents who wrote about the cold, damp mountain air, Boettiger dealt with the Olympic Park proposition.

From the *Post-Intelligencer* stories it seemed the president was not sounding out public sentiment but was promoting it. He talked about the park not only to Port Angeles school children but to every group, large or small, that thronged around him on the trip. And he talked not merely about *a* national park but about the largest national park it was possible to establish. He let his feelings fly at visual evidence of tree-butchery. Driven past one scene of devastation, he was quoted as saying, "I hope the lumberman who is responsible for this is roasting in hell."

The area was not pinpointed in the narrative but was easily identifiable when I followed Roosevelt's route eight months later, on a side road running up the Hoh River valley. Here the piled-up slash—too dangerous to burn—presented so frightful a spectacle that the Forest Service had temporarily moved the national-forest boundary sign three miles up the valley to keep the president from knowing that this devastation—though on private land—occurred within the Olympic National Forest.[4]

From the Boettiger articles Schulz learned that in advocating the largest possible park, the president seemed "to have qualified his statement with the provision that commercial use be made of timber in certain [unspecified] areas." Mr. Wallgren was then quoted as stating (after talking with the president) that he would "no longer ask for just 1,000 [square miles] as at present, but 1,400." That would produce a park of 896,000 acres, compared with 732,000 in Wallgren's original bill, and 642,000 in his second bill then before Congress.[5]

While Schulz was writing his long letter to me, he learned of a remarkable shift in the attitude of the Washington state government. He said he had just then read a *Post-Intelligencer* report that the state planning council "yesterday went on record as unanimously backing up the President's stand for a larger park, and one in which commercial use of timber would be permitted. . . . What does all this mean? . . . I can't believe that the President would try to institute any kind of a policy of permitting timber cutting in the national parks."

I replied that, on principle, I was opposed to the commercial use of park timber. It created a bad precedent. But if the park were to be extended to take in the entire winter range of the Roosevelt elk, this would bring in land primarily of economic value, which might justify the policy. Congress in considering the bill could either eliminate the provision for commercial use or eliminate from the park areas of primary commercial value. It was impossible, Schulz responded, for him to go ahead with his campaign until he knew whether the president was set on this new concept, or "until I hear further from you. . . . I am still wondering if you can get to the President?"

On October 29, in reply to my letter of the fourth in which I had quoted Schulz, Secretary Ickes put himself squarely on record; he wrote about his and the president's attitude with a fervor and content that cast decided doubt on the correctness of the Seattle interpretation of FDR's remarks. Said Ickes:

"I thoroughly approve a larger area for the park. You may count on my support being placed squarely behind this movement." Anything I could do to break up the "sinister combination of despoilers" who were thwarting the park project would be a "public service." Ickes wrote that FDR had "a most sympathetic understanding" of the value of the park. His visit to Washington state would exert "tremendous influence" for early establishment of the park by focusing public interest on the project.

Secretary Ickes furnished an extra carbon of his letter, which I sent to Schulz with the admonition that it could be shown but not publicized. The secretary made no mention of FDR's suggestion of selective logging in portions of the park, but the whole tone of his letter, including the paragraph praising the president, was inconsistent with any such plan. At the same time, Schulz's letters showed plainly that Roosevelt's proposal was being construed in Seattle in a way totally conflicting with his purpose of preserving the rain forest in its primeval grandeur.

I had just completed the writing of my Olympic pamphlet for the Emergency Conservation Committee in which, without taking a stand for or against the selective-cutting idea, I had treated it as an incidental matter affecting only marginal areas. Convinced now that the president had been misled and his proposal distorted by park opponents, I revised that portion of the manuscript, opposing any commercial logging, and contrasted what I thought Roosevelt had in mind and what the Forest Service would give him. I commented to Mrs. Edge, "I do not think the President will push his logging proposal after he understands what it would mean in the Olympic forests, in which case the principal effect of his statement will be to wipe out the small-boundaries talk."

I wrote similarly to Schulz on November 4, saying that I intended to send Roosevelt a memorandum on selective cutting and on the effect of commercial activities on national-park standards. However, I would wait about it until Fred Overly, forester of the Mount Olympus National Monument, had time to verify my description of what the Forest Service called selective cutting. And I gave Schulz a word of advice to be passed along to the Park Service personnel: "One thing for the Park Service to keep in mind, in presenting arguments about the park to the President, is that owing to his physical disability he has a particular interest in accessibility of scenic areas by highway. He spoke of that at once when I referred to it as a wilderness without roads."

On that occasion I had spoken in particular about preserving the Bogachiel Valley as a roadless wilderness. "How would I get in?" FDR asked. "You," I replied, "would go eighteen miles up the Hoh River valley on a paved road. That makes the only difference between the two valleys." That was not quite correct, for the Hoh Valley firs and spruces were older and slightly larger, while the rivers were quite unlike. The Bogachiel was a clear stream, the Hoh eternally gray with glacial silt. The silt had made it impossible to utilize their combined flow in a wood-pulp industrial center.

Though Schulz was feeling better about Roosevelt's intentions, he wrote me, also on November 4, that he was having second thoughts about setting up a pro-park committee—it would be too hard, he concluded, "to keep control of the reins." But he was about to accept an invitation from Irving Clark to join a new statewide organization, and might take on its publicity work, though retaining his independence. The state planning council, he found, was losing favor, thanks to the presidential visit: "With the President's words acting like a magic charm to sweep away much of the opposition, the battle is now half won. Everybody wants a park. The Port Angeles people have assured Wallgren they will back him on any sized park he asks."

I doubt whether Schulz had the full story of Port Angeles developments. Editor Charles Webster of the *Evening News* sent me his October 29 reprint of a letter from the Port Angeles Chamber of Commerce to President Roosevelt congratulating him on his plan for a national park and saying that, if adopted in full, it would "end the present disagreement over this matter." The next sentence was a deceptive hundred-word mouthful but would have been perfectly logical had it been directed openly to promoting the Forest Service program of timber management and collateral commercialism. The chamber felt that planned commercial activity would "better develop scenic beauties" and recreation, with forest growth "aided and controlled" by sustained-yield logging.

A resolution resembling the Port Angeles letter was sent to the White House from Port Townsend. Arrival of these masterpieces of misrepresentation coincided with my receiving from Fred Overly the material I had requested for my letter to FDR. Overly confirmed my views about the contrast between selective cutting in the Black Forest of Germany, which the president had in mind, and that practiced on the Olympic Peninsula. I wrote to the president on November 19 that I had received "enthusiastic reports" about the park sentiment that he had stirred up. I also warned that his views on selective cutting were being distorted.

Citing the Port Townsend resolution addressed to him, I said that in half a dozen details it was "too artistic a work of deceit to have come from any source except the Forest Service. The main trouble appears to be that selective cutting as you understand it—the Black Forest variety—and selective cutting as practiced on the Olympic Peninsula . . . are two entirely different propositions." I pointed out that earlier I had urged the Forest Service to adopt "selective cutting of the kind you have in mind"—cutting individual trees. They told me that in forests of the Olympic type this was an impossibility. Owing to the enormous size and dense growth of trees, the felling and dragging out of one tree destroyed or damaged scores of others. Tractors were as bad as high leads in that respect—they merely increased the salvage. The slash was so enormous that it had to be burned on the ground. Opening the forest by partial cutting exposed the remaining trees to windfall. Finally, Douglas fir would not reproduce in shade. All of these factors, they said, forced them to cut down everything if they cut down anything. So the Forest Service used a special kind of selective cutting—clearcuts "on selected areas"—for the Olympic region. This method "absolutely destroys the forests as scenic assets." I asked the president whether the Forest Service had told him the same thing they told me about selective cutting, or had said "nothing about what they meant by it in the Olympic National Forest." Since the proposed park did not jeopardize the local economy, I hoped that he would "capitalize" on the effect of his trip in promoting a larger park. A few presidential words to Congressman Wallgren would end the misuse of Roosevelt's other statements.

I turned then to the delicate subject of timber cutting in national parks, concerning which FDR had verged on compromise: "I believe that the National Park Service ought to be kept clear of commercial activities, except for the public visiting the parks." Otherwise, the agency would slowly be infiltrated by a commercial point of view; this would be an "entering wedge" for encroachments elsewhere.

Two days earlier, I told Mr. Roosevelt, I had attended a meeting in Chicago devoted to assisting his program of government reorganization. Some of those present, I said, hoped to talk with him about it, but I could not be with them. I believed that the most far-reaching results would flow ultimately out of changing the name of the Interior Department to Department of Conservation and establishing standards which the department must live up to under all presidents. I hoped that he would continue to press for authority to regroup bureaus. All this repeated what I had written to Mr. Roosevelt on March 24, 1933, three weeks after he took office, about the establishment of a Department of Conservation that would include both the Forest Service and the National Park Service.

By this time talk was spreading in the Seattle region about joint administration of an Olympic park by the National Park Service and Forest Service. It was the opinion of Superintendent Tomlinson of Mount Rainier National Park, relayed to me by Schulz, that this was "a scheme of the Forest Service to get its hand in the parks, and operate them as national forests, yet capitalize on the tourist drawing power in the name 'national park.'"

The manuscript of my Olympic pamphlet was by this time in the hands of Mrs. Edge, who had raised funds for the printing and distribution of twelve thousand copies. She wrote me on November 4 that she admired "the restrained emotion of its opening." In the pamphlet, I argued as forcefully as I could that (1) the judgment of the Forest Service had been distorted by its hostility toward the Park Service, (2) the commercial orientation of the Service resulted in sound forestry practices but led to a bias against noncommercial values, and (3) decentralized administration tended to let narrow regional views become Forest Service policy. The lumber industry was an essential one, I said; the problem was that its leaders could not accept aesthetic values as legitimate, and too many foresters felt the same way. In their view, "mature" trees had to be cut to keep them from decay; stands of Douglas fir had to be clear-cut to prevent gradual replacement by hemlock. This ignored the essential role of decay in the life of the forest, and the natural shift from Douglas fir to hemlock and back to Douglas fir, which "is part of an ecological cycle covering thousands of years. To preserve that cycle is one of the purposes of a national park." I closed the pamphlet by asking that this land be left for posterity as "something better than an indestructible mountain surrounded by a wilderness of stumps."

Olympic National Park (photograph by Ansel Adams, courtesy Ansel Adams Publishing Rights Trust. All rights reserved.)

CHAPTER SIX

THE OLYMPICS
IN CONGRESS

Supporters of the Olympic National Park project were doing quite a bit of worrying as the year 1938 opened, but the opposition was also uneasy. On December 30 the *Port Angeles Evening News* published a lengthy statement issued by Congressman Martin Smith at Aberdeen, Washington, two days earlier. On the surface, it seemed to indicate new and damaging developments. "It is true," said Smith, "that President Roosevelt favors the establishment of a large Olympic National Park area. However, [he] is forest-minded and possesses a more comprehensive knowledge of timber growing as a crop and its varied uses, including those of industry, than any president we have ever had."

Smith told of Roosevelt's early interest in forestry as practiced in Germany, his program of reforestation as governor of New York, and his forestry experimentation at Hyde Park. On his tour of the Olympic Peninsula the president had indicated that he would favor a joint control of the park, timber, and other resources of the peninsula. Now, Smith predicted, Roosevelt would ask for joint administration of the park by the Forest Service and National Park Service. It was "logical and natural" that this would include selective logging of pulpwood and "over-ripe" timber.

To complete the picture, Smith gave Secretary Ickes a new image—no longer that of a frightening ogre. Ickes was still "known as an ardent conservationist, but he is also considered to be one of the ablest and most practical members of the President's cabinet and an official who considers every element of the problems presented to him." Moreover, Secretary Wallace had "previously expressed views similar to those held by President Roosevelt." Since the president and members of his cabinet, according to Congressman Smith, would probably recommend special legislation to allow commercial activities within the park, "The lumber and pulp and paper industries will have no cause to feel insecure and alarmed on account of the proposal to still further increase the already large area of the park."

The key word in Martin Smith's statement was "over-ripe." If national-park timber was to be cut down when it became "over-ripe" for cutting, trees with a natural life of up to a thousand years would be lumbered at the age of eighty-one—one year after they passed the age of highest profitability under the established sustained-yield cycle. To my mind, Smith was living in a dream world as far as President Roosevelt was concerned, provided the president knew the facts—but the congressman had powerful allies who would work with him to make the dream come true.

On January 10 the *Aberdeen World* published an Associated Press dispatch quoting Congressman Wallgren as saying that he wanted a "MILLION-ACRE-PARK." (The headline could be read at something less than a quarter of a mile.) In its accompanying news story, the *World* said that "facing the danger of Grays Harbor losing one of its greatest potential natural wealth areas, Harbor leaders plan an immediate appeal to the state's congressional delegation, urging them to oppose any increase in the proposed park's limits."

Thinking back to Congressman Smith's endorsement of a national park in which selective lumbering by the Forest Service would be permitted, I wrote to Secretary Ickes on January 16 that this was quite a concession, coming from the bitterest opponent of the park. But "it reveals the danger—misstatement of the position taken by President Roosevelt, and a concerted effort by all former enemies of the park to get their interpretation of it put into the act creating the park." I hoped that Ickes would "have a chance to get in some licks on this, to see that nothing is put over, either in commercial concessions to the timber interests and Forest Service, or in cutting down the park if they don't get their way on lumbering." Congressman Wallgren, I told Ickes, had written to a Seattle man that he wanted to see the president about the bill. "I hope you'll be present," I said, especially since a visitor from Seattle had told me that the Park Service "appears friendly but shows no spirit." However, according to Schulz, "Major Tomlinson is working aggressively for it."

Mrs. Edge wrote me on January 25 that she had spent three days in Washington attending the national-park conference of the American Planning and Civic Association, during which the proposed Olympic park was not mentioned. Forest Service officials were given "an open platform for the dissemination of anti-park propaganda skillfully administered in a mild form," and Secretary Ickes was introduced at the association dinner by former NPS director Horace Albright "in such a flippant style that Ickes rebuked him and left without giving his speech."[1]

More pleasing was Mrs. Edge's statement "Your Olympic pamphlet is a grand success." It had brought in one hundred dollars from Mrs. Bruce Ford of the DuPont family, she reported. In a follow-up letter, Mrs. Edge said that Irving Clark and Schulz had raised fifty dollars for the printing of two thousand copies of my pamphlet to be sent to the state of Washington. (On March 8, the pamphlet would be placed in the *Congressional Record* by Senator Joseph Guffy of Pennylsvania; a total of twenty thousand reprints were distributed.) Out there, I heard, I had once more become a nonperson. Just as duck-clubbers said that "Irving Brant" was a pen name taken by Dr. Hornaday, just as the Audubon Association's defense committee called me the "purported" author of a critical pamphlet, so Washington state opponents of the Olympic pamphlet were saying that it was written by Irving Clark. Nobody explained why Clark should adopt an obscure cognomen in place of his prestigious name. By this time Bill Schulz had placed a splendid two-page spread on the park in the nationally circulated *Christian Science Monitor*. With his approval, I spent part of his expense allowance in furnishing him with several thousand copies.

On the last day of January 1938, I left my position with the *St. Louis Star-Times* and moved to Washington, D. C., to begin full-time work on a biography of James Madison. (Two years, I thought, would be spent on the book. Actually, it expanded to six volumes and took twenty-three years.) Although I remained contributing editor for the *Star-Times*, I expected to have more time to work for conservation. It turned out that I put in so many hours on the Olympic park project—by this time an administration affair—that I was working half-time for the White House without being paid for it.

The prospects of the Olympic park took a leap forward on February 8, but with factors of uncertainty, when the entire Washington congressional delegation, together with Park Service director Arno Cammerer and Forest Service chief Ferdinand Silcox, conferred with the president on that subject. The newspapers reported that Roosevelt spoke out for a large park and urged congressional action during the current session of Congress. Again, according to published reports, he spoke favorably of selective cutting in the park. Silcox opposed joint administration by the National Park Service and the Forest Service. Wallgren said he would ask for a park of about eight hundred thousand acres. It was agreed that congressmen Wallgren and Smith would meet on Saturday morning, February 12, with Cammerer and Silcox, to draw boundaries.

The reference to commercial cutting in the park alarmed me. It looked as if my November 19 letter to Roosevelt had produced no effect. At the close of the next White House press conference, on February 11, I stopped at the president's desk and asked him about it. The published report, he said, was utterly false. He had said nothing about tree cutting within the park and was totally against it except for protective purposes. Furthermore, he said, he wanted all timber harvesting in the Olympic National Forest to be done by the Forest Service itself, none by private loggers, and he would like to see all clear-cutting in that national forest abolished. After Roosevelt's explanation the false report about lumbering in the park was easy to account for. Congressman Smith had invented the story for consumption by his Grays Harbor constituents.

Wallgren invited me to take part in the Saturday conference on boundaries and I sent an account of it that same day to Schulz. The meeting, I told him, was greatly aided by the attitude of Chief Forester Silcox, who was very friendly to the park. But Regional Forester Buck, who flew in from Portland to help draw the boundaries, "kept saying that there was nothing left of the Olympic Forest. Every line that was drawn drew blood from him, although he said nothing argumentatively." At the insistence of FDR, the park was to extend through Hoh and Bogachiel river corridors to the sea and a seashore strip of the park.

Wallgren, I reported, "was running backward all the time. He would have given in to Smith on every point," even abandoning upper Queets lands included in the cut-down second Wallgren bill, but Cammerer balked at that. Chief Forester Silcox agreed to add all of the disputed land to the park, but Wallgren was ready to eliminate the lower part of the Queets and Lake Quinault itself.

Describing this controversial feature of the conference to Dr. Van Name upon his return from the Philippines, I said: "Smith and Wallgren both wanted the whole Quinault-Queets area out; I secured the compromise by which the park runs down to Quinault without taking in the ridges between the Quinault and Queets rivers. To have held out for that, and the lower Queets, would have imperiled the whole proposition."

Schulz sent me a clipping from the *Aberdeen World* making dire predictions of calamity to Grays Harbor from the proposed boundaries. He and his close associates (Tomlinson, Macy, and Clark) were highly pleased with the boundaries. They thought it best not to fight for the lower Queets River area if it would endanger the park, and he underlined the words: "We will be guided by your advice in this matter." They were urging Wallgren to issue a public statement about the expansion, to clear up confusion among supporters of the park and put an end to wild exaggerations about its size. But already, the Democratic clubs of Washington were joining park supporters and sending wires to Wallgren.

Irving Clark wrote that the proposed boundaries "will make a magnificent park," and added, "We are very fortunate to have your pamphlet as ammunition. . . . P.S. We are mighty glad to have Schulz here helping us."

Schulz wrote on February 23 that he still had a thousand of my pamphlets and said that Irving Clark was wiring Secretary Ickes, suggesting that his department put out and distribute a factual statement that would supplement the pamphlet. Now that the Forest Service and Park Service were agreed, "It should be proper for the government to issue such literature." Some people, Schulz said, believed (but he did not) that the Forest Service's new cooperative stance was a strategy measure to enable the bureau to take over administration of the park after overloading it with commercial enterprises.

The true explanation was much simpler. Secretary Wallace independently concluded that he had been misled; Chief Forester Silcox followed him willingly; and the Forest Service bureaucracy, both in Washington and in the Northwest, was silenced. Back of it all was the influence of President Roosevelt.

Knowing that Wallgren was seeking an appointment with Roosevelt, I rushed a memorandum to the president on February 25 to bring him up to date on the congressman's attitude and intentions. At the February 12 meeting of Cammerer and Silcox with Wallgren and Smith, I told the president, Silcox supported a good park. "Wallgren retreated before Congressman Smith right from the start, though why he should choose Smith to retreat from is beyond me." Cammerer stopped the retreat, "and the upshot was that only one important region was cut out, on the lower Queets." (This was an area that should have been in the park for added protection to elk and because it included a scenic timber stand—though not the best.)

Now, I said, a new complication had arisen. The Bogachiel and Hoh corridors to the sea consisted largely of private lands, partly timbered, including thirty farms (mostly in the lower Bogachiel Valley); most of the timber was owned by Port Angeles pulp mills which wanted the Sitka spruce to whiten wood pulp and feared loss of their supply. Farmers were (falsely) told they would lose their private rights and school taxes if their lands were inside the park. Chris Morgenroth of Port Angeles, a well-informed friend of the park and an honest man, was in Washington objecting to the corridors.

Morgenroth, I told FDR, was saying that the farmers' fears could be quieted by an official statement defining their private rights, but the pulp-mill owners feared ultimate government purchase of the spruce stands. Wallgren, I said, was "ready to eliminate the ocean front altogether." Then I told how at a Wallgren-Morgenroth meeting which I had attended the day before, there had been a suggestion to eliminate the corridors and add a longer strip along the sea, detached from the rest of the park. That had satisfied Wallgren and pleased Morgenroth. So maps were drawn, one showing the agreement of two weeks earlier, another Wallgren's present solution. My own proposal at this meeting, I said, had been—"if it seems necessary to make concessions"—to retain the Hoh corridor, as a connection with the enlarged ocean frontage. This would "greatly reduce private holdings in the park, give Port Angeles a permanent supply of spruce, and still maintain a continuous park from mountain top to ocean." (Best of all, of course, would have been two corridors and the longer frontage.) A public statement, I concluded, was greatly needed to clear up fears in Washington state; this would "take the heart out of the opposition." As for Wallgren, "What he needs is a stiff push from you."

Attached to my letter in the Roosevelt presidential papers are three maps of the Olympic Peninsula. These are identified in the letter as "No. 1. Boundaries . . . as agreed to . . . two weeks ago. No. 2. Boundary Wallgren suggested yesterday. No. 3. A suggestion I offered." Attached also is a March 21 memorandum from FDR to Cammerer and Silcox, written after the president had met with Wallgren. He understood, he said, that they were in substantial agreement on the Olympic park project. "If this is true, will you join in giving the Bill a push in both Houses?"

A memo from Cammerer followed, saying: "Silcox and I are in complete agreement, and Secretary Ickes has reviewed the boundaries developed under your instructions. From now on every effort will be centered on putting [the bill] through Congress." The stapling of these memos to my February 25 letter to the president appeared to link that letter with Roosevelt's conference with Wallgren, held March 1 at the White House, at which Secretary Ickes and I were present.

I reported the results on that day to Mrs. Edge and Schulz. To the former I wrote, "The President worked out the final plan himself and presented it to Wallgren, knowing from my memorandum what Wallgren was going to present to him." I told Schulz of my earlier suggestion that the president insist on keeping the Hoh corridor inside the park and said concerning his decision, "I think it is better than my suggestion." Under the plan drafted by Roosevelt and accepted by Wallgren and the Park and Forest services, "The Hoh and Bogachiel corridors are excluded from the park proper, but the bill provides that land in them may be added to the park by the President whenever they are acquired by gift, purchase or otherwise."

The bill would allow manganese prospecting in the park for five years, but claims not developed within two years after being taken out would lapse. I argued against this at the conference, I told Mrs. Edge, "and so did Secretary Ickes but Wallgren wanted it as a political defense for himself. He said, and I think it is true, that the manganese boom is a phony built up by the Forest Service, and no claims will be developed. Ickes finally agreed when assured of ample administrative control. (Don't mention this, of course.)"

New falsehoods were in circulation at this time. Ross Tiffany, executive officer of the Washington State Planning Council, charged in an Associated Press dispatch of February 25 that the park would lock up two hundred thousand acres of state school lands. Secretary Ickes asked me to draft a letter from him to Wallgren countering this adverse propaganda. My draft (ca. March 4, 1938) congratulated the congressman on his bill, approved by both Agriculture and Interior, which would give the state of Washington the only national park that included both mountain glaciers and seashore, and that preserved for the nation "a fragment, a magnificent fragment, of the northwestern wilderness of 300-foot firs, spruces, hemlocks and cedars." There was every evidence, I wrote for Ickes, that the park was overwhelmingly supported by public opinion in the state of Washington, but some of the letters received had expressed fears concerning the effect the park would have upon private property and business interests. It was obvious that a propaganda organization was secretly at work, I said, because the letters followed a set pattern, repeating the false assertion that private owners would lose their property rights. Rumors were also being circulated in Washington state that the park would "bottle up" 200,000 acres of state-owned timber. The truth was that only 5,754 acres of state school lands were included in the park, and that nothing blocked their use.

A further source of misapprehension (the letter-draft for Ickes went on to say) concerned two manganese mines near Lake Crescent, inside the park boundaries. These were worked for some years and shut down in 1926. "If, after the park is established, the owners of these mines decide to re-open them, they can do so as freely as if there were no park."[2] All other holders of mineral rights in the park could exercise them, subject to U.S. mining laws.

Schulz began a letter of March 8 with the words: "We are wondering about the Senate." Major Tomlinson, he said, feared that the opposition had worked on senators Bone and Schwellenbach so as to hold up Senate action and thus defeat the park. There was a feeling, among park supporters in Seattle, that the two senators "have played opportunist roles, at least until very recently. . . . People feel that they lacked courage and statesmanship, and that they (the senators) have pretty much played in with the opposition. . . . Irving Clark has wanted all along to make this a political issue, so we could put them directly on the spot; but so far that hasn't been possible."

I had been too busy with Wallgren and the drafting of his bill to see the senators, but now I obtained an appointment with Bone. It turned out to be with his administrative assistant, Raymond A. Seelig. This apparent shunting to a subordinate disturbed me until I was told of a remark made by Mrs. Bone: "Mr. Seelig is the real senator from Washington." The interview was satisfactory. He listened intently, asked intelligent questions, and came very close to committing the senator to support of the park.

A week after Schulz and Tomlinson did their worrying about Senator Schwellenbach, Schulz discovered that the senator had revealed his support of the park a month earlier in a letter to its most powerful enemy, the Aberdeen Chamber of Commerce. The *Aberdeen World* quoted him on February 12 as saying that there was sufficient information on the park; its creation should not be delayed for more study. Schulz commented: "That is magnificent, and you have no idea how gratifying, as well as enlightening, that is to us out here."

With the firm backing of President Roosevelt, and aided by full agreement between the National Park and Forest services, Congressman Wallgren on March 25, 1938, introduced H.R. 10024, his third and most inclusive Olympic bill. It called for creation of a national park of 938,000 acres, including a detached seashore area extending from the Quinault Indian Reservation northward, to and including Lake Ozette. There was no deviation from strict national-park standards.

However, the second Wallgren bill, H.R. 4724, was on the calendar, and to avert a long delay it had to be dealt with until H.R. 10024 could be substituted in committee. The immediate need was for clearance by the Bureau of the Budget. On March 16 I put in a telephone call to the White House which was summarized as follows in an aide's memo to Marvin McIntyre:

"Irving Brant 'phoned [then, quoting me] I understand that the Olympic Park bill is now before the Bureau of the Budget. Some time ago I heard Mac [McIntyre] make the suggestion that when it got there, he would try to speed it up a bit. They are waiting for a report on it before Wallgren makes any move in the House."

Stapled to this is a memorandum to McIntyre from D. W. Bell, acting director of the Budget, dated March 19, saying that he had received a draft of Interior's report to the House public lands committee on the bill and was waiting for the word from Agriculture. Attached also is a March 25 telegram from McIntyre at Warm Springs, Georgia, FDR's "other White House," giving this resultant order to aide Rudolf Forster: "Please phone Danny Bell [that] the president requests him to speed up Agricultural and Park Service H.R. 4724."

With the bill in the hopper, Secretary Ickes immediately sent the Interior Department's approval to the Bureau of the Budget. I called Secretary Wallace's office and was told that he would sign a clearance that night. Wallace approved the bill, reversing the stand he had taken in 1935.[3]

When the text of H.R. 10024 reached the state of Washington, hell broke loose. Grays Harbor newspapers screamed. Governor Clarence D. Martin, anti-New Deal Democrat who had kept quiet for three years, wrote to President Roosevelt on April 2 asking that the park's size be cut in half—down to the 450,000 acres recommended by the Washington State Planning Council. (He could as well have said "asked for by the timber industry.") The governor wrote that the proposed park would "seriously interfere" with the income from 200,000 acres of school land, the state's tax structure, and use of other resources.

Martin enclosed an area map showing his proposal for a park that consisted of the national monument plus 140,000 acres with hardly more than a sampling of the gigantic trees the Olympic park had been designed to preserve. Only a very attentive observer would have noticed that the 200,000 acres of state land, which according to Martin would be "seriously interfered with," were outside the boundaries of the Wallgren bill and would be unaffected by the park in any case.

On the day of the governor's intervention state senator Joe L. Keeler of Hoquiam (Grays Harbor) and F. V. Mathias, chairman of the Grays Harbor County Planning Commission, were "barnstorming" in Wallgren's congressional district with speeches against his bill. A lengthy interview with Keeler in the *Seattle Times* carried this clever exaggeration: "It is all right to make a park ON the peninsula, but not to make a park OF the peninsula." Keeler, a power in state politics, had grazed sixteen hundred sheep in the Mount Olympus National Monument (while it was administered by the Forest Service), until the lush meadows of Deer Park were so completely denuded that four years after the permit expired, the grass had not started a comeback.

The governor's intervention was considered a ten-strike by the opposition. Schulz learned the preliminaries to it. A group of lumbermen, he reported to me, called on Colonel William B. Greeley, general manager of the West Coast Lumbermen's Association and former head of the Forest Service. "They arranged for Greeley and one or two others to visit the Governor, and to persuade him to intervene. Hence the Governor's action."

Governor Martin wrote also to the entire Washington congressional delegation and secured a week's delay in the House hearings on the Wallgren bill, reset for April 19. Schulz wrote me on that date, "The press here [in Seattle] has largely strangled all pro-park news." It had carried not a line about a resolution of the national DAR supporting the park. But, said Schulz, "Thousands of people are indignant at the Governor's interference." John Boettiger, the president's son-in-law, was not one of them. He came out once more for selective cutting in a park jointly managed by the Park Service and Forest Service.

I took no part in the House hearings because I was out of town, but hoping to lift Congressman Wallgren's morale, I wrote him on April 18 that a high administrative source was replying to Boettiger, for publication, in a way that would make it look as if Wallgren and the president were "regular buddies" in bill drafting.

Actually I drafted the Ickes reply to Boettiger. It described four meetings that Wallgren took part in during the revisal process, the first and fourth being with the president. It told how the park acreage was built up by general agreement, and then was cut back by the president himself, eliminating corridors to the sea. This took out large tracts of private land that he really wished to bring into the park. If oil deposits existed, as was claimed by Boettiger, they were on this eliminated private land and were open to development. The draft also strongly refuted the notion that the president supported the destructive sort of "selective logging" practiced on the Olympic Peninsula. Sending this draft for Ickes to Undersecretary E. K. Burlew I remarked, "It was a tough one to write, as I wanted it to challenge Boettiger without antagonizing him, present the President's position without speaking for him, and advocate the park without encroaching on the domain of Congress."

When I returned to Washington on April 28, letters were at hand from Mrs. Edge, who had attended the hearings, and from Schulz; they told of a serious setback. Governor Martin, Ben Kizer (of the Washington State Planning Council), and others of Martin's group had made "grossly unfair" statements at a two-hour House hearing on the morning of April 19. At noon Governor Martin, Ben Kizer, congressmen Wallgren and Smith, and senators Bone and Schwellenbach conferred with the president. At the close of that conference (Schulz wrote) Martin gave out a press statement, saying that Roosevelt "had agreed in the main to his plan for a park of 450,000 acres. This caused consternation out here [in Seattle] especially when Wallgren told the press he would throw out his present bill and go back to H.R. 4724 [and] 600,000 acres."

Schulz had immediately wired Ickes, who wired back that the boundary question was not settled. He also, said Schulz, "urged me confidentially to keep on insisting on a larger park." (That meant Roosevelt still wanted it.) Since then, scores of telegrams had gone to Wallgren and the president urging a return to the larger boundaries. Grays Harbor interests, Schulz said, had choked off a University of Washington radio drama on the Olympics which did not even mention a park. Not a single Washington-state newspaper was supporting it, but they had to give news space to a pro-park rally by organizations representing a hundred thousand members.

Mrs. Edge reported that after the Martin–Roosevelt conference, the NPS staffers held a meeting (which she attended) where "it was frankly and specifically stated that the President's reversal was for political reasons." To win the support of Governor Martin, a Democrat opposed to the New Deal, Roosevelt "throws Wallgren to the dogs."

After reading these letters I hurried over to see Congressman Wallgren. He told me that the president's supposed "reversal" was a mere misunderstanding. Roosevelt had told Governor Martin that he wanted "the bill on the calendar" to be passed. That was the second, small-acreage bill, but Roosevelt thought it was the third, the big one. That explanation, I wrote that day to Dr. Van Name, "doesn't quite account for what took place." I suspected haste and confusion. It turned out that Wallgren was confused. Senator Schwellenbach cleared it all up in a letter to Irving Clark of which Schulz sent me a copy. At the White House meeting, the senator said, there was a discussion of Governor Martin's proposal of a small park, with selective cutting of timber outside it in the national forest. The president then proposed that the House should pass the second Wallgren bill; the president should be given authority to enlarge the park in consultation with the Forest Service, Park Service, and governor; and land around the park should be logged selectively.

"Everyone on both sides," wrote Schwellenbach, was willing to accept the president's proposal. This had surprised the senator, because "I thought . . . it meant giving to him the power to fix the boundaries of the park." Afterwards, Schwellenbach continued, the conferees left together, Governor Martin and Ben Kizer were dropped off at the Willard Hotel, and the four members of Congress returned to the Capitol. During that drive Bone, Wallgren, and Schwellenbach found that they were in "complete disagreement" with Smith on the meaning of "consultation." Their position was that the word gave the president authority to fix boundaries after consideration in good faith of recommendations from the Forest Service, Park Service, and state of Washington. Later that afternoon, Ben Kizer called on Schwellenbach, and they discussed the disagreement. Kizer said he was certain that Governor Martin believed that "consultation" gave him veto power. Schwellenbach attempted to explain that the federal government could not turn over that sort of power to the state.

Two days after Schwellenbach wrote that letter, the House lands committee reported the third Wallgren bill for passage, with amendments that cut out the seashore strip, eliminated the president's power to make additions, and removed the Bogachiel rain forest. Total acreage remained above that of the first Wallgren bill—large enough to make Grays Harbor and the *Seattle Post-Intelligencer* groan with anguish, too small, unless built up in the Senate, to meet the expressed desires of the president. The immediate need was to get a decision from the Rules Committee to allow the bill's consideration by the House, and I advised Mrs. Edge to ply that committee's chairman, John J. O'Connor, with requests for action. It would be useless for me to talk to him, I said, "because I have written too many editorials showing him up."

With Wallgren in a yielding mood, there was no chance of getting the House to put the Bogachiel back in the bill, but I said I would try to get Bone and Schwellenbach to restore it in the Senate, which would do whatever they wanted. The two senators "will do what they think the people of their state want."

A week later, on May 6, I wrote to Schulz that arrangements were completed for Secretary Ickes to make a recorded speech to be broadcast by CBS radio stations in Seattle and Tacoma, at a date still to be fixed. I said I thought that the speech would deal with the governor's "double-dealing" on the meaning of "consultation" and with the attitude of the Seattle newspapers and lumber interests.[4] This was more than conjecture. When I asked Ickes to deliver the speech, desired by Seattle supporters of the park, he answered, "I'll deliver it if you will write it." I did so.

The speech, delivered on May 17, was designed not only to correct the governor but to let the people know what the Seattle newspapers had been concealing, and to do it without charging concealment. So Ickes led off with the statement that the people already knew—though in fact few of them knew—that the Olympic park had been endorsed by the Wilderness Society, the Mountaineers, the Washington State Grange, the International Woodworkers' Association, the State Federation of Teachers' Unions, the Seattle Federation of Women's Clubs, and many other societies—evidence "that the well-informed and public-spirited people of the State of Washington are overwhelmingly in favor of its establishment."

Ickes then described the propaganda campaign of the lumber companies against the park. Lumbermen had not only "made a shambles" of part of the state but they also wanted to "destroy the last wilderness." There was a false claim that sustained-yield forestry required this logging, when in fact timber supplies outside of the park were from four to five times in excess of mill capacity. Ickes chastised the newspapers for biased reporting that favored industrial views. He then turned to Governor Martin, recounting the details of his visit with the president where the concept of "consultation" was introduced but later distorted.

Ickes ended with legislative realities, explaining that the House Committee on Public Lands had promptly reported the third Wallgren bill for passage. If the Senate decided to give the president discretionary authority, FDR would establish the largest park possible. Ickes hoped that his listeners realized the "complete unity of purpose" among the president, Bone, Schwellenbach, and Wallgren.

In writing this final paragraph for Secretary Ickes, I omitted the fact that Congressman Wallgren, yielding to pressure from Port Angeles wood-pulp interests, had induced the House committee to eliminate thirty-three thousand acres of the finest scenic forest. Still, he was united with the others in purpose; what he lacked was courage. When I turned the speech over to Secretary Ickes on May 11, I said (and so wrote to Dr. Van Name) that Wallgren's action, taken without consulting anybody, made it useless to attempt to restore the Bogachiel Valley in the House debate. Ickes agreed with me "that the best way to handle that was to try to include a provision in the bill to give the President discretionary power to add forest lands to the park. If that can't be done, we should work for a Senate amendment [to the bill]." I told Van Name that the real lesson to be learned was that "a national park bill should never be introduced by a congressman from the district in which the lands affected are located."

The House Rules Committee allowed the third Wallgren bill (H. R. 10024) to come before the House under suspension of the rules, which meant that it could not be amended and must receive a two-thirds majority to pass. Consideration was set for May 16. Writing that day to Dr. Van Name, I said that congressmen Eicher of Iowa and Cochran of Missouri (my close personal friends) "rallied a couple of groups of supporters and Eicher passed out several dozen of my pamphlets after the House convened."

Lands committee chairman De Rouen spoke for five minutes in support of the bill. Englebright of California, Fred L. Crawford of Michigan, and Adolph Sabath of Illinois gave it a few favorable sentences; nobody spoke against it. Thereupon the motion to suspend the rules and pass the bill was put and carried by the necessary two-thirds majority.

"As soon as the House voted," I wrote to Van Name, "I went to see Senator Adams, chairman of the Senate Lands committee, about the Bogachiel. He was called to preside at a conference committee meeting, but I am to see him again at his office." At our second meeting, Adams asked me to write him an explanation of the moves that led up to House amendments to H.R. 10024. My three-page, single-spaced letter of May 21 covered the same ground as the speech I wrote for Ickes, centering on the misrepresentation by Governor Martin that put the Washington senators in a difficult position, and on the elimination of the Bogachiel. The true reason for eliminating the Bogachiel, I told chairman Adams, was, presumably, that a Port Angeles pulp mill hoped to get hold of the national-forest timber in the valley adjoining its own small holdings.

I enclosed a copy of my Olympic pamphlet, saying that it was written when the Forest Service was fighting against this park, and dealt with the economic arguments raised by that bureau, which were now being used by the lumber industry.

The day after the House passed the Olympic bill I relayed a request to Irving Clark to write to all members of the Senate lands committee, "urging action at this session, discounting the opposition of the governor, and urging inclusion of the Bogachiel or granting of discretionary power to the President." Clark promptly sent off an excellent letter along that line, and made this comment to me about a closely related matter: "Secretary Ickes' radio speech on the Olympic National Park was all that could be desired and I feel sure will be tremendously helpful. Nothing has been heard from the Governor or Mr. Kizer on the subject so far."

Schulz wrote that the speech "caused quite a sensation out here. . . . The P-I gave it a splendid play on page one, top head"—thanks to the fact that managing editor Peters "is in favor of the park, but his hands are tied." Then presidential son-in-law John Boettiger "came out next day with an editorial saying the speech only confused the issue more."

Irving Clark's letter to chairman Adams of the lands committee harmonized with what I had said to the Colorado senator about giving the president discretionary power to enlarge the park. The clerk of the committee asked the Interior Department to prepare such an amendment to H.R. 10024; Secretary Ickes asked me to draft it. On May 28 I delivered a text that allowed the president to add to the park any lands within the boundaries of the national forest and any gifts or purchases of land; it specified that these additions should be permanent. The text also provided that before issuing such a proclamation, the president should notify the governor and the secretaries of agriculture and interior, who would be given opportunity to respond.

The wording had two special purposes. First, it foreclosed any possibility of some future president usurping the power to remove those lands from the park by proclamation, as President Wilson had done with Mount Olympus National Monument. Second, it avoided the "consultation," whose meaning had been distorted by Governor Martin.

With Congress approaching a June adjournment, there was need for speedy senatorial action on the Olympic bill. Chairman Adams of the public lands committee was in charge of the relief bill, then undergoing prolonged debate, and that delayed the meeting of the lands committee. Senator Bone told me that he had a couple of amendments which he wanted to place before the committee, but wished first to talk with the president about them.

Hoping to speed this up, I telephoned to Marvin McIntyre's office at the White House on May 25 to say that Bone and Schwellenbach were going to ask for an appointment to discuss the bill, public opinion in the state of Washington, and the attitude of the Senate lands committee. I offered to bring the president up to date.

Then I wrote a letter to FDR covering the situation, but did not deliver it. Senator Adams, freed of the relief-bill chore, had called an executive session of the lands committee for the next Monday, May 31, and I decided to hold back my letter for that event. At the opening of the Monday session, I was told, Senator O'Mahoney of Wyoming read aloud my letter of May 21 to chairman Adams, to post the committee on late developments. In a revised letter of June 1, I told the president that when the committee met to discuss the park bill, they called up Senator Bone. The senator asked them to postpone action "until he could talk with you about the amendment on discretionary power." Bone had told me afterward that he simply wanted this amendment added to the House bill. He gave me the impression, I added, that "he hoped you would use it extensively." The committee would meet whenever Bone was ready. "Senator Murray [of Montana] said he hoped it could be Friday."

I then told the president how Congressman Wallgren, "who has good intentions where his backbone should be," had induced the House lands committee to remove thirty-three thousand acres in the Bogachiel Valley from the park, at the instance of a wood-pulp company. The land thus eliminated "contains the finest scenic forest of Douglas fir on the peninsula, the most unspoiled wilderness, and one of the chief feeding grounds of the Roosevelt elk herd." I also told of Governor Martin's distortion of the president's position on discretionary power, adding that "Schwellenbach told him where to head in"; but, I said, the repetition of the misrepresentations in Seattle had created a political hazard, because "Schwellenbach fears that if the park is restored to proper proportions by action of Congress . . . the newspapers will accuse him and Bone of doublecrossing the governor." Presidential discretionary power, if granted, would take care of that problem, but, I ended, "The need at present is to press for action, and insist on the discretionary clause."

I handed this letter to President Roosevelt at the close of the June 1 press conference and went next morning to see Senator Bone. He said that he had been unable to get an appointment with the president and that he must have one before submitting his amendments to the Senate committee. I telephoned presidential secretary McIntyre, who said that Bone hadn't asked for an appointment.

I urged that the president call Bone in at once, if the bill was not to be lost for the session. Next morning I went to Bone's office. He had not yet come in. After a time the telephone rang. His secretary spoke only a few words: "This morning at 11:40. He will be there." His deferential and positive tone told the story. I went back to Bone's office in the afternoon. He greeted me with: "Well, I finally got that appointment with the president." Schwellenbach had been with him. Everything was satisfactory. The two Washington senators would meet with the committee and push for passage of the Olympic bill.

Years passed before I learned what followed my June 2 phone call to Secretary McIntyre. His assistant Henry Kannee wrote a memo for the president, saying that I had urged that the president call Bone in for a talk if he wanted action this session of Congress.

Roosevelt instantly sent a longhand memo to Steve Early: "Call up Schwellenbach & Bone and tell them I hope they will press for the passage of this bill—H.R. 10024—and ask if there is anything I can do to help." Early brought back the message that Bone and Schwellenbach thought that "five minutes with you tomorrow" would help them materially in pressing for passage of the bill. They were given ten minutes. Senator Bone gave me copies of the amendments he had left with the president. One was a simple grant of power to enlarge the park by proclamation. The other followed a similar grant with the amazing proviso that any timber set aside would be available for commercial use under Forest Service supervision.

This amendment, Senator Bone told me, had been drafted by Regional Forester Buck of the Portland office of the Forest Service (apparently without the knowledge of Chief Forester Silcox), and he and Schwellenbach had endorsed it to the president, whose views they thought it represented. When I began to point out its destructive nature, Senator Bone got out his memorandum of the April 19 conference of Governor Martin and President Roosevelt, and read a passage in which the president was said to have made a general advocacy of selective logging in the national park. The wording of it instantly brought to mind what the president had said to me in February, that he was opposed to any timber cutting in the park for commercial purposes, and that, in addition, he would like to see clear-cutting abolished in the entire *Olympic National Forest* outside the park. That, I was sure, was what he had said at the conference with Governor Martin.

When I finished my analysis of the Buck amendment, Bone said he would like to drop it and suggested that I communicate with the president. This I did in a letter of June 6, telling FDR of my talk with Bone and giving him the origin of the amendment, which "is full of dynamite, political and otherwise." It would take far too much of his time, I said, to describe everything that had been buried in that amendment, so I would deal only with its most deceptive provision. That was the clause calling for selective logging "necessary to maintain a forest cover" (wording clearly based on FDR's known admiration of Germany's Black Forest).

The "selective logging" that Buck actually had in mind to provide a "forest cover," I said, was described perfectly in a letter from Sacramento, published two days earlier in the *Washington Star*. The writer of it was "protesting against Forest Service logging methods, and said that 'on all Government fir areas exploited to date' the methods employed 'leave a mangled mass fire trap of priceless young trees.'" This carnage, I told the president, was a "forest cover" meeting the requirements of the Buck amendment, and it was selective logging when combined with "checkerboarding" or the cutting of alternate blocks to leave seed areas.

Under the power to make rules and regulations, I said, the president could prevent this; but: "His successor could permit damage that it would take 400 years to repair." The worst feature of the amendment, I told FDR, was that it established a commercial principle of "sustained-yield management" of a thousand-year-old scenic forest and turned it over to a bureau absolutely committed to a sustained-yield cycle of eighty years for sawtimber and forty years for wood pulp. Under such conditions, no president could prevent a slow transition to practices that would mean the "ruin of the park as an agency for preserving the primeval wilderness."

I pointed out a "joker" in the opening sentence of the Buck proviso setting up sustained-yield management of national-park lands by the Forest Service. It applied to "*all lands* so set aside by Executive Order." With that in the law, the president would have no specified power or duty to protect scenic areas in the added lands, even though, owing to reduction of the size of the park as defined in the pending bill, "practically all of the really fine trees will have to be added by proclamation."

Summing up, I said it appeared that the two senators accepted the Buck amendment "because they thought you wanted it, and my impression is that you accepted it because you thought they wanted it. I hope you will feel like suggesting to them that they concentrate on the amendment giving you discretionary power to enlarge the park and drop the other."

After talking with members of the Senate Committee on Public Lands, I wrote to Schulz that the committee probably would substitute the second Wallgren bill for the third, by means of an admendment. This would reduce the fixed area of the park from 898,292 acres to 648,000. But they would report another amendment giving the president discretionary power to enlarge the park. This they did, reporting the bill favorably on Saturday, June 11. The enlargement amendment was the one I had drafted for Ickes to give to Senator Adams, with one change. The requirement to "communicate" with the Washington governor became a requirement to "consult." However, my specifications of what the governor could do were incorporated without change.

Congress was scheduled to adjourn on Wednesday, June 15. That left three working days for the Senate to pass the amended bill and for the amendments to be either accepted by the House or subjected to conference proceedings.

Under "one-step-a-day" rules, the Senate passed the amended bill on Monday; the House received notice of the passage next day. On Wednesday chairman De Rouen was to move that the Senate amendments be concurred in. Unanimous consent was needed for that action, and Congressman Martin Smith had promised Wallgren that he would not object. With House confirmation a mere formality, I had time for other things.

Walking through a Capitol corridor, I met a St. Louis acquaintance who was in Washington as lobbyist for the railroad unions that supported Senator Crosser's bill for unemployment insurance. He was in anguish. The railroad companies had persuaded the president that they could not stand the cost of insuring part-time workers. Now the bill was stalled in the Senate and would be dead on adjournment. It occurred to me there was a way of interpreting the bill's requirements that would satisfy both sides. I telephoned Tom Corcoran at the White House. If I held a letter on the subject to half a page, he said, he would see that the president read it that afternoon. My memo to FDR was handed to a Western Union messenger at 3 p.m. on Tuesday. If the president wished to act, the Crosser bill could come before the Senate next day, in spite of the crowded end-of-session schedule.

About noon on Wednesday, the Olympic park bill was brought up in the House. Smith did not object. An upset came, instead, from minority leader Bertrand Snell, who hated Roosevelt. He would willingly vote for a larger acreage, but was absolutely opposed to giving discretionary power to the president: "Have you fellows no responsibility yourselves? . . . Mr. Speaker, I object."

This seemed to spell defeat. The bill had to go to conference, but with Congress adjourning there was no time for that. I described what followed in a long letter to Dr. Willard Van Name. De Rouen, talking with Wallgren and me, had suggested a quick shift by the Senate back to the bill passed by the House (H. R. 10024, without the Bogachiel). At that moment word came that the Senate had postponed adjournment for one day. The Crosser bill, it turned out, was to be debated that afternoon. This meant that the Wallgren bill also had a chance. The extra day's session, said De Rouen, "puts a different face on the matter." Invoking a rule known only to a few old-timers, he would get permission to file a conference report up till midnight. That would give the report privileged status and remove the need to suspend the rules by a two-thirds majority. As I phrased it to Van Name, De Rouen said "they could go ahead, hold a conference during the evening, make the report, act on it Thursday."

De Rouen got a satisfactory House conference committee appointed, then asked me to suggest some senators whom he could recommend to chairman Adams. I named Adams himself, O'Mahoney, Murray, and Hatch of New Mexico, all friendly to a large park. De Rouen telephoned at once to Adams, who said he and O'Mahoney were too busy to serve but he would put on Murray and Hatch.

So, as I wrote to Van Name, "I chased over to the Senate and talked to Murray and Hatch, saying Adams had said they were to be appointed." They were anxious to get the bill through, but said that the report from the House had not arrived. (De Rouen had ordered it expedited.) That delayed the naming of the Senate conferees for an hour and a half, by which time Adams and O'Mahoney were through with their rush. Immediately after the passage of the Crosser bill, Adams asked for a conference on the Olympic bill, and named himself, O'Mahoney, and Hatch as conferees, along with Senator Pittman of Nevada.

I had given Murray a lengthy fill-in, which was wasted. The conferees were to meet at seven and it was getting along toward that hour. I got hold of O'Mahoney, who was strong for the park, and gave him a quick briefing. He asked me to go with him to the Capitol and stay near the conference room. I sat outside its door for an hour. Then De Rouen came out and told me how things stood.

Senator Pittman had objected to the plan of accepting the House bill, which would have created a park of 898,292 acres, and suggested that they stick to the Senate's version, for a park of 648,000 acres with power given the president to make additions from the national forest. (Roosevelt himself had suggested this to the Washington delegation.) The problem was that this would permit the inclusion of the entire Olympic National Forest, thus authorizing a park of 1.5 million acres. That would lead to the conference report being thrown out on a point of order that it created a larger park than was authorized by the House bill.

Senator Pittman, De Rouen said, proposed to solve this by limiting the park, with presidential additions, to a maximum of 898,292 acres—the exact figure in the House bill. What did I think of it?

I could hardly credit what I heard. I had mistrusted Pittman, the buddy of Nevada gamblers, and he had presented a perfect solution. Chairman Adams incorporated the acreage limit in his amendment on discretionary power, the conferees agreed, and everything was lovely. Or so it seemed.

On Thursday, June 16, 1938, the House met at ten o'clock and promptly agreed to the conference report. Shortly afterward I encountered chairman De Rouen. He was looking for me, in dismay. Senator Bone had discovered a fatal clerical error in the printed report of the Olympic conferees. By accidentally changing the words "total area of" to "total area to be added to," the bill was made to say that the president could ADD 898,292 acres to the 648,000 specified by Congress. Uncorrected, the bill was dead.

The only chance for correction was by a concurrent resolution, passed by both houses. This posed no problem in the Senate. Immediately after adopting the conference report, the senators passed a resolution correcting its "technical errors." The hazard came in the House. Unless the concurrent resolution was agreed to unanimously it would have to get a two-thirds majority. In effect, one vote against the resolution would kill the Olympic bill. The amendment Snell had objected to was still in the bill, and Snell was on the floor. So was Martin Smith, arch-enemy of the park. During a four-hour recess, De Rouen told me his plan of action. Fortunately, he said, nobody knew about the conference snag except himself, Wallgren, Speaker Bankhead, and majority leader Rayburn. When the House reconvened, my wife and I were in a gallery; Major Tomlinson and national-park forester Fred Overly were cata-cornered from us. I described developments to Dr. Van Name:

"I saw De Rouen walk over and shake hands cordially with Snell, saying goodby and a pleasant summer, old pal. Martin Smith thought it was all over and wasn't there. . . . Controversial stuff came on, and the House voted down an appropriation [for Lake Tahoe] with apparent relish. Then it became evident (from Wallgren's movements) that Rayburn had sandwiched the Olympic resolution in with some unanimous consent stuff to which nobody was paying any attention. Wallgren finally moved to take up S. Con. Res. 42. The clerk read it (Wallgren said afterward that at this point everybody on the floor seemed to be turning to look at him) and the instant the reading stopped, Bankhead said, 'Without objection the Senate resolution is concurred in and a motion to reconsider is laid on the table.' Bang! That was over. Tomlinson and Overly and my wife and I all jumped up at the same moment, I let out a yip, and we left before anybody called the police."

So the Olympic National Park came into being, with 648,000 acres placed in it by act of Congress, and the president authorized to proclaim the addition of 250,292 more, for an overall total of 898,292 acres.

In my June 17 commentary to Van Name, I summed up attitudes. It was my definite impression that the chief obstacle had been outside influences operating on people who didn't know the facts. The public lands committees of both houses were friendly. Ickes and Undersecretary Burlew were A-1 plus. The National Park Service wanted the best bills obtainable but lacked forcefulness and political acumen. My own work, I said, "consisted chiefly of pulling things out of the way of it. The big push came from Seattle and vicinity. Schulz's work was vitally important." Wallgren "except for his temporary cave-in to that Port Angeles woodpulp company, has done a fine job." But the single overwhelming influence was that of Franklin D. Roosevelt, who had devoted greatly disproportionate time and attention to pushing the bill through. He was responsible for defeating delays, and he gave the Washington State delegation stamina to resist pressure from lumbermen and chambers of commerce. Secretary Ickes' role was second only to the president's.

Irving and Hazeldean Brant with daughter Robin (center) in the Sierra Nevada, 1941; the Brant family made many such wilderness expeditions during the course of Irving Brant's work in behalf of the American conservation effort (photograph courtesy Robin Brant Lodewick).

REPORT ON ENLARGEMENT
OF OLYMPIC NATIONAL PARK

The week that followed congressional approval of the Olympic National Park was one of mutual congratulations among its supporters. Schulz praised Irving Clark of the Wilderness Society, who contributed liberally of both time and money; his inside knowledge of Washington state politics made him the "most valuable single ally we had." Schulz added, to me, that there never would have been a park "if you hadn't been in Washington to steer things." My reply gave Schulz no more than his just dues. Sending him a final Van Name remittance, I told him he had brought out the public sentiment in Washington state that kept the park movement going.

In writing to me, Mrs. Edge was exuberant: "Your name should be across the glaciers of Olympus like 'Prudential' across Gibraltar." I replied with greater factual accuracy about her own contributions in stirring up sentiment for the Olympic Park. To Van Name I said, with some deviation from pure conservation principles, "Your name ought to be carved on the biggest tree in the park."

Ickes (who had just returned from a honeymoon in Ireland) sent a note of appreciation for my "very effective efforts." He had recently been urging me to become director of the National Park Service. The secretary had taken a strong dislike to Director Arno Cammerer, about whom he used epithets associated with excessive weight. But the reasons were only symbolically physiological. "Cammerer," he said, "has no guts. He is afraid to disagree with me. He tries to guess my position and support it." Cammerer's attitude was in harmony with an impression widely held in the Interior Department that it was dangerous to disagree with the ardent secretary.

That depended on estimates of worth, as one incident a few months later proved. Ickes showed me a letter blistering him for policies in the fisheries end of the Fish and Wildlife Service. It came from Kenneth Reid, prominent in the Izaak Walton League. "That is the kind of man I would like to have at the head of fisheries," said Ickes. He spoke seriously of offering him the job. Nothing came of the idea, perhaps because Reid's health began to fail.

Ickes renewed the national parks offer to me, telling me that I could go under civil service and have lifetime security. Mrs. Ickes joined in the request. The next time Ickes spoke about it he said that President Roosevelt wanted me to take it. Tom Corcoran told me that Arthur Demaray (who kept the bureau running) could do the work, and I could take assignments from the White House, principally speech-writing for the president.

I had several reasons for refusing. I was determined to keep on with the Madison biography. I felt reasonably secure without salary. I did not like the idea of taking a position and not filling it. And I felt that it would push me into "channels," cutting off the easy access I had to President Roosevelt—easier, I had reason to believe, than some cabinet members possessed. But I was willing to accept a part-time position.

The result was an arrangement that I should become a consultant, technically attached to the National Resources Board but transferred to the Public Works Administration upon its establishment later in the year. This was a bookkeeping arrangement to divide my salary between the Interior Department and the White House. My actual work was to be as personal assistant to Secretary Ickes and speech writer for President Roosevelt. The appointment was for ten days' work a month, which was almost immediately raised to twenty. The standard salary was fifty dollars a day, but I had a quixotic unwillingness to take more than the forty-five dollars I was receiving from the *St. Louis Star-Times*. I could have kicked myself for this, because the publisher, Elzey Roberts, raised my stipend to fifty dollars as soon as he heard of the government appointment.

Three national-park projects lay immediately ahead: (1) the enlargement of the Olympic National Park by exercise of the president's power to add 250,292 acres to it by executive proclamation, (2) the purchase and preservation of a magnificent grove of giant sequoias on miscalled Redwood Mountain in the southern Sierra Nevada—a grove threatened with destruction because the conservation-minded owners were no longer able to pay taxes on the land, and (3) establishment of the long-sought Kings Canyon National Park, whose boundaries would be in contact with both Sequoia National Park and Redwood Mountain.

To promote the second and third of these projects, I was hopeful that

Secretary Ickes would put William Schulz on the department payroll to do the same kind of work in which he had been so effective in the campaigns for the Carl Inn sugar-pine grove and Olympic National Park. Ickes had told me several times that he wanted to become acquainted with Schulz. So, when Van Name's one-man park-publicity bureau wrote that he planned a trip to Washington after visiting his old home in Springfield, Ohio, I advised him to time it to follow Ickes' return from Europe. He did so and was immediately appointed field representative, connected with the National Park Service for payroll purposes, but not subject to its control. That left him free to continue his correspondence as before, with Secretary Ickes and with me.

Of more immediate concern was an assignment given me as an official consultant by Mr. Ickes. I was to go to the Olympic Peninsula, study the lands adjacent to the new national park, and recommend areas to be added by presidential proclamation. The six-week mission was to end in a swing to southern California for a less formal examination of boundaries for the Kings Canyon-Redwood Mountain park project. Five national-park officials—two park superintendents and three technicians—were to be in the Olympic party. Permission was given for my wife and younger daughter to go along, at our expense.

We reached Seattle on July 20; work started next day at Port Angeles. There Preston Macy, lately superintendent of Mount Olympus National Monument, occupied temporary headquarters as "resident acting superintendent" of the national park. Soon afterwards he was formally appointed superintendent. A rugged mountaineer, Macy refused to let chronic phlebitis hamper his movements.

Besides Macy, our initial expeditionary force included Major Owen A. Tomlinson, superintendent of Mount Rainier National Park and acting superintendent of the new Olympic park. A veteran of service in Philippine tribal areas, he would become noted for knocking out the U.S. Army Corps of Engineers with one toss of a "hand grenade." The major on that occasion sat for hours at a public hearing in which the corps explained and defended its plan to build a south–north military highway straight across the summit of the Olympic Mountains to forestall a possible Japanese expeditionary force marching on Seattle along the Strait of Juan de Fuca and Hood Canal. Finally Tomlinson rose from his chair and asked, "What will you do if the Japanese make their landing during the ten months of the year in which this military highway will be buried under a hundred feet of snow?" The presiding engineer had a ready answer: "The hearing is adjourned."

The others in our party were Ernest Davidson, regional architect of the National Park Service; Lowell Sumner, regional wildlife adviser; and David Madsen, supervisor of national-park fish resources. Formerly Wyoming state fish commissioner, Madsen had experienced difficulties in that position that were a testimonial to his conservation principles.

The Olympic Mountains massif, centered in the great peninsula west of Seattle, is divided into two distinct climatic areas by the effect of the mountain barrier on rainfall. The eastern side of the mountains is semiarid, with an annual precipitation of about 18 inches. On the western slope to the Pacific, rainfall rises from about 80 inches per year at sea level to 150 inches near the summits.

This variation in rainfall produces a profound effect upon forest growth. Old-growth Douglas fir on the eastern slopes exceeds 200 feet in height, in dense stands, but is seldom more than 2 feet in diameter. Old-growth Douglas fir on the rainy slopes is not much taller—about 250 feet—but reaches its maximum diameter at almost 15 feet. Similar contrasts mark other conifers and the difference extends to the undergrowth—far lusher in the rain-swept west. Swift rivers flow out of the mountains in all four directions.

The park as defined by Congress was almost roadless, as were the prospective additions. It was to be in the main a wilderness park. Macy and Tomlinson had planned the logistics of our trip—by automobile in the eastern half and around the perimeter, on horseback up the western valleys. For convenience, two horseback trips of several days' duration were sandwiched between day-long motor drives totalling two thousand miles. However, in preparing my report on boundaries, I defined nine consecutive additions in geographic blocks running counterclockwise around the national monument, plus park headquarters in Port Angeles.

Choice of lands to be added was governed by five principles: (1) whether lands were important to the park by reason of scenic, scientific, preservative, or recreational value; (2) whether the inclusion of such lands was practicable; (3) whether their inclusion was damaging to other interests, and if so, how might they be harmonized, or which should prevail; (4) whether lands, not otherwise important to the park, were needed to protect the approaches to it, or for other administrative reasons; (5) what relationship the park would have to the national forest, state land, private land, highways, tourist resorts, packers, fishermen, hunters, etc.

In my report, I stated that the park was being created primarily to preserve the wilderness rain forest and the winter range of the Roosevelt elk. It was therefore essential to include large areas of commercial timber, whose value would ordinarily be used as an argument for exclusion. Both rain forest and elk range could be protected only by taking in lands at low elevations. Finally, I declared, it was necessary to consider the relationship of the park and national forest to the economic needs of the Olympic Peninsula and its lumber industry.

Before the investigative trips began, I came in contact with various pro-and-con groups. Bankers and officers of the Port Angeles Chamber of Commerce were unitedly opposed to extensive additions in the western valleys and advised me to pay special attention to the interest of the Crown-Zellerbach Corporation, which owned much of a strip of land one mile wide and nine miles long, running up both sides of the Bogachiel River and containing magnificent stands of Sitka spruce. Editor Charles Webster of the *Port Angeles Evening News* did not join in this pressure. The entire Port Angeles community desired the inclusion of their hometown mountain, Mount Angeles, and of the twenty-thousand-acre Morse Creek watershed lying at its base and furnishing the Port Angeles water supply.

Civic and political leaders in Seattle urged large additions on the eastward side of the national monument, including all of the mountain peaks visible from their city. Though legitimate, this coincided with the wish of the lumber companies to reach the statutory limit of additions without taking in the industry-coveted western rain forests. The Seattle people, however, merely wanted to say to themselves and eastern visitors, "Those white peaks are all in our national park."

I recommended ten additions to the park. First, 6,720 acres to the Lake Crescent–Sol Duc area, to protect the mountain slopes north of Lake Crescent from future lumbering visible from the lake. Second, 1,820 acres to the Soleduck-Calawah divide area, to protect nearby scenic values and to provide a better administrative boundary between the park and national forest. Third, 30,400 acres in the Bogachiel-Hoh valleys, which was the most controversial of all the proposed additions. The president had pressed for inclusion of the entire corridor containing the Bogachiel and the neighboring Hoh, as a connecting link with his cherished ocean-front strip, but lumber interests also coveted the valleys.

I had worked in Congress to keep the Bogachiel Valley in the park, but concluded without on-the-ground inspection that the president had been too many ranches and too much non-scenic private forest land. Our tour of the area terminated seaward at the western boundary of the nine-mile privately owned strip, lying along the river.
owned strip, lying along the river.

Our party drove eighteen miles up the Hoh River valley to the road's end at the Jackson Ranger Station (the same ground covered by FDR in 1937). We then went on horseback up the Hoh, headed for Bogachiel Peak and a return ride down the Bogachiel River valley. We camped the first night at Hoh Lake (no tents), where Dave Madsen hauled in enough trout for supper. At Bogachiel Peak, next day, the young fire lookout demonstrated the use of his swivel-mounted telescope. "I swing it like this," he said, "looking for fires—THERE'S ONE NOW," he exclaimed and darted to the telephone. Getting the Forest Service guard station on the highway, he learned that the fire had already been spotted in the Soleduck region and covered ten acres. (It later spread over ten thousand acres.)

Next day we rode down the North Fork of the Bogachiel River, with its deep pools and foaming cascades, and lunched on the rocks at Flapjack Shelter, where the fork joined the main stream of the Bogachiel. From that point, a short side hike took some of us onto the Snyder–Jackson Trail, which crosses the mountain ridge between the Hoh and the Bogachiel. This taught me something new about scenic forests. From a lumberman's point of view, or that of the Forest Service, it was a "beat-up" area demonstrating the inferiority of Mother Nature in her reproduction of trees—a one-time forest of Douglas fir of which nothing remained except scattered dead snags, among western hemlocks that had taken possession two or three hundred years before. But to persons who see more in nature than commercial board feet, the transition was indescribably beautiful.

As our party rode on downriver, we passed through forests of gradually increasing beauty and majesty. The trunks swelled in size, the crowns rose higher, overhead rooting (a distinctive feature of rain forests) became more conspicuous, festoons of moss swayed more deeply from the maples. We spread our sleeping bags that night under the 250-foot Sitka spruces that surrounded the Bogachiel Guard Station.

Following this pack trip I had a long talk about the Bogachiel Valley with Crown–Zellerbach's vice-president for production. I found him to be an honest man, working for an honest company—devoted to its interests, but fair-minded. He was of course opposed to extension of the park down the Bogachiel River, along which Crown–Zellerbach and a Michigan-based company owned nearly all of the nine-mile private corridor. His company, its vice-president told me, had sufficient pulp timber, but this corridor was of particular future value to it because of its heavy stand of Sitka spruce, which was used in paper making as a whitener in the sulfite process.[1] With Sitka spruce disappearing elsewhere, the trees in this corridor were looked upon as a final reserve in the whitening process. "What will you do when it is gone?" I asked. "We will use a chemical whitener," the vice-president replied. "Why can't you do that now?" "Spruce whitener," he said, "has publicity value."

This argument did not impress me, and I put a proposition up to him: If the entire valley should be added to the park by the president, I said, the privately owned corridor could be logged by its owners at will. The president would have no authority to place the corridor in the park unless the government had previously acquired it by purchase or gift. Neither method of acquisition was practicable. But if the publicly owned portion of the valley should be added to the park by proclamation, and the private corridor left out, land in the corridor could lawfully be acquired by the government through an exchange of standing timber for it; or the lumber company, if unwilling to trade, could go ahead and log it. What did Crown–Zellerbach think of such alternatives? The vice-president responded that in that case they would favor an exchange; it would be too expensive to log the corridor without logging the whole valley.

Knowing President Roosevelt's wishes, I felt that Crown–Zellerbach's semi-agreement settled the matter; my report therefore was devoted to advancing the timber exchange. Having ridden the length of the corridor, I found the final three miles of it a little less scenic than the rest. So I cut this off as an immediate objective, reducing the initial cost of the timber exchange. I reported that the recommended 30,400-acre addition would bring the finest rain-forest wilderness into the park, yet exclude private timber holdings along the Bogachiel. This would carry the park six miles west of the statutory boundary, compared with twelve miles proposed in the original H.R. 10024.

Jutting into the park between the Hoh and Bogachiel additions, but still a part of the national forest, would be six miles of the nine-mile private corridor. This area, I recommended, should be acquired by the government through a timber exchange and added later to the park to prevent despoliation of the river valley, which was "the purest wilderness area on the Olympic Peninsula." I concluded by saying that if the private land could be acquired, the park should be extended three miles westward by a later proclamation. This would take in more of an important winter range for the Roosevelt elk.

Continuing my description of addition number three, I turned to the Hoh River valley. There the park, I said, ought to be extended to the original limits set in H.R. 10024. That would carry the boundary four miles down the Hoh and bring in five miles of the road from the peninsular highway. "This will offer the motoring public the same type of 'rain forest' wilderness found in the Bogachiel River valley, which is and always should be roadless." The Hoh and Bogachiel valleys, I said, ought to be considered as a unit, though serving, in the main, different groups of people, because "they are ideally located for hiking and pack-horse trips covering both valleys."

The highly scenic Hoh River road through the national forest, I said, needed to be protected by the Forest Service "through a vigorous policy of timber exchange, as most of the timber land below the recommended park boundary is privately owned, and is being destructively lumbered." (It was here that President Roosevelt expressed his wish that the lumberman responsible for this scene should be "roasting in hell.")

The fourth addition was 8,960 acres in the Queets River valley. None of this proposed addition was in H.R. 10024. The valley was the locale of our second packing trip on horseback. From the ocean, I reported, "A road winds twenty miles up the Queets valley, past huge spruces, hemlocks and maples, terminating a mile inside the national forest. . . . Above the road is an almost untouched wilderness extending thirty miles up the river to the snow mountains. Two small ranches, a trapper's cabin and a banker's summer home . . . represent the only invasion of this part of the national forest." The Queets appeared to have washed its valley out of deep glacial deposits. Old landslides, still bare, showed that the lower slopes consisted of loose gravel. The fall of one giant hemlock in the dense forest had bowled down and splintered eleven others, in a six-hundred-foot swath. Lumbering here, practically speaking, was infeasible.

The Queets River, by reputation which our trip confirmed, was far and away the best fishing stream in the Olympic area. We camped the first night at the mouth of a large creek. As Dave Madsen was rigging his five-ounce rod with a three-pound breaking-test leader, our guide, a rancher named Kelley, said to him, "I'll bet you two dollars that the first fish you strike will be more than twenty-four inches long." Madsen took the bet and began casting. At the second drop of the fly a fish struck. Madsen played it for thirty-five minutes with his delicate gear, then drew it to shore—a twenty-six-inch-long steelhead. The next day he pulled in a thirty-six-inch salmon. My photograph of Sumner photographing a Dolly Varden trout held by Macy, while Madsen, behind them, played a second trout, was used in my report to the president, and showed up some years later as a picture postcard at Port Angeles.

My fifth recommendation was that twenty-eight thousand acres be added in the Quinault River valley. Lake Quinault, whose nature and setting made it one of the most beautiful bodies of water in the United States, belonged to the Quinault Indians, whose reservation, extending fifteen miles from the lake to the sea, took in only the seaward side of the lakeshore. On both the North Fork and the East Fork of the Quinault, roads branching off the peninsular highway below the lake reached fifteen miles or more into the national forest.

My recommendation included only half of the Quinault area covered by the original H.R. 10024. The south shore of the lake was closely built up with tourist facilities on land leased from the Forest Service. The first few miles of the (southerly) East Fork road ran through private timber holdings which, I wrote in my report, "are being so frightfully butchered by the removal of the larger trees that they would constitute nothing but a handicap to the park under present circumstances." Considering these factors, I concurred in the judgment of Superintendent Tomlinson that administrative difficulties made it unwise to carry the South Fork addition farther west than Bunch Creek. The decision made a park vista of the lake itself and its panoramic northern skyline of wooded mountains, putting the mountains, but not the lake, in the park. It also left no question about the prior rights (e.g., fishing) of the Indians over the lake itself. I did not know until years later how closely our judgment coincided with the expressed views of President Roosevelt. In 1961 I visited the lake with a Grays Harbor professional man who had originally opposed the park; he said as we looked across the lake, "In September 1937, I stood on this exact spot beside Franklin Roosevelt. I heard him say, as his arm swept the lake and mountains, 'All of that ought to be in the park.'"

Since FDR was surrounded then by opponents of the park, his remark traveled no farther than his voice. Coincident with this opposition there was a growing movement in the Quinault resort area for tourist developments conflicting with wilderness principles. I added to my report that the roads extending into the rain forest on both forks of the Quinault would "make the area popular for motorists in contrast with the roadless Queets, thus preserving a balance between pure and modified wilderness." But there was heavy pressure by Lake Quinault resort owners to continue the East Fork road (already too long) up the Quinault and down the Dosewallips River to the Hood Canal, so as to bring Seattle tourists over the mountains to the Quinault region. "Such a road," I said, "would be in utter violation of the principles on which the Olympic National Park is being established." The recommended additions, I continued, served by existing roads, would bring the forks of the Quinault inside the park and would add "a splendid scenic area of Sitka spruce, western red cedar and maples." An illustrative photograph in my report depicted a Quinault roadside cedar thirteen feet in diameter.

My sixth recommendation was that 19,840 acres be added at the southeast corner of the park. This included a tract five by six miles in area along the North Fork of the Skokomish River, plus a square mile reaching the shoreline of Lake Cushman, a reservoir maintained by the city of Tacoma. Although this lakeside had been appallingly mistreated, I said, it could be restored with the aid of WPA labor.

Addition number seven was to be 55,040 acres including the Dosewallips River (flowing east) and the "Seattle skyline," which would assure the people of Seattle that the Olympic peaks they saw from their homes were in the park. Not only was the Dosewallips valley beautiful, it was the logical entrance for those driving west from Seattle.

Within the last few months, the Forest Service had extended a road up the valley aiming toward Lake Quinault. A great scar was left where the precipitous wall had been dynamited beside Dosewallips Falls. Work had stopped when the park bill was passed, and much of the damage, where talus slopes now ran down to the river, could be repaired. (I was told in Seattle that the road extension was strategic. It was meant to persuade Lake Quinault residents that the Forest Service intended to continue the road across the mountains.)

Next, I proposed adding 10,240 acres comprising the high plateau area of Deer Park (elevation 6,000 feet) on the north side of the park. This addition would provide for winter sports and allow auto access. Motorists could see a panorama of snow peaks, Puget Sound, Vancouver Island, and the San Juan Islands.

The ninth addition was 65,600 acres including Hurricane Hill, Obstruction Point, and the Elwha River valley. This added high mountain country similar to Deer Park and with similar panoramic views. The two areas, I advised, should be treated as an administrative unit. Completion of a partially built road would unite Hurricane Ridge and Deer Park in a one-way loop drive from the Olympic highway.

The final addition was a 36-acre administrative area, which had been offered by Clallam County in the suburbs of Port Angeles. In conclusion, I summed up the recommendations: area authorized by Congress, 898,292 acres; area included by Congress, 648,000 acres; subject to addition by presidential proclamation, 250,292 acres; total proposed additions, 226,656 acres; held in reserve, 23,636 acres. That reserve was too small, but I left the correction of it to the future.

Secretary Ickes, on his way to Alaska, spent August 2 on the Olympic Peninsula. I had wired him an invitation on July 21 from Margaret Thompson, head of the Northwest Conservation League, to be the principal speaker at a banquet in honor of Congressman Wallgren, at a date to suit the secretary's convenience. Ickes telegraphed his acceptance and asked me to prepare "some material" for him to take on his trip to Alaska.

I wrote his Conservation League speech between pack trips. Arriving on August 2, the secretary surveyed the entire peninsula in a Coast Guard plane. Late in the day he and I, by invitation, went to the Lake Crescent home of Thomas L. Aldwell, president of the Port Angeles Chamber of Commerce, to discuss park boundaries with a delegation from that body. Aldwell, launching an argument against their westward extension, said he had gathered such statistical material as he could, by means of long-distance phone calls, about the importance of the pulp-and-paper industry to his community. His figures, he said, were subject to revision. Ickes quietly suggested that he work out a statement and send it to him after he got back from Alaska.

Secretary Ickes' August 26 speech at the Wallgren banquet received a great play in the *Seattle Post-Intelligencer* next day—a three-column, page-one story and, separately, six columns devoted to the text. In writing this speech for the secretary, I had several objectives in view: to build up popular support for the additions yet to be made, to give Congressman Wallgren his just due for putting the public interest above political opportunism, and, above all, to protect a magnificent wilderness against impairment by misplaced catering to the tourist business. Both the dominant theme and the conflicting commercial trend (useful within limits) were given play in the *Post-Intelligencer*'s three-column news heading: "'Keep Olympic Park / A Wilderness,' Ickes / Urges in Talk Here / Region to Draw / Thousands / of Visitors."

The day Ickes returned from Alaska, Schulz was in Seattle and read in the paper that members of the Washington State Planning Council were to meet the secretary at the dock. "I knew immediately," he wrote me, "that some mischief was up." He grabbed a taxi, but missed Ickes by fifteen minutes. From the ship, the group had gone to John Boettiger's office at the *Post-Intelligencer*. By phoning the newspaper and pretending that he and Ickes had expected to meet but had missed connections, Schulz managed to get the secretary on the phone. They talked casually for a minute or two and then Ickes said suddenly and gruffly, "Come on up—right away."

The planning council, said Schulz, "was plainly amazed." He did not speak until Ickes called upon him; thereafter he spoke freely. The council members "were all armed with maps and whole portfolios full of facts and figures." Ickes responded to them by plying Schulz with questions. Schulz had the answers, and Ickes "seemed to relish the fight." He was "adamant" to the council's pleas, refusing to go into conference with them to produce a report for Roosevelt on park additions. If he agreed, he said, he would have to submit "a minority report of one." The meeting lasted about an hour, with the council getting nowhere. It was, Schulz said, "a grand treat for me to see the secretary in action."

Ickes' speech at the Wallgren banquet stirred up a lot of comment, some strongly favorable, some equally adverse, in the Olympic area. Superintendent Tomlinson of Mount Rainier Park wrote me that the occasion "gave the Secretary an opportunity to outline his views and lay down a policy for the new park," and that was worth more than everything else. "We have something to back up our views and actions, and we are already using the Secretary's speech to offset pressure which is developing for a road in the southern end of the park."

The first offsetting move was made by Irving Clark, who asked for and received assurance from Regional Forester Buck that no more work would be done on the Dosewallips road until it was decided whether or not this river valley would be added to the park. Later, Supervisor Bruckart of the Olympic National Forest told Major Tomlinson that, in his opinion, the road ought to be extended and he intended to extend it. I reported this conflict to Ickes and told him what lay behind it, that this road work was started as a Forest Service maneuver to line up Lake Quinault resort-keepers against the Wallgren bill.

Ickes sent my memorandum to the White House. The president sent a memo to Chief Forester Silcox (with a notation on the retained copy that my letter should not accompany it) saying that he understood that work on the road was being resumed. If so he wanted it stopped until there was a general government agreement. Silcox investigated and reported that no work was under way or planned "and none will be done until after the Park boundaries are settled and a general agreement can be reached."

The incident was trivial but therein lay its significance. Amid the arduous labors of the presidency in a period of domestic and international crises, Franklin Roosevelt could give time and personal effort to preserve the wilderness values of a region he could never visit except on the highway whose construction he forbade.

The sharpest protest against the policies set forth in Ickes' Seattle speech came from the Hoquiam (Grays Harbor) Chamber of Commerce. That body, after seven "whereases" opposing park additions and denouncing the preservation of a large roadless wilderness, resolved unanimously "that the Park Service plans be required to guarantee a program of development, including proper national advertising, that will amply compensate for the loss to the Olympic peninsula and other state communities from the locking up within park boundaries of the great wealth in developed natural resources." It was further resolved to request Governor Martin "to take immediate action that will require sufficient development of scenic roads and accommodations for the traveling public within the Olympic National Park that will make readily accessible the high areas of the Olympics as well as the timbered slopes."

On September 26 Thomas Aldwell of the Port Angeles Chamber of Commerce furnished Secretary Ickes with the requested exposition of the effect enlargement of the park would have upon the pulp-and-paper industry. Sending me an almost identical copy of his fifteen-hundred-word letter to the secretary, he reminded me of his visit with Ickes and me on August 2, at his home on Lake Crescent, and said that the letter to Ickes "is really a letter to you both as you are collaberating [*sic*] all the facts." His communication to Ickes gave a long account of the upbuilding of Port Angeles through development of the wood-pulp industry, but the thrust of the argument was contained in similar paragraphs in the two letters, explaining that the boundary could not be moved farther west without handicapping the pulp and paper mills that were in competition with Canadian mills.

Accompanying the letters to Ickes and to me were photographs of pulp mills and "statistics with respect to certain pulp and paper mills on the Olympic Peninsula." These covered the operations of three companies: the Crown–Zellerbach Corporation at Port Angeles and Port Townsend; Fibreboard Products, Inc., at Port Angeles; and Rayonier Incorporated at Shelton, Tacoma, Port Angeles, and Grays Harbor. Their combined annual payrolls amounted to $6,189,936 for 3,464 employees. Yearly production of pulp and paper was 493,281 short tons, from a total investment of $48,861,030.

Aldwell's figures no doubt were accurate, but the alarmist conclusions that he drew came from another source. The menace to the peninsular woodpulp industry existed only in Forest Service propaganda, whose falsity had been dragged out of Regional Forester Buck by President Roosevelt at their Lake Crescent meeting in September 1937. And when I talked with Crown–Zellerbach's vice-president a few days after Ickes and I met with Aldwell, the only argument he presented against these projected additions to the park was loss of the publicity value of Sitka spruce as a whitener of wood pulp.

On October 30, 1938, I sent a carbon of my report on enlargement of the Olympic Park to Acting Superintendent Macy with a request that he and park forester Fred Overly "look it over and report at once whether you see any inaccuracies or weak spots in it. It is to be printed . . . as soon as possible, because the President said he wanted to discuss the park with me soon after election."

They reported several errors in boundaries and acreage already corrected in the interim by the Park Service in Washington. The book publication was not a routine job. As a part of the economic recovery program, the Interior Department was operating a WPA printers' training project at Manteo, North Carolina; also, the National Park Service had press facilities in its regional office in Richmond, Virginia. The printing trainees set up the type by hand.

The end product was a book of folio size (fourteen by eleven inches) of 114 pages, illustrated with 48 full-page mounted photographs (not reproductions) taken by me, every photograph protected by an onionskin sheet.

Twelve copies were produced, strongly bound, some of them in leather; President Roosevelt, Ickes, Cammerer, and the chairmen of the House and Senate public lands committees were on the distribution list.[2]

My Olympic report was silent concerning the corridor to the sea and the ocean-front strip because these would require public expenditures and because I wanted to do a little missionary work at the White House. In my first talk with the president after returning to Washington, I urged him to shift from his projected Bogachiel-Hoh corridor to the sea, to the more scenic and unpopulated Queets River route. He neither sanctioned nor opposed such a transfer, but showed interest in what I said about the Queets and linked it at once with his previously expressed desire to put a stop to the devastating lumbering methods in the adjoining Quinault Indian reservation.

Administration moves on the seashore project soon followed. On November 19, the *Seattle Post-Intelligencer* carried the headline "U.S. to Extend / Olympic Park / Announcement Comes as Surprise; / Suggested by Roosevelt." The story dealt with a Queets Valley corridor to the ocean and a seashore strip. The *P-I* said that Frank A. Kittredge, NPS regional director at San Francisco, had sprung this "startling surprise" at a public hearing being held by the Washington State Planning Council on an unrelated matter.

Saying that the corridor and seashore strip were suggested by President Roosevelt following his trip to the peninsula, Kittredge described the proposed park extension as follows: "A corridor two miles wide along the Queets River from the western boundary of the park to the ocean. An ocean strip one mile wide and forty-five miles long from the mouth of the Queets River to the north end of Lake Ozette." The Park Service, Kittredge said, "is working on the plan now . . . looking up the ownership of private lands in the area." Considering antecedent events, this action constituted in effect a postscript to my report on enlargement of the park.

The president received my Olympic report from Secretary Ickes sometime before December 10, when he first commented on it. An undated handwritten note by attaché D. Jones about the receipt of it reads: "This book is to go on the table in the President's office." Two uncertainties lay ahead: How would the president receive it? I felt sure that his reaction would be favorable. How would Governor Martin of Washington react to the recommendations? Adversely, beyond a doubt.

Lush rain-forest growth of the Hoh area; during the Roosevelt administration, this area and others like it were the subject of political debate (photograph by Marc Gaede, courtesy the photographer).

CHAPTER EIGHT

THE BATTLE OVER
OLYMPIC ENLARGEMENT

On December 10, 1938, after reading my Olympic report, President Roosevelt partially clarified his position regarding the choice between the Bogachiel-Hoh and the Queets corridors to the sea. Without choosing between them, he wanted legislative authority to add either or both areas to the park and also wanted to protect the Indian forest lands. He sent a memo to Ickes that outlined three areas of concern. First, still needed was legislation to preserve the coastline. Second, either a strip the length of the Bogachiel-Hoh valleys or a strip down the Queets from the park to the ocean should be added. Finally, the remaining timber in the Quinault River valley and most of the timber on Quinault Indian reservation land should be preserved. The Indians currently could sell their timber to lumber interests; the government should buy the lands at a fair value.

Secretary Ickes referred the president's memorandum to the Park Service and sent me the reply he received three days later from Associate Director Demaray: "We are having legislation drafted to accomplish the objectives set forth by the President."

NPS regional director Kittredge's mission to Seattle, planned before the Queets issue came to the fore, had a broader objective. Kittredge was to discuss Olympic Park boundaries with the Washington State Planning Council, with a view to reducing opposition to the intended extensions. Informed of this purpose, I wrote to Kittredge on September 22 that I did not think he would have much difficulty in his conference with the planning council "because their ideas are so ridiculous that you will never get close enough together to have a real discussion unless they totally alter their tactics."

I heard nothing about Frank Kittredge's conference in Seattle until Interior field agent Schulz wrote me on December 28 from San Francisco. He said that Kittredge, who had not yet made a report on his dealings with the planning council, was to go to Washington in a few days to attend a gathering of national-park superintendents and wanted to report personally to Secretary Ickes. Parks director Cammerer was preventing this; so Kittredge had asked Schulz to see if I could arrange a meeting with Ickes. This request, Schulz thought, absolved him from confidentiality regarding Kittredge's negotiations in Seattle, about which he was greatly alarmed.

Kittredge, Schulz wrote, had "twice conferred with Ross K. Tiffany, executive officer of the Wash[ington] State Planning Council," who was "adamant in refusing to yield any more on the west—that is, in the Hoh and Bogachiel." Schulz was "positive that Tiffany has . . . just about gotten Frank to agree to trading the coastal strip for the Hoh and Bogachiel proposed additions"—so, no park enlargement in those two river valleys. Kittredge explained to Schulz that he would like to see the Hoh-Bogachiel rain forest added to the park; but "to ask for it would bring a violent storm of protest from many who have been staunch park friends, and would create much bitter feeling, especially against Secretary Ickes."

This seemed to explain why Kittredge was so anxious to make his report direct to the secretary; he wanted Ickes to save himself from a torrent of criticism by giving up the Hoh and Bogachiel. On that point (without mentioning this controversy) I answered a double inquiry from Mrs. Edge by remarking that the president was not likely to be influenced by Ben Kizer and "Ickes is just as likely to apologize to Hitler as to back up on the Hoh and Bogachiel." On the same day (December 31) I replied to Schulz that I was surprised that Kittredge would advise yielding after a victory. I also wrote that the president's inquiry about corridors and the coastal strip was made after he had read my report and showed that he was inclined to expand the park. However, I said, because of the increased opposition I would recommend against new legislation until after the additions were proclaimed. If a strip was added later it should go down the Queets.

Stirred by news of the Kittredge-Tiffany negotiations, Irving Clark wrote to Secretary Ickes on January 4, 1939, urging "that there be no yielding on the subject of the inclusion of the great primeval forest of the west side"—specifically in the Bogachiel, Hoh, and Queets valleys. It was, he said, to preserve this forest that tens of thousands of people had been striving, and of these valleys the most important was the Bogachiel—virtually untouched by man. It contained all of the main forest trees of the region in all stages of growth, and all leading game species of the peninsula. "The Bogachiel is the only large stream in the Olympics of clear water, unclouded by glacial silt."

Clark voiced his disagreement with my recommendations on the Bogachiel addition, saying it should also include the portion "below the lower forks of the river," since logging in the lower valley would tremendously increase fire hazard and remove the best Sitka spruce.

Somebody misinformed Mr. Clark. My recommendations carried the park six miles below the forks of the Bogachiel and advised, concerning the remaining three miles within the national forest, "If this private land can be acquired, the park should be extended three miles farther west by a later proclamation."

Clark was strongly critical of the Kittredge–Tiffany negotiations, doubting that Kittredge was fully aware "that the Washington State Planning Council has led the fight against the park ever since the guns of the United States Forest Service were silenced." I wrote to Clark, on January 20, that in reality the Kittredge–Tiffany joint statement took no stand against my westward recommendations. The two men had agreed completely on the eastern, northern, and southern additions and made separate reports about those to the west. "Kittredge supported the recommendations I had made, and Tiffany objected to anything being taken in." The damage resulted from Kittredge's oral disclosure that he favored a compromise.

I told Clark that a copy of his letter to Ickes reached me at an opportune time. Ickes had been able to make use of it at the White House even before he got the original. And—"I was glad that you criticized my report for not taking in enough on the Bogachiel, as that fitted well into plans under consideration."

My remark on Ickes having made effective use of Clark's letter did not exactly reflect what happened. The secretary and I had gone together to talk with the president about his cherished corridor to the sea and the seashore strip. Mr. Roosevelt readily accepted my conclusion that the Hoh–Bogachiel route was too heavily developed in ranches to make a suitable park corridor. He definitely accepted the Queets River valley for that purpose and proposed that this corridor and the ocean front be acquired by the government as a Public Works project, with construction of a scenic highway as the link with the national recovery program. This placed it under the direction of Ickes as PWA administrator. It was agreed that land-acquisition options should be taken at once, without publicity, to avoid price hikes through speculative buying by private interests.

I brought up the subject of a three-mile westward extension of the Bogachiel Valley addition, which I had approved in my report but had not formally recommended pending a decision on the purchase of the private land involved. "Put it in," said Roosevelt. Since all of these additions would more than exhaust the reserve acreage provided for in my report, it was agreed that I should make a supplemental report including the new areas and eliminating the least valuable acreage already recommended. Most of this could be achieved, I said, by moving the eastern boundary westward without excluding the mountain tops visible from Seattle.

Irving Clark, writing to Schulz on January 24, reported an upsurge of opposition to the park in the state of Washington. The Seattle Federation of Women's Clubs had a new president whose attitude had been influenced by the state planning council. Clark himself had been allowed to speak for ten minutes before the federation in defense of the park additions, but one strong supporter "was denied permission to hand out copies of Irving Brant's pamphlet at the meeting."

Clark was more and more convinced, he wrote to Schulz, that it was unsafe to defer the making of the additions to the park, and he was disturbed to hear from Schulz that I had suggested postponement of the conference with Governor Martin, which by the Olympic Park Act could not be held before mid-March. Schulz's report had not accurately presented my position. At the bottom of an April 24 letter from Clark to me I penned the following notation: "I pressed FDR several times in regard to inviting Governor Martin to a conference, but he said it must be carefully timed and it was too early." Roosevelt had not wanted to hold the conference while Congress was in session, lest it get mixed up with pending legislation.

In one of these conversations with the president he told me that in preparation for the required consultation with the governor he wanted a thoroughgoing report on the wood-pulp requirements and supplies of the Olympic Peninsula. "Do you think I can trust the Forest Service to make it?" he asked. My thoughts went back to September 30, 1937, when Regional Forester Buck made his unsuccessful attempt to deceive the president at the lodge by Lake Crescent. I replied:

"I think you can trust them if the study is to be made in Washington, but not if it is made in Portland."

FDR looked at me sharply and asked, "Is that fellow still there?"

"Yes," I said.

The president picked up the telephone and said, "Get me Henry Wallace." FDR held the phone. Then—"Henry," he said, "what did you do about that fellow I told you to transfer out of Portland a year ago?" A long silence. Then, in a tone of incredulity: "You didn't?" Another long silence. And finally, speaking slowly and emphatically: "Well – I – want – it – done." And he put down the receiver.

It was done. On April 1, 1939, Regional Forester C. J. Buck was moved to the Washington office of the Forest Service as special inspector, which preserved his salary grade and took away his power. Occasional mention of Buck's name as regional forester had meant nothing to Roosevelt, but he never forgot "that fellow" who deliberately lied to him at the September 1937 conference at Lake Crescent.

Park opponents had begun talking about the "Kittredge-Tiffany line" as if such a line existed, and tried to build up its status by contrasting it with an also-hyphenated "Brant-Tomlinson line." There was some reason for this. Major Tomlinson had been a wonderful working companion, and although I had sole authority to recommend additions, I had invariably been governed by his opinion in excluding areas on account of administrative difficulties. Now the linking of our names reacted against the park opponents because Tomlinson was known and highly regarded throughout the state of Washington while I was an otherwise unknown "eastern tree-lover." The Park Service began calling it the "Brant–Tomlinson line," and so did I.

In Kittredge's conference with Tiffany, it was agreed that Tiffany should make a separate report on the areas concerning which they disagreed—that is, on the westward extensions asked for in my report. Tiffany sent this paper to Secretary Ickes on March 16. Kittredge left again for Seattle on June 1, to renew their talks, but on that day Tiffany died.

I was scheduled to leave for Europe on June 22, to conduct a tour for the National Public Housing Conference, of which I was vice-president. Secretary Ickes piled up two rush assignments: to analyze and answer Tiffany's March 16 report, and to make supplemental recommendations taking account of the Queets corridor, the ocean strip, and the Bogachiel enlargement, approved by the president in the previous winter.

In his report, Tiffany raised seven objections to enlarging the park; my replies are shown in parentheses. (1) A congressional ceiling of 898,292 acres did not mean the park should be that large. (Since the size had been cut down from 1,500,000 acres, the maximum was probably intended.) (2) Possible manganese deposits would be locked up. (Eighty-one of the eighty-eight sites mentioned were outside the park, the rest worked out or unworkable.) (3) Enough rain forest was already in the park; the rest should be left outside to form a block of timber large enough for sustained-yield management— besides, the trees were over-ripe. (The only rain forest in the park would be on the lands to be added. Since the sustained-yield timber could be harvested in any-size units by truck, the "block" was needed only for clear-cutting to finance a logging railroad—and "over-ripe" trees grow on, magnificently, for centuries.) (4) Clear-cutting increases elk browse. (What the elk needed was safety from hunters.) (5) Uncut corridors along streams and roads would save enough scenery. (A good idea, if applied to approach roads.) (6) Counties would lose taxes. (Tiffany's figures were ten times what the counties actually received.) (7) The Washington State Planning Council would lose credibility. (Enlarge the park, I said, and in four months the state will be boasting of its size.)

My other memorandum, of June 20, finished in New York, was for use in case the president enlarged the park during my three months in Europe. It described the actions taken "in accordance with the suggestions made by the President last winter." It should be read, I said, in conjunction with my reply to Tiffany's protest against the westward extensions.

My original recommendations, I pointed out, left a total reserve of less than twenty-five thousand acres, of which ten thousand would be needed to cover the nine-mile strip of private land along the Bogachiel River and to carry the park boundary three miles farther west in that valley. To cover the Queets corridor and ocean strip in addition, the reserve would have to be built up to over sixty thousand acres.

There was, however, a disturbing factor. The high-mountain country had never been surveyed. Section lines existed only on maps. Acreage in this area was guessed at. If subsequent surveys showed that the president had exceeded the statutory acreage limit, the whole action might possibly be invalidated. To guard against that, I was eliminating 47,000 acres instead of an estimated 42,000. The net result would be an initial addition of about 187,000 acres, with 63,000 held in reserve.

To achieve this was easy, but slightly painful. I moved the eastern boundary of the park three miles west, losing some fine campgrounds along the Dosewallips River but keeping the waterfalls and road end. These changes took out about thirty-five thousand acres. Ten thousand acres were eliminated on the north side, excluding low mountain slopes south of overdeveloped Lake Sutherland.

"All of these changes," I told Ickes, "have been discussed with Mr. Granger of the Forest Service and agreed to by him, as in accord with the policy outlined to him by Chief Forester Silcox." This memorandum was followed by a note of June 21 to Ickes ending with: "Sailing tomorrow—and have you kept me busy up to the last minute!"

Returning from Europe in mid-September, I found myself being congratulated on my "appointment as Co-Ordinator of Wild Life." Ickes scotched the story to reporters, remarking, "It might be a good idea after all." Ira Gabrielson of the Fish and Wildlife Service thought the rumor originated as part of the enraged reaction of duck-clubbers (who wanted to restore baiting) to my June 1938 pamphlet, *Sportsmen's Heaven is Hell for Ducks . . . Baiting is Murder from Ambush*.

In regard to the Olympic enlargement, little had happened during my absence in Europe. Thomas Aldwell of the Port Angeles Chamber of Commerce wrote to the president at great length on August 4, substantially repeating the arguments against westward extensions that he had presented to Secretary Ickes in March. Later in the month, the press reported that the president might visit the Pacific Coast or even Alaska. This inspired Governor Martin to inquire of Roosevelt, on August 21, whether it would "fit in with your plans" if the conference on park boundaries were held during "your forthcoming trip to the Pacific Northwest." It was the governor's understanding that Kittredge and Tiffany had agreed on everything except "a comparatively small area on the western side of the Olympic National Park." Roosevelt asked Ickes to prepare a reply. Besides doing so, Ickes briefed the president in detail on my amended recommendations for enlargement.

The president did not make the projected western trip. Opposition intensified on the Olympic Peninsula when the progress of land acquisition along the Queets made it necessary to disclose the corridor and seashore projects.

Then in mid-October (as Schulz described it to me) "a storm of abuse, invective, lies and misrepresentation" burst out in Washington state newspapers against a suggested North Cascades national park, centering in Mount Baker. That project, merely in the study stage between the National Park Service and the Forest Service, was tied to the Olympic extensions in hostile propaganda secretly fed to the press, so Irving Clark thought, by the Washington State Planning Council.

This mounting opposition increased my anxiety for action on the Olympic additions. On November 20, learning that Irving Clark was coming to Washington, I suggested he go to the White House and ask to see press secretary Stephen Early, to urge quick action on the park. Early, I said, might be tied up, but the call would at least furnish a basis for writing to the president about it later. The only obstacle I knew of was "that the President is concentrating so completely on international affairs and national defense that it is almost impossible to get anything else before him. There is no indication that the Washington State campaign to cut down the size of the additions has had any effect."

Two days later I was told that the president had invited Governor Martin to confer with him at the White House on December 6 (later changed to the ninth) or send his representative. Informing Mrs. Edge of this, I said that Roosevelt had timed the conference to follow the adjournment of a special session of Congress.

Secretary Ickes asked me to present the arguments for the enlargements at the December 9 conference with the governor. Also, to help the president prepare for it, I was asked to write a comprehensive statement, anticipating and answering the governor's probable arguments. I completed a sixteen-page memorandum on December 6, together with a summary. Ickes sent them to the White House next day, with an accompanying note to the president naming me as author.

My memorandum opened with a listing and analysis of opposition groups and their motives. In general, I said, all those who had opposed creation of the park now declared their support of it but opposed the projected enlargement. The Washington State Planning Council, closely linked with the state's chief industry—timber—encouraged the inclusion of timberless high mountain areas and lower lands of indifferent timber value. Their apparent purpose was to use up available acreage and make it impossible to add the scenic forests of the Bogachiel, Hoh, and Queets river valleys. For this same reason they were even willing to include in the park what they called a "manganese belt"—in order, I wrote, to "exclude certain timbered areas."

Turning to Grays Harbor, I said that its opposition "is a reflex of the dying condition of the sawmill industry, due to exhaustion of sawtimber reserves through excessive cutting by an over-expanded industry and destructive lumbering methods that prevent natural reforestation. The sawmill industry hopes to prolong its life a few years by lumbering in the Olympic

National Forest, hence opposes the protection of scenic forests. Grays Harbor has abundant woodpulp reserves."

The Port Angeles Chamber of Commerce, I said, "reflects the position of its chief industrial company," Crown–Zellerbach, which desired to lumber the large Sitka spruce of the Bogachiel and Hoh valleys so as to "postpone the transition from natural to chemical whitener in its print paper." The chamber of commerce also wanted to push its pulp-timber exploitation as near Grays Harbor as possible by construction of a logging railroad. Opening these western valleys to sawmill lumbering would help to finance the project.

I told of the negotiations that took place over what came to be called the "Brant–Tomlinson line," and my modification of that line in June of 1939 to meet the president's desire for larger additions in the west. My original report had called for the immediate addition of 226,656 acres, of which 39,360 acres were in the Bogachiel, Hoh, and Queets river valleys on the west side, with 23,636 acres to be added later. My modified report called for a total immediate addition of 187,411 acres, of which 50,625 acres were in the Bogachiel–Hoh–Queets region and 136,786 acres on the three other sides, with 62,881 acres reserved for later acquisition.

To block the addition of these superlatively fine western valleys, Ross Tiffany had proposed the addition of 202,292 noncontroversial acres on the north, east, and south. Not satisfied with this, George Yantis of the Washington State Planning Council had lately written twice to Frederic A. Delano (Roosevelt's uncle), who was chairman of the president's Council on National Resources; he wanted to raise the Tiffany figure to 233,320 acres. If his proposal were accepted, Yantis told Delano, the small area left in dispute would be reduced to "a tempest in a tea cup."

Describing to President Roosevelt this planned exhaustion of available acreage, I said that if the planned Tiffany–Yantis additions were made, they "would effectually block the proposed westward additions either now or in the future." To justify his second letter to Delano, Yantis had declared that "a new factor of importance has now developed"—the discovery of large deposits of manganese in the proposed additions. Governor Martin wanted provision to be made for developing these "highly important strategic minerals."

The "new discovery," I told President Roosevelt, had been set forth in detail in Ross Tiffany's March 16 statement to Secretary Ickes. The claims thus made had been studied by the Geological Survey and found to be misleading; of 118 manganese locations shown on the Yantis map, 92 were outside the park and proposed additions. Of 5 locations within the park thought worth exploring, 3 were of unworkable bementite; the fourth had been worked out and abandoned; the fifth could be mined under prior rights whether in or out of the park. If extraction from bementite should ever become commercially feasible, vastly larger fields of more easily extracted ores in Montana and New Mexico would be exploited first.

I devoted all this space to manganese in my memorandum not because of its importance, but because it was so overemphasized in the state of Washington. My memorandum finally turned to the general wood-pulp industry of the Olympic Peninsula. Its growth was limited not by the supply of pulpwood but by lack of silt-free fresh water for the sulfite process. It had nearly reached that limit. The timber problem could not be solved by logging fifty thousand acres of scenic forest. The problem was to restock hundreds of thousands of acres of virtually waste cutover lands which, according to a 1938 Forest Service report, had been denuded by destructive lumbering methods and not restocked. If the scenic western valleys proposed for the park were lumbered, they would, after lumbering, "be worth no more for sustained-yield purposes than any other area of equal size in that region." I emphasized that in spite of all the talk about sustained-yield and selective cutting, nobody had any intention of deviating from the practice of clear-cutting. "'Selective cutting' on the Olympic Peninsula means 'area selection' for clear-cutting, either on an economic basis or to encourage regrowth." It had been fully demonstrated, I wrote, that the preservation of these western river-valley areas would have no adverse effect upon the economic life of the community. Either the two wilderness corridors should be added to the park or they should be abandoned to lumbering; there really was no way to compromise between the two extremes.

President Roosevelt's consultation with the governor of Washington, required by law as a preliminary to enlargement of the Olympic National Park, took place as scheduled, on Saturday morning, December 9, 1939. Present, aside from President Roosevelt and Governor Clarence D. Martin, were the governor's two aides, Ben Kizer and George F. Yantis of the Washington State Planning Council; Secretary of Agriculture Wallace and Chief Forester Silcox; Secretary of the Interior Ickes; Director Cammerer and Associate Forester Overly of the National Park Service; and myself. Present also as a guest participant was Irving M. Clark of the Wilderness Society and Seattle Mountaineers.

On Friday afternoon, following the White House press conference, I had had a few words with Mr. Roosevelt. I told him that on the day the governor left for Washington, D.C., the Seattle newspapers had said he would lay heavy emphasis on manganese in the Olympic area. To support this, the governor would make a strong appeal for extension of the five-year limit on prospecting in the park and in the proposed additions.

In the conference, Messrs. Yantis and Kizer led off for Governor Martin. Yantis's first sentence contained the word "manganese." He got no further. Turning to Governor Martin, the president said:

"Now, Clarence, you know and I know that there is nothing to this manganese business. I don't want to hear another word about it."

He didn't.

Yantis turned next to the subject of "rain forests," employing for that purpose a set of large wall charts. They revealed (correctly) the gradual increase of rainfall from 80 inches a year near sea level to 150 inches near the mountain summits. All except the lowest levels were in the park by act of Congress. Therefore, Yantis argued, the best portions of the "rain forest" whose protection was called for by the Interior Department were already protected. Yantis and Kizer pointed to the inclusions shown on their maps—twelve miles of the Bogachiel River's main fork, and eight miles of the North Fork, already in the park, which thus contained the superlative scenic forests of the Olympic Peninsula, as was proved by their rainfall charts.

As I listened to this, I thought the two men were deliberately trying to deceive the president, but it developed that neither they nor the governor had ever visited the western Olympic valleys. They did not know what a "rain forest" was, or where it was or what produced it.

When my turn came to speak, I simply set forth the facts. The rain forest—lush forest growth of gigantic size, deep with moss—was produced *by heavy rainfall AT LOW ALTITUDE in a moderate climate*. Their maps and charts, instead of proving the presence of rain forests in the park, proved their absence. The level of 150-inch rainfall, which they regarded as the climax of the rain forest, bore stunted alpine fir and treeless meadows, buried under snow during ten months of the year.

I told of the trip taken with Tomlinson and Macy from Bogachiel Peak down the North Fork of the Bogachiel River. It was a trip from snowfields and alpine meadows down through small-growth timber of gradually increasing size. The huge conifers and moss-covered maples of the true rain forest began at the mouth of the North Fork, right at the boundary of the existing park, and gained in magnificence as one advanced through the proposed addition. The entire rain forest lay outside the park, except for fringes of the private strip.

Taking up a Yantis–Kizer argument that the Bogachiel Valley should be left out because it was so small that it would not be missed, I said that if it was too small to be missed, scenically, it was too small to affect the economic life of the peninsula. It was valuable to the park, not for size, but for its superlative scenic quality.

Yantis, Kizer, and the governor (who joined at times in the dialogue) finally shifted ground. The Bogachiel and Hoh valleys should be left out to allay the alarm felt in the state of Washington over other proposed national parks there—specifically in the North Cascades. If they should give up the western Olympic valleys, it would be taken as an invitation to unceasing withdrawals of commercial timberland from the state's economy.

That was a defeatist attitude, but defeat of the governor was in the air. At times during my presentation, Roosevelt would turn to the governor and cite Horning's study of the Forest Service's Olympic timber survey, showing that the western valleys were not essential to the peninsula's economy. Instead of challenging Horning, Kizer and Yantis belittled the scenic importance of the areas. They barely mentioned what was to be their main argument the next day, the need to unite the park's proposed 50,000 acres in this region with 200,000 acres of state school lands and 250,000 acres of contiguous national forest in order to create a sustained-yield unit large enough to keep the wood-pulp industry alive (actually to amortize the high cost of a new logging railroad).

President Roosevelt had been alerted in my December 7 memorandum to the facts behind this sustained-yield argument. The total five hundred thousand acres of state and national-forest land, I had pointed out, consisted almost entirely of pulpwood—hemlock and silver fir—which under prevailing conditions could be marketed profitably only as a low-priced byproduct of Douglas fir logging. Handled as pulpwood and trucked out, the timber on these joint state and federal holdings could be logged in any-sized units, large or small. Why, then, sacrifice a scenic forest to subsidize a railroad whose only required use would be to destroy the scenic forest itself?

President Roosevelt strongly approved the idea of federal-state cooperation in sustained-yield forest management, but wanted more facts. At the conclusion of the conference, therefore, he asked Yantis and Kizer to remain in Washington for a Sunday meeting with Silcox, the National Park people, and me. He wanted us to come as close as possible to an agreement on all points. In particular, he wanted a report by the Forest Service on the bearing of these western valleys upon federal-state development of sustained-yield forestry.

The Sunday meeting was held as scheduled. Present were Kizer and Yantis; Chief Forester Silcox; NPS officers Arno Cammerer, Arthur Demaray, and Fred Overly; two other Park Service men; and myself. The session opened with Silcox asking me whether the president had decided to make the additions. I said I had received the impression, from what the president said, that he would; Silcox said he had formed the opposite impression. He asked the same question later, several times.

As a meeting of minds between the representatives of the governor of Washington and the secretary of the interior the meeting was a complete flop. On Monday I sent a memorandum to the president describing the delaying tactics that had been used which pivoted on the sustained-yield study the president had asked for. The Washington men insisted that the western additions were not to be made until the study was completed. They also disclosed, I told the president, that on leaving the White House they had gone to C. J. Buck, former Pacific Northwest regional forester, who had supported them in their factual claims about the Bogachiel, Hoh, and Queets valleys. Forest Service subordinates, clearly, were still "sabotaging the park." It was my understanding, I added, "that you wished to act at once on the park additions."

On that same day, Monday, December 11, White House aide Henry Kannee sent a memo to General "Pa" Watson for the president. Yantis had called at the offices and said they were unable to reach an agreement at the Sunday meeting. "He is therefore submitting his [and Kizer's] report. He understands Mr. Silcox is preparing a report on the whole situation." Yantis wished to know if the president wanted him to remain for further hearings. The answer was jotted on the memo: "OK for him to go."

The next morning I received an excited phone call from the Interior Department. Yantis and Kizer, in their joint report to President Roosevelt, had accused me of replying to Silcox's inquiry with a flat assertion that the president was going to add all of the disputed areas to the park. Fortunately, I was told, associate NPS director Demaray had taken extensive notes at the Sunday conference, and they contained the exact exchange between Silcox and me.

The upshot was that on that same day, the president received a letter from E. K. Burlew, acting secretary of the interior, saying that he considered the Yantis–Kizer statement "so prejudicial that I inquired personally of five of the six representatives of the National Park Service, who had attended the meeting and who were available today, and find that there is no basis for this assertion."

Without mentioning names, Burlew gave Roosevelt an accurate account of what I had said. He told how a representative of Interior was asked "if you [Roosevelt] had made up your mind as to the lands to be included." The representative's reply was that "he formed the impression from your reference the day before to the fact that the lands under discussion represent about one-half of one per cent of all the lands on the Olympic peninsula that you had decided what you were going to do." According to Burlew, the questioner said in reply "that he had formed a contrary opinion." Burlew added, "Later in the meeting Mr. Silcox repeatedly asked whether you had reached a decision and the answer uniformly was that nobody knew."

President Roosevelt said nothing publicly, but within the confines of the administration he revealed his intentions without waiting for the Silcox report. Coming upon the name "C. J. Buck," he exploded with anger. The anonymous "that fellow" whom he had ousted from Portland for deceiving him was no longer nameless. Addressing a memorandum of December 12 jointly to the secretary of agriculture and the Honorable F. A. Silcox, the president said he understood that after the Sunday meeting (it was really after the Saturday meeting at the White House) Kizer and Yantis had gone "immediately to consult with C. J. Buck, the former Regional Forester of the Northwest area, and . . . Mr. Buck supported them in their contention that the 50,000 acres of pulp wood land which is in question on the west side of the park would be absolutely necessary to a sustained yield program on the basis of fifty year rotation for pulpwood trees." The president asked Wallace and Silcox to recall that "as you know, I became firmly convinced when I was out there that Mr. Buck has long been definitely on the side of the lumber and pulp mill people. Everybody in the State of Washington thinks so too." Mr. Roosevelt then gave his opinion on the Yantis–Kizer–Buck position; even if fifty thousand acres were added on the west side of the park there would be more than enough pulpwood acreage left to sustain the mills. He felt "certain" that the Forest Service would get its report to him in a few days.

On that same day, December 12, I drafted a report from Acting Secretary Burlew to the president, giving my own detailed account of the Sunday conference with Kizer and Yantis. At this meeting, the Burlew report said, Yantis and Kizer accepted the additions on the northern, eastern, and southern sides of the park. But when asked if their agreement applied also to the Queets addition, they had said they would accept it "only on the basis of compromise for the exclusion of land in the Bogachiel-Hoh region." This was unsatisfactory, the letter-draft said, but it reduced the discussion to the Bogachiel–Hoh area. Here, they did what they had been expected to do at the White House conference—"laid heavy stress upon the possible need of this tract to sustain the woodpulp industry." (On this subject a brief factual summary accompanied Burlew's letter.)

To reinforce their plea of economic necessity, the letter told the president, the governor's representatives repeated the claim they had made at the White House that the best portion of the Bogachiel rain forest was already in the park. They now "laid still heavier emphasis upon this claim, apparently resting the main weight of their position upon it. Today, therefore, Mr. Brant submitted their assertions to Irving M. Clark . . . one of the leading citizens of Washington and past secretary of the Mountaineers." Clark's reply, quoted in the letter, was that he was personally familiar with the area and "not one foot" of Bogachiel rain forest was inside the present park.

My draft said that Clark had branded as "completely contrary to fact" the claim that the Bogachiel rain forest extended twelve miles inside the park. At a point twelve miles east of the park boundary, Clark said, the Bogachiel River "is a high mountain brook in open country where the snow is many feet deep in winter and lies on the ground until July. . . . The entire Bogachiel 'rain forest' lies within the proposed extension of the park." Burlew, who was responding to a request by Roosevelt to Ickes, then closed with a paragraph that stated Ickes' recommendation on enlargement, which singled out the Bogachiel–Hoh and Queets additions as essential.

With Burlew's letter at hand, all statutory requirements for enlargement of the park had been fulfilled except for a report by Secretary Wallace. That, in turn, depended on a report from Silcox to the secretary. Silcox completed the dictation of his report on Wednesday, December 13. That evening he suffered a massive heart attack. His report to Wallace was taken to his sickbed and he signed it. He died on December 20, and on that day I wrote to Dr. Van Name, "Why do the best men have to die? He was worth all the rest of the F.S. staff put together."

Only a few weeks earlier I had testified before the House Committee on Agriculture in support of a report by Silcox, made after a two-year study authorized by Congress, in which he recommended federal regulation of private timber production and cutting. The argument against public regulation of private lands, I said, "is always presented by lumbermen with the best timber practices. The devastators never come before a congressional committee."

Silcox had chosen a private forester to head the working force that made the study. During the course of it I asked him why he had not put a Forest Service man in charge. "There is nobody in the Forest Service that I could trust," he replied. His report stirred a panic at the annual convention of northwestern lumbermen. It was quelled when a high regional official of the Forest Service took the floor and said, "Don't worry about that report. Nothing will come of it." Nothing did.

Secretary Wallace sent his report on park enlargement to the president two days before Silcox died. The heart of it was a finding by the Forest Service on peninsular wood-pulp needs. On the basis of a ninety-year growth cycle, the existing stands of merchantable pulp timber "would last the existing mills 125 years, without considering volume added by new growth." This would permit a mill expansion of 38 percent, which would be reduced to 30 percent by the proposed withdrawals in the Queets, Hoh, and Bogachiel valleys. As the proposed pulp cycle was fifty years, the expansion could be far greater, even without the reforestation of hundreds of thousands of acres of cutover lands. The Silcox–Wallace report thus completely destroyed the Kizer–Yantis claims; it virtually duplicated the figures with which Roosevelt had overwhelmed C. J. Buck at their Lake Crescent discussion in September 1937.

Wallace's report then explained Buck's meeting with Kizer and Yantis. The two men had called on Silcox, who brought Buck in to give an estimate of the length of Bogachiel Valley rain forest inside the park. Buck thought that Ross Tiffany might have exaggerated a little bit, but for all the western valleys in the park he would place the total rain forest at eighty linear miles. Thus the president faced a choice between an estimate by Tiffany, who had never been in the Bogachiel Valley, supported in the main by Buck, and a conflicting assertion by Irving Clark, who had hiked the valley from ocean to mountain tops.

Tiffany estimated that twenty miles of rain forest already lay within the park along the Bogachiel River and its North Fork. Clark asserted that "not one foot" of Bogachiel rain forest lay within the park. Mr. Roosevelt already had taken a step to resolve this conflict. On the day before Wallace submitted his report, FDR asked me to give the National Park Service a directive that would send a photographer into the Bogachiel Valley, to take a picture every half mile from the western boundary of the national forest up to the mouth of the North Fork of the river. "Tell them to get the photos to me by next Tuesday."

The message was sent by radio. The photographers took the pictures in a heavy rainstorm. They were printed and packed—and the continuing storm grounded all airplanes. Informed of this on Monday, I dug into my own films and selected a set at shorter intervals than half a mile. In addition, because Kizer and Yantis claimed that the "rain forest" extended eight miles up the

North Fork, I extended the set of photographs up that branch of the Bogachiel to the snowfields.

With a collection of ten-by-twelve-inch prints made by the National Park Service, I went to the White House Tuesday morning and started to explain the significance of the pictures, starting at the proposed western boundary, with the land elevation gradually rising. FDR picked up the whole batch and put them down one at a time, with a correct rain-forest appraisal, twice as fast as I could have presented them.

Letters next day (December 20) to Dr. Van Name and Mrs. Edge informed them that the final White House conference on the Olympic additions was held that day, and the president probably would issue a proclamation while my family and I were canoe-camping along the Gulf of Mexico. If the newspaper stories said that the president was adding 187,411 acres, they would know that the prized western valleys were included. One of the letters contained this sentence:

"Secretary Ickes and I saw the President again today, and went over the final memoranda."

More than that was involved. President Roosevelt disclosed his intention. Every acre that I had recommended was to go into the park. The president asked Ickes to draft a letter for his signature, to Governor Martin, announcing these decisions. He wanted it at once. Ickes asked me to draft it. I did so that day. In it, I tried to combine firmness with conciliation, and to present the two men as being as close to agreement as facts permitted. The opening paragraphs dealt with the only matter in serious contention—the western river valleys. My draft emphasized the Forest Service figures which showed that the additions would not deplete commercial timber supplies. I then described the president's "personal enquiry," which convinced him that the rain forest lay west of the present park boundary. Roosevelt's decision should satisfy the governor, since only the facts had been in question.

I then turned to a less controversial feature of the enlargement, the acreage held in reserve for later inclusion in the park. Highway and railroad rights-of-way across the Queets corridor would be granted to protect economic interests. I closed by expressing appreciation for the governor's "co-operative" attitude.

The letter was signed and mailed next day. Before having it typed, Secretary Ickes revised one sentence without altering the meaning—a foible he always indulged in when I wrote speeches or important letters for him.[1] President Roosevelt made one meaningful change. At the suggestion of Secretary Wallace, to whom he submitted the draft, he inserted the word "pulp" before "industries," in order (Wallace told him) to avoid the possibility of "someone challenging your statement because of the possible effect of the withdrawals on the diminishing sawmill industry." Roosevelt underlined the word.

On January 2, 1940, President Franklin D. Roosevelt proclaimed that, the terms of the act of June 29, 1938, having been complied with, "the following described lands, in the State of Washington, are hereby added to and made a part of the Olympic National Park." The lands thus described were, acre for acre, the 187,411 acres recommended in my 1938 report, as modified by my supplemental report of June 1939. A week after the proclamation was issued I wrote to Dr. Van Name, appraising FDR's attitude and actions in the final critical period: "The President, I think, did a masterly job in allaying Washington State opposition to these extensions. In the conference here, at which the governor was given an opportunity to state his objections, Roosevelt practically won him over, and after the proclamation was issued Martin made a statement indorsing it."

Still available for future presidential additions were 62,881 acres. Designed to be added, out of this reserve, were the Queets corridor, the ocean strip, and the nine-mile Bogachiel corridor of private land which President Roosevelt had ordered acquired by the Forest Service through an exchange of national-forest timber. The great task, however, had been completed. The magnificent western valleys, with their gigantic trees and beautiful rain-forest growth, had become, as far as Roosevelt and the Congress could make them so, a perpetual treasureland for the whole American people.

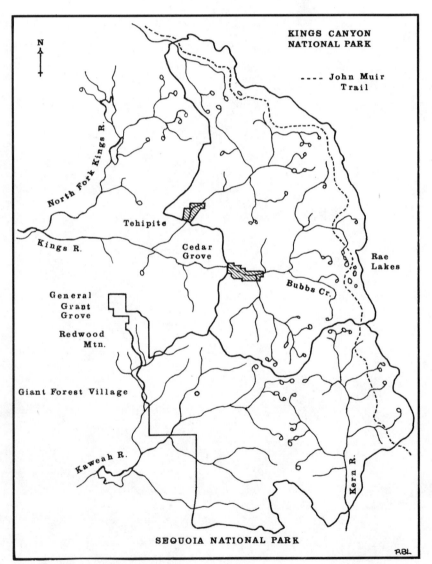

Kings Canyon National Park

CHAPTER NINE

KINGS CANYON
NATIONAL PARK

Sequoia National Park was established by act of Congress in 1890, primarily to protect groves of giant sequoia in the national forest reserve. A year later the great naturalist and mountaineer John Muir, who was largely responsible for its creation, proposed that it be extended northward in the Sierra Nevada, to take in the great mountain peaks and deep canyons of the Kings River country in the mountains directly east of Fresno, California. In *Century Magazine* Muir called on "our law-givers" to "make haste, before it is too late, to save this surpassingly glorious region for the recreation and well-being of humanity, and the world will rise up and call [you] blessed."

In 1921, a move was made in both that and the opposite direction. A bill was introduced in Congress to create the "Roosevelt–Sequoia National Park." It would have extended the Sequoia National Park northward to take in the Kern River and Kings River country as a memorial to Theodore Roosevelt, but would have cut the pre-existing Sequoia National Park to half its size by southward eliminations. Both the Forest Service and the National Park Service supported this bill. Dr. Willard Van Name, asking about the reduction, received an answer on December 21, 1921, from Robert Sterling Yard of the National Parks Association, who explained that the Park Service had only accepted the Forest Service's last proposal in order to avoid even greater demands by its rival agency.

That bill died, but later in the 1920s Sequoia National Park was cut down in the south and enlarged in the north by addition of the Kern River canyon. Two more bills to add the Kings Canyon area were introduced but failed. During the long controversy three successive Forest Service chiefs—Henry S. Graves, William B. Greeley, and Robert Y. Stuart—testified before congressional committees, strongly approving proposals to protect the Kings River region in a national park. Greeley told the House Committee on the Public Lands that he had become quite familiar with the region as a local Forest Service official. He spoke of the region's stunning array of mountains, canyons, lakes, and forests as having "fixed this area in my mind for a good many years" as appropriate for a national park.

By 1932 the Forest Service had abandoned that idea. It was ready to classify the highest regions as a roadless primitive area, but the accessible canyons were to be developed along lines that the National Park Service was trying to get away from. On April 6, 1932, forest supervisor Frank P. Cunningham stated his plan for the construction of two hotels: "One of them should be prepared to cater to the class that has plenty of money, and wants to spend it; the other to those who wish to enjoy themselves with comfortable, but not over-expensive accommodations."[1]

In other words, Kings Canyon was to be an imitation national park, with the worst features of the concessionaire system.

Twice more, in 1935 and 1938, bills were introduced in Congress, aimed now at creating a Kings Canyon national park. Action was frustrated at first by the fallacious notion of the metropolitan power companies that dams on these narrow canyons would produce cheap electricity. When they realized at last that dams without storage reservoirs would be limited in output to the minimum stream-flow, their abandoned entries for the power sites were replaced by those of the Kings River Water Association. These irrigationists wanted a power plant and large reservoir at Pine Flat, many miles below the proposed park. But they needed supplemental water from wells and hoped to lift it with power from dams at Cedar Grove and Tehipite Point, on the South and Middle forks—the scenic gems of the whole Kings River. There were better sites on the North Fork, but the association leaders paid no attention to them. In 1935 Interior secretary Ickes addressed himself to both conservationists and farmers with a public statement pledging administration of a national park along wilderness lines and advocating boundaries that would take account of the economic needs of the San Joaquin Valley.

It was with these two principles in mind that I went to the Kings River country in August of 1938, after the Olympic trip, to look over the country and make general recommendations on boundaries. Our party, aside from the Brant trio, consisted of Frank Kittredge, regional director of the National Park Service; his wife and daughter; Dr. Joel Hildebrand of the Sierra Club and the University of California; his teenage son Roger; and a father-daughter team of packers.

Irving Brant in Kings Canyon, 1938; the author made it a point to personally investigate the natural areas whose causes he championed (photograph courtesy Robin Brant Lodewick).

The proposal before Congress, introduced that year by Congressman Rene De Rouen, was to create a national park embracing the three forks of Kings River, the small adjacent General Grant National Park of giant sequoias, and the magnificent privately owned sequoias of misnamed Redwood Mountain and Redwood Canyon. Our six days on horseback over the mountains were followed by a motor trip and hike through the sequoia groves.

With the South Fork canyon highway not quite completed, we had to ride over a mountain trail to get down to Cedar Grove, a wonderful recreation area of park-like yellow pines. Its level floor gave way to sheer side walls several thousand feet high. The river's narrow exit was subject to waterpower entries, and a study of the feasibility of boring to a solid-rock dam footing was being made by the Bureau of Reclamation. The Forest Service had ambitious plans for development of what would be left above water if a dam 150 feet high should be built (instead of a much worse 300 feet). National-park advocates wanted no dam at all, while Regional Forester S. B. Show (rhyming with "now") supported the irrigationists in order to kill the park.

A lone Forest Service guard named Snow, stationed there, had ideas of his own. Looking up at the mighty Jeffrey pines and the towering cliffs, but pointing toward the unfinished road's end, he said to me: "The dam will never be built. When that highway is completed, the people of California will come in here by the thousand, and they will never allow this land to be flooded."

I agreed with him. What a fine regional forester he would have been. Snow instead of bitterly anti-park Show.

Our route took us five miles up the broad level valley to Zumwalt Meadows, flanked by still higher sheer walls, then turned sharply up miles of switchbacks along Bubbs and Vidette creeks. More open country amid a panorama of peaks took us to Kearsarge Pass, beyond which several hundred miles of Nevada desert spread out. Retracing our steps, we stopped for lunch at a small lake, in whose icy waters Kittredge and I went swimming (about ten strokes) for the sake of boasting about it. We camped that night back at Bullfrog Lake, where everybody except the packers ate two rattlesnakes (tasting like tough chicken) that had scared our horses.

Next day we turned north, led our horses through snow over rugged 11,000-foot Glen Pass, and traversed the beautiful Rae Lakes basin. From there we headed down Woods Creek to its junction with the South Fork of Kings River, through vista after vista of towering snowy peaks. This route took us through well-named Paradise Park and brought us on our sixth day back to Cedar Grove.

There was no time for a much-desired circle trip to the mountain top above Tehipite Canyon, but unanimous testimony made that area the crown jewel of the whole Kings River country. On the map it looked easily accessible by trail up the Middle Fork, yet we were told that only five white men had ever been able to make that journey. This isolation did not deter waterpower interests from marking the canyon for destructive development; isolation alone was not enough to save it.

A single day on Redwood Mountain and in Redwood Canyon was enough to prove that here was a situation calling for immediate action by Congress. The sequoia stand was the largest grove in existence; it contained the largest individual tree in the world—the Hart Tree, estimated to be four thousand years old. Traversing the canyon below the mountain, we came upon an Indian cutting grape stakes from a sequoia whose fallen trunk had been lying on the ground for perhaps a hundred years. The broadside of the log towered fifteen feet above his head.

That forest was privately owned. The owners had been holding it for years, without cutting a living tree. Now they were desperate, with back taxes unpaid and unpayable, wanting the trees preserved but unable to preserve them. Nobody—count them, nobody—wanted these trees cut. The Indian had several months' work ahead of him, and at least that much time was left for rescue by the government.

The problem of Kings Canyon boundaries, I concluded, was 99 percent political. From the standpoint of national-park standards, one could put markers anywhere along hydrographic ridges, and if the markers were far enough apart, they would produce a park of superb beauty. The political problem was double: the contest between the Forest Service and National Park Service for custodianship, and the contest between the environmentalists and the irrigationists for Cedar Grove and Tehipite Dome and Canyon. Had the two bureaus been united, they could have saved both scenic gems by persuading the irrigationists of the truth—that better power sites existed on the North Fork of the Kings River, outside the proposed park. Instead, the Forest Service backed the demand for dams at these two points.

Much less important was the inclusion or exclusion of the Sugarloaf Creek area, which had been stripped out of the pending bill. Regional NPS director Kittredge thought it might be desirable to compromise, but he reported to Arno Cammerer my argument that grazing and hunting in that region were too limited to justify eliminating it from the park proposal.

The Sierra Club, whose support was vital, had refused to support the pending bill because of divided jurisdiction between Park Service and Forest Service in the Cedar Grove area. If the dam were built, the Forest Service was to manage the unflooded portion of the reclamation area while the Park Service administered the adjoining land. The Sierra Club foresaw duplication and confusion. Naturally, Dr. Hildebrand emphasized this in extended discussions with Kittredge and me during our week together. The nature of our relationship was described by Hildebrand in a letter to Secretary Ickes. Writing on August 29, the day after I returned to Washington, he said that while he had known Kittredge before, he had enjoyed meeting me for the first time "in the informal atmosphere of trail and campfire." He went on to say that, although the club's "relations with members of the Park Service in this region have always continued intimate and cordial, we have recently felt ourselves somewhat out of touch with the makers of policy in Washington," and had reluctantly chosen not to endorse the latest Kings Canyon bill. However, he foresaw that the "extended and friendly discussions between Mr. Brant, Mr. Kittredge and myself may . . . gain our whole hearted support for the project. The Kings River region compares favorably with Sequoia and Yosemite, and the Sierra Club will gladly assist as called upon . . . to preserve it in its natural grandeur."

Dr. Hildebrand made it clear that the Sierra Club's principal concern was for boundaries and administration that "promise safeguards of its great natural features better than those existing under its present well-planned administration by the Forest Service."

Writing to Dr. Van Name a couple of days after my return, I said that the park boundaries in the pending bill "are puzzlingly bad. I can't figure out the reason for some of the defects, unless it was just plain jitters, an inferiority complex." The Forest Service, I said, had nothing to do with this retreat. It was fighting the whole park project.

William G. Schulz, taking up his field work for the park on September 4, gave me the probable explanation five days later. In the absence of Regional Director Kittredge, he had been given a fill-in by the assistant director, B. F. Manbey, who had been working for six months to overcome opposition in the San Joaquin Valley. Manbey, Schulz wrote, wanted a good park. To secure it, he "has played a game at all times of moderation and conciliation, and thus gained the support of the irrigationists," by agreeing with them on boundary concessions. Schulz did not approve of this policy and, Manbey told him, neither did Kittredge. Schulz wrote:

"To my mind, *Manbey is too timid and conservative*. He has yielded too readily. . . . now he is afraid to change his views lest the irrigationists and Chambers of Commerce down in the San Joaquin Valley accuse him of double-crossing.

"The opposition, aided and abetted by the Forest Service, has built up the tale from the very start that the National Park Service could not be trusted, that they were liars and double-crossers; that once the people in the Valley agreed to a park, and decided on boundaries, the Park Service would merely use this as a wedge and afterwards demand more and more.

"Now Manbey lives in fear that you may recommend to Secretary Ickes boundaries larger than those he worked out with the people in the Valley. If you do, then he says you will precipitate a big fight and perhaps lose most of the support gained at such effort. . . . You and I and Mrs. Edge and Secretary Ickes know from hard experiences that these things have got to be brought out into the open and a final fight made before any real ground can be gained. Manbey is afraid to have a fight come, but it will have to come anyway, just as it did on the Olympic park."

Earlier in the letter, Schulz had listed and described the California organizations that, unlike the irrigationists, were working primarily to kill the park. He suggested the weapon against them—another pamphlet, to be published by Mrs. Edge's Emergency Conservation Committee. Someone outside the government, he said, "must do the exposing of the greedy, selfish opposition. You are the man to write that pamphlet."

Replying to Schulz on September 15, I said that the irrigation angle had to be handled very carefully. "Nothing should be said or published that will turn the irrigationists against the park, for they represent the only body that, if antagonized, would be strong enough to defeat [it]." The proposed Pine Flat dam and reservoir, below the park, would probably take care of the complete flow of Kings River, and the supplemental power needed for irrigation would be furnished by the government without interfering with either Cedar Grove or Tehipite. However—"That is up in the air now, and not a word should be said about it," until after the Bureau of Reclamation made a report late in the fall.

In my letter I agreed with Schulz that "a pamphlet should be published, and it should be for a real park." But I thought that since I had made a survey of park boundaries for the government, it might be best for me to keep out of the pamphlet end of the business. Meanwhile, in preparation for a pamphlet, we needed information about the amount of grazing in the affected area. Schulz should find out from the Forest Service the number of cattle in each meadow from Sequoia Park northward to the limits of the proposed park, also get the rate of stock reduction in past years. Needed also was the number of deer killed in this region.

In dealing with Redwood Mountain and Redwood Canyon, I advised, the arguments should be confined to those areas alone, not tied in with Kings Canyon, because the acquisition of sequoias was noncontroversial except for cost and should be kept clear of controversial issues. One question remained: was there an organization in California that would fight for both projects?

The sharpest controversy over Kings Canyon at that time concerned alternative plans of the Reclamation Bureau for a Cedar Grove power dam 150 feet high or one of 300 feet. In a choice of evils (if both could not be beaten) there was no question which side conservationists would take. The low dam would leave a good part of the canyon floor exposed for recreational development; the 300-footer would flood everything. The pending bill excluded the whole reclamation area. The Sierra Club was adamant against a high dam, and I felt the same way. The problem in writing a new bill, I wrote to Hildebrand on October 1, was how to define provisional boundaries with the height of a possible dam unsettled. "However, no bill will be drawn, and there will be no map [of shore lines], until the Reclamation Service has made its report this fall, so it is too early for definite action on boundary proposals."

The Bureau of Reclamation was in Ickes' department; but the secretary could not frustrate the building of a dam if Congress authorized one, and, to win the support of the irrigationists, he had quite properly promised them that their interests would be protected. The rub was that he did not—could not—tell them HOW they would be protected, and Manbey's ill-judged verbal concessions had been taken by Kings River ranchers and chambers of commerce as cabinet-level promises.

Two days after I wrote to Hildebrand he repeated, to NPS director Cammerer, the Sierra Club's firm stand against a 300-foot dam and added his own personal view of the alternative: "I believe that the lower dam, only 150 feet high, backing up the water to a point below Cedar Grove, could hardly be regarded as objectionable." Speaking for the club, he said they realized that a limitation to the lower level could not be written into the bill. (Too much technological uncertainty.) Their hope was that the Reclamation survey would show the 300-foot height to be unnecessary. "Persuasion and negotiation," Hildebrand remarked, "may accomplish much that cannot be accomplished by law or by force." If park boundaries were to be described in terms of the higher water level, he hoped that the lower-level lines would also be described, "to keep the more desirable project before the eyes of everyone concerned."

Responding to a suggestion I made to him, Schulz arranged with the John Muir Association that he should handle its publicity (without pay) in the campaign to save the Redwood Mountain sequoias. If this worked out well, the arrangement could be extended to cover the project for Kings Canyon Park. By direction of Secretary Ickes, I instructed Schulz not to send out press material under the imprint of the Interior Department. Assuming (correctly) that he had disclosed his government connection, I said he should make it clear to the Muir people that his cooperation with them did not commit any government agency to the policies advocated.

Meanwhile, I wrote a speech for Ickes to deliver at the dedication of the Dr. Edmund A. Babler State Park in Missouri on October 10, 1938.[2] Jacob Babler, a wealthy Missouri politician, had donated the land for the park to the state in memory of his brother. The speech focused on cooperation between the federal and state governments in park planning and praised private citizens such as Babler and John D. Rockefeller, Jr., for helping to save scenic areas for future generations.[3] Coming from alleged rich-man-hater Ickes, the conciliatory speech amazed the American press.

Ickes followed the Babler Park speech with a trip to San Francisco, chiefly designed to bring about close cooperation with the Sierra Club in support of a Kings Canyon national park. In preparation for this I wrote a five-page memorandum on the history of the club and its recent and current relations with the National Park Service. The club, I told Ickes, had taken the lead in establishing Yosemite Park. It desired wilderness status for the Kings River country, and would support whatever administration—Park Service or Forest Service—seemed more likely to sustain that status.

Until recent years, I said, the Sierra Club worked closely with the Park Service; of late it had been closer to the Forest Service. Elements of estrangement had been a lessening of contact by the Park Service, ardent wooing by the Forest Service, and problems in the California parks—the intensive commercial development in Yosemite National Park, the Yosemite packhorse monopoly, ultra high-grade road building in the parks, building of expensive hotels, and lack of small shelters and hikers' supplies in the high mountains. Most of these grievances dated back to the period of NPS director Mather.

On the other hand, I said, there were definite trends toward a restoration of the old attitude of the Sierra Club toward national parks. Establishment of the NPS regional office in San Francisco helped this, and apprehension was developing in the Sierra Club that the Forest Service would not stick to its declared principles of wilderness protection. Only strong protests by the club had halted construction of a road, already begun, that would have frightfully gashed the high Kings River mountains. And Hildebrand and I had found stakes set for cabins (so an FS guard told us) where the Forest Service had promised there would be none.

Also, the Sierra Club had been strongly impressed by "recent statements of national park wilderness policy" (i.e., by the Ickes speech of August 28 in Seattle). To cement this renewal of cordial relations, the Kings Canyon bill should include (a) prohibition of roads east of Cedar Grove Flat, (b) prohibition of non-government-owned buildings, (c) a declaration against packhorse monopoly, (d) a promise of boundaries that would unify the administration of the Cedar Grove recreation area, (e) a stand against a high dam there, and (f) general Kings Canyon boundaries that would both satisfy irrigation needs and produce maximum protection of scenic areas. It would be well, I said, to advocate the inclusion of wilderness preservation in the park bill.

Secretary Ickes met with the Sierra Club directorate on October 21. This was a meeting which Schulz called "probably the finest thing that has happened for national parks in California in many years." Present were ten directors of the club, also Kittredge, Schulz, Reclamation commissioner John C. Page, and Newton Drury, secretary of the state park commission. Schulz reported that after an informal dinner Ickes talked for an hour, going into "the most intimate and confidential matters of the Department and the National Park Service, his dissatisfaction with much that was done in national parks. . . . It was all rather astounding, that the Secretary of the Interior should tell frankly such confidential matters."

Schulz told how the Sierra Club directors then aired their views, including a series of grievances and fears regarding national parks and present trends. On many of these matters the secretary promised early action, and on others he promised investigation. Thus, he agreed that all competent packers should have access to the parks, and that no one concessionaire (as in Yosemite at that time) should have exclusive rights.

On Kings Canyon as a wilderness park, the Sierra Club directors "saw that his views coincided in all essentials with theirs," and they assured him that they wanted a Kings Canyon national park. In the discussion of Cedar Grove and Tehipite boundaries, it was agreed that no immediate change could be made from the old bill, but Reclamation commissioner Page said he was beginning surveys on the North Fork which he hoped would result in "evidence that dams could more feasibly be built there than on the Middle or South Forks. If so, we have just about won the day in getting boundary enlargements."

Without affecting the building of the dam, Secretary Ickes agreed to have Cedar Grove's unflooded areas withdrawn from reclamation use. That would take them out of Forest Service jurisdiction and ease the way to future inclusion in the park. In Schulz's words: "The whole thing was a grand triumph, on both sides." Dr. Hildebrand expressed, in a letter he wrote a couple of days later, "our hope" that the Interior Department, working through the Reclamation Bureau, would meet the legitimate needs for irrigation and power "elsewhere than on the floor of the canyon above Cedar Grove."

There would have been no need for Secretary Ickes to woo the Sierra Club if its directors had seen the Porterville, California, *Recorder* of October 11, quoting the regional office of the Forest Service in what I called "some desperate propaganda" against the Kings Canyon park project. After asserting that the Forest Service had established a large, fully protected, roadless primitive area which "preserves the priceless High Sierra as a wilderness," the regional office announced policies for the Kings River drainage as a whole:

On irrigation: "The water must be impounded back in the mountains. Many reservoirs, not a single one, will be required to fully regulate and use the water."

Electric power: "The river as a whole is the major untapped source of power in the region and State. Fully developed, the Kings River will produce about as much power as Boulder Dam."

Flood control: "[This] will undoubtedly require a comprehensive series of reservoirs throughout the drainage. . . . A permanent flood control program can hardly be carried out if the land is dedicated to a single purpose [a park], as now proposed."

In other words, the Forest Service intended to maintain an untouchable wilderness filled from top to bottom with irrigation, waterpower, and flood-control reservoirs. And the monumental construction job would be performed without building a foot of road.

Schulz sent me this statement along with newspaper clippings that revealed an intensified organized publicity campaign against the park. A new group called the California Mountaineers, Inc., containing no mountaineers except some deer hunters, had invited the principal newspaper publishers to an all-expenses-paid two-day trip in Kings River country. The results were manifest in these sample headlines in California newspapers of October 12, 13, and 14:

Oakland Tribune: "KINGS RIVER / PARK FOUGHT / Campaign Launched / to Keep Area Under / Forest Service Control."

San Francisco News: "KINGS RIVER / CANYON PARK / PLAN FOUGHT / Mountaineers Resist Secre- / tary Ickes' Move to Take / Over Wilderness."

Exeter Sun: "PUBLISHERS SEE / KINGS CANYON AS / GROUP'S GUESTS / Buckman, Elliott, Point Out / Park Plan Resistance / Over Weekend."

President Buckman of the Mountaineers was a Visalia insurance broker; Elliott was a Forest Service official. The bias of the articles was typified by the *Oakland Tribune*'s characterization of the park movement as a land "grab" and the opposition to it as a fight (quoting Buckman) "against seizure of land of great economic and recreational value" by the Interior Department.
the opposition to it as a fight (quoting Buckman) "against seizure of land of great economic and recreational value" by the Interior Department.

The day after these clippings reached me I wrote to Mrs. Edge that I would write a Kings River–Redwood Mountain pamphlet for the Emergency Conservation Committee; Dr. Van Name had told me he would bear the expense of publication. It might be that I would not sign the pamphlet, on account of having made a boundary report for Interior. Later I consulted with Ickes and was advised not to sign it.

The manuscript was almost completed when the secretary sent me to New York on November 10 on a double mission—to sound out the possibility of a gift from John D. Rockefeller, Jr., for purchase of the Redwood Mountain grove of giant sequoias and also to talk with two officers, A. R. Owen and Carleton Blunt, of the Del Norte Company, which owned the Mill Creek grove of coastal redwoods in Del Norte County, California. Van Name had notified me of their impending trip to New York. The two projects presented remarkable similarities. They involved the two species of sequoia, both groves were located in California, and both were owned by people who wanted the trees preserved by government but were being forced toward cutting or sale to meet defaulted taxes. I spent an hour or more with Arthur W. Packard, manager of Rockefeller's conservation affairs, and left with him a letter from the Redwood Mountain owners describing their tract of 2,680 acres and saying, "We have long felt that any forest of such unique character and such a large number of the finest specimens of their species should be in public ownership." They suggested a price of $750,000, but left it negotiable, with no agents involved.

Mr. Packard agreed to put the matter before John D. Jr., but said he was pretty sure to run up against the decision, resulting from business conditions, "that no new matters would be considered on their merits until past commitments are cleared up." That afternoon he wired me in Washington that Ickes was going to spend Sunday with Rockefeller, who promised to talk with him about the matter. They talked, and Rockefeller said to Ickes what Packard had said to me.

During that day in New York I spent five hours with the Del Norte Company officers at the Waldorf Astoria. They went into their tax troubles in great detail, showing delinquencies, partial or total, running back to 1931. The rank and file of stockholders, the officers said, had given up their dreams of wealth. The officers wanted to sell the most scenic areas to the state or federal government, for enough, after taxes, to enable them to retain other portions. Their valuation of stumpage seemed low.

The general attitude of these men was reflected in a remark made to me by Carleton Blunt. His wife had accompanied them in a hiking inspection of the forest. At the close of it she turned to him and said, "If you allow these trees to be cut, I'll divorce you." They were not cut. Nothing came of the idea of a national monument financed by private philanthropy, but the state of California bought the Mill Creek grove for a little more than the defaulted taxes, and it became one of the choicest parts of the state's redwood-park system.

A bit of private philanthropy for public purposes did, however, come out of my one-day invasion of New York City. Willard Van Name gave me an initial check of six hundred dollars toward the Kings Canyon pamphlet, specifying (since he was in one of his periodic tempers with Mrs. Edge) that it be anonymous. I made and kept that promise, saying to Mrs. Edge that "we both laughed (the donor and I) at the word anonymous, but it made him feel better."

Schulz wrote shortly after this that he had arranged to furnish an article on Kings Canyon to the *Christian Science Monitor* (as he had done with the Olympic Park fight), including an appeal that means be sought to obviate the need for dams at Cedar Grove and Tehipite. I advised him at once either to tone that down or get somebody else to sign the article. If he put in such a plea while connected with the Park Service, the Forest Service would circulate it as a statement of Interior Department plans, charging bad faith. If the areas were to be included in the new bill, it would be as a result of a report by the Reclamation Bureau that might change the attitude of the irrigation people. Schulz made appropriate alterations and produced a fine article.

General Hugh Johnson, ex-NRA head turned columnist, published a strong plea for Redwood Mountain in November. Sending this to Ickes, Schulz wrote that "there is a great flood of enthusiasm among individuals and groups" in support of that project. Schulz was writing a pamphlet on the subject for the John Muir Association, whose secretary, Mrs. Linnie Marsh Wolfe (Muir's granddaughter), found wide support during an eighteen-day lecture tour of southern California. Newly elected Republican congressman Hinshaw told her that he would introduce a bill for purchase of the forest. The California State Chamber of Commerce, surprisingly, invited Kittredge to speak on Kings Canyon at its annual meeting.

The Kittredge speech, it turned out, came at the end of an all-day attack on the Kings Canyon bill, and national parks in general, by Regional Forester Show and the misnamed Mountaineers. Kittredge, Schulz reported to me on December 1, spoke in terms of moderation and conciliation that went far to offset the attacks by the Forest Service and others. I could have condensed Show's five-page, single-spaced speech into three words: "Reservoirs, reservoirs, reservoirs." Schulz summed it up in two sentences:

"National parks have only one value, recreation, whereas national forests have not only recreation but much else.

"The Park Service would tie up the whole Sierra from Sequoia Park to Yosemite in a national park if it could."

Every person present was given a copy of Show's speech. This onslaught on the proposed park followed a meeting at which chamber of commerce leaders sought to dissuade a prospective new sponsor from offering a new park bill. The unsatisfactory 1938 bill, drafted by the National Park Service, had been introduced by chairman Rene De Rouen of the House Committee on the Public Lands at the request of Secretary Ickes. The man now interested was Congressman Bertrand W. ("Bud") Gearhart of Fresno, whose district included two-thirds of the proposed park area. He had sounded out his constituents and found overwhelming support of the project. Conversely, its principal congressional opponent was Congressman Alfred J. Elliott, whose district embraced the southern third of Kings Canyon country.

Kittredge reported to Washington that Gearhart had told the opposing businessmen that "they were hurting their community and hampering his actions in Congress for the community's good," by hostility to the park. Gearhart had followed this with a statement to the *Los Angeles Times* that he would introduce a Kings Canyon bill when the new Congress convened in January.

Following the chamber of commerce meeting, Kittredge, Manbey, and Schulz drafted a suggested nine-point statement of Kings Canyon park policy to be put out by Secretary Ickes in contrast with Forest Service proposals. Ickes asked me to analyze it. I said that it was in the main an elaboration of a statement made by Ickes in 1935, in connection with an earlier Kings Canyon bill, on wilderness policies to govern the proposed national park, plus a call for statutory limitation of roads and prohibition of entrance fees. It was defective, I said, in being too specific and detailed; wilderness features that were not mentioned might be challenged later. What was worse was that administrative guidelines could not protect against changes in policy.

Ickes asked me to draft a statement for his signature. My draft summarized the 1935 statement, pointed to the Olympic and Isle Royale park wilderness precedents, and called for legislation to establish stronger safeguards for wilderness policy than administrative orders could provide. For Kings Canyon the law should prohibit roads within the park; require that buildings be erected only with government funds; allow no housing except trailside shelters and a few simple rental cabins; provide equal access for all public and private packers; and make admission free of charge.

A few days after submitting this draft to Ickes I wrote to Mrs. Edge that the manuscript of my Kings Canyon pamphlet would be sent to her after final approval of a policy statement by the secretary which I had seen and taken account of. Four days later (on December 16) Regional Director Kittredge furnished the Sierra Club with the National Park Service's draft of a Kings Canyon park bill that was to be submitted to Congressman Gearhart. Dr. Hildebrand wrote to me after reading it:

"I suspect that you were not consulted in the preparation of the draft recently sent out by Demaray. The Park Service boys seem more eager to get a bill passed than to provide for the proper use of the floor of King's Canyon. The Sierra Club has no interest in furthering such a project."

Two days after receiving that letter I wrote to Schulz that Ickes had asked Dr. Hildebrand to come to Washington to discuss the park's boundaries. I had not seen the draft of the new bill until a week after it was sent out. "It did not surprise me," I told Schulz, "that the Sierra Club kicked about it." The new version established no statutory wilderness and cut the Cedar Grove park boundary off at right angles to the canyon, making no provision for national-park administration of unflooded lands. At Ickes' request, I said, Demaray and I had gone over the bill and made these changes: (1) the "wilderness national park" principles to be announced (next day) by Secretary Ickes were to be incorporated into the bill; (2) the park boundaries were to follow the high-water line of the Cedar Grove and Tehipite reservoirs if those dams were built; (3) as long as no dams were built, the land within the reclamation withdrawals was to be administered by the Park Service; (4) if a dam was built, the president was to include all lands above high water in the park, and if existing water entries were abandoned "he shall proclaim the entire area in the park."

Still undecided was the name of the proposed park. There was strong support in California for naming it after John Muir, the godfather of Yosemite, Sequoia, and General Grant national parks. I favored the idea, although a hyphenated "John Muir–Kings Canyon" name seemed clumsy. I also wrote to Schulz that I would be meeting with Ickes and the president to discuss the park's name, and planned at the same time to ask for FDR's help in getting the Forest Service not to oppose the park.

The White House meeting was held, and the president readily endorsed the idea of making the name a memorial to the great naturalist. The discussion of the park took a general turn and stretched out. I forgot the curbing of the Forest Service. Ickes walked out a little ahead of me. Just as I reached the doorway FDR asked, "Is there anything I can do to help with the park bill?" My wits returned. It was too late to resume the conversation, but I turned and said, "Nothing, unless you call off the Forest Service, as you did in the Olympic fight."

Next day I encountered Secretary of Agriculture Wallace on a downtown street. He jumped on me with these words: "When you have a complaint to make about my department, why don't you talk to me first, before going to the president?" I asked him how he knew that I talked to the president about the department. He replied:

"When I read on the ticker that you and Ickes are to see the president at 11:30, and he calls me half an hour later, do you think I can't put two and two together?"

160

There were reasons for not complaining to Wallace first. Some time earlier I had told him some of Interior's shortcomings. He said, "Tell me what is wrong with my department." I replied that it was too big "and you can't control the Forest Service." It was not too big, he commented, "but it is true that I can't control the Forest Service."

That, he said, was due to its regional setup, aggravated by the distance of the Portland and San Francisco offices from Washington, and, still more, by the close political relationship enjoyed by the regional staffs with West Coast politicians and business interests. He could well have added, by the favors the Forest Service men were able to bestow or take away, in relation to grazing licenses and leases of forest sites for summer homes. All this made the regional offices virtual independent satrapies, initiating and carrying out their own policies, sometimes in flagrant disregard of the opposing views of the chief forester.

At the same time, the Washington press had begun to report that Ickes and Wallace were no longer getting along. Several weeks earlier, I had responded to an inquiry from Schulz on the subject by suggesting that Wallace's presidential ambitions for 1940 might be getting him in trouble with other New Dealers, or at least might account for his reluctance to rein in politically influential subordinates.

President Roosevelt's order to stop Forest Service opposition to the Kings Canyon bill was transmitted promptly to San Francisco and just as promptly publicized in the California press to aid the park opponents. The presidential stop-order reached the regional office just as Regional Forester Show was preparing to testify before a state senate committee in support of a joint resolution introduced by Senator Fletcher of San Diego County, which memorialized the president and Congress to oppose the new Gearhart bill, not yet introduced. When I learned of this on Friday, January 13, I handed the president a letter at his afternoon press conference suggesting that he order the Forest Service employees not to attend the hearing "or submit any statement whatever." I then described the working partnership of Regional Forester Show with Ernest Dudley and Parker Frisselle, who, besides organizing the California Mountaineers, Inc., to work against the Kings Canyon park, "sent Charles G. Dunwoody to Washington to lobby against the reorganization bill last winter, and financed his campaign." Of Show I wrote, "The man seems to be suffering from delusions of grandeur, but he is doing great damage because it is assumed in California that he speaks with official sanction." Ickes supported my request for direct intervention in a memorandum to the president the following Monday.

The president in fact had taken action on the previous Friday, calling up Secretary Wallace within minutes, apparently, after I handed my letter to him. Wallace wrote to the president on Monday, with reference to what "last Friday you spoke of having heard" concerning the legislative hearing. The regional forester, Wallace said, had been invited to be present or represented, and could not appropriately avoid supplying facts and opinions when asked to do so. However, the secretary concluded: "I am told that your instructions to the Forest Service to refrain from public opposition to the proposed park have been conveyed to the Regional Forester at San Francisco, and I have no reason to believe that they are being violated."

The next day, January 17, 1939, President Roosevelt sent a lengthy memorandum to Chief Forester Silcox, summarizing what I had written him about the teamwork of Regional Forester Show with Dudley and Frisselle, and about the reversal of the regional office and Show in fighting the Kings Canyon park: first because the area should be kept a wilderness and later because it should be opened to economic exploitation. The president's memo ended with a question: "What can you do?"

On the day that memorandum was written, press dispatches from Sacramento revealed that an unnamed Forest Service official had testified against the park at the rules committee hearing on the previous evening. Secretary Ickes telegraphed to Schulz in San Francisco asking for the name of the witness. Schulz wired back, "J. H. Price."

When word of Price's action came to Roosevelt, he almost blew his top. On January 24 he sent the following memorandum addressed jointly to the secretary of agriculture and Chief Forester Silcox:

"I am told that at the Senate Rules Committee meeting of the State Senate in Sacramento, California, Regional Forester J. H. Price of San Francisco appeared in opposition to establishing the Kings Canyon National Park.

"How long are the orders of the President, the Secretary of Agriculture and the Chief Forester to be disobeyed? F.D.R."

Price was number two, not regional forester. Presumably, being of greater fortitude and deeper conviction than Show, he had volunteered to take the rap for disobeying orders. The rap came. As he had done in the case of Regional Forester Buck in Portland, Roosevelt ordered Secretary Wallace to move Jay Price out of California. He was brought to Washington to await an opening suitable to his salary grade, and some months later took over as regional forester at Milwaukee, thus raised in rank but left powerless concerning Kings Canyon.

The Fletcher resolution, which caused all this commotion, was adopted after park supporters took nearly all the punch out of it. The Sierra Club had prevented the California Senate Rules Committee from voting without a hearing. The club then sent three witnesses to testify against the resolution. They succeeded in having it watered down to such an extent that after reading the final text I wrote to Hildebrand: "I don't think the California legislature's resolution will do any harm down here. It tried to please both sides and wound up by saying nothing. But it is most important to get letters to California congressmen in reply to the organized propaganda against the bill."

Bending a bit before those opposing forces, Congressman Gearhart made several weakening changes in his bill as it had been worked out by Demaray and me. Principally, the Cedar Grove valley was excepted from the prohibition of hotels in the park. These changes required some minor revision of my Kings Canyon pamphlet, whose publication was being held back until the bill should take final form. Sending the alterations to Mrs. Edge on February 7, I closed my letter with these words:

"Wallace and Silcox agreed today to support the bill. It is not safe to put that in the pamphlet, but I think some public announcement will be made within a week, and it would be possible to put in a slip. For the present, keep this confidential." Gearhart's bill was laid before Congress that same day, and twenty-four hours later Wallace wrote to Ickes approving the park.

Thundercloud over the North Palisade, Kings Canyon, 1933 (photograph by Ansel Adams, courtesy the Ansel Adams Publishing Rights Trust. All rights reserved).

CHAPTER TEN

THE GEARHART BILL

Representative Bertrand W. Gearhart's bill to establish the John Muir–Kings Canyon national park, H. R. 3794 of the 76th Congress, was introduced on February 7, 1939, and was referred to the House Committee on the Public Lands, of which Rene De Rouen of Louisiana was chairman.

The bill embraced three distinct but closely related projects. The first, and by far the most extensive, was the transfer of 445,500 acres from the Sierra and Sequoia national forests to a Kings Canyon national park bordering the northern side of Sequoia Park.

According to Section 2 of the bill, the 2,548-acre General Grant National Park, established to protect the Sherman Tree and several other super-giant sequoias, was to become the General Grant Grove in the new park. This proposal was not controversial. The third objective, set forth in the same section, was to save Redwood Mountain and Redwood Canyon from despoliation by authorizing the president to add 10,000 acres to the General Grant Grove. This involved, but did not authorize, the purchase of 4,297 acres of privately owned land containing seven thousand giant sequoias. These trees could be lumbered, even though inside the park, unless the government acquired title to the land. The rest of the 10,000 acres was national forest. There was no organized opposition to this project, and strong specialized support for it.

Sections 3 and 4 of the bill provided that "to insure the permanent preservation of the wilderness character" of the park, "no hotels, permanent camps or other similar physical improvements" should be constructed therein, "except upon ground used for public housing purposes." And there should be constructed no "new roads, truck trails, or public housing structures other than simple trailside shelters"; but these limitations did not apply to the South Fork canyon below Copper Creek (i.e., to Cedar Grove) or to General Grant Grove.

No privileges (concessions) were to be granted for more than one year. All authorized structures should be built only by the federal government. All existing grazing permits were to be renewed during the lifetime of the present permittees.

Section 5 provided that the National Park Service should administer, "for public recreational purposes," the lands withdrawn for the Cedar Grove and Tehipite Dome reclamation projects, "subject to the dominant use of such lands and waters for reclamation purposes." If either or both of these dams were constructed, the lands above high-water mark could be added to the park by proclamation of the president. If either or both were abandoned, the president, on certification to that effect by the secretary of the interior, and after notice to local irrigation interests and public hearings, could add the lands to the park.

At the same time Gearhart introduced an important irrigation bill related to the park bill, which authorized the construction of an irrigation, power, and flood-control reservoir at Pine Flat, impounding all the waters of all three forks of the Kings River at a point twenty miles below the proposed park. This bill provided also for the construction of dams at Cedar Grove and Tehipite Valley, on the Kings South Fork, to create power for pumping wells to supplement Pine Flat in periods of low water. All of these projects were to be built by the Reclamation Bureau.

On the day before, the chairmen of the House and Senate public lands committees had introduced identical bills authorizing the president to set aside wilderness areas within national parks and national monuments, where there should be no construction beyond basic trails and shelters. The idea had come to me from Congressman Lacey's 1904 attempt to give the president the power to create national parks. I drafted the bills, Ickes requested their introduction; but they got nowhere during a period of reaction against presidential authority.

Gearhart's Kings Canyon bill received the enthusiastic support of the Sierra Club, which recognized the strategic necessity of omitting the Cedar Grove and Tehipite reservoir sites from the park. Except among those set on defeating the bill, boundaries were not an issue. Everything was set for a push to passage.

My unsigned pamphlet, *The Proposed John Muir–Kings Canyon National Park*, was dated January 1939, but the Emergency Conservation Committee brought it off the press a few days after the Gearhart bill was introduced in

February. Over the page from a portrait of John Muir was a picture of the Hart Tree on Redwood Mountain, believed to be the oldest and largest living thing in the world.[1] The Sherman Tree exceeded it in diameter at the base but tapered more rapidly. If the Hart Tree had been cut off sixty feet above the ground (so the Otis Elevator Company informed me) 157 persons could have stood on the cross section of its trunk. Preservation of Redwood Mountain and the Hart Tree stirred no controversy in Congress; on the contrary, the threat to them was a mighty influence toward passage of the Gearhart bill.

After a description of Kings Canyon, "one of the greatest mountain panoramas in the world," the pamphlet took up the eighteen-year fight for and against the park. During the first decade three heads of the Forest Service supported the park proposal; currently, the California regional office of that service was fighting it. During the early period, private-power companies worked to control the area, but later gave up their rights in the mountains because of the absence of areas suitable for water storage. San Joaquin Valley irrigationists then turned to the two scenic spots, Cedar Grove and Tehipite Canyon, for power to supplement the projected storage reservoir below the park. The irrigationists, I suggested, would "naturally shift to the North Fork" of the Kings River, outside the park, if (as expected) a study in progress by the Reclamation Bureau showed superior power sites on that branch of the river.

The Gearhart bill sanctioned the building of power dams at Cedar Grove and Tehipite if Reclamation called for them. Thus the legitimate needs of the San Joaquin farmers were fully provided for. The Kings River Water Association, the only organization rightfully concerned, had ceased its opposition to the park. Who, then, was conducting the violent propaganda campaign against it? The opposition, I said, had dwindled to a few "minor but extremely vocal elements" who were making very limited use of the area already: farmers using summer pastures for cattle, deer hunters, and leasers of summer-home sites (actually outside the boundaries of the Gearhart bill). There was also the San Francisco regional office of the Forest Service.

I went on to say that the chief ally of the regional office was the organization calling itself California Mountaineers, Inc. Its initial argument was that only the Forest Service could be trusted to preserve the wilderness character of the Kings Canyon country. When the regional office, on October 11, 1938, came out for reservoirs throughout the mountains, California Mountaineers followed suit. After Regional Forester Show made his December 2 speech protesting that a national park would "lock up resources vital to the welfare and prosperity of the people," the Mountaineers (I said) dropped all talk of wilderness protection and cried out that the area "was needed for *lumbering, power, irrigation and grazing.*"

This, I wrote, "is mystifying until you know who are back of California Mountaineers, Inc." Its secretary and principal organizer was Ernest Dudley of Exeter, California, a banker and former Forest Service official. Co-organizer was Parker Frisselle of Fresno, another retired Forest Service man.

"These two men practically ARE California Mountaineers, Inc."

Dudley and Frisselle, I pointed out, held key positions in the state chamber of commerce. They and Charles C. Dunwoody, the chamber's professional lobbyist, controlled the conservation committee of the chamber and used it as a propaganda machine against national parks. I wrote:

"Dunwoody is being sent to Washington, D.C., to fight the park project in Congress. . . . His propaganda facilities in California are causing a flood of letters against the plan to go to California congressmen. Dudley and Frisselle represent the working management of the opposition to Kings Canyon National Park. They are strategically situated to create the appearance of a widespread, spontaneous opposition, though in reality an overwhelming majority of San Joaquin Valley organizations support the park, and many of its strongest supporters are in the State Chamber of Commerce."

The revolt of the Forest Service's regional office, I said in conclusion, had created the impression that the struggle over the Kings Canyon Park was a contest between government bureaus. Nothing was farther from the facts. It was a choice *for the people to make* between two methods of use, two concepts of protection, under radically different sets of national law. If it was true, as the regional office of the Forest Service contended, that reservoirs for irrigation, power, and flood control must be built throughout the mountains, and that the area was vitally needed for grazing and lumbering, then Kings Canyon should not be made into a national park. "But if, as three chiefs of the Forest Service have testified, and as any competent engineer would testify, none of these things is true, and the region is what they say it is—a scenic wilderness of unexampled beauty—it should be made into a wilderness national park."

Secretary Ickes put the California campaign for the Gearhart bill in high gear on February 15, when he responded to what he called the democratic equivalent of a royal command to speak before the Commonwealth Club of San Francisco. In his speech, which I wrote, he told how deeply he had been impressed, during the few days he had been in California, with two aspects of the proposal for a Kings Canyon National Park. The first of these was "the very high character of the support given to it by the people of California." This required him "to pay a tribute to the principles and standards of the Sierra Club," which insisted that "any project it supported should be of the highest type," established by the best law obtainable. The other thing that impressed him was the way in which the discussion of this park by its California supporters had diminished opposition to it by eliminating the basis of opposition. On practically every word in his bill that related to irrigation, Ickes said, Congressman Gearhart consulted the Bureau of Reclamation and the Kings River Water Association. That was essential because it was necessary to leave the park boundaries indefinite at two points until final studies by Reclamation engineers should fix the location of power dams (which had to be outside the park) supplemental to the Pine Flat storage reservoir, to which he pledged unqualified support. In short, said Ickes, the bill was "a triumph in conciliation."

Secretary Ickes praised the Commonwealth Club for its strong published stand in 1936 for protection of wilderness areas against too many roads and announced that he would have preferred to exclude hotels, which were "grandiose mistakes," from the floor of Kings Canyon at Cedar Grove. (I put this passage in his speech, I told Ickes in a memo, both to encourage the San Francisco people to work for restoration of the "no hotel" clause which Gearhart struck out and to show that the secretary was not responsible for its elimination.) In the Gearhart bill, Ickes emphasized, protection of the wilderness was "written into the law, instead of being entrusted to the changing and changeable personnel of any administrative body." The wilderness provisions of the bill "embody, in general, the principles worked out by the Sierra Club during several years of study, with due regard to the interests of the general public." Areas of equal magnificence would be accessible to motorists.

Ickes held informal public hearings and delivered several other radio addresses in California cities, directed toward special audiences. One that I wrote for him predicted that the hostility of cattle interests to national parks would disappear as soon as stockmen accepted and acted on conservation principles in the management of their grazing ranges. To counter the argument, dinned into the stockmen by Forest Service officials, that national forests were being wiped out by transfers of land to national parks, I put a statistical comparison into the speech:

"If you added all the national parks in the continental United States together, it would make an area 10 percent larger than Inyo County, California. If you added all the national forests in the continental United States together, it would make an area larger than the combined areas of Maine, New Hampshire, Vermont, Connecticut, Rhode Island, Massachusetts, New York, New Jersey, Delaware, Maryland, Virginia and South Carolina—twelve states of the Union—and there would be enough national forest land left over to take in Inyo County, California."

Ickes said that although stock grazing was incompatible with national-park standards, he had agreed to a provision in the Gearhart bill extending present Forest Service permits for a few hundred cattle during the lifetime of the holders. Commercial grazing in the proposed park had disappeared years earlier. In the Roaring River watershed, where twenty thousand sheep grazed in 1891, a burro now had to carry its own feed.

Secretary Ickes' visit to California, Schulz wrote five days after the speech to the Commonwealth Club, "has entirely changed the whole park outlook. It is vastly improved." The *Fresno Bee*, long friendly but lukewarm, had come out strongly for the park, "largely because Secretary Ickes gave such strong assurances behind the Pine Flat dam." The *San Francisco News* and *Long Beach Sun* had done likewise. Numerous organizations were giving similar support, including the Los Angeles Federation of Women's Clubs, the Martinez Chamber of Commerce, and large Bay Area Democratic clubs.

Opposition to the park was weakening. On February 17 its most powerful adversary, the San Joaquin Valley Council of the California State Chamber of Commerce, unanimously adopted a resolution that in fact gave the park qualified support: Since the irrigationists "have become convinced that their best interests now rest in the hands of Mr. Ickes . . . be it resolved" that the council "is unalterably opposed" to creation of the park unless the Pine Flat bill "goes hand in hand therewith through Congress to successful completion." That was precisely what Gearhart and Ickes had pledged.

Qualified though it was, the San Joaquin action thus represented a severe setback for Ernest Dudley and Parker Frisselle, the Forest Service alumni who had dominated the council. However, the about-face of this regional body did not commit the entire state chamber of commerce, which was swayed by lobbyist Dunwoody. Also, saboteurs were at work against the park in strange places. The *Wilderness News*, organ of the Wilderness Society, edited by Robert Sterling Yard, devoted its February number to an attack on the Gearhart bill as a crafty device by Ickes to purchase irrigationist support by sacrificing Cedar Grove and Tehipite. This, said Yard, roused the opposition of "those who argued that the worst way to preserve a wilderness area was to give it the glamour and publicity of a national park. . . . The Forest Service is still faithfully preserving the whole Kings country as it has these many years." This article, in which every sentence attacked national parks, was an ostensibly impartial request to Wilderness Society members for letters of guidance to the society's council. The article was in fact a covert attempt to utilize the Wilderness Society in opening the Kings Canyon wilderness to destruction. I doubt whether one in a hundred of its members knew the facts about Yard which I appended to my copy of the *Wilderness News* article in a notation headed Chain of Control:

"Robert Sterling Yard (a well-meaning man) drew his pay from the National Parks Association, which depended for its support on [William H.] Wharton, an honest, simpleminded Massachusetts millionaire. Wharton took all his policies from Ovid Butler, formerly of the Forest Service, and head of the American Forestry Association, a 'good name' organization which received its money and its lobbying policies from the West Coast Lumbermen's Association and the National Association of Lumber Manufacturers."

The next figure in the "Chain of Control" soon got into the picture. On March 10 the McClatchy Newspapers Service (friendly to the park) carried a San Francisco dispatch with this opening paragraph: "The California State Chamber of Commerce reported today that the National Parks Association [presided over by Wharton] has gone on record against the creation of the proposed John Muir–Kings Canyon National Park. The association has its headquarters in Washington, D.C." Schulz wired the information to Mrs. Edge (who asked what I could do); he told her that the announcement was doing great harm since the association was generally believed, from its name, to be a government agency.

Wharton had been induced by Ovid Butler in June 1938 to wire President Roosevelt urging him to veto the just-passed Olympic Park bill. Two months later the association was circularizing for support funds as one of the creators of that park. Since Butler worked through Wharton, and Wharton through Yard, in both the National Parks Association and the Wilderness Society, I was hitting at Yard in both offices when I sent a government radiogram to Irving Clark in Bellevue, Washington, with a copy to Joel Hildebrand of the Sierra Club, asking for the mailing list of the Wilderness Society "to enable a fair statement to be sent," in answer to the "grossly unfair description" of the park bill that Yard had sent to the membership.

Schulz notified me that Regional Forester Show, disregarding the orders of Chief Forester Silcox, was traveling around the state, working against the park without publicity. He was accompanied by W. E. Stewart, director of conservation for the state chamber of commerce, whom Ickes had lately accused of willfully lying about him. Schulz suggested that I say nothing to Ickes about Show's connection with Stewart lest the secretary "hurl some of his thunderbolts" at a time when it was well to avoid controversies with minor government officials. (Good advice.)

Opposition to the park, however, had been sinking to lower levels. With House hearings set for March 15, congressmen were flooded with telegrams opposing the park, in the name of local chapters of two organizations whose officers denied sending or authorizing them. Similar wired protests came from four other organizations known only as names in a list of park opponents published by the state chamber of commerce. That publication was their undoing. Suspicious that these organizations were non-existent, park-supporter James Fauver, president of the Tulare County Water Commission, had sent registered letters to their listed addresses. Not one was deliverable to anybody.

In preparation for Secretary Ickes' testimony at the House hearings, I analyzed the types of organizations for and against the national park, and gave the identifiable motives for the positions taken. Summarizing, I divided the passers of resolutions into three groups. Mixed for and against were service clubs, chambers of commerce, general farm organizations, and veterans' organizations—usually depending on the attitude of a few individuals. Opposed to the park were deer hunters, stockmen's organizations, leasers of summer-home sites in national forests, and county supervisors affected by possible loss of tax revenues. Favoring the park were mountaineering and hiking clubs, conservation organizations, women's clubs (with several million members), garden clubs, county supervisors influenced by tourist revenues, and hotel and other commercial interests similarly affected.

A resolution of the California legislature, as I remarked in an accompanying memo, was in a class by itself. As amended in committee to secure passage before the contents of the Gearhart bill became known, it displayed a general tone adverse to the park, but the second half was favorable enough to national-park objectives to win the votes of several strong park supporters. For what it was worth, it might be contrasted with Governor Olson's unqualified endorsement of the park.

Also at the request of Ickes, I compiled a three-thousand-word factual memorandum for him to use in answering possible questions. Under "quality of proposed park" I quoted the well-known praise of it by John Muir, and this from the naturalist-writer Emerson Hough: "I have seen all the passes and parks in this country and clear up to the Arctic Ocean, and Europe, and there is no country on the face of the earth that compares with the country in this proposed park." The Interior Department was well represented in the list of witnesses by Secretary Ickes, associate national parks director Arthur Demaray, and Reclamation commissioner John C. Page. I did not testify at the House hearing, but sat at chairman De Rouen's elbow as a special assistant borrowed from the Interior Department. That assignment had indeed been made weeks earlier, at De Rouen's request. It was the conventional way of adjusting to a rule which restricted the lobbying activity of government employees.

Redwoods, northern California. Stands of magnificent redwood and giant sequoia were the subject of bitter management debates between the Forest Service and the National Park Service (photograph by Ansel Adams, courtesy the Ansel Adams Publishing Rights Trust. All rights reserved).

CHAPTER ELEVEN

THE HOUSE HEARINGS

Secretary Ickes opened the House hearings on the Gearhart bill on March 15, 1939, with a brief explanatory statement, presumably prepared by the National Park Service. He emphasized that Gearhart's bills for the park and for the Pine Flat irrigation and power projects must go forward together to avoid either one damaging the other. He outlined the history of cooperation on the combined recreation and economic proposals by the two bureaus most directly concerned—the Reclamation Bureau and the Park Service—as well as by local landowners and water users, national conservation organizations, and the Department of Agriculture. Ickes closed by pointing out that since the opening of the state highway to Cedar Grove would bring throngs of visitors to the area, an early and final decision about the future of the Kings River canyon wilderness was vital.

At the request of Secretary Ickes, chairman De Rouen ordered two lists of supporting organizations to be printed in the record. They made a total of 159 organized groups, including the all-important Kings River Water Association. Seventy pages in small type were devoted to publication in full of various resolutions of support from collective bodies, governmental and private (representing millions of citizens), also group petitions bearing hundreds of signatures, and half a dozen newspaper editorials.

Ickes added a telegram received that morning from William Schulz, who had compiled the combined sworn circulation—820,000—of nineteen

California newspapers supporting the park; Schulz also named the *San Francisco Chronicle* as the only large daily in opposition. Chairman De Rouen added a strong telegraphed endorsement just received from California governor Culbert L. Olson.

"Is there any question?" Ickes asked. There were enough to fill the next forty-one pages of the hearings record.

Congressman Alfred J. Elliott, the most extreme congressional opponent of the park, said he would like to see the originals of the letters listed by the secretary because a number of those who wrote them had rescinded their support. Ickes, offering to furnish all that were in the department files, remarked that there had been rescissions on both sides and many of those supporting the park had formerly opposed it. Elliott then filled four pages of testimony in a futile attempt to trip Ickes into saying that he would punish the irrigationists if the park bill failed. All he got was repeated assurances that all projects would be considered on their merits, and a remark that cooperation was the best policy.

Congressman Compton I. White of Idaho then complained about keeping the Olympic Park an inaccessible wilderness; that policy could be better applied to the North Pole. Ickes said he preferred taking in the new land at the South Pole: "That is a happy thought of yours."

White thought Kings Canyon ought to be held as national forest because the Forest Service was better equipped to handle forest fires. He cited recent disastrous fires in Glacier National Park. Demaray whispered to Ickes, who replied, "Mr. Demaray tells me that the fire started on the national-forest ground and spread into the national park."

White complained that the expense of horseback riding would limit that mode of transportation to "playboys, capitalists, and Hollywood actors and actresses." Ickes doubted that many Hollywood actresses could sit on a horse; he himself was no playboy but used to spend his summers on horseback in Wyoming. Congressman Horton of that state interrupted to say that he had seen Ickes on horseback, "and while he does not do it particularly well, he is not a playboy." Ickes rejoined that the quality of his riding depended on the horse: "I rode one of your horses at your place." White then proceeded to attack the national-park concessionaire system and entrance fees. Ickes' response was he would like to get rid of them, but doing so depended on congressional appropriations.

After some further criticism (which Ickes agreed with) of the concessionaire system, Congressman Elliott brought the Gearhart bill into the discussion. Would the secretary object to open public hearings in California, where the committee could view the ground involved? That, Ickes replied, would be a good way to defeat the bill. Not a single new fact could be adduced if the whole Congress went out there.

Elliott asked if the witness knew why the *San Francisco Chronicle* was opposed to the park. Ickes did not know, but said he suspected it was because of who was secretary of the interior. (He was not alone in that suspicion.) After a few more irrelevant questions the committee adjourned until next day, when De Rouen resumed the hearing by suggesting that they stop wasting time.

Congressman Horton wanted to know why all the national-park lands in California could not have been left in the forest preserves; when they were parks all that people could do in them was fish. Ickes replied that the Forest Service was supporting the bill. Horton rejoined that in a national forest, "no charges are made. . . . You can do just as you please. . . . Now in the national park you have no rights whatsoever." Chairman De Rouen suggested that members ask the witness only "germane" and specific questions, but Ickes was willing to address Horton's general comment. He said that Congress had imposed two differing rules: the national parks were supposed to be self-supporting, whereas people enjoyed the national forests at the expense of the government—and he would be delighted to have that system applied to the parks. Recurring to the concessionaire system in a dialogue with Congressman Englebright, Ickes said it would be a happy day for him when Congress made it possible for his department to take over all such facilities and operate them without profit for the benefit of the public. He denied that national parks catered to the rich. And he wanted road building in national parks held to a minimum.

De Rouen choked off a digression by Elliott to the Kings Canyon resolution of the California legislature. Englebright then asked the first question in the hearing that had direct relevance to the bill before the committee. Why did the secretary think the Park Service would sustain this wilderness area better than the Forest Service?

Ickes saw no controversy on that point. He had faith and confidence in Secretary of Agriculture Wallace, who had gone further in setting up wilderness areas than any of his predecessors. "The only point I am trying to make is that under the law he can rescind that order tomorrow, or a successor could revoke it the day after he took office. There is no assurance in perpetuity of maintaining one of the few outstanding wilderness areas in the United States unless we set it up as a national park." Englebright rejoined that Congress could change the law. "Of course," Ickes replied; but to make it a national park "would be considered an earnest of the will of Congress to set it up and maintain it as a national-park area."

Supporters of the park took little time. Republican Jacob Thorkelson of Montana entered four favorable resolutions and letters, and fellow Republican Fred J. Douglas of New York said, "For once I agree with the policy of the secretary of the interior."

Congressman Elliott reported that he had just come back from California, where those with whom he conferred were "unanimous in the feeling that the people of California were not given a fair hearing when you appeared in California about three or four weeks ago."

That charge, Ickes replied, "touches me on a very sensitive spot." He had held a hearing in San Francisco and then by request, at great inconvenience, another in Fresno. There, in large measure, he heard the same people he had heard in San Francisco. "I challenge anyone to say to me, face to face, that he asked for an opportunity to be heard and that at either of those hearings he was denied that opportunity."

Sticking to his obviously baseless accusation, Elliott said the feeling of "my people" was so intense that he must insist on a committee hearing being held in California. In the light of that feeling, "Do you still feel that such a move is insincere, as inferred by yourself yesterday morning?"

"I am really surprised," Ickes replied, "that a question should be couched in such language as that. I have never made any implication or any suggestions, let alone any open statement, charging the congressman with insincerity. I ask to be excused from answering a question couched like that."

Said Elliott, "All I want, gentlemen, is the truth of this thing, and so help me God I am going to find it before I leave Washington, D.C." He declared that he needed the facts before he could vote on the bill.

Further questioning was blocked by the twelve o'clock bell calling the House into session, and De Rouen announced that Chief Forester Silcox would be next day's opening witness.

Silcox was accompanied to the hearing room on Friday, March 17, by a number of Forest Service men, including the assistant chief forester for land acquisition, Leon Kneipp. Jay H. Price was there—the assistant regional forester whom President Roosevelt had ordered removed from California because of his persistence, against orders, in fighting the park. The group from the Forest Service stayed in the background.

The testimony of the chief forester was to be crucial. Silcox could back up Secretary Wallace's approval of the national park, by giving it wholehearted support, or he could subtly undermine it. He opened by saying that he did not want to repeat the long history of the park movement given by Secretary Ickes, with which he was "in agreement as to the essential statement of facts." The area in question, he said, became a forest reserve under Interior in 1893 and was transferred to Agriculture and put under the Forest Service in 1905. About forty miles long and eighteen miles wide, a "canyonous . . . rocky, mountain area," it contained "practically no resources so far as commercial timber is concerned."

As to other resources, Silcox said that in 1905 about twenty thousand sheep grazed in the park area. "Practically all of these sheep have been removed over the years"—the only grazing left was by a small herd of cattle, about eight hundred. He personally was "very much in favor" of national-park development of "certain spectacular areas that are large enough and primarily valuable for scenic and recreational purposes."

Kings Canyon, the chief forester said, was already being "handled on the basis of the primary purpose for which we think it is valuable; that is, for its high scenic and recreational values." A satisfactory boundary line "has been worked out between the Park Service and ourselves." The issue of water development could be handled by an act of Congress. Secretaries of agriculture and three chief foresters had endorsed the park. Silcox said he was inclined to believe that very little more factual material could be developed by further examination on the ground: "This proposed park has been an issue for a long time, and as chief of the Forest Service I would like to see it settled."

Out of four hundred thousand acres, he said, all except sixty thousand on lower ground was classified as wilderness. As for loss of national-forest revenues by California counties (a scare issue raised by several county governments), this would amount to only $250 a year. Most of the hunting areas and virtually all timber would remain in the national forest.

Silcox's testimony did not leave the park's congressional opponents a leg to stand on. Elliott asked him if the Forest Service would "do something to take away the beauty, if there is any there," if the area remained in their custody.

"Certainly not," Silcox replied; but "where an area like this . . . is outstanding scenically, and large enough to constitute a complete administration unit," and where the use was primarily recreational, there he personally "would rather prefer to see the Park Service manage it. I would rather spend time, from the Forest Service standpoint, on timber areas, with recreation, grazing, and all other uses incidental to the timber use."

Mrs. Edge told me that she had been sitting in the audience at the hearing next to a man who kept sending notes to Elliott. At about this point, the note-passer remarked to her that "Silcox doesn't mean a word he says; the president fixed him, and Elliott is going to bring it all out." Elliott then addressed to Silcox a question which "you do not need to answer," since, said Elliott, it might be embarrassing. Had not the heat, he asked (as reported word-for-word in the hearing transcript), "been turned on to your department to such an extent on you people in the Forest Division, to feel so friendly toward making this transfer; isn't that right?"

Silcox said he would "answer this way." He was in the Forest Service from 1904 to 1917, then came back in 1933. Part of the historical development concerning Kings Canyon took place while he was out of the service. After returning, "I critically examined this record when this controversy arose, and became personally convinced that this area is an area that has very little timber." It also had "very little grazing, little or none." Silcox learned that chief foresters Graves, Greeley, and Stuart had agreed that it was of national-park caliber, and—"I found that secretaries of agriculture Houston, Meredith, and Hyde, H. C. Wallace, and later H. A. Wallace approved of this area as a park."

At one time, he said, when a report was made to the Federal Power Commission on the development of water resources, controversy over irrigation use had given "the appearance of a violent scrap between the Park Service and the Forest Service." Files were "that thick. . . . And the decision has always been the same. That is, the Forest Service has never taken the position, so far as I can find in the official record, nor has any secretary of agriculture, of opposing the creation of this area as a national park. Secretary Ickes was quite right when he cited the same record."

After a speech by Congressman Horton praising the Forest Service, Englebright asked Silcox if it was not a fact that Secretary Wallace had rendered an adverse report on a Kings Canyon bill on June 6, 1938, and that "the letter was presented to the California legislature a month or so ago and was presented by Mr. Price in behalf of the Forest Service, reporting adversely on the creation of this park."

"That is essentially true," Silcox replied. But, he said, at the time it was written there was a long gap in his personal experience and he had not gone far enough back in the files. "I was frankly ignorant of the fact [that] this bill had been approved by different secretaries of agriculture." He said he went back to the files after learning this fact from Secretary Ickes, and verified it. He would like to have Wallace's letter inserted in the hearings, so that the committee would have a full understanding of the circumstances, for which, he said, "I am partly to blame."

He then repeated his explanation that (in drafting the letter for Wallace to approve and sign) he had not known the "long historical background of this case." When the issue arose again, with the Gearhart bill, "I took the whole record to Secretary Wallace, and he made the decision then—on the basis of material which I do not think he had on his first letter—that he agreed with the others [four secretaries of agriculture] that it should be a national park."

This stand against a particular measure, later reversed by the same secretary, did not invalidate the statement that the Forest Service had never opposed a Kings Canyon national park in itself.

Toward the end of his testimony, Silcox admitted he had not seen the Redwood Mountain sequoias himself. Englebright and another congressman demanded to hear about the trees from "one of the local men." Silcox then suggested Colonel White, superintendent of Sequoia National Park. The two congressmen preferred Forest Service testimony. Silcox said that Price had been over the area. Even before his name was mentioned, former San Francisco assistant regional forester Jay Price jumped to his feet and, still bent over, almost ran to Silcox's chair, where he stood with a hand on the back of it, looking expectantly at the chairman.

Only a few minutes remained before the noon recess. Hugh Peterson of Georgia (a friend of the park) suggested discussing the matter later. De Rouen remarked casually, "Let's put it in the record"—meaning as printed information rather than testimony. The anti-park congressmen changed to requests to "put him [Price] on later."

What the hearing record does not reveal is the silent activity that went on during this exchange. I was sitting about two feet from De Rouen. The instant Price stood up I scribbled a few words and handed the note to the chairman. It read: "They want him to sabotage Silcox." De Rouen glanced at the note, then maneuvered out of the trap. Later he made a ruling (not shown in the record) that the committee should get all Forest Service testimony from the chief forester.

I recounted the whole episode to Dr. Hildebrand on April 6, the day the hearings closed. After the failure of the attempt to put Price on the stand, I had tipped off Silcox to what was going on. He ordered Price to go to Milwaukee, to take up his new duties there as regional forester. Price did so, but returned almost at once to Washington, still hopeful of being called to the stand. At any rate, he told me during this visit that Englebright had asked him to testify.

Three times, during the last days of the hearings, committee members attempted to introduce testimony by "a witness from the Forest Service." Each time, the chairman ruled against them.

If Price had once gotten into the witness chair, Englebright would have drawn out all the misleading arguments that he had put before the rules committee of the California State Senate in defiance of the president, the secretary of agriculture, and the chief forester. At the least, Price would have disrupted the testimony of his immediate superior, who made a magnificent witness for the park. Standing up under hostile questioning, Silcox gave up nothing that fell within the rightful functions of the Forest Service, claimed nothing that rightfully inured to the Park Service.

Taking the stand on Tuesday, March 21, Congressman Gearhart gave a word-picture of the proposed Kings Canyon park, ranging in elevation from 5,000 to nearly 15,000 feet, presenting "the most beautiful and awe-inspiring scenic recreational area in all the world." Coupled with these mountains, in the park area, was a different sort of grandeur—that of seven thousand giant sequoias, some of them "thousands of years old when the Christ was born." He called these trees "too great to cut" but worthless as timber. Felled with dynamite (he said), when they came crashing to the ground up to 90 percent would splinter into kindling, the rest would become fence posts and grape stakes.

Gearhart then went into the arguments against the park, which formerly came from irrigationists. Their desires, he said, had been satisfied by the exclusion from the park of two reservoir sites. Now they were asking for a Kings Canyon national park because its preservation as a wilderness area would safeguard the water resources they must have to sustain a considerable population. He answered other arguments. The park area contained no commercial timber, no minerals; had an annual deer-kill of 159 compared to 2,800 killed in the surrounding national forests; grazed 300 sheep compared to 3,000,000 slaughtered annually in the state; and grazed 987 head of cattle and horses compared to 1,250,000 cattle slaughtered in 1938.

Gearhart said he would like to discuss the relationship between the park bill and two other bills of his, one for the Pine Flat dam and one for participation in the Central Valley project, which together "present a most compelling argument for the passage of the park bill." That fact, he said, explained why Elliott, the day before, had obtained a rule that witnesses should confine themselves to one bill. O'Connor of Montana wanted to hear about the connection. And so did Englebright, to find out "what the people have been promised here [by Gearhart and Ickes]." Elliott promptly consented to waive the rule.

Past opposition to the park, Gearhart said, had grown out of fear that irrigation rights would be locked up. His three bills represented "a program for the comprehensive conservation of the water resources of our Kings River watershed." Passage of the first bill, creating a wilderness national park, would conserve the water supply. Passage of the second bill, for the Pine Flat reservoir, would improve the use of that water. Passage of his third bill would make the San Joaquin River also available to local farmers for irrigation. But the three bills, although interrelated geographically, were not necessarily dependent on each other. "One can pass, two can pass, or all three can pass," with increasing benefit. "Some people in the opposing camp" had made "the

Grape stakes were sometimes the ultimate use of a 4,000-year-old sequoia; scene witnessed by Irving Brant at Redwood Canyon in 1938 (photograph courtesy Robin Brant Lodewick).

ridiculous and absurd charge that some people have felt compelled to withdraw opposition to this or to that bill" in order to promote passage of another. That motive, said Gearhart, had played "no part at all" except with some persons who were "chronic opponents of all public-developed conservation programs." He called them "bent upon creating trouble in the hope that they can break down and prevent the passage of all three of these bills."

These people had filled the public with fear, but, Gearhart said: "That fear is rapidly being dissipated." He could confidently say that 90 percent of the people of the San Joaquin Valley "who have had a chance to inform themselves" were supporting all three bills, and 90 percent of those who were familiar with "the wondrous mountain country of Kings Canyon" wanted it made a national park.

Before his bill was drafted, Gearhart pointed out, the California legislature had adopted a resolution memorializing Congress against a national park in this area. A careful reading of the resolution showed that it was actually a memorial for preservation of the area as a wilderness; it was a resolution "against the destruction of all the things which this bill not only endeavors to, but will, protect." So he drew his bill "within the four corners of that memorial"; and the governor of California had sent an endorsing telegram to every member of the committee. Elliott, he said, had presented ninety resolutions against the park, seventy of them adopted before Gearhart's bill was drafted; and it was drafted to accomplish the very things they asked for.

Gearhart quoted the *Fresno Bee*'s headline, "Phoney Agencies, / Bogus Telegrams / Fight Park Bill," over an article saying that non-existent organizations with impressive letterheads were sending resolutions to Congress and that twenty to thirty presidents of genuine clubs had denied sending the anti-park telegrams signed with their names. Nobody knew who was guilty of these near-criminal actions, but no less reprehensible, in Gearhart's view, were the tactics of the California State Chamber of Commerce, which "represents the great commercial exploiters of California." Officially, it had swung over to qualified support of the park on the day after Secretary Ickes, by his Fresno speech, "won everybody to our side." But its Fresno secretary, Bill Halleen, and "a fellow by the name of Hugh Trawcek" began at that time to hand out slips to members urging them to "write an airmail letter [in opposition] immediately to each of the following"—naming five members of the House Committee on the Public Lands.

The letters were to be written longhand, to show that they were spontaneous and unsolicited. Gearhart said he had refrained from asking committee members about the response to this action, but the secretary of Delegate Anthony J. Dimond of Alaska told him that he received fifteen such letters in one day, all airmail and all in longhand. The state chamber, Gearhart commented, was still "using the same cheap methods which have characterized the actions of every discredited lobbyist that has sought to propagandize us into doing that which would serve their [the chamber's] purpose." But the chamber's statement was worded so that it very nearly supported the park: it opposed the park bill "unless the Pine Flat bill goes hand in hand" with it through Congress.

After a few friendly questions about Redwood Mountain the hearing recessed. When Gearhart resumed the stand on March 22, he read a letter from his predecessor in the House of Representatives, Henry E. Barbour, strongly approving the park, then said that he was ready to answer questions. I told Dr. Van Name what followed: "Congressman Elliott forced the adjournment of the Kings Canyon hearing yesterday by raising and sticking to the point of 'no quorum.' That just isn't done in polite congressional society, and it won't make Elliott any more popular with the committee." I added that Englebright was fighting the bill as hard as Elliott, and nobody knew why.

When the hearing was resumed on March 28, it was Elliott's turn to ask questions. But Gearhart said that he would like first to answer a question of Congressman O'Connor's concerning the acreage lying within the districts of the various congressmen, stretching in a line down the Sierra Nevada. Out of a total of 454,600 acres in the proposed park, not an acre was in Englebright's district, 357,425 acres were in Gearhart's district, 82,560 in Elliott's.

Elliott took some time, before questioning Gearhart, to deny reports in the *Fresno Bee* that he had gone to Congressman Cochran of Missouri, high-ranking member of the Committee on Accounts, to protest the Kings Canyon and Pine Flat bills. De Rouen cut short the digression by telling Elliott that correcting newspaper stories was a waste of time, but the issue involved me indirectly, because I had provided the information to Ralph Kelley, the reporter for the *Bee*. I immediately wrote to the paper's editor that Cochran had confirmed, in conversation with me, Elliott's opposition to the dam, though Elliott referred to the Pine Flat bill not by name but as "that $25,000,000 dam." And I said it was Cochran who had gone to see Elliott (not vice versa), in order to rule out a subcommittee junket to California.

At the hearing, Elliott began his questioning of Gearhart. Two hours and twenty-seven pages of testimony brought out one relevant bit of information—proof over the signature of Gearhart that he had refused to introduce a park bill until he felt sure it was overwhelmingly approved by the people of his district. That disclosure did not hurt the bill.

The first scheduled witness on March 29 was Charles G. Dunwoody,[1] lobbyist for the California State Chamber of Commerce. However, Congressman Gearhart asked and was given permission to make a brief statement "of tremendous importance to me." It was indeed. He said:

"A few moments ago, I was advised by the chairman and chief engineer of the Kings River Water Association [W. P. Boone and Charles L. Kaupke], an organization which includes in its membership a large proportion, perhaps as many as 90 percent of the users of water in that drainage area, that neither bill is satisfactory to that organization. In view of this startling information and in view of the fact it is the irrigationists alone whom I desire to serve, I think those gentlemen [Boone and Kaupke] should be heard by this committee at this point."

Gearhart did not say what their complaint was, but suggested that, as Elliott and Englebright had requested, a subcommittee be sent to California to study and report on the situation. That, chairman De Rouen replied, would require approval by the House leadership and a resolution appropriating money. He then revealed that he had discussed the dispatch of a subcommittee earlier, with the expenditures committee, and they had objected that it was not necessary and would prove a costly precedent; there were also "many other reasons" (which he gave) against it. So, they would proceed to hear Mr. Dunwoody. Writing that afternoon to the managing editor of the *Fresno Bee* in defense of Ralph Kelley, I gave my reaction to the disconcerting development announced by Gearhart:

"I did not suppose it was possible for anybody to perpetrate such a blunder as the irrigation people did today, in suddenly coming out with a statement that they were dissatisfied with the two bills, and compelling Congressman Gearhart to hold up his support of them. As matters stand today the Pine Flat bill is absolutely dead; killed by its own backers. The national park bill is almost dead. The execution was done, I am told, by somebody named Smizer [R. F. Schmeiser] out in California, but who led him into the trap I don't know. Gearhart thinks it was P. G. & E. [Pacific Gas & Electric] but I suspect that it was cooked up by the Dudley-Dunwoody-Show organization."

The mystery began to clear a few minutes after I mailed that letter. Schulz wired from San Francisco: "Have learned that Boone and Kaupke are leaning strongly to have army engineers build Pine Flat dam." The full story took shape in a series of NPS radiograms and telegrams in the next two days. Apparently the Sacramento office of the Army Corps of Engineers had given Boone and Kaupke "high hopes" of getting their irrigation dam and reservoir *free of cost* if the Pine Flat project could be shifted from Reclamation to the engineers as a flood-control undertaking.

Schulz confirmed my conjecture (voiced to him as well as to the *Fresno Bee*) that Regional Forester Show, lobbyist Charles G. Dunwoody, and forester-banker Ernest Dudley played managerial roles in the manipulation of Boone and Kaupke after they took the army engineers' "free dam" bait. To give the proposition an impressive front, Dudley's associate R. F. Schmeiser had organized and headed a Southern San Joaquin Valley Water Association claiming to speak for all concerned farmers. Schulz identified Schmeiser as head of the San Joaquin Valley branch of the Associated Farmers of California, an anti-labor organization.

Schmeiser, by pre-arrangement with Boone and Kaupke, sent them a wire-letter which they were to present to Congressman Gearhart, demanding delay on the Kings Canyon bill until final reports were received from the army engineers and the Reclamation Bureau on power sites.

Underlying the whole affair, in the expressed opinion of the *Fresno Bee*, was the effort of the "power trust" to block the construction of a public-power facility at Pine Flat. That, if true, led straight to Charles G. Dunwoody, whose official position as conservation director of the California State Chamber of Commerce was a cover for lobbying in behalf of any reactionary organization that put up enough money to buy his services. With such credentials, Dunwoody followed Congressman Gearhart to the witness stand.

Dunwoody opened the hearing on March 29 with a denial of Gearhart's assertion that the chamber represented "big business," not the small businessman or the farmer. To refute it he detailed the source of the chamber's income, 6.3 percent from farmers, 17.3 percent from manufacturers, 4.5 percent from utilities (i.e., the "power trust"), and so forth through sixteen categories. Eighty percent came from contributions of less than a hundred dollars a year. No "big business" domination there. In his testimony Dunwoody repeated the stock arguments against the park that had been circulated by the chamber of commerce and the regional office of the Forest Service, but the committee seemed more interested in (and skeptical of) his description of the state chamber of commerce.

Dunwoody apparently thought no one would look further than his own testimony for information about his activities. But Paul Y. Anderson, the most brilliant investigative reporter of the period; the Senate Lobby Investigation Committee; and now Kenneth Crawford's new book, *The Pressure Boys*, had all probed Dunwoody's methods. I had provided much of the information on Dunwoody for Crawford's book, using the research of Anderson, who had died. Now with Dunwoody testifying, Ickes asked Crawford for a pen-portrait of the lobbyist. At Crawford's request I prepared a draft. Technically, Dunwoody could claim to represent small businesses only because his large contributions went into a "special fund" for specific campaigns rather than being funneled through the chamber's general fund. In 1938 Dunwoody had carried on a high-pressure campaign, in Washington, against Roosevelt's government reorganization bill. He had been financed in this, Anderson found, by West Coast lumber interests. I summarized Dunwoody's alignments and strategy to Mrs. Edge: "Dunwoody and the state chamber crowd do not represent the irrigation people at all, but are trying to sabotage the irrigation movement for the benefit of the private power interests."

On Thursday, March 30, Elliot had again raised the point of "no quorum" and wasted most of the day. On Friday the opening witness was John C. Beebe, representing the Federal Power Commission. Without further identifying himself, he summarized a study by Ralph R. Randell, senior engineer of the commission, which had concluded that the South and Middle forks of the Kings River could eventually produce 3.6 billion kilowatt-hours for 3.3 mills apiece. Thus, said the FPC witness, the area proposed for inclusion in the national park "controls a power resource approximately equal to that of Boulder Dam." Pointing to a map on the wall, he explained the Randell study. Low dams were to be built at virtually all of the lakes in the high mountains, storing water which would be gradually released into the flowing streams and ultimately conveyed through a tunnel system to power plants. There would be four main reservoirs above Pine Flat, at Simpson Meadows and Tehipite Valley on the South Fork, at Paradise Park and Cedar Grove on the Middle Fork. In 1935, Beebe said, Eugene Logan, a Forest Service engineer, verified the Randell study but raised the estimated cost of electricity to 3.56 mills per kilowatt-hour.

In this study of power resources, said Beebe, engineer Randell "made an extensive field trip over the area and assembled all known data relative to its power possibilities." But qualifying this statement, he told the committee that the investigations and reports prepared by Logan and Randell were "not based entirely on actual instrumental surveys," nor were the dam sites drilled; but in estimating costs an allowance had been made for "those unknown factors."

The first friend of the park to question Beebe, Representative Hugh Peterson of Georgia, asked him what position he held with the Federal Power Commission. "Chief of the Division of Power and Flood Control Surveys." Did he speak from actual contact he had had with the Kings Canyon area? "Yes, sir. I used to be with the Forest Service."

If the committee had pressed its inquiry into background and personal contact, and if Beebe had answered fully and frankly, these facts would have come out about him and Randell:

Beebe until February 6, 1939, had been assistant regional forester in California. In that position he had been part of the Show-Beebe-Price campaign against the Kings Canyon national park and of the regional-office revolt against orders from Wallace and Silcox. But what was Randell's personal knowledge of Kings Canyon? And how accurate were his facts?

Randell's estimate of potential power volume was probably correct. He had obtained his statistics on water flow from the Geological Survey and he needed only a pencil to convert that into kilowatt-hours. The real question was cost of construction by packhorse in a roadless mountain wilderness. That could be determined only through the "extensive field trip" which, according to Beebe, Randell made.

Were such trips made? If so, why did Beebe devote only those three words to what should have been a major feature of the Randell report? The conclusion was obvious that no such ground study was made and the cost estimates were guesswork. Beebe came close to admitting as much when he said that the investigations and reports of Randell and Logan were "not based entirely on actual instrumental surveys" but estimates of cost "were made proportionately higher to cover the lack of definite information." How could a proportion be struck between the known and the unknown? The committee failed utterly to follow up these revealing leads.

The Randell report had been made in 1930 at the joint request of the

Forest Service and the National Park Service, and as usual, the Park Service people were played for suckers. Ralph Randell was a capable engineer but his report was not an engineering study. It was a combination of irrelevant engineering facts and an engineering fantasy, put together to help the Forest Service regional office defeat an early Kings Canyon park bill.

The House public lands committee came close to discovering this in the final minutes of questioning, but did not quite make it. Congressman Horton, a park opponent, remarked, "This is very rugged country, which means that it is pretty hard to transport materials right up to the little lakes. . . . Is the cost going to be prohibitive?"

"No," Beebe answered, "the cost was figured by Mr. Randell and Mr. Logan both, assuming that there would be no method of transportation in that high area at all except saddle horses and packhorses."

So, with his pencil and without instruments, Randell had figured out the cost of transporting thousands of tons of cement and iron on the backs of horses, carrying each two-hundred-pound sack over precipitous trails, across passes 12,000 feet high, to build hundreds of dams on unvisited lakes, to blast scores of tunnels through unexamined mountains—finding as a result of this extrasensory perception that it would cost just 3.3 mills per kilowatt-hour to produce as much electricity as was obtained from Boulder Dam.

The witness who followed Beebe was equally marvelous but totally different. Charles L. Kaupke, secretary-treasurer of the Kings River Water Association, testified that the association had withdrawn its support from the bill for the Kings Canyon park because it contained a different boundary than had been agreed upon and omitted certain matters "relating to the storage of water."

Representative Hugh Peterson asked Kaupke whether "your group" would favor passage of the bill "if this bill was amended so as to incorporate the agreement which was entered into between all of the interested parties."

"Probably," Kaupke replied, but he was "not authorized to speak for them to that extent."

Peterson pointed out that both Interior and Agriculture were in agreement and that "if you [did have] an agreement with those departments" upon this legislation, the committee should, in his opinion, amend the bill in accordance with that agreement. Would that satisfy all parties? Kaupke thought it would. So, asked Peterson, "There will be no further objection to it on your part?" Kaupke demurred; he did not "like to give you a positive answer" since he represented a lot of people.

But, persisted Peterson, "your people did agree upon a bill" to which the two departments did not object. "That is right," said Kaupke.

Congressman Elliott, challenging Gearhart's claim that 90 percent of the people of the San Joaquin Valley favored the park, asked Kaupke how many of the listed resolutions supporting the park had been obtained by "your organization"—the Kings River Water Association. "Approximately sixty" was the reply. Elliott then asked whether the people who passed those resolutions would rescind them if they "all knew the condition that is confronting you and Mr. Boone here in Washington." "They certainly would," replied Kaupke.

Elliott drew from Kaupke a statement that he would "certainly favor" additional hearings in California. Rene De Rouen then took over.

Did the witness believe, asked the chairman, that testimony in California would "develop more matter"? He went on: "I understand you are testifying for a large group of people. Who else would be more interested there that are not [included] in your organization?"

Kaupke replied, "I do not believe there is anyone."

If there was any logic in Kaupke's stand, it had to be looked for outside his testimony. He and Boone had turned against the park because of dissatisfaction with its boundaries. But, knowing what those boundaries were, they had induced sixty organizations to endorse the park. What was the situation "confronting" them which, if known, would cause those resolutions to be rescinded? They were now confronted with an offer by the committee to amend the bill to meet their wishes. All this led to the inescapable conclusion that Kaupke and Boone were fishing in the waters of a reservoir to be built for them cost-free by the U. S. Army Corps of Engineers.

John C. Page, commissioner of reclamation, was the next to testify. At the request of the Kings River Water Association, in 1937, his bureau had studied the possibilities of water storage and conservation and of power development on the Kings River. He said that the secretary of the interior had directed him to "work out the best plan we could find for the conservation of water and the development of power" on that river, "considering also the possibility of conflict between the desires of the irrigation interests and the proponents of the proposed Kings Canyon park. That was the only instruction we had."

At that time, Page said, the army engineers were studying flood-control features of Kings River, and his bureau had worked closely with them on plans for a combined structure that would serve flood control, water conservation, and irrigation. Their reports were certain to show that a large reservoir at Pine Flat (twenty miles below the park) would control the entire flow of Kings River for both flood control and irrigation.

In addition, said Page, it would be necessary to develop electric power to operate twelve thousand pumping plants to supplement Pine Flat in the dry season. "The best-appearing sites are those on the North Fork, which are outside of the proposed park boundaries." These dam sites had been drilled (to determine their ability to sustain a dam) and plans had been sketched. The North Fork sites, he said, were definitely superior to and cheaper to develop than Cedar Grove and Tehipite, although he understood there would be no objection to excluding the latter two power sites from the park.

Page presented correspondence between Boone and the National Park Service down to January 24, 1939, showing agreement on exclusion of Cedar

Grove and Tehipite from the park. He said he was fully sympathetic with "the irrigation and power . . . demands on that river." He believed that the Reclamation report, to be made in about six weeks, would be "so much more favorable than the irrigation interests originally conceived" that a full agreement could be reached when the time came to sign the contract.

Congressman Robinson of Utah, ranking Democrat, wanted to know the effect upon the park. Page replied:

"Well, in my own mind I am convinced that the plans we will bring out and which will do the things which the irrigation people want have no connection, or will have no infringement on this park area."

White of Idaho wanted to know the effect upon excessive pumping rates. Page replied that the planned developments would take care of the pumping demand "for many, many years . . . at a figure which is materially lower than the prices they are now paying."

James A. Foote, executive secretary of the National Parks Association, then took the stand and obeyed the order handed down to him from lumberman Greeley through Butler, Wharton, and Yard. His association, he said, numbering 1,000 members and 250,000 affiliated members, strongly favored a Kings Canyon national park that would be a realization of the efforts of John Muir and Stephen T. Mather. In these respects the present bill "unfortunately fails."

The proposed park, Foote said, "is a compromise between unproven, future industrial needs" and the most important policy promulgated by Mather in 1918, "that the national parks must be maintained in absolutely unimpaired form for the use of future generations as well as for those of our own time." Foote cited as fatal defects the exclusion of Tehipite Valley and Cedar Grove from the park and inclusion of the Cedar Grove reservoir shoreline. And if the rest of the park was to be a wilderness area, it might as well be left under the Forest Service.

Opposition committeemen drew from Foote many repetitions of these objections. Then Knute Hill, a park supporter, asked if it was a fact that William P. Wharton, president of the National Parks Association, had "telegraphed the president of the United States, Mr. Roosevelt, asking him to veto the bill that created our Olympic National Park."

Foote replied that Mr. Wharton "did not understand all the terms of that bill" and later retracted his telegram.

Said Hill: "And your association opposed the Olympic National Park. I would respectfully submit you ought to change this National Parks Association to Anti-National-Park Association."

Foote repeated that "it was just a misunderstanding . . . and we retracted and published our retraction. And we went on and we helped you and other people there in Washington [state] to put the Olympic Park across." Wasn't that remarkable! The association's president urged President Roosevelt to veto the park bill, and then, after it became law, the National Parks Association "helped to put it across." I thought of the *Alice in Wonderland* sequence "sentence first—verdict afterwards"; it fitted the circumstances well. But there was a difference, as well as a likeness, between Foote and Wharton. Both did what Ovid Butler told them to do. Foote knew what he was doing. Wharton did not.

At the conclusion of his testimony James A. Foote went out with a friend to have a drink. I was told of his plaintive remark to that friend: "Is there any way a person can make an honest living in conservation?" A day or two later, Mrs. Edge wrote to Ickes that the Emergency Conservation Committee was constantly receiving letters asking why it was that two government agencies, the National Park Service and the National Parks Association, were on opposite sides in the Kings Canyon fight. At her suggestion, the secretary put out a public statement, on April 3, saying that the "so-called 'National Parks Association'" had no association with the government. He told of its attempt to get the president to veto the Olympic Park bill and said, "It may be a stooge for the lumber interests, but it does not represent and cannot speak for the National Park Service." De Rouen inserted the words "not a Federal agency" after its title in the index to the House hearings.

Following Foote's testimony Miss Harlean James, past executive secretary of the American Planning and Civic Association, placed in the record a statement by its president, Horace M. Albright, former director of the National Park Service. Albright endorsed the distinction between Forest Service and Park Service functions and policies that was made by Chief Forester Silcox, which had led Silcox to approve the Gearhart bill. Rebutting the argument that California had enough national parks, Albright said that national forests in that state contained 19,423,135 acres, national parks only 1,246,538, and two of the four national parks were overcrowded. An attempt by Congressman White to show that Miss James (being a woman) didn't know anything about the high country brought out the fact that she had ridden horseback over the whole Sierra from Yosemite southward—territory on which White had never set foot.

On April 4, W. P. Boone, chairman of the Kings River Water Association, placed in the record five telegrams from branches of that organization, each one revoking its resolution supporting the park and calling for delay until final reports were received from the Army Corps of Engineers and the Reclamation Bureau. Owing to illness, Boone made no formal statement but answered questions with clarity of language and obscurity of thought. Pages and pages of questions failed to bring out any specific reason, other than a desire for delay, for the irrigationists' withdrawal of support from the Gearhart bill.

Told that Kaupke had said he favored the park at one time but reversed his position because the bill did not contain agreed-on boundaries, Boone responded that if Kaupke had favored the park at any time he was very much surprised, since "we both took a noncommittal stand on the park matter."

Their organization, he said, "withdrew its objection to the park" because of the expected power development on the Kings River. Chairman De Rouen asked him how the park would affect irrigation when the bill excluded the only practical reservoir sites (Cedar Grove and Tehipite Valley) in order to allow the building of dams there.

Boone replied: "The project has a great many phases and we want to see whether or not those things can be straightened out in order to enable us to organize our local people to carry it out."

De Rouen finally drew out that Boone had heard that the Reclamation Bureau would report those two sites were "impractical for use." Should that be true, said Boone, in order to get power development, "We have to go higher up. The North Fork [outside the park] is there of course. . . . But it at present is under the control of the Pacific Gas & Electric Company and they have one small plant there."

Congressman Murdock of Arizona, pursuing the theme, secured from Boone a repetition of the thought that "we might need higher reservoirs" and this in addition: "Of course, Mr. Page tells us he thinks he can make a deal [with the power companies] for the North Fork . . . and if we can make a satisfactory arrangement, the park would not find any trouble with us."

This was sufficient to explain a desire for delay, but not the drastic change of position regarding the park, nor Boone's totally unexplained assertion that the Gearhart bill violated an agreement "signed by the Park Service chief and approved by Mr. Ickes." So serious were the deviations, said Boone, that if he advocated the Pine Flat bill alone and said nothing about the park, "I would be run out of the country when I came home."

Strangely enough, nobody asked what these monstrous deviations were. Gearhart had introduced his bill on February 7. It embodied all agreements with Ickes and the park people up to that time. Boone had it in his hands within three days. More than a month later, on March 22, 1939, seven days after the hearings opened, Boone wrote to Senator Hiram Johnson of California:

"Kindly be advised that the irrigation interests on Kings River withdrew their objections to the creation of the John Muir-Kings Canyon National Park when they were assured that the Tehipite and Cedar Grove reservoir[s] had been excluded from the park and would be available for their use for water storage and power development. Copy of resolution and letters forwarded by air mail."

That letter, proving that the irrigationist leader unreservedly approved the Gearhart bill a month after he read it, two weeks before he turned against it, was placed in the record by Secretary Ickes, who resumed his testimony immediately after Boone left the chair. Ickes was in his best fighting mood. He introduced the Boone-to-Johnson letter by reading one of February 15, 1939, from Boone to Congressman Gearhart, describing the recent Fresno meeting addressed by Ickes on the subject of Kings Canyon and Pine Flat. "Everybody," Boone wrote of the secretary, "praised his ability, and he made many friends and some soreheads. In short, he broke the backbone of the group opposing Kings Canyon National Park. He took Frisselle and Dudley for a hard fall. . . . The hotbed of opposition in Tulare County . . . will turn over a new leaf and now spend their time trying to convert their friends to park advocates."

"Quite 'noncommittal,' " Ickes remarked, echoing Boone's use of that word to describe his and Kaupke's closest approach to support of the park. Then he resumed reading Boone's letter:

"The irrigation interests were entirely satisfied and much pleased with Secretary Ickes' definite promise of active aid in all our plans for Kings River development. . . . There was some talk by some of the members of the local [Fresno] chamber of commerce tying park and water to a single channel, but we expressed faith in the secretary's good intentions and said that would not be the procedure adopted by the irrigationists."

All this was written by Boone to Gearhart after he knew every dot and comma of the Gearhart bill, which, he said two weeks later, would cause him to be run out of town if he failed to oppose it. Ickes next placed in the record a telegram from R. F. Schmeiser to Boone and Kaupke (obtained through Gearhart) saying that the Southern San Joaquin Valley Water Association was urging support of the water-storage program (the whole Kings River development) "as a flood-control project to be constructed under the exclusive jurisdiction of the United States army engineers" and that the association was discouraging "advancement of Reclamation Bureau project at this time or until report of army engineers has been made available and carefully considered."

Ickes then, by permission of George Aydelott of Hanford, California, read a telegram from Boone to Aydelott calling on him to "have organizations wire us requesting delay and hearing on park bill in California." In combination, Boone's letter and Schmeiser's telegram let the cat out of the bag, and Ickes proceeded "to do a little more interpreting." The irrigationists at first had been satisfied with the Bureau of Reclamation project and Gearhart's park bill. "Then some bright person got the idea that if they could get the army engineers in there it would not cost them a nickel."

"In other words the irrigationists want the United States government, contrary to the established policy of building irrigation projects and letting the users pay the cost over a long term of years—they want to put both hands into the grab bag, and by having the army build this flood-control project, charge it all to Uncle Sam."

Ickes then threw a blockbuster: "Now, Mr. Chairman, I took the liberty of asking the War Department for what may be regarded as an interim report, addressed to you. You have not seen it yet. But with your permission I would like to read it into the record." He wished to read aloud only the last paragraph. Although Elliott interrupted to ask the relevance of the report for the park bill, De Rouen overruled him. Ickes then finished reading the paragraph. It stated that the Corps of Engineers' policy required "suitable payment to the United States by those who benefit from the conservation of water for other purposes than navigation and flood control."

The report was in the form of a letter signed by Major General Schley. In the portion of the letter not read aloud, General Schley said it appeared that any works that might be undertaken by the War Department "will be outside of the proposed John Muir–Kings Canyon National Park, so that the report of this Department could have no bearing upon H.R. 3794 [the park bill]."

Ickes then read a letter from Chester H. Warlow, a prominent Fresno banker, saying that several people had said to him, and a number had said to former congressman Barbour, that Boone and Kaupke "were getting 'off the reservation,' making fools of themselves." Asked whether the writer of that letter understood that it was to be used in the hearing, Ickes read further: "It is with Mr. Barbour's permission that I use his name in this respect. I say quite frankly that the feeling here . . . is that you folks in Washington ought to go right through with Gearhart's measure in accordance with the original plan, regardless of anything that these two men might attempt to do."

Elliott rose to a point of order. It should not "be placed in the record and go out from this committee that those gentlemen have made fools of themselves." Ickes offered to withdraw the letter. Congressmen Fred J. Douglas of New York and Jacob Thorkelson of Montana thought it should be printed. Boone, through Elliott, said he "would like to have the letter stay in the record." It stayed.

With support from Commissioner Page, who was present, Ickes rebutted the Kaupke idea of power dams on the Middle Fork above Cedar Grove. To obtain a steady flow of power, there must be a steady supply of water. That would be impossible without very expensive high-mountain reservoirs which also would interfere with maximum use of water at Pine Flat. And, finally, the secretary had been informed by Page that plenty of power, and cheaper, was available over on the North Fork outside the park.

The committee, Ickes said, might have divergent views about some of the testimony, but he thought all would agree on one thing: "This national-park bill is opposed by a very powerful and a very shrewd and a very far-reaching lobby," working both in Washington and in California. The purpose of this lobby: "To use the irrigationists to defeat the park and the park to defeat the irrigationists. It is very shrewdly conceived and very cleverly carried out."

The secretary said he would like to develop something he had said earlier, that the private-power interests had a hand in all this. Utilizing a memorandum from an unidentified Californian, he said that the recently formed Southern San Joaquin Valley Water Association (one of the organizations which had telegraphed Boone to oppose the park bill) had as its prime mover a Bakersfield banker, Arthur Crites, who headed a real-estate subsidiary of the Southern California Edison Company. The secretary suggested that the "power lobby," represented by Dunwoody, was ultimately behind the recent opposition to the park. He recommended closer scrutiny of Dunwoody's motives and methods.

Englebright raised a point of order against this questioning of "Mr. Dunwoody's integrity" and thought Dunwoody should be allowed to reply. Park supporters joined in the request, O'Connor of Montana because "we were promised something would be dragged out of the dark," Hill of Washington because "we will ask some questions." Englebright dropped the subject.

Ickes closed his statement by placing in the record the signed memorandum I had prepared for him, analyzing the resolutions for and against the park, describing the character and motivations of the groups analyzed. It filled three pages of fine print.

So came the final day of the hearings, April 6, twenty-two days after they began. On account of this stretching out, Mrs. Edge withdrew her request to be heard on behalf of the Emergency Conservation Committee. This was both a sacrifice and a loss, because her gift of repartee always made her a lively witness. I obtained permission for her to enter a written statement, and wrote it for her because the hearings transcript was to go to the printer in two days. In it I discussed several matters not adequately dealt with in the hearings and followed with a condensation of our ECC Kings Canyon pamphlet. I summarized the opinions of hydraulic engineers I had consulted about the Randell report, who said that it grossly underestimated costs at the high-mountain sites and ignored more promising sites outside the proposed park.

And how, I asked, were these hundreds of high-mountain Randell dams to be built? "Every sack of cement and every iron rod used in the construction of dams [must] be transported on pack horses from 20 to 30 miles over high mountain trails. All of this heavy material must be carried over trails so steep and rugged that they often form precipitous rock stairways up and down the mountains, with steps 2 feet high and switchbacks every 20 feet. Anybody who has seen a horse jumping from step to step under the weight of a 200-pound tourist who hasn't the decency to walk . . . will understand some of the cost items that are inadequately figured in the Randell report." I also pointed out the likelihood that the final report from Reclamation, concerning reservoirs at Cedar Grove and Tehipite, would show that glacial deposits were too deep at those sites to permit dam construction.

Congressman Elliott, as the hearings closed, placed in the record thirty-one pages of resolutions against the park, answered numerous trivial or irrelevant questions, and enumerated his objections in detail. Several others went on record: Congressman Englebright entered another nineteen pages of opposition resolutions, Congressman Charles Kramer of San Francisco stated his support of the park, G. H. Collingwood registered the opposition of the American Forestry Association, and Ickes delivered a letter to the committee chairman asking for a favorable report on the bill.

Thus on April 6, 1939, after twenty-three days, ended one of the most controversial congressional hearings, hotly contested on issues which from a national standpoint were virtually nonexistent.

Lake near Muir Pass, Kings Canyon, 1933. Power companies, irrigation interests, and federal agencies wrangled over proposals to dam these high mountain lakes (photograph by Ansel Adams, courtesy the Ansel Adams Publishing Rights Trust. All rights reserved).

CHAPTER TWELVE

THREE PLOTS THAT FAILED

On the day that Congressman Gearhart virtually abandoned his park bill (March 29, 1939), I had written to the managing editor of the *Fresno Bee* that the Pine Flat bill was "absolutely dead" and the national-park bill "almost dead." By the time the hearings ended, Pine Flat was still dead but the park bill had returned to life. Governor Olson of California stood by it. The California State Grange reaffirmed its support, and—more significantly—the local granges of the San Joaquin Valley followed suit. The vote in the Tulare County Grange (Elliott's home county) was almost unanimous for reaffirmation. Numerous women's clubs took similar action.

In the hearings, Secretary Ickes had knocked out power-lobbyist Dunwoody. Boone and Kaupke had not offered a single understandable reason for their sudden withdrawal of support. The War Department had punctured their real reason—inflated hopes of a free irrigation dam. Most important of all, Congressman Gearhart wired the John Muir Association, "The fight goes on."

Stimulated by the news, Linnie Marsh Wolfe, secretary of that association, went to work on a new round of publicity. And, in response to a flood of requests, Mrs. Edge printed five thousand more copies of my Kings Canyon pamphlet. I wrote to the president of the Sierra Club, Joel Hildebrand, summing up the hearings and predicting that "the bill will be favorably reported, possibly with no more than four votes against it." The bill as reported probably would not allow the president to add Cedar Grove and Tehipite to the park. However, Reclamation commissioner Page had told Boone—and Boone had repeated it—that dams could not be built at either site "because of the depth of the glacial deposits." It would not be hard to add the sites later by action of Congress.

Still, I saw Boone and Kaupke as a real threat to the park, because they would ask for a dam at Paradise Park if the Kings Canyon park bill did not pass: "They are a peculiar pair. They know—in fact they say—that Cedar Grove and Tehipite are out of the reclamation picture, but they react emotionally in defense of those sites, and if they were taken away completely, they would look immediately for a substitute higher up [inside the park]."

Writing to Mrs. Edge on the same day (April 6), I listed Elliott and Englebright of California, Horton of Wyoming, and Dworshak of Idaho as the only committee members likely to vote against a favorable report. The prevailing thought of the majority appeared to be that the area's scenery was of park status and the park would not really damage the interests of irrigationists. Most of the committee realized that the opposition of Elliott and Englebright was based on fear that tourist business at national parks in their home districts would suffer from competition with a new park nearby; Elliott was, in addition, "sore at Gearhart." The most significant opposition, I told Mrs. Edge, was from the private-power interests, who wanted to avoid a public-power project in their backyards.

The crisis stimulated the Sierra Club to fresh exertions in a needed direction. I had sent Dr. Hildebrand a copy of a telegram to Irving Clark suggesting an exposure, to Wilderness Society members, of Robert Sterling Yard's attempt to deceive them about Kings Canyon. It brought a response by wire, signed by J. H. Hildebrand and William E. Colby, which I transmitted to Clark. Sierra Club officers, the wire stated, had learned of charges that Gearhart's bill did not adequately protect wilderness values. The club leaders disagreed; they insisted that the bill was one of the "strongest and most encouraging" wilderness proposals that Congress had considered in many years. It deserved unqualified support.

In a follow-up letter to Irving Clark, I pointed out the problem of the Wilderness Society's interlocking directorate, involving the links between Yard, its executive secretary, and the lumbermen William G. Greeley and A. R. Watzek through William P. Wharton of the National Parks Association and Ovid Butler of the American Forestry Association. I told Clark that I had asked one of Wharton's most intimate associates whether he was "a clever dissembler or an honest dumbbell," and he replied: "An honest dumbbell. He would be astonished to discover that he is a tool of the lumber interests, but there is no chance of his discovering it. I have talked to him for hours trying to get a simple proposition through his head, and it is useless." As a result, I told Clark, both the National Parks Association and the Wilderness Society were led into taking the lumber industry's position on parks issues.

These admonitions were not needed. On the day Hildebrand and Colby sent their telegram, March 25, the Wilderness Society adopted a resolution supporting the Gearhart bill. Countering this to a minimal extent, Jimmie Foote's undercutting testimony was printed and sent out by the NPA to its entire unsuspecting membership. Four days after Ickes denounced that organization in the House hearings, its president, William P. Wharton, wrote him an aggrieved letter of protest, revealing that this too was being sent to all members of the association. In it he repeated Foote's assertion that Wharton's request for a veto of the Olympic Park bill was based on a misunderstanding. Wharton declared that the association had worked for passage of that bill and asserted that now he favored creation of a Kings Canyon national park but opposed the Gearhart bill because it permitted the construction of the two reservoirs on the floors of Cedar Grove and Tehipite Valley.

Secretary Ickes asked me to draft a reply to Wharton. In doing so, I summarized Wharton's letter, requested that the reply to it likewise be sent to the association membership, and then wrote that "whenever Congress proposes to establish a national park that trenches upon any important commercial interest, the opposition to it comes from two groups: Those who say, 'We are against it,' and those who say, 'We are for it, but—.' The National Parks Association can always be found in the latter group." It had happened with the Olympic Park in 1937-38, and it was happening with Kings Canyon. Wharton had claimed that the nonwilderness development allowed at Cedar Grove and Tehipite was the reason for withholding his association's support for the Gearhart bill. In fact, a new highway through Cedar Grove prevented its ever being wilderness again. Wharton's position would open the entire Kings Canyon area to power dams. "Why don't you tell your members," I asked, "that the actual choice is whether this entire wonderful country shall be left open to wreck and devastation, or saved by a bill protecting all that it is possible to protect now, and leaving Cedar Grove and Tehipite in a far better status, certainly, than if the park is not created?"

I closed this draft for Secretary Ickes by turning to the personal side: "Mr. Wharton, I believe that you are an honest and sincere man, but I think you are getting and following some very bad advice." For six years the National Parks Association, at some crucial point in a conservation campaign, had taken a position which dovetailed perfectly with the opposition of commercial opponents. If he could remember who advised him that a nine-hundred-thousand-acre Olympic park would be injurious, who told him that the Carl Inn Grove of sugar pines was in no danger, and who wanted him to ask Roosevelt to veto the Olympic bill, he would know, I suggested, who was misleading him on Kings Canyon. William P. Wharton was capable of identifying the individual—Ovid Butler—but he undoubtedly continued to trust him.

At the close of the House hearings, the Gearhart bill was plainly headed toward a new hazard, which developed into "Plot No. 1." In his testimony against the bill, engineer Beebe had revealed that Congressman Elliott had asked the Federal Power Commission to present its opinion and views on the future of Kings Canyon. "They are preparing a letter now," he said, to be addressed to chairman De Rouen. It would "cover that point." This seemed to mean that Beebe himself, as chief of the Division of Water Power and Flood Control Surveys, would have a predominant influence upon the commission's report to De Rouen. With that in mind, as soon as the hearings ended, I got hold of the printed Randell report on which the commission's report was certain to be based. The revelations in it were so astounding as to be almost incredible. The report showed that Randell (like Beebe) had never set foot in the Kings Canyon country above low-level Cedar Grove. He had made a seven-day pack trip to that valley before the trail was supplanted by the not-yet-opened state motor highway. The "extensive field trip" (Beebe's words) that Randell took among the hundreds of mountain lakes consisted of a one-day airplane flight over them.

Randell determined the cost of building these hundreds of high-mountain dams by multiplying their estimated acre-feet of storage capacity by $100, a figure obtained from the acre-foot cost of building three small dams by packhorse at Mineral King, a summer resort south of Sequoia National Park. I submitted the Randell material to a PWA engineer, Mr. Field, who had built power dams by packhorse in Colorado. The Mineral King dams were within three miles of a road, and the largest (and most economical) of them cost $52.17 an acre-foot. Field said that the cost of these dams, built before 1909, would be double in 1939, while to build dams thirty miles from a road would add at least 50 percent to the cost. The economically feasible limit for power-dam construction, according to Field, was generally put at $50 an acre-foot. Other engineers in San Francisco agreed. They told Walter Starr of the Sierra Club that the Randell report no doubt was accurate on water flow, since the figures were taken from the Geological Survey, but on cost the report offered "mere guesses . . . and absurdly low guesses at that."

Writing to Van Name later in April, I said the indications were that the Kings Canyon bill would be reported favorably by the House committee, by a vote of about fifteen to six, less possible absentees. "Gearhart is working strongly for it again. Congressman Elliott is out in California, spouting against the bill and claiming it is beaten in committee"—but working, I thought, for a face-saving compromise he would not get.

Beebe's influence in the Federal Power Commission, however, now became apparent. The *San Francisco Chronicle* of April 16 carried a United Press dispatch from Fresno saying that the commission had "today" made a report to the House Committee on the Public Lands on power development "upon the upper reaches of the Kings River in the mountain fastness of the Sierra Nevada range." This was called "the next major step in the development of electrical energy in the West." The commission reported that its engineering staff had "determined that additional power resources must be developed in California soon" and there was "no undeveloped block of power comparable to the Kings River resources close to the California market."

The commission's letter, as described in the dispatch, carried no reference to the proposed national park, but the implications were all adverse. Its call for early power development could be met by the Gearhart bill for Pine Flat and for power plants on the North Fork, outside the park area, but the project of power development in the "mountain fastness of the Sierra Nevada range" covered the entire national-park wilderness area.

Federal Power Commission intervention in the park fight took a far more serious turn on April 20, when the acting chairman of the commission, Clyde L. Seavey, wrote personally to Congressman Elliott in response to his request for an opinion on park-versus-power in the Kings Canyon country. Basing his reply principally on the Randell report, Seavey strongly urged that action on the Gearhart bill be postponed until the Federal Power Commission should make a thorough study of the power resources of the region covered by it.

It was the commission's belief, based on Randell's study, that "3,600,000,000 kilowatt-hours of primary, and an indeterminate amount of secondary electric energy" could be developed annually in the park area. This could be done, he wrote, and still "preserve unsullied for this and future generations the primeval recreational features of this Kings River territory." In other words, the mountains would still be there.

Because pending legislation was involved, Seavey did not mail the letter at once, but sent it to the Bureau of the Budget for administration clearance. Things happened fast after that. The director of the budget sent the letter to Secretary Ickes for comment. Ickes sent it to me on April 22. On that day, after receiving it, I wrote a five-page letter to President Roosevelt—the longest I ever wrote to him—and sent a carbon to Secretary Ickes. Ickes sent his copy to the president on April 24 with a cover letter asking for the president's immediate attention to the issue. My letter linked the anti-park lobby, led by private-power interests, and the organized fight, led by the Forest Service, to defeat the president's government-reorganization bill. I also summarized the careers of the opposition's main spokesmen: Dunwoody, behind-the-scenes opponent of Roosevelt on reorganization, supported by contributions from private-power companies and the lumber industry; and John C. Beebe, who had resigned as assistant regional forester at San Francisco to join the Federal Power Commission. Beebe had presented the 1930 Randell report, based on one airplane flight over the Sierra Nevada, as a true assessment of the power potential of Kings Canyon. The report, I told the president, was made at the joint request of the Forest Service and the Park Service, "with the Park Service in the usual role of sucker. It was useful for nothing, and has been used for nothing, except to feed anti-park propaganda in California." Even if Randell's figures were right, they would show that it would cost 50 percent more to produce power within the park area than outside it, on the North Fork. Yet this report had led Acting Chairman Seavey to write a letter to Congressman Elliott opposing the park—and that letter was only temporarily stalled in the Budget Bureau for approval.

I pointed out that the irrigationists, who controlled all of the Kings River water rights, were opposed to any power dams in the park because they would interfere with irrigation storage at Pine Flat. Thus the project was politically impossible as well as being economically unfeasible and ruinous to scenic and recreational values. I did not think that anybody in the Federal Power Commission was "designedly aiding the private power interests," but if Beebe "doesn't know that Dunwoody is a private power lobbyist, he at least knows that he is one of the cleverest anti-Roosevelt lobbyists in the United States."

Seavey's letter, I thought, was written by general counsel David W. Robinson. I had recently talked with Robinson, who had argued that the commission could not repudiate the Randell report once it had been filed. Robinson said the problem should have been taken up with Seavey; I had talked to Seavey twice and he said he was consulting Robinson. "There seemed no reason to pursue the matter further in the Federal Power Commission," I ended my letter to Roosevelt, "so I am reporting the situation to you."

After the president read my letter, or during the reading of it, he directed his secretary, "Pa" Watson, to get in touch with Seavey. Watson reported back to him the same day in a memorandum to which a copy of Seavey's letter to Elliott was attached. He said that Seavey had estimated the proposed study would take four months. He had warned Seavey that his letter to Elliott would "be used by the opponents of the proposed park to kill legislation this Session." However, said Watson, Seavey "believes the power question involved here is so important that it should be given the serious consideration he suggests."

The Park Service, Watson went on, had told Seavey "that you are personally very interested that the legislation creating the park go through this Session. . . . If you are interested, he would like to talk to you about it—presenting his views; or at least he would like an indication of your views, after you have considered the very important power angle."

The next day, April 25, Roosevelt sent a note to Ickes asking him to prepare a memorandum of reply to Seavey. Ickes asked me to draft the letter. I did so, letting my feelings get the better of my judgment. Ickes telephoned to say that he would have to revise the letter. "The president," he said, "cannot write so roughly to a subordinate."

Ickes then drafted a firm, persuasive, courteous letter in which the president said the creation of the national park would protect a unique, magnificently scenic area in the High Sierra. Speaking of the area's natural beauty, the ulterior motives of the park opposition, and the fact that cheaper power sources were available elsewhere, he wrote that "it would be, therefore, very unfortunate if by some act of the Federal Power Commission the bill failed of enactment." He requested that the letter Seavey drafted should not be sent and that the commission do what it could, conscientiously, to support the park. Now that the only valid cause of opposition, by irrigationists, had been removed, Ickes "strongly urged" in a memorandum that his enclosed draft or a similar letter be sent to the Federal Power Commission. Roosevelt sent the letter, and Seavey did not send his. Thus failed Plot No. 1.

Part of Congressman Elliott's "spouting" in California, about which I wrote to Van Name, consisted of a vicious personal attack upon Secretary Ickes as a secret conspirer with the private-power interests. Gearhart sent Ickes the charges as outlined in a letter from Mr. H. B. Williams, a Kings County farmer. Ickes asked me to draft a letter to Elliott for his signature. In this instance there was no reason to avoid plain speaking.

What Elliott had said was that Ickes created a phony private-power lobby against the park bill in order to conceal a conspiracy between himself and private power to block development of public power within the park area. This conspiracy was to be consummated through the clause in the Gearhart bill authorizing the president to add abandoned power sites to the park. The ultimate motive, Elliott intimated, was to give Ickes some sort of job after he retired from public office. Following a summary of these accusations, my draft for Ickes was strongly worded.

If the charges against Ickes and the innuendo against FDR, I wrote, were not "subject to word-of-mouth spreading by the ignorant tongue of slander," they might be ignored. Intelligent people would see through the falsehood, but malicious accusations had a "creeping vitality." If Elliott knew that the visible opposition of the private-power lobby to the park bill was part of a conspiracy to get the bill passed, why, I asked, had he defended the power lobbyists during the hearings? Why had he used the written promptings handed him by their chief lobbyist (Dunwoody) in cross-examining park supporters?

The Ickes letter closed with a reference to the confusion over the Pine Flat and North Fork irrigation and power projects: "I know of no single element that has added more to the confusion, or done more to jeopardize the interests of the farmers dependent on irrigation and power, than your own attitude toward the bills introduced by your colleague, Representative Gearhart."

That colleague was the next victim of Alfred J. Elliott's talent for slander. This became Plot No. 2—one of the most bizarre, laughably idiotic, yet most damnable incidents in congressional history. When the House convened on May 2, 1939, Congressman Gearhart rose "to a question of personal privilege." When asked by the speaker to present the charges, Gearhart said that he had been portrayed by his colleague from the tenth California district, Mr. Elliott, as "a cheap, money-taking, grafting, self-serving politician in the worst sense of that term"; he had been assailed in public and had affidavits and letters to prove it, and wished to present the evidence in chronological form. Speaker Bankhead ruled that he must first produce enough evidence to support his charges. The result was that Gearhart had to dip into his affidavits, which he did, and the Speaker ruled that a question of privilege was involved and could be presented.

The proceedings filled eleven pages in that day's *Congressional Record*, but at the outset few members understood what was going on. The case becomes clear, however, if one simply recites what happened and omits the mountain of supporting evidence by which Gearhart successfully supported his charges.

On March 4, 1939, Mrs. Gertrude Achilles of Morgan Hill, California, an elderly, wealthy member of the Sierra Club, wrote similar letters to congressmen Gearhart and Elliott, urging them to work for establishment of the Kings Canyon national park. By mistake she addressed to Gearhart a letter offering financial support, but sent a letter actually giving such support—in the form of a check for a hundred dollars made out to Gearhart—in an envelope addressed to Congressman Elliott. When he saw the contents, Elliott had the check photostated by the FBI. J. Edgar Hoover promised to send him a copy of the endorsement. Lobbyist Dunwoody then took the letter (headed only "Dear Sir") and the check, put them in a plain envelope addressed by typewriter to Congressman Gearhart, and found someone to mail the envelope and its contents from San Jose (fifteen miles from Morgan Hill). Gearhart simply returned the check to Mrs. Achilles. He knew nothing of the plot until an anonymous caller warned him not to cash the Achilles check: "He is out to frame you, Buddy."

Affidavits from California portrayed Elliott as waving the copy of the check before public gatherings, charging Gearhart with corruption. The clincher was an affidavit from Mrs. Achilles, in which she swore that she did not own or use a typewriter, nor did her secretary, and that she had never seen the envelope in which her letter and the check reached Gearhart. By the time Gearhart was half through his statement, most members of the House had grasped the situation. When he sat down Elliott was given forty minutes to reply. He presented three defenses: (1) everything he did was in the public interest, (2) he did not personally send the check back to California, and (3) he suspected that Ickes and Mrs. Achilles had a money interest in the government's intended purchase of Redwood Mountain for four hundred thousand dollars.

More than half of Elliott's reply to Gearhart consisted of denunciations of Ickes. His absurdities caused the *Congressional Record* to be punctuated with "(Laughter)." After many questions, Elliott was asked if he had given Dunwoody the letter "with instructions to mail it . . . from Fresno." "No." "What were the gentleman's instructions?" "From San Jose." Sitting in the gallery, I had a private laugh. To prove the corruption of Ickes, Elliott waved a circular of the Emergency Conservation Committee, which solicited funds to promote the park campaign, and three times he called it the Emergency Conversational Committee.

"Honest Harold" of course was furious about Elliott's assault on him and asked me to write his response. Summarizing the congressman's brazen attempt to bring discredit on Gearhart, I quoted Elliott against Elliott to refute his defense that he suspected the sale of Redwood Mountain would financially benefit Ickes and Mrs. Achilles. My draft showed that Elliott's opposition to the acquisition of Redwood Mountain had developed since April 6, the date that he testified before the public lands committee that he had "always thought this Redwood area [Redwood Mountain] should be . . . a national park." I supplied Ickes with a final rhetorical question: Had any member of Congress ever known the secretary to use his control of "more than six billion dollars in federal funds" since 1933 to influence votes?

Thus ended Plot No. 2, in total discomfiture of Elliott and in the destruction of Dunwoody. Congressman John J. Dempsey of New Mexico remarked to me that he did not believe there would be fifteen votes against the Gearhart bill. However, Plot No. 3 lay not far ahead.

I employed the Elliott-Dunwoody conspiracy as a reason for writing to President Roosevelt on May 5, 1939, about the current attitude toward the limited powers already given him to reorganize the government. Tom Corcoran handed my letter to FDR. In it I pointed out that Dunwoody, who led the fight of the San Francisco office of the Forest Service against a strong government reorganization bill the year before, had been "destroyed . . . as a lobbyist" by his attempt to entrap Gearhart. The Forest Service lobby in California was demoralized. If the president still intended, as he had told me in 1936, to "deal with the Forest Service," now was the time to do it. Roosevelt's reaction was friendly but noncommittal. Steve Early's reply read: "The President has asked me . . . to thank you for your memorandum of May fifth. He, also, requested me to say that he wants to see you soon."

After the Elliott-Gearhart imbroglio the public lands committee moved rapidly toward final action on the park bill. Gearhart submitted a number of amendments, and Secretary Ickes asked me to analyze them and draft a report by him to chairman De Rouen. Amendments No. 1, removing one square mile from the park for administrative reasons, and No. 2, allowing the secretary (but not requiring him) to grant concessions for five years rather than one, were not objectionable.

Amendment No. 3 was designed to clarify the wilderness provisions excluding roads and structures from the high country. I had talked this feature over with President Roosevelt. Owing no doubt to his physical handicap, he shied away from total exclusion of roads above low-lying Cedar Grove, specifying the need of them for elderly persons. I described the devastation that would result—gouging out mountains for hairpin turns—if the Park Service carried out the Forest Service project of a highway over the Sierra via Bubbs Creek. The president finally agreed to the prohibition but said: "Mark my words, that highway will be built within twenty years." His prophecy was not fulfilled.

My report approved the purpose of this amendment but proposed that, in view of the Budget office's warning against expensive hotels built at government expense, the wording be further altered to limit housing structures at Cedar Grove to "simple accommodations . . . for sleeping, eating, assembly and utility purposes" below Roaring River.

Amendment No. 4, opening the park to reclamation projects, was condemned. My report pointed out that it was patterned after a 1915 act designed to permit a diversion tunnel to be channeled through a mountain in Rocky Mountain National Park. "The Congress," I wrote, "has full power, whenever it believes such action necessary, to authorize reclamation or power projects in any national park." Sovereign power was sufficient to assure any future economic use that might be essential to the public welfare.

Amendment No. 5 eliminated the president's power to add Cedar Grove and Tehipite Valley to the park if those reclamation withdrawals were abandoned for power production. Without this power, my report-draft said, abandonment of the reservoir sites would give rise to many questions about underlying jurisdiction over the lands affected.

Boone and Kaupke approved all five amendments, saying that they met the principal demands of the Kings River Water Association. Nevertheless, the association was unwilling to withdraw its objections to the bill until the army engineers and Reclamation should make their final report.

On May 25, 1939, the House Committee on the Public Lands reported the Gearhart bill for passage. There was no recorded opposition. In the final hours of action the committee dropped the words "John Muir" from the name of the national park. It stripped the wilderness provisions out of the bill, but De Rouen succeeded in establishing the designation "Kings Canyon Wilderness National Park," thus creating a presumption of wilderness status.

The fifth section of the bill, dealing with the administration of Cedar Grove and Tehipite, had been revised, the chairman told me, by an amendment offered by James W. Mott of Oregon. Its meaning was unchanged, he said, but the dedication of the areas to reclamation was more definitely stated. I read the revised section. It stipulated that the National Park Service should administer "the lands withdrawn"; but "nothing herein" should prevent construction upon "said lands" of works recommended by the army engineers or the Bureau of Reclamation.

I pointed out that the revised section did not limit reclamation to Cedar Grove and Tehipite, because there was no definition of "lands withdrawn." De Rouen had not noticed that. The omission of the names, he said, must have been accidental. It made the whole section meaningless and would have to be corrected on the floor of the House.

That evening I made a study of the entire revised bill and discovered Plot No. 3. A week earlier, I remembered, one of the Gearhart amendments had taken out the sentence immediately preceding Section 5. That sentence had described Cedar Grove and Tehipite as "the lands withdrawn." I ran backwards through the bill for an earlier use of these words and found them in its opening sentence, reading: "The tract of land in the State of California particularly described as follows . . . is hereby reserved and withdrawn [from the national forest for the park]."

Omitted from that quoted sentence are eight pages of real-estate description. Mott by his amendment was opening the entire park to every type of reservoir.

I took an airmail letter to the post office that night, alerting Dr. Hildebrand and the Sierra Club to what was happening. "It is my opinion," I wrote, ". . . that Mott and Englebright (who I think engineered this) knew what they were doing. I think it would be well not to say anything about this for the time being, until a line of action is planned here."

Chairman De Rouen was astounded at this news. It was too late, he said, for correction in committee. The committee report was not yet written, but House rules prohibited a report from opposing any part of a reported bill. It was permissible, however, to describe the exact effect of this revision without taking a stand for or against it.

So, De Rouen asked me to write a clear statement of that effect for inclusion in the committee report. Also, he wanted me to draft a substitute amendment restoring the original purpose of Section 5. Then, he said, when the bill came up for action on the floor he would make a speech opposing Mott's amendment, after arranging for introduction of the substitute.

I talked with several members of the lands committee. None of them had realized the effect of the amendment and all expressed opposition to it. Then I went to see Mott, making no accusation. Would he agree to insertion of a limitation to Cedar Grove and Tehipite? He would not. I told him that the committee thought it was voting on an amendment referring only to those two spots. He replied (I quote here from a second letter to Dr. Hildebrand) that "he was not responsible for what the committee may have thought, that it expressed what he had in mind, to open the entire park."

I advised the Sierra Club "to denounce the emasculation of the bill all over the place" and concentrate on the California delegation in both House and Senate. The lesser issue of roadlessness should be dropped in view of Roosevelt's stand-offish attitude on that, but on the reservoir issue, "The President will go to bat." Within the next day or two I had identified Voorhis of California and Robinson of Utah as Mott's principal supporters, aided by White, James O'Connor, Murdock of Arizona, and Ellis of Arkansas. Several of them, I was told, "wish they hadn't."

I wrote the explanatory statement about the amendment that De Rouen asked for and drafted a new Section 5, which not only limited the section to Cedar Grove and Tehipite but solved the administrative problem caused by elimination of the president's power to add those areas to the park. My explanation of Mott's amendment went into the committee report in these words:

"This amendment provides that nothing in the act shall interfere with the construction upon the park lands of dams and reservoirs for flood control, irrigation, or hydroelectric power. The effect of this amendment is to open the entire Kings River Canyon Wilderness National Park to dams and reservoirs."

In writing my substitute for the Mott version, I decided it was not feasible to restore the president's conditional power to add Cedar Grove and Tehipite to the park—too much opposition. Without it, however, ultimate authority over the reservoir withdrawals was left in doubt in case they were abandoned as reservoir sites. To remove that uncertainty, I wrote in what was now Section 3 (renumbered from 5):

"The lands withdrawn for the Cedar Grove and Tehipite Dome dam and reservoir projects shall be administered by the National Park Service, under rules and regulations to be prescribed by the Secretary of the Interior, for purposes not inconsistent with the development and dominant use of the lands for reclamation projects." Furthermore, buildings on any lands needed by the Bureau of Reclamation should be removed by the Park Service. Sending this draft to Secretary Ickes for official submission to De Rouen, I explained its purpose and effect. Instead of limiting NPS jurisdiction to recreational use, the effect was to transfer all of the residual authority possessed by the Forest Service, "while the naming of the Bureau of Reclamation excludes other agencies."

With administrative control by the National Park Service broadened, I said, there was no need to restore the eliminated provision that lands above high water should be added to the park, "and much less need for a provision giving the President power to add the entire withdrawals to the park if the reclamation projects are abandoned." It would be unwise, I thought, to revive that proposal in the absence of strong need for the power.

In another memorandum to Ickes of the same date (May 29) I suggested a plan (already approved by De Rouen) for getting the provision against high-mountain roads restored. Regional Director Kittredge (who was a highway engineer) had given me an estimate on the cost of extending the new Cedar Grove highway to the Rae Lakes: $8 million plus immediate high maintenance costs. Roads were now forbidden east of Copper Creek, I told Ickes, because the secretary of agriculture had established a primitive area there. An economy-minded congressman like Jack Cochran could point this out and add that a highway past Copper Creek up to the Rae Lakes would cost $10 million. The congressman could then easily offer an amendment excluding roads from the portions of the park where they were now excluded under Agriculture. De Rouen had told me, I reported, that he would wait about sending in a report and asking for a rule bringing it before the House until all matters then in suspense were cleared up. The delay gave time for heavy solicitation against Mott's emasculation of the bill. The Emergency Conservation Committee put out (on June 2) fifteen thousand copies of a two-page, large-type call for letters to prevent "The Impending Ruin of Kings Canyon." Mrs. Edge reported a week later, "I have never had so prompt and *high class* a response to any appeal. The right people have written just the right letters. The Massachusetts Forests and Park Association of which Wharton is President wrote to every Massachusetts Congressman."

While the "Wharton organization" was taking a constructive stand, Wharton himself wrote in early June to Ickes and to members of Congress, in the same old negative way, as president of the National Parks Association. Again I wrote the secretary's reply, saying that "your entire argument to Congress was negative. Your letter contained not one word to inform the recipient that you want Kings Canyon made a national park. . . . This is the advice you gave: 'We most earnestly call upon every congressman who values the national parks to oppose this bill in its present form. It must not pass.'

"Those two sentences were written by a very adroit man. If I thought you had written them, I would not waste time writing to you. The purpose of the first sentence was to make you think that you were opposing the bill only 'in its present form.' The purpose of the second sentence was to make the members of Congress think you were asking them to defeat the bill irrespective of its form. That was the actual effect of the letter, as I have been informed by the author of the bill." The letter pointed out that the Sierra Club had recently resigned from the National Parks Association, which could not "long exist as Public Enemy No. 1 of the national park system. Private Enemy No. 1 is your chief adviser, and if you wish to understand the chief point in his technique, it is that he always sticks your neck farther out than he projects his own."

The Sierra Club sent a strong letter against the Mott amendment to all members of Congress, and the John Muir Association spread an appeal in California. Mrs. Edge supplemented her "Impending Ruin" publication with a news release to all newspapers of more than twenty thousand circulation. General Hugh S. Johnson, writing in his newspaper column, said he didn't know "who jimmied this joker into the bill," but he called for its removal: "—quick!"

On June 9 I was able to write to Van Name that "the House Rules Committee has granted a rule to bring the Kings Canyon bill to a vote, probably next week. Indications are that the dam amendment will be taken out on the floor. From talks I have had with members of the Senate Committee there is a good prospect of such action there if the House does not do it." Following the granting of the House rule, Ickes asked me to prepare a memorandum for use by the president in a scheduled conference with majority leader Rayburn and Speaker Bankhead.

I delivered the memorandum to Ickes on June 12, along with a copy (for the president) of my substitute for the Mott amendment. With them went this comment: "Thinking that he [the president] might wish to give [the memorandum] to Rayburn, I have omitted all identifying marks. De Rouen is confident that this amendment will be adopted if Rayburn offers it, but says it is important that the President speak to [Speaker] Bankhead." My memorandum for the president explained the difference between the original purpose of the disputed section, to allow the Park Service to administer the nonsubmerged areas around any lakes created by power dams, and the effect of the new version, which would permit construction throughout the whole park. My proposed substitute for the committee amendment would reinstate the original purpose. Concerning Cedar Grove and Tehipite, I warned that inter-bureau conflicts would occur unless the Park Service had exclusive control of their recreational use.

The day was fast approaching when I was to conduct the tour of Europe long scheduled by the National Public Housing Conference. As part of my preparation, I drafted arguments to be used in seeking restoration of wilderness provisions in the Gearhart bill, including a ban on roads. De Rouen outlined parliamentary procedures most likely to succeed; I sent the suggested plan to Congressman Cochran. Bills of more pressing importance kept crowding in, and it was evident that no vote would come before I sailed on June 22. However, I found time for two digressions. Dr. Van Name, in reply to a letter of which I have no copy, had written to me on June 13 agreeing that there was need to educate the public on the positive roles of predators in maintaining the balance of nature. Although he thought such a campaign would take many years to show results, the harm done by the Biological Survey's poisoning program "should be made known to the public very soon." My thought reflected that of James Madison, who had expressed the same concern in 1818 as president of the Agricultural Society of Albemarle County, Virginia. The interdependence of different forms of life, Madison stated, made it necessary, in building the new nation's agriculture, to work within "the established system and symmetry of nature." He spoke of invisible "animalcules" and vegetables whose existence was probably connected with the visible forms of life, and asked, could either exist without the other? In line with Madison's thought and Van Name's suggestion, I wrote to Secretary Ickes from New York on June 21, proposing a "careful study of the predatory-animal and rodent-control programs," which had expanded under pressure from stockmen but were "condemned by 90 per cent of the mammalogists of the country."

The other digression was distantly related to this one. In mid-June, Mrs. Edge asked for my help in obtaining the president's endorsement for her "new, and *swell*, Eagle Unit," written by Ellsworth Lumley, a naturalist in Mount Rainier National Park. At my suggestion, presidential aides tried to save the president time and trouble by having his endorsement of the first eagle pamphlet transferred to the new one. But instead, Roosevelt had Secretary Wallace's office draft a new letter, addressed to Lumley and expressing his support for eagle preservation. Mrs. Edge may not have exaggerated when she remarked to me some years later that she believed the president's letter, occupying the title page of the eagles pamphlet, led to passage of the law forbidding the killing of America's national bird.

The Kings Canyon bill came before the House of Representatives on July 18, 1939. Being in Moscow on that day, I had neither telegraphic nor telepathic knowledge of the proceedings. However, a letter written next day by Park Service associate director Demaray reached me in western Europe, bringing the welcome news that the bill had passed the House, 205 to 140, after the Mott power-dam amendment was stricken out. In taking that action the House struck out all of Section 5 that related to Cedar Grove and Tehipite Dome, leaving only a superfluous statement that "the lands withdrawn" (for park purposes) were to be administered by the National Park Service. On that subject Demaray wrote: "I have just had the opportunity to discuss the bill with the Secretary, who states that he would prefer that the bill be passed in its present form by the Senate, if that can be done without Senate Public Lands Committee hearings. It is his view that if the bill can be thus handled, we can seek legislation next year to provide for Park Service administration of the reclamation withdrawals for recreational purposes." On account of the turn thus taken, Demaray had decided not to send a letter I left with him for Senator Adams, but Secretary Ickes had conferred with Adams about expediting Senate action. Demaray closed by congratulating me on the bill's success to date.

Further information reached me from William Schulz. He had arrived in Washington on the day the House acted, and sat in the gallery with Frank Kittredge. They had listened to two hours of the "most confused debate imaginable." They felt few could have understood the arguments, and even friends of the park were in error on their facts and figures.

Running through the *Congressional Record* after we returned late in September, I noted confusion, and noted also that several supporters of the park referred to a bitterness not apparent in the printed words. Elliott and Englebright of California, Horton of Wyoming, and White of Idaho almost monopolized the vocal opposition to the park, aided by a few economy zealots who sided with Elliott in his opposition to "an entering wedge" toward the purchase of Redwood Mountain. Apart from that issue, the opponents centered on hydroelectric development, in addition to which Elliott extended his attack on Secretary Ickes, whose threats, promises, and paid assistants, in Elliott's opinion, produced practically all of the park support that did not emanate from the Sierra Club. Item: "Dr. Palmer [of the Biological Survey] has spent most of two months contacting congressmen, urging them to support H.R. 3794. Irving Brant, a newspaperman on the payroll of Ickes, has continuously circulated around the Hill and the departments urging support."

Robinson of Utah, a member of the lands committee, took the floor to say that "none of these individuals to my recollection or memory ever called on me or said one word to me about this bill." Wadsworth of New York asked Robinson to add his name and perhaps the names of several other members of the committee "as amongst those who were not approached by anyone from the outside."

The only member of that committee whose support I had solicited was Congressman Karl LeCompte of Iowa, a college classmate. My only contact with other members was as an "assigned by request" aide to chairman De Rouen in promotion of the bill, discussing strategy with park supporters and seeking (fruitlessly) to change the mind of Congressman Mott regarding his amendment.

That amendment, as expected, was the focal point of debate and caused most of the confusion. Chairman De Rouen attacked it in opening the debate, then swung into general support of the measure. Robinson, Wadsworth, O'Connor, and Voorhis spoke along the same line, extolling the grandeur of Kings Canyon and Redwood Mountain. The fight over power dams developed when the Committee of the Whole took up the twelfth amendment (Mott's). Number eleven had produced in the *Record* only one line: "The committee amendment was agreed to." Strategy on the Mott amendment had been worked out by De Rouen and by Cochran of Missouri; they were just about the only members of the House who appeared to understand the procedure.

As soon as the clerk finished reading the amendment, Cochran offered an amendment to the amendment, striking out every word of it. His amendment was read, and he spoke upon it. The committee amendment, he understood, had been adopted by a margin of one vote. It had aroused a national protest. It was denounced by every national-park enthusiast in the country:

"They assert that parks should be parks and not areas of commercial exploitation, least of all for such works, dams, reservoirs, and transmission lines. They fear the inclusion of such an amendment in any national-parks bill will create a precedent most destructive of national-park standards."

Cochran cited statements by the chief of the army engineers and the commissioner of reclamation, received since this amendment was adopted, that it was "absolutely unnecessary, that it is not needed in this bill. In view of that announcement, why should it be included here?" Retention of it would "serve no good purpose whatsoever, but . . . set a bad precedent."

Robinson of Utah supported Cochran's position and White of Idaho argued for power dams, but chiefly the House got into a snarl over parliamentary procedure. Chairman De Rouen finally straightened this out, making it clear that Cochran's motion was in order and that it wiped out the committee amendment. The Cochran amendment was adopted. The planned strategy had been for Cochran to offer the amendment I had drafted and Ickes and De Rouen had approved, conferring administrative authority on the National Park Service over the Cedar Grove and Tehipite withdrawals. Probably to avoid adding to the complexity of the proceedings, that idea was dropped and Section 3 (formerly Section 5) as amended became meaningless. The wisdom of this course became evident when a motion to recommit the bill to the public lands committee received a nine-vote majority, 90 to 81. De Rouen instantly objected on the ground that a quorum was not present. A call of the House brought 345 members to the floor, and the motion to recommit was voted down, 205 to 140. The bill then passed without recorded opposition. In shape it was less than satisfactory, but it had passed without the power amendment, and nothing else mattered.

After my return from Europe I worked closely with Senator Alva Adams of Colorado, chairman of the Senate Committee on Public Lands. He was thoroughly committed to the bill without anybody's urging, as was his administrative assistant Raoul Camalier. Adams had his problems, or subserviencies, but they did not involve trees. One day as I sat talking with Camalier, the doorway darkened and the 350-pound congressional lobbyist of the American stockmen's organization entered the room. Without a preliminary word he said, "I want a meeting of the committee next Thursday." "Yes, sir," said Camalier. The cattle-and-sheep agent then said a few words about the purpose of the meeting and rolled out of the room.

With Adams wholeheartedly for the park and very influential in the committee, and with California senators McAdoo and Downey both committed to it, passage of the Gearhart bill in some form seemed virtually assured. I strongly advised passage of it without amendment. It was so reported by the Senate lands committee, favorably, in November. I wrote to Mrs. Edge on the sixteenth that although the bill was far from perfect, it would be risky to let it go back to the House for another vote. But if the Senate passed the lands committee bill, the park would be established and the fight would be over.

Apprehension was growing among conservationists that Redwood Mountain would be lumbered before the bill could become law. I advised Mrs. Edge, confidentially, that there was no danger of this. The sequoia grove could be protected "through the combined use of two other powers placed in the President." Efforts should center on saving Kings Canyon, I said, because "if the appeal for the park bill is based on the saving of the sequoia grove, and it is brought out that it can be saved anyway, there might be a reaction against the bill."

This was the truth but not the whole truth. I did not dare tell her, lest the news reach Congress, that because certain special funds would soon be unavailable, Redwood Mountain had already been bought and paid for.

The Gearhart bill received another lift in January 1940, when the executive committee of the Wilderness Society forced editor Robert Sterling Yard to open the *Wilderness News* to a resolution urging "every member to write to his Senators asking that the two superlative scenic features of this whole Kings River country [Cedar Grove and Tehipite] should be incorporated in the park."

Yard, controlling publicity of both the Wilderness Society and the National Parks Association, had been saying "defeat the bill" because these scenic areas were left outside the park. The effect was entirely different when their inclusion was asked for in a broadside headed "WE URGE THE SENATE TO SAVE KINGS WILDERNESS."

Early in the morning of January 8, 1940, I delivered a memorandum to the White House, suggesting that the president speak to Senator Barkley about avoiding any procedural obstacles to the bill's passage when the calendar was called that day. (In the presidential papers this memo has been heavily marked beside the words about Barkley.) Senator Pittman had blocked the bill the previous summer, in the same situation, by refusing unanimous consent. Now, from the same two motives—hatred of Ickes and anger at the president—he once again refused unanimous consent for the bill and it was laid over. Camalier told me that Pittman had asked him for the anti-park bulletin of the National Parks Association, which opposed the Gearhart bill ostensibly because it omitted Cedar Grove and Tehipite Dome from the park. Giving Pittman more credit than I thought he deserved, I wrote to chairman Adams of the lands committee that, on the basis of this bulletin, the Nevada senator might conceivably support the bill if these areas were brought into the park; or he might seek to have the bill sent back to committee in order to delay it. Requiring descriptions of land, such amendments could not be drafted on the floor.

There would have been good reason, I continued, for Senate passage of the bill in the previous summer without amendment, because there was then no time for a conference between the houses. But I had just talked with chairman De Rouen of the House committee, who said that "if the Senate adopts amendments acceptable to the Department of the Interior, and appoints conferees friendly to the amendments, he is confident they will be approved in conference, and . . . they might be accepted by the House without a conference."

Moved by this prospect, I asked the National Park Service to draft two amendments: one to bring Cedar Grove and Tehipite into the park, the other to restore the original provision for the Park Service to administer those withdrawals for recreation purposes. Submitting these amendments to Senator Adams, I said that the Interior Department would not ask for their adoption, since that would go beyond the understanding reached a year earlier with the Kings River Water Association. If the two areas were placed in the park, it would represent the judgment of the Senate on the recent findings of the Bureau of Reclamation that they were infeasible for reclamation.

At this moment opposition to the park intensified. The California State Chamber of Commerce sent a new highflying lobbyist to Washington, to replace Dunwoody, who had destroyed himself in the "planted check" plot against Congressman Gearhart. E. J. Wallace, executive secretary of the non-mountaineering California Mountaineers, bore a remarkable resemblance to his predecessor Dunwoody in morals, methods, and capacity for action. In February 1939, E. J. Wallace had been a central figure in an unsavory imper-

sonation of Secretary of Agriculture Henry Wallace for the purpose of sow-
ing discord between the secretary and workers for the preservation of Redwood Mountain.

This began to come to light when Linnie Marsh Wolfe of the John Muir
Association received a letter from Secretary Wallace bitterly denying her sup-
posed charge to state senator Fletcher that Secretary Wallace had testified
falsely in telling a state senate committee that she had turned against the park.
Mrs. Wolfe promptly replied that her letter to Fletcher referred only to "Mr.
Wallace," with no more precise identification of the person—*not* Secretary
Wallace—who was referred to.

Who forwarded that letter to Secretary Wallace? Fletcher? E. J. Wallace?
Or some third person? Nobody would have known had not Henry Wallace
pursued the matter further. The upshot was a letter from his aide Paul
Appleby to Mrs. Wolfe saying that Secretary Wallace understood perfectly
how the unfortunate situation was brought about by enemies of the park.
The Department of Agriculture, Appleby added, could not be held responsible
"for the acts of former employees." That remark, Bill Schulz commented to
me, "points directly to Ernest Dudley," former employee of the Forest Service,
and "the most bitter and rabid of the park enemies." It pointed no less directly
to E. J. Wallace himself, No. 2 man in Dudley's California Mountaineers.

I suggested to Mrs. Wolfe that she write to all members of the Senate, exposing this affair, and sent her a suggested draft for that purpose, linking the
Mountaineers with the private-power interests. She replied from Michigan
that, being without secretarial help, she was writing the letter only to the two
California senators and Senator LaFollette. Her letter included this sentence:

"Sometimes we feel baffled, here in California, when we realize that important conservation projects are being fought under cover by powerful,
selfish men who snap the whip over local politicians and have the money and
the skill to create an appearance of public backing when they have none."

That factor lay right at the heart of E. J. Wallace's work in Washington.
His first action there was to give every senator a sixteen-page statement
against the Gearhart bill. Senator Adams allowed me to copy it. The Sierra
Club wired, asking for a copy, and I furnished one also to Ralph Kelley of the
Fresno Bee. In this document Wallace barely fell short of revealing his ties with
the private-power interests. After describing the Gearhart bill with emphasis
on provisions that had been taken out by the House, he launched an attack
on the *Bee* and other McClatchy newspapers, quoting an adjuration in their
founder's will that they should battle for public ownership of electric power
"at any and all times no matter against what odds." It was an opinion "common among the people of this area," said E. J. Wallace, "that Congressman
Gearhart is, either consciously or unconsciously, being influenced by this
voice from the grave." (Yes, a voice from the grave, warning against the voice
of the power lobbyist.)

E. J. Wallace then listed the groups—cattlemen, sportsmen, sellers of sporting goods, National Parks Association, National Reclamation Association—that were opposed to the bill. The remainder of his paper quoted testimony from the House hearings designed to show that the arguments for and against the park represented a contest with Secretary Ickes and the garden clubs on one side and California farmers and businessmen on the other. The power lobbyist closed with a disclaimer of self-interest: "This outline was prepared by myself without compensation, and purely out of love for the outdoors and my regard for fellow farmers who already are bearing a cross."

Wallace went back to California and reported on February 2 to the San Joaquin Valley Council of the state chamber of commerce. Senator Pittman was fighting the park bill, he said, but it probably would pass unless the California senators turned against it. Redwood Mountain, he reported, had been purchased for $457,000, with slum-clearance money he believed. The council adopted a resolution asking for a federal law requiring approval by the state legislature and governor before a national park could be created in any state.

Without knowing about this meeting, I wrote next day to the Sierra Club that nothing could defeat the bill except renewed opposition by the California legislature "followed by a change of attitude by the California senators, but they do not seem concerned about what the legislature may do."

On February 12 the Bureau of Reclamation and the Army Corps of Engineers both made their final reports to Congress on water conservation in the Kings River. Both agencies advocated a big dam at Pine Flat and nothing on the forks that entered the park. The Reclamation Bureau reported that it had bored 190 feet deep through sand and gravel at Cedar Grove without reaching bedrock. It had bored 100 feet deep at Tehipite with similar results. Neither site was feasible for a dam, but as I reported to Mrs. Edge, it was likely that Boone and Kaupke would immediately ask for a worse dam, higher up, at Paradise Park, if Cedar Grove and Tehipite Valley were put back in the park.

The Senate calendar was to be called again on Wednesday, February 19. The Kings Canyon bill would be brought up, and I was hopeful, I told Mrs. Edge, "that if Pittman blocks it then, a motion will be made to make it the unfinished business of the Senate." Adoption of such a motion would remove the power of a single senator to delay consideration. As that day approached, Pittman told majority leader Barkley that he was going to ask for permission to speak against the bill for longer than the five minutes permitted by the rule. That was a good omen, since all he needed to do, to prevent action, was to utter the words "I object." Senator Ashurst of Arizona gave notice that he was going to speak against the bill, but, he explained to me, he did not intend to hurt it; he was just going to put in some stuff to protect himself from attack because of government purchase of private lands in the Grand Canyon National Monument.

The calendar was called as scheduled. Pittman orated for half an hour, spilling his animus against Secretary Ickes by saying that this was a case of one man against the state of California. But he sat down without objecting to a vote. Committee chairman Adams then asked that the subcommittee's favorable report be placed in the *Congressional Record*. The report was signed by Pittman's Nevada colleague, Senator Pat McCarran. Adams also cited the support of California's two senators and the inclusion in the park of an imperiled "5,763 acres . . . of giant sequoias," which were a "minor part" of the park's acreage but a "major part" of its scenic value.

The *Congressional Record* concluded the story:

"The Presiding Officer: Is there objection to the present consideration of the bill?

"There being no objection, the bill was considered, ordered to a third reading, read a third time, and passed."

The third reading, of course, was by title only. Thus the Kings Canyon National Park came into being, after fifty years of controversy. Either Senator Adams was unaware of a fact known to the leading lobbyist against the bill, or he did not choose to share his knowledge with fellow senators—the fact that the Redwood Mountain sequoias already were owned by the federal government. But why did Senator Pittman drop his objection to the bill? By indirection, he revealed the reason when he said, "Mr. President, I realize that this is a futile attempt on my part so far as this bill is concerned. . . . I even have dear friends who are anxious that it go through in a hurry that they may forget it; [they] urge me to let it pass, and I want to help them all I can." In other words, senators from all over the country were receiving such a deluge of pro-park mail that they begged Pittman to let them off the hook.

Why did Boone and Kaupke continue their refusal to support the Kings Canyon National Park after every visible reason for opposition had evaporated? That came out when congressional attention turned to Gearhart's Pine Flat bill, with which the national-park project was closely linked. The regional office of the army engineers had promised Boone and Kaupke that if they helped shift the construction job from the Reclamation Bureau to the engineers, the two of them would be put in permanent charge of the completed project. The army engineers did get their contract, Boone and Kaupke were given their sinecures, John Muir's lifelong dream was fulfilled, and the American people obtained a marvelously beautiful national park.[1]

Hoh River meets the Pacific Ocean, Olympic National Park. This was part of the corridor to the sea that the author and FDR discussed during strategy sessions concerning the Olympic area (photograph by Marc Gaede, courtesy the photographer).

CHAPTER THIRTEEN

BACK TO THE QUEETS

As in the case of the Olympic park, primary credit for bringing Kings Canyon into the national-park system belongs to Franklin Roosevelt. In both instances, his interventions to smooth the way were made in periods when affairs of state were in two of the greatest crises of the century—the Great Depression, and recovery from it, in the one instance; Naziism and the beginning of World War II in the other. Fortifying all of Roosevelt's conservation activities was the work of Harold Ickes as secretary of the interior.

The unremitting work of Mrs. Edge through the ECC had been a big factor in the outcome. Also, creation of the park, and particularly the saving of the Redwood Mountain sequoias, crowned twenty years of ceaseless endeavor by Dr. Willard Van Name. Sending the news to him on the day the Senate voted, I closed by saying, "If you have any conservation medals, pin one on yourself for Redwood Mountain. Some people, anyway, know how long you worked for it." He replied that looking back made it clear just how much had been achieved. He had just written congratulations to Ickes, but "No, I do not pin any medals on myself."

Secretary Ickes closed the subject, as I thought, in a single sentence to me: "Just a word of appreciation to convey to you my very real thanks for the tremendous and tireless help that you gave in support of the bill to establish the Kings Canyon National Park." A month later Regional Director Frank

Kittredge returned a check I had sent him to pay for a fishing license he had bought for me at the time of our camping trip up Kings Canyon. "Thought I had returned it more than a year ago," he wrote. "That fishing license was my treat—didn't want either of us to be arrested in a National Forest. . . . That would have been too good a joke on the Park Service, & us." He told me that my sympathetic understanding of their ideals had brought the Sierra Club into active support of the park.

Well, it was Frank Kittredge's sympathetic understanding of the feeling and true interests of San Joaquin Valley irrigationists, combined with tact and acumen in dealing with honest but misled opponents, that caused group after group to revoke hostile resolutions and support the park. I had once severely criticized an error of tactics by Kittredge in dealing with the unfamiliar Olympic situation, but where he knew the ground his work was faultless and crucially important. William Schulz also deserved great credit.[1]

By now—March 1940—research was completed for the first volume of my Madison biography. Concentration on the writing of it would make it impossible to continue a fourteen-hour working day—seven hours as a consultant, the remainder on Madison. I had decided to resign as a consultant as soon as Kings Canyon was out of the way. Right then, however, Secretary Ickes told me that consultant funds had been reduced by a budget cut, and he asked whether it would be convenient for me to reduce my time from twenty to ten days a month. That made it easy to bow out completely.

I reported my resignation to President Roosevelt on March 6, in a memorandum which, I said, "represents entirely my personal views, unaffected by any departmental connection. Reports on the Hill are that you do not intend to transfer the Forest Service to Interior this spring." These reports reflected the effect of renewed propaganda against the transfer by lumber interests and by the Forest Service itself, operating, I said to Roosevelt, "through conservation groups unfamiliar with the facts." Assuming that the decision was against an early transfer, I reminded him that the Taylor Grazing Act of 1934 gave the president unqualified authority to transfer grazing lands in the national forests from Agriculture to Interior. By transfering 30 million or more acres to Interior, "You . . . would knock the political power of the Forest Service on the head," since that power was largely based on granting favors to stockmen.

The president replied on April 25 from Warm Springs, his letter expressing "regret that the very great press of business has prevented an earlier reply," and saying that "the views which you expressed . . . [summarizing them] were of definite interest. You may be certain that this material will receive proper consideration in any further analysis that may be made of this subject."

The "very great press of business" that delayed the reply was not presidential business. FDR had sent my letter on March 11 to the director of the Bureau of the Budget to draft a reply for his signature. That route was chosen presumably because he did not want either secretary—of agriculture or of the interior—to handle a matter that involved an undecided conflict between them. The draft of the reply was sent to him six weeks later at Warm Springs. The president's desire to transfer the Forest Service was well known, but either method of dealing with the problem was too hot to handle.

Although my work as an Interior Department consultant ended at once, the lesser, formal connection with the White House was to run on until July. Calling my attention to the fact, the National Park Service asked me to write a speech for the president to deliver at the dedication of Kings Canyon National Park. The next time I passed his desk at the close of a White House press conference I stopped and said, "You don't know it, but I am writing a speech for you." For what occasion? he asked. When I told him he said, "Well, here is something I want you to put in." He then set forth, at considerable length, a line of thought about which I had been asking myself: Do I dare put this in without an authorization?

The speech never was delivered because the fall of France aborted Roosevelt's trip to the Pacific Coast. But included in my draft almost verbatim is what the president said to me about federal administration of land that "belongs . . . to all the people." State and community interests were an important part of the national interest. "Often what appears to be a clash between nation and community is really a conflict between long-range interest and short-range desire."

Enemies of the Olympic National Park obtained some ammunition in the spring of 1940 through false charges growing out of secrecy in the taking of options on land sought for the Queets River corridor and the ocean strip. Officially, the National Park Service had nothing to do with acquisition except to designate the areas desired. Reports were circulated, nevertheless, that Secretary Ickes intended to push affected residents off their farms.

Representative Warren G. Magnuson, whose district lay in eastern Washington, tried to allay these fears. He felt sure, he told the Aberdeen, Washington, chamber of commerce, that the settlers would be given a life lease on property purchased from them. This assurance, the anti-park *Aberdeen World* reported, "brought little comfort for Aberdeen opponents of the park extension program."

On March 22, a placard-laden motor caravan of fourteen persons proceeded to Olympia to lay a protest before Governor Martin. They were from the Anderson and Northrup families of the Queets and Clearwater valleys; they were Fletchers of the Hoh; and one was famous John Huelsdonk, "the Iron Man of the Hoh," whose land was not affected. They made big headlines by petitioning the governor to call out the national guard, if necessary, to keep federal marshals away.

The *Port Angeles Evening News* devoted its next three issues to deflating the Grays Harbor "blow-up" of the caravan. The "50,000 acres of their lands" that were being taken away from the "embattled settlers" were almost entirely owned by distant landlords (lumber companies); some were owned by the state. Only about a dozen families, according to the newspaper, lived in the areas affected by the Queets corridor and ocean front. They would have life tenure of the property on which they lived. The Hoh and Bogachiel valleys, whose ranchers were upset, would be untouched except within an unpopulated ocean-front fringe.

The final article in the *Evening News* was headed "Hoh's Iron Men and Women Denounce / 'Honest Harold' Ickes as Land Grabber." It quoted John Fletcher, president of the protesters' organization, as saying that the delegation calling on the governor was smaller than hoped for because of the fear of many settlers opposed to the park program that "if they openly fight Ickes and the virtual confiscation of their property, the agents will crack down harder when condemnation begins."

"Condemnation prices," the pro-park newspaper explained, "are set by juries, not by officials." But Lena Fletcher (wife of Fred) had an even more frightening objection. She had long suspected that behind all of the national-park extensions, "subversive influences" were at work, "interested in having strategic resources of the nation locked up." Lena may have been the demonstrator who carried a placard reading "This is not Russia."

All reported protests, the *Evening News* commented, were aimed at Secretary of the Interior Ickes, "although it is well known that President Roosevelt himself is the mainspring behind the ocean parkway extension. He has taken a close personal interest in the Olympic National Park, as indicated again by what Governor Martin told the delegation Friday."

Next day (March 26) the *Evening News* printed an open letter from publisher Charles N. Webster to Secretary Ickes urging him to clear up the apprehensions of the Queets-corridor settlers by giving them definite assurances that would eliminate their fear that "they are about to be evicted from their homes." It is hard for city dwellers to appreciate, said Webster, "the intense attachment developed by isolated settlers for lands which they have cleared and improved with their own hands." All that was needed was an assurance that "lifetime leases such as exist in other parks for similar situations" would be given; also official confirmation of verbal assurances "that rights-of-way will be guaranteed across the corridor in both directions."

Secretary Ickes replied to Webster on April 15 and his letter was published a week later, along with one of April 12 from me to Webster. A few days before this, by direction of Ickes, the Interior Department's agent in charge of these land acquisitions furnished the *Evening News* with specific information about the project. It was financed by a presidential allocation of $1,750,000 from the Public Works Administration. As far as possible, lands were to be acquired through negotiations with the owners.

There were only nine farms in the Queets River valley, ranging from twenty to thirty acres of cleared land. The *Evening News* quoted purchasing agent E. Baldwin Myers: "A few additional families live in the ocean beach strip between the Queets and Ozette rivers, but this involves practically no cleared farmland." Of the 50,000 acres desired, about 25,000 were owned by large timber companies, 14,000 by small owners (about 225 acres cleared), and 11,500 by state and counties. The best timber cruisers obtainable were determining the prices offered by the government.

This information formed a useful prelude to publication of the Ickes letter three days later. "I share with you," the secretary wrote to Webster, "a genuine sympathy for the small number of pioneer settlers who have a natural and understandable desire to remain in their homes." Therefore he had instructed National Park Service officials to give "every consideration consistent with existing authority" to applications from landowners who wished to continue occupancy after acquisition by the federal government.

Because of the nature of the purpose for which the lands were to be acquired, Ickes wrote, "it is not possible to make a general commitment now. Each case will be handled on its merits." Occupancy problems in eastern national parks had been "handled in an orderly manner." And almost without exception, "Former owners have appreciated the consideration given them and the cooperation extended by park officials." Also, Ickes had asked for legislation to ensure rights of way across the proposed scenic highway.

Publishing my letter along with that from Ickes, Webster identified me as an "eastern editor and conservationist who temporarily served the government as special consultant on Olympic National Park boundaries." My recommendations, made after "a month traveling over Olympic mountain trails," had been "important in determination of the final boundaries."

My letter emphasized that Mr. Ickes had "taken action to see that the interests of the ranch owners are protected and as all government branches involved are working in harmony, there will be no difficulty on that score. As to the construction of a logging railway across the Queets corridor, Governor Martin obtained a personal pledge from the President that this would be provided for." (I had drafted the president's "full approval" of Martin's request for this assurance.)

The Huelsdonk–Fletcher Olympia caravan came back into the news when Richard Neuberger of the *Portland Oregonian* described it in the *Saturday Evening Post* of June 15, 1940, and Grays Harbor congressman Martin Smith placed the article in the *Congressional Record*. Under the heading "How Much Conservation?" the future United States senator cited the searing conflict thirty years earlier between Gifford Pinchot and Interior secretary Richard A. Ballinger and asked, "At what point does conservation stop and the arbitrary bottling up of land and resources begin?" He drew his answer from the "Iron Man of the Hoh," who came into the story again and again as a symbol illustrating the dilemma.

The Huelsdonk farm did not lie within fifteen miles of the area sought for the park, but the future senator pursued his thesis, attacking the additions already made by President Roosevelt in the Olympics. He pictured the creation of Kings Canyon National Park as a seizure and locking up by Ickes of a vast storehouse of electric power and other economic resources.

Mrs. Edge was terribly upset by the article. I wrote to her, even before reading it, that I knew Neuberger well and was sure that he did not write the article as anti-park propaganda. But he might "have been misled by the Portland office of the Forest Service." That became evident when I read the article. My copy of the clipping from the *Congressional Record* bears this marginal note: "When Neuberger's knowledge of facts increased, he became a strong defender of the Olympic National Park." His article furnished one bit of information that I had missed: John Huelsdonk's placard in the state-capitol demonstration bore the wording "Stalin took Finland. Hitler took Poland. Don't let Ickes take our homes away from us."

In July, with purchase negotiations still proving difficult, the government decided on a drastic change of tactics. Instead of negotiating purchases where possible and using condemnation proceedings when necessary, it was decided to carry out the entire acquisition by a "declaration of taking." That shifted the judicial process of price fixing from a federal-court jury to a federal district judge. It also created a peril. In condemnation proceedings, if a jury fixed an excessive price, the government could refuse to buy. Under a declaration of taking, the government had to buy the property at whatever price the judge fixed.

No worry was felt in this instance because the $1,750,000 PWA allocation was considerably more than the carefully appraised valuation placed on land and timber by competent foresters. If awards were too low, the brunt of criticism would be borne by the judge, not by the Interior Department. In any event the verbal onslaughts upon Secretary Ickes would come to an end.

In due time—or, better say, after undue delay—the "declaration of taking" came before a federal judge in Seattle. Secretary Ickes told me the outcome. The judge made awards so vastly in excess of appraisals that the PWA allocation fell six hundred thousand dollars short of covering them. The government had to buy every acre covered by the awards. The question, said Ickes, was whether to ask Congress for a deficiency appropriation or sell enough timber in the acquired strip to overcome the deficit. Selling it would narrow the two-mile-wide parkway by perhaps half a mile. Which should he do?

Without a moment's hesitation I let political discretion get the better of environmental valor. "Sell the timber," I said, "and say nothing to Congress about it." That is what he did, and nothing happened except that, after Ickes died, an occasional uninformed conservationist would make the "discovery" that the secretary had ravaged the corridor in a surrender to the timber interests.[2]

Late in July Secretary Ickes did what he had wanted to do for more than two years—squeezed figurehead Arno Cammerer out as director of the National Park Service. Associate Director Demaray was too valuable to promote. My refusal of the office in 1938 had been final and it was not offered again. What was my opinion of Newton Drury? A good opinion, I told Ickes. He would be a strong defender of national-park standards, and had done excellent work in the Save-the-Redwoods League. He had too favorable an opinion of the Forest Service (which had traveled rapidly backward since Chief Forester Silcox died), but he would get over that. However, I suggested that the secretary look carefully into the qualifications of Lawrence C. Merriam (son of Dr. John C. Merriam of the Save-the-Redwoods League), who had recently been appointed superintendent of Yosemite National Park. Writing to Mrs. Edge after Drury was appointed, I said, "From what I hear, only the internal difficulty of jumping a newcomer in the Park Service to the head of it disqualified [Merriam]." But I was well satisfied to have Drury the director.

A fresh menace to conservation became visible after Republican nominee Wendell Willkie opened his campaign for the presidency. Willkie was a man of honest principles, with no political background, who jumped into new positions at every swing of the skipping rope by his advisers. He mastered the subject of conservation from A to Z in a one-day train ride with Republican congressman (and re-nominee) Horton of Wyoming.

The result was a speech at Butte, Montana, on the national domain and national parks. In order to ensure "using those public lands as much as is economically possible for private uses, within proper regulation," Willkie made a pledge that if elected president he would appoint as secretary of the interior "a man from the western country who grew up in and understands the atmosphere of this great section of America."

In my one-day-a-week capacity as contributing editor of the St. Louis Star-Times, I quoted Willkie's promise and wrote that this was the same sort of language used by cattlemen and sheepmen who overgrazed and by power interests who wanted to invade national parks. "Not less ominous is the fact that Mr. Willkie has been taking his conservation counsel from Congressman Horton of Wyoming, who recently introduced a bill to abolish the Grand Teton National Park."

Soon, however, the election brought defeat for Willkie, Horton, and the sheepmen and a renewed mandate for Roosevelt and conservation. To the brief alarm of Van Name and Mrs. Edge, Ickes (with other cabinet members) went through the form of offering to resign. But he remained in office, a strong, aggressive adviser to the president.

Mt. Clarence King, now included in the Sequoia—Kings Canyon Wilderness, as seen in 1925 (photograph by Ansel Adams, courtesy the Ansel Adams Publishing Rights Trust. All rights reserved).

CHAPTER FOURTEEN

WAR CLOUDS GATHER
OVER THE FORESTS

When English colonists first set foot on Jamestown Island and Plymouth Rock, in the early 1600s, the entire eastern third of what became the United States of America was an unbroken wilderness of virgin hardwoods—oaks, elms, maples, ash, beech, birch, hickories, chestnuts, and numerous other deciduous trees—along with white and yellow pine and various other conifers. These vast forests were the hunting grounds of Indian tribes. Their culture fitted a landscape in which little patches of cleared ground made scattered breaks in a canopy of green. The mature trees were of enormous size. Among the mossy logs of decaying giants, slender saplings competed for sunlight.

By the year 1940, only one large virgin forest of northern hardwoods was left in the United States. This consisted of close to two hundred thousand acres on and around Porcupine Mountain (or mountains)[1] at the western extremity of the northern peninsula of Michigan, directly north of Wisconsin. All of this area was inside the boundaries of the Ottawa National Forest, a government entity which existed in name and staff only. The forested land was entirely in private ownership. The Ottawa National Forest had been set up for purchase in annual installments. However, the Forest Service found the timbered land so expensive that it decided to buy nothing except cutover tracts. Thus, by the time the whole forest was purchased there would be no forest.

Porcupine Mountain rose in the northerly portion of this heavily wooded area. Its rugged fifty thousand acres were of superlative beauty, with hard maples and oaks four to five feet in diameter. The mountains were cut by three swift rivers, the Presque Isle, Big Carp, and Little Carp, which flowed through deep canyons broken by waterfalls and finally cascaded down to the waters of Lake Superior. Crowning the mountain summit was sparkling Lake of the Clouds.

Porcupine Mountain had long been recognized to be of national-park caliber. A hundred years earlier, the first government surveyors had interjected comments about its beauty in their statistical reports. Early in the 1930s the National Park Service drew up a national-park bill that got nowhere in Congress. Then Representative Frank Hook of Michigan, entering Congress in 1935, undertook to bring Porcupine Mountain into the national-forest purchase program. His bill authorized a special appropriation of $10 million to buy Porcupine Mountain lands for addition to the Ottawa National Forest. This bill made considerable progress in committee but was struck down by the director of the budget. A letter of June 7, 1938, from President Roosevelt to Representative Hook stated that a special appropriation in addition to authorized annual purchases for the forests would be a bad precedent. Reintroduced in the next Congress, the bill met with a similar rejection by the Budget Bureau in 1939 and died in committee.

After that Congressman Hook shifted his approach. He and Senator Brown of Michigan introduced companion bills directing the Reconstruction Finance Corporation to lend the secretary of agriculture up to $30 million over a ten-year period. The sum, to be repaid within forty years, was to be used to purchase 1.5 million acres of hemlock-hardwood forest lands in northern Michigan and Wisconsin. Sale of timber on the lands thus purchased, which were to be maintained on a sustained-yield basis, would repay the loan. The Forest Service promised Hook that it would look with favor on setting aside a scenic area of twenty-five to fifty thousand acres, with cutting forbidden.

Such was the situation when I first heard of Porcupine Mountain in February 1941, through reading a booklet on the subject from the pen of nature writer Ben East. I went at once to talk over what I had read with Secretary Ickes. He showed quick interest and asked for more information. My suggestion to him, as I described it on February 22 to Mrs. Edge, "was that an attempt be made to work out a combination purchase, of the surrounding area for selective cutting by the Forest Service and of the scenic region for a national park." There was probably no chance to do any actual buying during the international emergency, I said, "but a public campaign should start soon."

I then talked with Congressman Hook, suggesting a joint Forest Service–Park Service operation. He said that he would gladly introduce a new bill along that line if the two bureaus would agree to cooperate. It seemed useless to try to place the matter before President Roosevelt at such a time. Only a few days earlier, Ickes had asked me to carry an important departmental matter to the president if I had the chance. "For six months," he said, "I haven't been able to get a word with him except at cabinet meetings, where it is impossible to bring up departmental matters."

By early 1941, Michigan conservationists had formed an association for the protection of Porcupine Mountain. Its secretary enlisted the aid of Eleanor Roosevelt. She wrote to Secretary Ickes, who sent me a copy of his reply, which stated that a tract of 175,000 acres "in the heart of the Porcupine Mountains" had long been considered suitable for national-park purposes. He listed hard maple and hemlock as the predominant species, followed by white pine, Norway pine, yellow birch, basswood, white cedar, black ash, American elm, red oak, white spruce, and balsam fir. The problem, he said, was to find means for acquisition of the lands. Federal acquisition would allow dedicating the superlative hardwoods for a national park; the remainder could be available for selective logging.

With little advance notice, a hearing on the Hook bill was called by the House agriculture committee for June 11. Mrs. Edge, chairman of the Emergency Conservation Committee, was then on a week-long visit to Porcupine Mountain. I was preparing my statement for the hearing when she sent a telegram asking me to represent the committee. The ECC, I testified, strongly supported the purposes of Representative Hook's bill. The heart of the forest, the area of the greatest scenic beauty, "should be acquired by the government and set aside as a perpetual wilderness, protected from all timber cutting whatsoever."

I said that the forested area around Porcupine Mountain, if left in private hands and lumbered by the usual method, would be reduced to one more stretch of worthless sand and scrub. The choice in the commercial field was between government purchase, paid for through perpetual timber cropping, or destroying it forever with a total loss of all value beyond the standing crop of timber.

Public support of the bill, I went on, had been aroused by the hope of saving the last forest of virgin hardwoods left in the nation. Yet Hook's bill in its present form carried no "guarantee of permanence." It proposed only an administrative order for protection. A single lapse by a single president, secretary of agriculture, or chief forester and the ancient forest could disappear. "Once it is cut, it is gone forever." But this was not an issue between Interior and Agriculture. I did not believe, I said, there was a person in the room "who would trust the question of lumbering in national parks to the discretion of a secretary of the interior [if] that means trusting to the discretion of all the secretaries of the interior who will be appointed in the next hundred years." Only by writing protection into the law could perpetual protection be assured.

I proposed that Hook's committee should ask the Park Service and the Forest Service to work out the "proper boundaries" between national park and national forest. I also suggested that the land for a national park be paid for out of the profits of selective logging in the national forest. But whether or not there was a national park, the scenic area should be protected by statute. Of course, if heeded, my suggestions made early congressional action less likely. The National Park Service, stimulated by Ickes, could be counted on to move promptly; the probable sticking points would be the Forest Service and the Bureau of the Budget. The Forest Service attitude was likely to be influenced to some extent by J. H. Price, regional forester at Milwaukee, the man who had tried to sabotage the testimony of Forest Service chief Silcox in support of the Kings Canyon bill.

Two reports reached me concerning Price. Raymond Dick, secretary of the Porcupine Mountains Association, wrote to Van Name on April 5, 1941, that he had guided the regional forester over Porcupine Mountain. They sat for a long time looking at the waterfalls and canyon of the Big Carp River—so long and silently that Dick thought his companion had fallen asleep. At last Price said, "It is so damn beautiful that I hate to move."

Mrs. Edge had a different experience. After three days spent visiting state forests in Wisconsin, a state in which women led conservation thought, her party was joined at Ironwood, Michigan, by the regional forester. In their encounters Mrs. Edge found Price "shy, amiable, and a little pathetic. . . . The conservation ladies all regarded him with reverence." When Price held a conference with the group he refused, in answer to Mrs. Edge's "bland and seemingly guileless questions," to commit himself "even tentatively" about areas that might be preserved. Mrs. Edge urged the need of Park Service protection, saying to the women that these Michigan foresters, whom they trusted, might very well be transferred. "A man from California, where Forest Service practices are very bad, might any day be sent to take charge of the Forest Service in the Middle West." Only the Forest Service people got the point, she felt sure, "since no one of the ladies realized Price's past history."

It finally came out, Mrs. Edge wrote, that the Forest Service had been telling Wisconsin conservationists that the Emergency Conservation Committee was working to defeat the Hook bill and prevent the preservation of the Porcupine Mountain forest. "An item in the Ironwood paper saying that you had appeared at the hearing in favor of the bill was very helpful—and very surprising to everybody."

The hearing produced no consensus. Predictably, the Forest Service undertook at once to sabotage my proposal. Raymond Dick wrote to a member of the ECC about Mrs. Edge's (alleged) conclusion that it would be inappropriate to bring the National Park Service into the project. Asked who gave him the false information, Dick said it came from the regional office of the Forest Service. The prospect looked bad—false tales spread by a government agency about a conservation plan whose fulfillment would depend on faithful enforcement by the bureau that was spreading the falsehoods. There the matter rested for some months.

After a family camping trip to Vancouver Island in the summer of 1941, we stopped at Port Angeles. Charles Webster of the *Evening News* told me of a new threat to the Olympic Park. In my report of additions to be made by presidential proclamation I had omitted the Morse Creek watershed, a twenty-one-thousand-acre forested rectangle that served as the Port Angeles watershed. Because of that use, it seemed immune from logging by the Forest Service. I left it out of the proposed additions, therefore, to be sure of acreage for the Queets corridor, the ocean strip, and nine square miles of private land in the Bogachiel River valley.

Linked with the Morse Creek watershed was Mount Angeles, which rose from the outskirts of the little city and commanded a view of the distant mountains of Vancouver Island and the North Cascades. Its western slope—a third of the mountain—already was in the park. Full inclusion was desired by all factions in Port Angeles. To promote this, a local outfitter invited us to be his guests on a horseback ride part way up the trailless mountain. We hiked on to the summit, breathtaking in both exertion and view.

Back in Port Angeles I wrote to Secretary Ickes, giving the reasons for omission of this area in 1938 and describing the present menace—a new plywood mill in Port Angeles. Its owners had persuaded the chamber of commerce to revise its previous recommendation that this area be put into the park. The Forest Service was ready to sell the timber, claiming that its new methods of selective logging would save the watershed from damage. The chamber falsely claimed that the Park Service no longer wanted the area.

I gave my opinion that the president, as soon as possible, should add the six thousand densely forested acres of the Ennes Creek drainage to the park, leaving the rest of the Morse Creek watershed, which was less attractive to loggers, for future action. This would bring the mountain summit and beautiful Lake Angeles into the park. The Ennes Creek valley, I wrote, "contains a fine scenic stand of large old growth Douglas fir, hemlock and western red cedar." But the Forest Service, after cruising the watershed with a lumber-company representative, had recently made a report grossly exaggerating the trees' commercial value by failing to list large and small old growth separately, thus giving the impression that the whole figure represented large "peeler logs" for plywood.

The day after I wrote that letter, Port Angeles people held what Webster called (in a letter to me) "a rouser" of a public meeting. "The opposition stacked our meeting," he said, but he reported that their comments had an opposite effect from what was intended. Congressman Henry Jackson took the lead in questioning chamber of commerce president Aldwell, who by his bumbling proved to be as usual "the park's best aide." It was two years later, on May 29, 1943, that President Roosevelt added the entire Morse Creek watershed to Olympic National Park.

This trip produced another recommendation, which I made by letter to the president. The already-purchased ocean-strip addition bordered the western side of Lake Ozette, close to the sea. The eastern side, heavily forested with giant cedars, was being knocked to pieces by lumbering for shingles. It occurred to me that this lake, six miles long and four miles wide, set in very low mountains near the ocean and Strait of Juan de Fuca, would be a good site for an emergency naval airbase, and acquisition of the eastern shore would stop the ruinous lumbering. I sent this suggestion to President Roosevelt, reminding him that "it was your desire to have this lake completely included in the Olympic National Parkway. That proved impossible because of lack of funds."

My letter, sent to the secretary of the navy on August 4 "for preparation of reply," brought an adverse response. The president changed the salutation from "My dear Mr. Brant" to "Dear Irving" (the first time he used that form of address) and informed me that the department had recommended against Lake Ozette, because of high construction costs. Also, the surrounding mountains would be a flight hazard under poor visibility conditions. The airbase was built at Neah Bay in the Strait of Juan de Fuca.

Back in Washington on October 1 (after a three-day backpack trip in the high country of Sequoia Park), I learned that the new Forest Service chief Lyle Watts had assured Senator Wallgren (promoted to the upper house in 1940) that there would be no cutting for plywood in the Olympic Morse Creek watershed. The Porcupine Mountain situation was deteriorating, but my attention was diverted from that by the rise of a more immediate crisis in conservation.

On November 10 Dr. Ira N. Gabrielson, chief of the Fish and Wildlife Service, came to my study room in the Library of Congress. The War Department, he told me, was engaging in a stupidity that threatened the extinction of the trumpeter swan. Spurning discussion with a coordinator appointed by the Fish and Wildlife Service, the department had picked on Henry Lake, Idaho, for experimental artillery practice in mountainous country. Gabrielson told them that "if they had searched the entire Rocky Mountain region, they could not have found a more disastrous location." Henry Lake was the only resting place on the migration route of the rare trumpeter swan between Red Rock Lake and Yellowstone Lake, both of which were sanctuaries. There was little chance that they would survive a disruption of their flyway by artillery fire.

The War Department replied that the army was engaged merely in advance planning of the range, which was to be used only if the army were enlarged. Gabrielson said that there were numberless similar sites in mountainous national forests and named five of them that would be superior. The army spokesman then shifted ground—the planning was too far advanced to be abandoned. "Gabe" urged me to try to get the matter before the president.

Thinking it best to have the complaint originate in a nongovernmental source, I asked Mrs. Edge to write to the president and send me any reply she might receive from the War Department, to which her letter would be routed by the White House. The answer came to her signed "E. S. Adams, Major

General, The Adjutant General." Adams gave the same two conflicting reasons why the site could not be abandoned. However, he soothed her, "appropriate action is being initiated" to have local military authorities and Fish and Wildlife Service representatives "confer on the ground for the purpose of arriving at a workable solution of the problem which will be satisfactory to all concerned." In other words, the swans would die.

This letter reached me on Monday, November 24, minutes after I had completed the draft of a tentative memorandum from Secretary Ickes to the president on the subject. I dropped that idea at once. On the previous Friday, President Roosevelt had made a nationwide appeal to the American people to deliver brass utensils to the government—every scrap of brass they could lay hands on—to be melted up for national defense. I now wrote to the president that, "if you are melting any brass hats at present," I hoped he would include the one worn by Adams. I explained that Adams, without consulting conservation agencies, had selected for an artillery range the "one and only spot where it is likely to result in extermination of the Trumpeter Swan"; other sites were available.

I handed this memorandum to Mr. Roosevelt at the close of the Tuesday morning press conference. He read enough of it right then to get the gist of it and there was a glint in his eyes when he laid it down. Three days later he sent my letter and the following memorandum to the secretary of war: "Considering the size of the United States, I think that Irving Brant is correct. Please tell Major General Adams or whoever is in charge of this business that Henry Lake, Utah [sic], must immediately be struck from the Army planning list for any purposes. . . . The Army must find a different nesting place!" Secretary Stimson replied on December 2 that the necessary orders had been issued. On the same day General Adams wrote to Mrs. Edge that "the matter has been given further consideration" and he was "pleased" to report that plans for the artillery range had been dropped.

The War Department by this time was being flooded with responses to a circular Mrs. Edge had sent out, asking that protests be made. Not knowing of the president's intervention, she thought that the ECC letters had turned the trick, and her letter to me opened with an ecstatic exclamation: "A VICTORY! One of the biggest victories that the Emergency Conservation Committee has ever won."

That letter crossed one from me containing a copy of my memorandum to the president. She promptly shifted the credit but thought that she might "have done some useful ground-work." She certainly made some groundwork for the adjutant general's secretaries, who spent weeks signing a multigraphed form letter acknowledging the protests that kept piling in.

On December 4, 1941, with the Library of Congress manuscript collection soon to be closed and hidden because of war hazard, I began to work as a Washington-based editorial writer on the *Chicago Sun*, launched that day by Marshall Field. Three days later Japan struck at Pearl Harbor.

In the name of national defense, early in March 1942, the Merced, California, chamber of commerce adopted a resolution calling for selective cutting in the Carl Inn Grove of sugar pines. NPS regional director Frank Kittredge headed off immediate support by the state chamber of commerce by proposing a general study of sugar pine for war purposes, and I predicted to Van Name that the assault would get nowhere. That proved true.

Far different was the situation revealed in the same month when the *Seattle Post-Intelligencer* printed (on March 18) a little story headed "Group Seeks Use / of Olympic Park / Resources in War." The brief article began: "Representatives of eleven Olympic Peninsula and Puget Sound communities yesterday formed a committee seeking to induce the government to open up the Olympic National Park area to selective 'harvesting' of its airplane spruce, oil and manganese resources as a war measure." On the peninsula, oil was a thimbleful, manganese an empty dream, but giant Sitka spruce rain forests formed the prime attraction of the beautiful Bogachiel, Hoh, and Queets valleys.

In the airplane industry, aluminum and magnesium, lightweight and strong, were just coming into full use in the manufacture of fighter planes and bombers; but to meet enlarged production of trainer planes and other aircraft, wood was still being used. Spruce best combined lightness with the needed toughness and resiliency. Aluminum, long held down in quantity and up in price by a corporate monopoly, was in short supply, but Sitka spruce was abundant.

The Seattle newspaper story went on to say that the committee proposed to ask the state director of conservation and development to invite National Park Service director Drury to "visit the peninsula and investigate the possibilities of their plan." The project gained force by the naming of the communities involved: Seattle, Tacoma, Bellingham, Anacortes, Everett, Aberdeen, Hoquiam, Olympia, Shelton, Port Townsend, and Port Angeles.

The National Park Service met this proposal, at the outset, by simply saying that no request for spruce from the park had yet been made by the War Production Board. In August an employee of the board, Roy S. Leonard, wrote to me in alarm about the threatened raid. (His information, however, did not come from the board itself.) He was a Seattle engineer who had worked to establish the park. I replied that the War Production Board would make the decision on spruce logging. Despite heavy local pressure for logging the easily accessible timber along the Hoh, there didn't seem to be any support on the board itself.

It was just at this time that Secretary Ickes was forced to narrow the Queets corridor by selling timber to offset the excessive price awards made in the federal district court. Part of this was achieved, I told Dr. Van Name, by selling spruce on lands acquired from the Polson Lumber Company. That sale would reduce the pressure for lumbering in the Bogachiel River valley and along the Queets parkway. Fortunately, no sale made then did any serious injury to the corridor.

On July 20, 1942, I reported to Van Name that "there is a sort of time race on, out in the Northwest, between the demand for Sitka Spruce in the Olympic area, for airplane manufacture, and the bringing in of spruce from southern Alaska. . . . By next spring, enough spruce should be rafted in from Alaska to prevent a demand on the park from proving effective." (The "Davis Raft," used for that purpose, built up the logs toward the center to give them something of the contour and towing ease of a heavy barge.)

By June 1943, Irving Clark of the Wilderness Society was expressing acute alarm. His own studies, he wrote on the sixth, convinced him that park spruce was not needed for war purposes, but there was a rumor in Seattle "of a scheme on the part of the U.S. Forest Service in Washington to cut out of the park the Hoh, Bogachiel and Calawah valleys." He believed that F. H. Brundage of the Forest Service, western log and lumber administrator, "would be glad to see this elimination made." Clark understood that national parks director Drury was about to make a report to Secretary Ickes on the spruce situation; although he felt confidence in Drury and Ickes, there was still danger "from political pressure and from Congress. . . . Are you prepared to step in if necessary?"

Early in July, in Chicago, I read Newton Drury's report to Secretary Ickes and was appalled. Drury explained to me, personally, that he was suggesting concessions to which he was opposed, but which he feared would become necessary later. I wrote at once to Secretary Ickes, repeating Drury's explanation, and then said, "I can't help feeling that this is a time for an 'offensive defensive' rather than the charting of a line of retreat." Labor shortages were the real issue: loggers had been drafted into the army and had been lured by higher wages into shipyards and airplane factories. The shortage of manpower was used as an excuse for logging only the most accessible trees. To deprive future generations of the rain forest because we hadn't "sense enough to send a few hundred men back into the work for which they were trained," I said, would be "as monstrous a failure of democracy as I ever heard of." I added that the real drive for spruce logging came from the timber interests' desire to "exploit and despoil." War Production Board decisions were made by people who had no interest in the park.

I then turned to the subject of presidential intervention, which was needed to push the War Department and the Manpower Commission to send lumberjacks back into the woods. The president would act, I was sure, once he understood that the cutting was "absolutely needless" and threatened the Hoh, Bogachiel, and Queets valleys with destruction. In theory, I told the secretary, Drury was right to say that if these valleys were lumbered they should be eliminated from the park. But a move in that direction by Congress would set all the anti-park "hounds of the Northwest converging on Washington." A legal ruling that the president could eliminate, by proclamation, lands which Congress had given him power to add by proclamation would unsettle all the national monuments in the country. The Wallgren bill had been carefully worded to avoid sanctioning President Wilson's cutting down of the Mount Olympus National Monument. Better "leave a despoiled area in the park than . . . open other areas to despoliation" through pressure upon future presidents.

I emphasized that it was not a case of "putting these forests ahead of the lives of soldiers." If any soldiers died because of lumber shortages, the fault would lie upon those who drafted the lumberjacks out of the woods, or allowed them to shift to higher paid war jobs which could be done by men and women without their training.

Ickes replied that he agreed with every word of my letter, and, "I am taking the liberty of sending copies to the President and to Anna Boettiger, the latter of whom, through the *Seattle Post-Intelligencer*, has joined, although not clamorously, in the cry of the lumbermen of the Olympic Peninsula. I agree with you about Newton Drury, too. He is a good man but not a fighter." Drury, Ickes said, had recently written for his signature so "weak and yielding" a letter about the cutting of spruce in the park that it was returned to him for strengthening.

In mid-July Mrs. Edge sent me a copy of a letter from Washington state treasurer Otto A. Case, asking me to get it to Ickes. Case said the drive for park spruce was the work of "the same old crowd" that tried to prevent the enlargement of the Olympic park. His figures showed that there were nearly 2.5 billion board feet of spruce available for cutting on private land in Washington, and nearly a billion more in state and national forests: "There is plenty of timber available without spoiling the beauties of the great Olympic National Park."

Late in July Irving Clark wrote to me about a three-day hearing held in Seattle on the spruce situation, by a subcommittee of the House Committee on Small Business. "We were fortunate in the congressmen who were here with that subcommittee. Both Kefauver of Tennessee and Stevenson of Wisconsin appeared to be strongly Park-minded, and Kefauver, particularly, showed an attitude very helpful to our side."

Clark seemed to think that he had failed in an effort to get a financial grant for publicity from the Robert Marshall Wilderness Fund, set up in honor of the leading advocate of the national-forest wilderness system, who had died a few years earlier. From what he said, its trustees were obviously dominated by Robert Sterling Yard. That added one more to the list of conservation bodies whose policies were either guided or obstructed by Ovid Butler of the American Forestry Association, whose bread and butter came from Colonel William B. Greeley, general manager of the West Coast Lumbermen's Association, and A. R. Watzek, head of the National Association of Lumber Manufacturers.

The list so dominated was indeed an impressive one: the American Forestry Association, the magazine *American Forests*, the National Parks Association (through Butler's control of Wharton), the Wilderness Society (through Yard's editorship of *The Living Wilderness*), and now the Robert

Marshall Wilderness Fund. All their deviations from conservation principles ran back to Butler's attitude developed during his years in the Forest Service. The Wilderness Society directorate, however, had broken free of the Butler-Yard guidance.

Clark reported that Colonel Greeley told the congressional committee that the Olympic National Park contained 3 billion feet of Sitka spruce. That figure was challenged later on by Assistant Forester Reino Sarlin of the National Park Service, who placed the figure at 758 million feet. Greeley accepted the correction. At luncheon that day Sarlin told Clark that even the revised figure (based on a survey made in 1917-18) was too high by several hundred million feet, and that only 80 million feet were of loggable spruce—3 billion reduced to 80 million.

It disturbed me that Sarlin had not put all this information into his testimony. I telephoned to NPS acting director Hillory Tolson, suggesting—and he agreed with me—that if the record of the hearing was to be published, Sarlin should amplify his remarks to include what he said to Clark.

The Associated Press reported on September 4 that Donald Nelson, head of the War Production Board, had demanded the transfer of certain Olympic National Park lands to the Reconstruction Finance Corporation. That was clearly an exaggeration, since such an action was palpably illegal, but it reflected a desire to get control of that park timber. Irving Clark, reporting the story to me, told of an article in the *West Coast Lumberman*, written by a Canadian, stating that British Columbia had sufficient mill capacity to meet the airplane needs of both nations.

Clark, continuing to pile materials on me, wrote on September 7 that if "loggers, particularly fallers and buckers," could be provided for spruce cutting in the Olympic Park, they could with equal ease be sent to Alaska or put to work on private holdings in Washington. Forester Sarlin had estimated that feasible logging in Alaska alone could furnish a two-and-a-half years' supply of needed aero spruce. Clark followed three days later with a reply to the WPB assertion that British Columbia spruce production could not be increased. He quoted the statement of Bob Filberg, head of Aero Products, Ltd., that their output would be doubled that year. Canada could produce all the lumber needed for the Mosquito bomber.

On my return to Washington from Chicago in September 1943, I confirmed my impression that the War Production Board was getting nasty about Olympic Park spruce, and that Ickes was valiantly holding them off. To help him do so, I suggested to President Roosevelt that he tell Ickes not to make any concessions without authorization from the president. At my suggestion, Ickes made the same request. FDR furnished the fortifying directive. Reporting this to Mrs. Edge, I described the situation that lay behind it, which was that Nelson of the War Production Board, lacking contrary information, had accepted the advice of his lumber advisers. It was quite plain that the primary interest of the lumber division was not getting spruce for airplanes, but "getting it from the park while getting it for airplanes."

On September 21, I wrote to Clark that apparently Nelson was unaware of Roosevelt's interest in preserving the park spruce, and that I intended to ask Ickes to get in touch with him. My information on Nelson came from Bruce Catton, his personal assistant, who was in a delicate situation. He was doing what he could, within the bounds of propriety, to enlighten his chief, but he could not become park propagandist. He and I had many discussions of his efforts to prevent the WPB from slipping into various errors. I have no record of how or whether the necessary word about Mr. Roosevelt's interest in national-park spruce was conveyed to Donald Nelson, but on October 29 I received a welcome notification from Park Service director Drury that "the War Production Board has reviewed the situation and has indicated that such logging is not at this time necessary."

The battle was over for the foreseeable future, and expansion of the aluminum industry soon put an end to the use of wood in airplane construction. As usual, the decisive factor had been Franklin D. Roosevelt's ability and willingness to keep a corner of his mind open to crises in the realm of nature while dealing with the greater political follies of mankind.

Pressure to log the forests of Porcupine Mountain stepped up during the war years. On January 14, 1942, I wrote to Secretary Ickes that "the campaign to save Porcupine Mountain in northern Michigan is at a critical stage," for lumbering was headed straight into the heart of the forest.

The Hook bill authorized a loan from the Reconstruction Finance Corporation to the Forest Service for acquisition of 165,000 acres. They were to be selectively cut, with preservation of a scenic portion promised. That bill, I said, "is getting nowhere. Its author is shuttled between Jesse Jones [head of the RFC] and the Budget Director, the latter being hostile." Passage of the bill would stop the immediate cutting, but it combined incompatible objectives. "If selective logging is relied on to finance both what is logged and what is not logged, it will result in logging all but a trifling part of the scenic area whose inviolate protection is the chief aim of the whole movement."

General Motors, I pointed out, owned about 37,000 acres, checkerboarded through the 165,000 acres covered by the Hook bill, and including most of the scenic area on the mountain itself. It was my opinion that "General Motors should be asked by the President to give this land to the government for a national park, as a goodwill token return for what it is getting out of the government in defense contracts." It was valuable land "but it is an invisible drop in the bucket of General Motors' war supply profits."

If this gift were made, I said, it would be sound policy to make an RFC loan for sustained-yield lumbering in the surrounding area. "Unless action comes soon, the lumber company will destroy the scenic values of the district by cutting its alternate sections. Then General Motors will cut, and the country will be a blighted wasteland of rolling sand." Secretary Ickes sent my letter to President Roosevelt along with a note urging him to read it.

Three days later the president directed the Bureau of the Budget to draft a reply to Ickes, saying in his memo to the director: "I think that Ickes and Irving Brant are right. We ought to save this virgin timber. F. D. R." Budget director Harold Smith communed with the Forest Service and sent a three-thousand-word report to the president on February 4, replete with facts and figures about purchasing price, costs of acquisition, interest payments to the RFC, and capital investment. The joint Forest Service-Budget study concluded that, extending the period of repayment from forty to sixty years, 1.3 million acres could be bought with a total outlay of $71,492,442. Receipts would amount to $52,440,000. The land and residual timber were valued at $16,500,000. That raised the assets account to $68,940,000, leaving a deficit of about $2,500,000.

Because the secretaries of agriculture and of the interior had made no report on the Hook bill, the matter was not officially before the Bureau of the Budget. However, Director Smith wrote that after the receipt of favorable reports from them he would advise the president to say that he had "no objection to their submission to Congress."

And how much, in this seventy-one-million-dollar project, was to be allocated to perpetual preservation of the scenic portion of Porcupine Mountain? On that subject Smith's report to the president was restrictive in size—only thirty thousand acres to be preserved—and completely hostile in tone and argument. He questioned whether "either economic or social justification" could be found for locking up more of the forest; it was not of national-park quality.

Commenting on my suggestion that President Roosevelt ask General Motors to donate its thirty-seven thousand acres of scenic forest, Smith said that he saw no objection to such an approach by interested individuals, or even at the departmental level of government. "It does not appear, however, that this . . . is of sufficient importance to warrant your personal intervention. For any Federal officer to suggest such a donation because of a corporation's sharing in defense contracts would be hardly within the bounds of propriety."

All of this except the final moral precept could have, and undoubtedly did, come from the Forest Service. Smith used the same argument employed against preservation of the virgin forests of the Olympic Mountains. Cut down a four-hundred-year-old, four-foot-thick hard maple and there are still "aesthetic values" in the four saplings that replace it. Exterminate elephants and lions; there are still aesthetic values in gazelles and hyenas. The issue was not selective lumbering; it was preservation of big trees and foaming rivers.

President Roosevelt sent the budget director's six-page memorandum to Secretary Ickes, asking for his comment. Ickes replied on March 2 that Smith's report was in the main an analysis in support of the Hook bill for an RFC loan to be repaid through sustained-yield lumbering. Ickes then turned his fire on Smith's statement (aimed at me by name) that it was questionable that "economic or social justification" could be found for setting aside more than thirty thousand acres for park purposes. There was no national park, the secretary pointed out, readily accessible to the large populations of the Middle Western industrial areas, and "An adequate national park in the Porcupine Mountains region would serve an enormous number of people."

Ickes was in sympathy with the proposal that purchase of important desired lands be made by means of an RFC loan, but he believed that the proposition would be much sounder if the outstanding recreational lands were managed for park purposes by the National Park Service. He suggested that Agriculture and Interior develop a mutually acceptable proposal for the president to consider.

President Roosevelt issued the desired directive, but in reporting to the secretary of agriculture the Forest Service dragged its feet on the division of administration. I met with FDR late in May. Chief object of the meeting was to urge, directly to him, the proposal that had reached him in my January 14 memorandum to Ickes and that was frowned on by Budget director Smith—namely, that the president should hit General Motors for a donation of its thirty-seven thousand acres of scenic forest on the mountain. On June 16, explaining to NPS chief Newton Drury that editorial duties would prevent me from making a trip to Porcupine Mountain with him, I gave a partial account of my talk with FDR, in which I told the president that "a prod was needed" to get the Forest Service to agree to the park.

The prod was given within a week. On June 1, 1942, FDR sent a memorandum to the secretaries of the interior and agriculture, asking that they "get together and present a united front." He suggested that General Motors—which ought to be "very liberal with the government"—might be willing to deed its acreage if allowed to selectively log the timber. "I am told that we ought to have 150,000 acres and that a large portion of this has already been lumbered and should be treated as a reforestation project. Also, I am inclined to think that 50,000 acres in the heart of it should be kept as a National Monument or National Park—in its original condition without cutting."

The memo made it evident that my statement to the president had not been clear. I had failed to say that the fifty thousand acres desired for a national monument or national park included the thirty-seven thousand scenic acres owned by General Motors. Of course, that corporation could be reimbursed out of the proceeds from selective cutting in other areas. And the words "ought to be very liberal with the government" implied that the stumpage should be priced at considerably less than its value in the commercial market.

Secretary Ickes sent the president's memorandum to Park Service director Drury with this notation: "Please note the attached. The man who knows more about this area is Irving Brant and I suggest that you get in touch with him." Drury replied that he would do so and drafted a memo from Ickes to the president saying that the national parks director would consult with the secretary of agriculture and believed that they could agree upon an adequate area for a national park.

Drury and I planned to confer in Chicago on June 19 by telephone but missed contact. However, he sent me a lengthy report from the National Park Service to the Bureau of the Budget. This provided for an RFC loan for acquisition of a Porcupine Mountain national park, of the same sort contemplated for purchase of national-forest lands. It was estimated that by an expenditure of $11.5 million an adequate national park could be set up, the whole debt to be liquidated in sixty years through automobile entrance fees and profit from government-run business operations. Receipts in existing state parks of Michigan and Wisconsin were cited to support these estimates. A month later (July 20) I reported to Van Name that "things are looking up for Porcupine Mountain." The National Park Service and Forest Service had agreed to an amendment to the Hook bill authorizing the president to set aside a seventy-thousand-acre national monument made up of forty thousand acres purchased by the Forest Service and thirty thousand acquired without cost to the government—it was hoped by gift from General Motors.

In mid-August Mrs. Edge sent me, for criticism, the manuscript of a waterfowl pamphlet she had written. It urged that, with duck hunting greatly reduced by shortage of ammunition, the "regulatory authorities" should put a total and permanent end to waterfowl hunting. I replied at once that if the president and secretary of the interior issued such regulations, "their powers would be taken away by Congress almost overnight."

When Mrs. Edge wanted to tone down the pamphlet, she reported, Van Name was furious. So I had the job of mollifying the country's number one conservationist (whose infallible judgment where trees were concerned was not matched by his appraisal of *Homo subsapiens*). I wrote to him that such a pamphlet "would destroy the influence of the E.C.C. both with moderate hunters, by ascribing to them a sadism they do not possess, and with the Fish and Wildlife Service and Secretary Ickes, by assuming that something legally possible was also politically possible." Van Name accepted the explanation in good spirit and the pamphlet was dropped.

In November a national crisis in conservation loomed up—this one emanating from the president himself. Press dispatches reported that he was on the point of making a cabinet shift, removing Secretary Ickes from Interior to handle the Manpower Commission, then headed by Paul V. McNutt, former governor of Indiana and unannounced aspirant to the presidency. McNutt was botching the job, especially through maldistribution of migratory farm labor, which was in short supply in critical areas. Along with this, Ickes was to have other duties (or virtually three jobs if he continued to hold Interior). If Ickes were transferred, it meant that McNutt might succeed him as secretary of the interior, a horrible prospect. I telephoned Ickes and told him that I was thinking of making a protest to FDR against the transfer. "If you are going to," he replied, "do it quickly, so it will do some good." So on that day, November 30, 1942, I sent a letter to Mr. Roosevelt outlining two reservations. First, if Ickes took on two new jobs besides Interior, he would be spread too thin. Second, I wrote (with McNutt in mind), no one with presidential ambitions could withstand the political pressures on Interior. Unsettling that department would be dangerous; only a man with experience could safeguard the nation's resources during wartime.

At my suggestion, Mrs. Edge sent a telegram urging retention of Ickes in Interior, where, she said, conservationists relied more than ever "on his experience his dependability his integrity and his true conservation spirit." Van Name, at the solicitation of Mrs. Edge, also telegraphed the president, wasting $1.14, he told her, in a "hopelessly useless" effort. Ickes, in his view "was the only redeeming feature in this blundering, corrupt, communist, racketeering New Deal administration, that has wrecked the nation and robbed us of our rights, our liberties, our national resources, and let the Japs defeat us." Thus, I noted on his letter, did a magnificent conservationist react to his "real grievance against the New Deal"—that its forcing down of interest rates had "enabled corporations to issue bonds for the re-financing of 7% preferred stocks (inherited by him) thereby cutting in half the thousands of dollars per year that he devoted to conservation." Mrs. Edge commented, "He would faint if he knew what I spent on telegrams yesterday."

Ickes was left where he was, I told Mrs. Edge a week later, chiefly "because he was unwilling to give up Interior and because of his argument that he could not take on two new and difficult jobs at once. Your telegram and others which no doubt arrived certainly did not hamper that result. One of F.D.R.'s secretaries told me that he would be sure that it reached him promptly."

In a postscript to my letter of September 2 to Van Name, I had said that Porcupine Mountain prospects were not very good, owing to the congressional zeal for economy. There might be some chance to get the national-monument authorization through by itself, with some special provision for matching gifts. By this time the Bureau of the Budget had turned down the National Park Service's plan for purchase through an RFC loan. Not even Roosevelt's expressed interest could overcome the speculative uncertainties of a sixty-year amortization based on automobile entrance fees and the profits of unbuilt hotels and filling stations.

Congressman Hook had been beaten for re-election (he made a comeback later), but his successor, Representative John B. Bennett, was equally ardent for preservation of the scenic forest and made a broader and more practical approach to it. He enlisted the support of the two Michigan senators in alternative projects—establishment of a national monument, federally financed, or purchase of the scenic forest by the Michigan legislature for a state park. And the president was still active. On March 9, 1943, I wrote to Mrs. Edge that FDR had "made a move" to save Porcupine Mountain, with possibly a 50 percent chance of success. The move was not identified except as carrying out a "suggestion" made a year earlier. This links it to my January 14, 1942, letter to Ickes and my talk soon after with the president. On the carbon of the Ickes letter, I noted: "I asked F.D.R. to talk with a General Motors executive (Knudsen) about this." He did so, the note added, but Knudsen replied that such a gift would be a "dissipation" of the company's property. Their discussion of it actually went on, intermittently, for weeks. Knudsen's solicitude for the company was touching indeed. Such a gift, chargeable to goodwill advertising, would not have opened more than a pinhole in the corporation's swollen war profits.

With emphasis shifting toward purchase by the Michigan legislature, I sought to promote interest in the northern tier of states by a two-page spread in the *Chicago Sun*. Raymond Dick furnished the illustrations—one a fine clear photograph looking across Lake of the Clouds to the heavily forested mountain panorama beyond it, another showing an outstanding group of tall hardwoods. The article was given wide distribution.

To further the Michigan purchase, NPS director Drury on November 9, 1943, provided Secretary Ickes with a final report on projected boundaries, worked out jointly by the National Park Service, the Forest Service, and representatives of the state of Michigan. They found 72,315 acres necessary "for the effective protection and administration of the superlative hardwood-hemlock exhibit." Concerning plans for acquisition, Drury reported that in August Representative Bennett had consulted with Governor Kelly and other Michigan people and thought the state might appropriate funds for land acquisition. Drury had agreed to meet with Director Hoffmaster of the Michigan Department of Conservation and Regional Forester Price of the Forest Service to discuss land values, a boundary, and the details of a possible state land acquisition program.

Those details had been worked out, said Drury, and he was ready to draft letters from Ickes to Representative Bennett and Senator Ferguson explaining the recommended areas and providing other helpful information. Secretary Ickes completed the shifting of the project from nation to state, and the state legislature provided the money. The last large stand of virgin North American hardwoods was saved, and Michigan obtained the most magnificent state park in the United States.

Although the efforts to save Porcupine Mountain through congressional action had failed, the work in that direction by President Roosevelt, Secretary Ickes, and the Michigan congressmen was decisive in arousing the people of Michigan and the legislature to the pitch of determination that resulted in triumph.

Grand Tetons and the Snake River, ca. 1942 (photograph by Ansel Adams, courtesy the Ansel Adams Publishing Rights Trust. All rights reserved).

CHAPTER FIFTEEN

JACKSON HOLE
NATIONAL MONUMENT

When I testified at a hearing in Washington, D.C., on February 1, 1930, in support of a southward extension of Yellowstone National Park, the region involved had various claims to fame. It lay within historically famous Jackson Hole, a broad valley of four hundred square miles flanking the eastern base of the Teton Mountains, from Jackson Lake on south beyond the little town of Jackson, Wyoming. The northerly part of this valley provided grazing for that portion of the great Yellowstone elk herd that migrated southward in the winter. A large part of Jackson Hole lay within the boundaries of the Teton National Forest, and nearly all of the land within the national forest was owned by the federal government.

In 1930, opposition to inclusion of the elk rangeland in Yellowstone Park came primarily from the Forest Service, which argued that sometime in the future thirty thousand acres of unmarketable lodgepole pine might acquire commercial value. Allied with the Forest Service were livestock grazers whose herds competed with the elk, big-game hunters, and dude ranchers who feared national-park competition.

Prevailing local sentiment some years in the past had been strongly protectionist. In 1923 the Yellowstone superintendent was invited to meet with Jackson citizens who urged that the government buy up private land in the northern part of Jackson Hole, to be added to the park for protection of the elk. In 1926 John D. Rockefeller, Jr., visited the area and was encouraged to make purchases for the same purpose. He conferred in the following year with state officials, with the Wyoming delegation in Congress, with President Coolidge, and with Secretary of the Interior Hubert Work. All of them urged him to proceed. President Coolidge withdrew the involved national-forest lands from public entry, to prevent commercial encroachment.

In 1928 Mr. Rockefeller began his purchases and speedily completed them, buying 32,117 acres in the low land near the Snake River, at a cost of $1,400,310.04. This land he duly offered as a gift to the nation. In 1929 Congress created the Grand Teton National Park, but avoided controversy with the Forest Service and local dissidents by confining the park strictly to the mountains. Not even enough foreground was taken in to provide a view of the Tetons from the park itself. In that same year Secretary of the Interior Ray Lyman Wilbur visited Jackson Hole and approved plans presented by the citizenry to preserve a representative portion of the region by federal action. President Hoover endorsed the project.

The following year, Mr. Hoover's commission on Yellowstone boundaries held its abortive hearing at which I testified, and the Senate Select Committee on Wild-life Resources made a trip to Jackson Hole. The Senate committee approved boundaries for elk protection drawn up by a citizens' group. The area thus marked for preservation contained something like a quarter of a million acres—more than twice the acreage of the Teton park.

In 1933 the Senate public lands committee, stimulated by Senator Robert Carey of Wyoming, visited Jackson Hole, and in the following year the Senate passed Senator Carey's bill adding to the park the Rockefeller area and surrounding national-forest lands. The House committee reported the bill favorably on the last day of the session.

The House report, however, included an amendment asked for by the Bureau of the Budget, striking out a clause reimbursing Teton County for taxes that would be lost through acceptance of the Rockefeller gift. On that issue the project remained stymied for the next nine years while all the local forces of politics and propaganda were at work against protection of the disputed area.

During those years the people of Teton County came to look upon Mr. Rockefeller in a new light. He was their largest and by far their richest taxpayer, furnishing more than nine thousand dollars out of their total county budget of forty-two thousand. They would not let him go. But after paying taxes for fifteen years, the nation's number one public benefactor informed President Roosevelt that he no longer felt justified in keeping up his investment. Such was the situation when on March 15, 1943, President Franklin Roosevelt signed an executive order proclaiming the establishment of the Jackson Hole National Monument.

The 222,929 acres thus converted into a national monument under the Antiquities Act of 1906 contained 173,065 acres of federally owned national forest, Rockefeller's slightly increased gift of 33,560 acres, 14,937 acres of other private land, and 1,367 acres of state school lands. Few people, aside from Secretary Ickes and Park Service personnel, knew that this action was to be taken. It struck the general community like a bolt of lightning. Governor Hunt of Wyoming wrote to the president that the local people "strenuously objected" to his proclamation, as did all of the people of Wyoming and its delegates to Congress. "A fundamental principle of democracy" had been violated, he claimed, by dispossessing American citizens of their homes.

The president of the Wyoming Stock Growers Association cried out, "The order virtually destroys a county, a town, and the hard-won homesteads of as fine a little mountain community as our nation owns. . . . All this in the name of idealistic democracy." Not surprisingly, opponents of the monument cast the onus of its creation upon the usual *bête noire*, and state senator Dexter Farr of Utah wrote to the president, "I feel sure you have been listening to the fanciful wiles and wishes of your Secretary of the Interior." That same thought was put in type in a three-page publication issued by the Jackson Hole Citizens Committee, a group without an address or named officers. They claimed that "Ickes wants to control the trade highways, cattle crossings, elk migrations, water shed and mineral resources," which would result in an "ejection of all settlers."

All this was wild exaggeration. The town of Jackson, Wyoming, was in the Teton National Forest. Private land within a national forest, a national park, or a national monument is still private land and retains all pre-existing private rights that do not interfere with the administration of public property. The one genuine impending loss to the people of Teton County was about nine thousand dollars a year of Rockefeller tax money, and that was sure to be made up by the growth of the tourist trade.

However, the revolt was on. Utah senator Farr's protest to the president climaxed with a plea: "I beg of you to undo this rash act." It was a plea based on a fallacy: that a presidential action, legislative in nature, authorized by an act of Congress, can be undone by the president without the sanction of a law. However, Wyoming's lone member of the House of Representatives had a more practical idea. "Scarce was the ink dry on the presidential edict," as the citizens' committee broadside phrased it, "before Congressman Frank A. Barrett of Wyoming had introduced . . . a bill abolishing the newly-created national monument." Wyoming's Senator Joseph O'Mahoney, who was friendly to national parks except in Wyoming, protected his political future by joining in the hue and cry, saying it was "an attempt to do by executive act that which the National Legislature repeatedly declined to do."

In reality President Roosevelt had taken an action in exact accord with the law—also in accord with the principle he asked me to embody in his undelivered speech at the dedication of Kings Canyon National Park, that all public land belonged to all the people.

When the proclamation was made public, the National Park Service put out a two-thousand-word news release emphasizing the blend of historic interest in Jackson Hole as an early-day trapping center, its value as a sanctuary for elk, moose, white-tailed deer, beaver, and other depleted wild animals, and its scenic beauty in relation to the magnificent Teton mountain range. To offset the previously "insurmountable obstacle" of the loss of school taxes through nationalization of the Rockefeller property, the NPS pointed out that thanks to acts of Congress passed in 1936 and 1940, the state of Wyoming was drawing $150,000 a year from the receipts of Yellowstone Park.

But recognizing the seriousness of that immediate loss, I wrote an editorial in the *Chicago Sun* of June 17, 1943. The attempt to overturn the president's action, I said, represented the combined efforts of those interested in school taxes, of cattlemen who were illegally grazing their stock in the national forest without permits, and of dude ranchers who thought national parks were bad for the tourist trade. Such shortsightedness, I wrote, was incredible, for tourists were spending $2.5 million a year in Yellowstone and Teton national parks and huge sums outside. But the county was poor and suffered from the change; the simple answer was in a pending bill that would allocate a portion of national-park receipts to counties to cover tax loss.

Although the initial furor died down, it was evident that the Wyoming delegation was determined to press for passage of the Barrett bill—its author moved by lopsided devotion to local interests, and the two senators out of motives of self-protection. Along with this there was an upsurge of the state-rights doctrine in a new or revived form—the notion that all lands and natural resources within a state (including wildlife) originally fell within the domain of state sovereignty and that federal authority in those fields represented an unconstitutional seizure of power.

Along that line *Conservation News*, the organ of the National Wildlife Federation, gave top position in its issue of March 1, 1944, to an article headed "Wildlife Belongs to the Individual State." Its editor, Carl D. Shoemaker, a good conservationist in spite of gun and ammunition affiliations, argued the case in legal terms. A state owned the wild animals in it for the benefit of all its citizens, and regulated hunting. The federal government could engage in conservation programs only on federal land or for "the general welfare."

The argument that wildlife belongs to the individual state, I wrote to Shoemaker (a personal friend), was based in part upon an assertion so completely at variance with historical facts that I begged leave for space to correct it. My letter quoted a paragraph he had written about the nonexistence of the national domain in 1787, when the Constitution was drafted, and rebutted it. The concept of public domain dated to 1776, when the Maryland legislature adopted a resolution that all the "back lands" should be "a common stock." Other states fell into line, ceding their western lands to the federal government.

Quoting resolutions in the Continental Congress on the acceptance of such transfers, I wrote: "Without considering the extent to which federal authority over wildlife on the public domain might . . . be held to extend, I find it hard to imagine an earlier or broader base for the authority now exercised by Congress and approved by the courts."

Cessions of state lands into the public domain were steered through the Continental Congress by James Madison of Virginia. At the time I wrote to Shoemaker, I had not yet discovered Madison's reply to Governor Edward Coles of Illinois, who wrote that various people in that new state were claiming that the public lands within the state rightly belonged to the state. (That was essentially the argument of the *Conservation News*.) Madison replied on June 28, 1831, that he had always viewed such a claim "as so unfair and unjust; so contrary to the certain and notorious [i.e., well known] intentions of the parties to the case and so directly in the teeth of the conditions on which the lands were ceded to the Union, that if a technical title could be made out by the claimants it ought in conscience and honor to be waived." So it seems that as early as 1831, people had forgotten the most agitating cause of domestic strife in 1782, which was the thought that if the vacant western lands belonged to individual states, the landed states could sell off the lands instead of levying taxes, and thus siphon away taxpaying citizens from the landless states. That fear produced the national public domain four years before the Constitution of 1787 was written, but the fallacy of 1831 was being repeated in 1944.

On March 28, the House Committee on the Public Lands made a report on the Barrett bill to abolish the national monument, recommending that it "do pass." The brief report said that because of Mr. Rockefeller's ownership of 33,800 acres (lately increased) the gift of his land would take away one-third of the entire tax base of Teton County. This meant that other property owners would have to pay that much more, or some of the county's six schools would close. As another drawback, permits for grazing within the monument would be continued only during the lifetime of the permittees and the lifetime of their heirs. Also it was essential that ten thousand cattle and horses be trailed yearly across the monument area to reach summer grazing territory in the mountains. The monument spelled destruction, and "In destroying the cattle business of the country [i.e., region], all other business will suffer in proportion."

The House committee report also included the contrary views of Harold Ickes. He surveyed the place of Jackson Hole in American history, its geologic significance, its scenic value as the forefront of the Teton range, and its use as the winter range of the Yellowstone elk. Private rights, Ickes said, would be undisturbed. He repeated the guarantees of livestock transit, grazing permits, and summer-home leases and the payment to Wyoming of $150,000 a year out of Yellowstone Park receipts. Teton County would get part of this, to offset the $10,000 loss of Rockefeller taxes.

Seven members of the House lands committee submitted a minority report signed by its new chairman, Representative J. Hardin Peterson of Florida. Although he believed it was better to establish boundaries by act of Congress rather than by executive order, wrote Peterson, "yet every President

249

beginning with President Theodore Roosevelt . . . established monuments by Executive order and many of them with far greater areas than this one."

The matter should be set at rest, the dissenters said, "and the passage of this bill does not accomplish this purpose." If it should become law, the president could immediately establish another monument with slightly different boundaries. But chairman Peterson argued further that the area deserved protection because "the Grand Teton Mountains and the adjacent scenery constitute one of the greatest scenic spots in the world." A portion of the land in the monument, Peterson went on, should be placed within the national park, a portion should protect the elk range, and a portion should be "definitely by law set apart as a driveway to be allowed for the drifting and grazing of cattle from one range to another [while] some portion of it should be taken out of the monument." Studies with this in view were being made, and "Every effort should be made to work this matter out on a reasonable basis, fixing the boundaries by law."

There was only one conceivable reason why this rational approach could not and did not prevail—it would not protect Congressman Barrett and the two senators from the anti-park hysteria they had helped to stir up. As a supplement to his minority report against the Barrett bill, Peterson took the floor in the House of Representatives on June 7 to describe a trip he made to Jackson Hole after the hearings closed. In talking with Jackson Hole residents he found only one serious objection to creation of the monument: it would cause Teton County to lose about ten thousand dollars a year in taxes on the Rockefeller property. That situation should be rectified and it was "up to Congress to rectify it," he said, referring to the bill that would apportion some national-park receipts to counties. (That was precisely what I had advocated in my *Chicago Sun* editorial a year earlier.)

To justify his statement that opposition to the monument was by no means unanimous, Peterson placed in his speech a letter strongly supporting the park, signed by eight long-time businessmen of Jackson. They supplemented their letter with an eight-point signed argument in support of the monument. The two papers bore the additional signatures of ninety-six endorsers. Peterson was told, personally and in an additional letter, "that many other people in Jackson Hole would support the monument openly if they dared."

The businessmen declared their support of the grazing industry but said they believed the economic future of Jackson lay in tourist appeal. They had seen it grow in fifteen years from a small cattle town into a thriving community with many activities for the tourists attracted by park publicity. But, said these businessmen, unless Jackson Hole was protected as a part of the national-park system, "these crowds of visitors and those trying to make money from them will, in short order, spoil the country." This spoilage was beginning to happen at Jenny and Leigh lakes and on the Teton peaks, where it was checked by creation of the national park; checked also by Rockefeller's purchase of the privately owned lands in the north part of the valley. Protected by national-park administration, and differing greatly from Yellowstone, Jackson Hole could take care of the increased tourist travel without damage to the community. "We earnestly urge you not to undo the Jackson Hole National Monument, but, if it needs bettering in any way, that you strengthen and perfect it by legislation."

Congressman Jack Cochran of Missouri, a strong defender of national parks, took the floor two days after Peterson spoke. As a member of the House Committee on Wildlife Conservation, he was naturally interested in the effect of the Barrett bill if it set a precedent. Eighty-two national monuments had been established by executive order since the passage of the Antiquities Act in 1906, and this was the first time any such action had been challenged in Congress.

On that account he had asked the Department of the Interior to prepare a fact sheet on past presidential actions under that law. This the department had done in the form of answers to a series of questions. Cochran was given

Grand Tetons (photograph by Marc Gaede, courtesy the photographer).

permission to include the fact sheet as part of his remarks. In effect, it constituted his speech. "What is Jackson Hole National Monument?" The answer gave its size and location, its public and private acreage, and the relationship to it of the Rockefeller tract. In answer to the next question, the statement quoted the Antiquities Act, authorizing the president to set aside as national monuments "objects of historic or scientific interest."

The answer to the third question, "Why was Jackson Hole National Monument established?" put the president's action in line with the purposes defined by Congress in its supplemental act of August 25, 1916, on national monuments: "To conserve the scenery and the natural and historic objects and the wildlife therein and to provide for the enjoyment of the same in such manner and by such means as will leave them unimpaired for the enjoyment of future generations."

The next question was a blockbuster for one side or the other: "Was the creation of Jackson Hole National Monument in accordance with established precedent?" This took account of a rising move to repeal the Antiquities Act. President Roosevelt, opponents were saying, had perverted a law that was passed to protect Indian cliff houses. The act, opponents pointed out, required that the "parcels of land" so set aside be "the smallest area compatible" with the care of the protected object. The purpose, it was said in Wyoming and Washington, was to provide a place in which to tie visitors' horses (or to park automobiles). Now Roosevelt, flouting law and precedent, had set aside 222,000 acres. Congressman Cochran named the largest single national monuments set up by various presidents under the restrictive wording of the 1906 law:

President Theodore Roosevelt,
   Grand Canyon National Monument, 806,400 acres;
President Woodrow Wilson,
   Katmai National Monument, 1,087,990 acres;
President Calvin Coolidge,
   Glacier Bay National Monument, 1,164,000 acres;
President Herbert Hoover,
   Death Valley National Monument, 1,601,800 acres;
President Franklin Roosevelt,
   Joshua Tree National Monument, 838,258 acres.

In answer to a question whether the Supreme Court had ever passed upon the president's authority in this field, Cochran quoted the court's dismissal of a case challenging Theodore Roosevelt's establishment of the Grand Canyon monument: "The act under which the President proceeded empowered him to establish reserves embracing 'objects of historic or scientific interest.' The Grand Canyon, as stated in his proclamation, 'is an object of unusual scientific interest.'" No problem had been found in the monument's size.

Congressman Cochran's statement gave abundant proof that Franklin Roosevelt's creation of the Jackson Hole National Monument was in accord with the Antiquities Act as applied consistently by five preceding presidents and construed by the Supreme Court. But no testimony had come from the author of the 1906 law, Representative John F. Lacey, whose eminence in his day as a conservationist was as great as that of his close co-worker Theodore Roosevelt. During a visit to Iowa City in the summer of 1944, I examined Major Lacey's papers in the library of the Iowa State Historical Society. My findings were reported to Senator Guy M. Gillette of Iowa on my return to Washington in September. I wrote to him that much of the confusion about the Antiquities Act resulted from an unclear record of congressional intent, which brought into question how broadly it could be interpreted.

In those papers was an article written by Lacey entitled "The Pajarito—An Outing with the Archeologists." It was this trip in 1902, he said, which led him to introduce his bill "for the preservation of aboriginal ruins and places of scenic and scientific interest," under which the Petrified Forest, the Olympic elk reserve, and many ethnological sites had since been designated national monuments.

The library's collection also included, in its *John F. Lacey Memorial Volume*, a letter of July 16, 1906, from President Theodore Roosevelt to Lacey, congratulating him upon passage of the bill which TR had signed five weeks earlier. "Certain gentlemen interested in the preservation of the forests of this country and . . . in the preservation of the wild-life of the country, and the objects of natural and historic interest which should be kept unharmed for the sake of those who come after us, have written to me expressing their deep sense of obligation to you." The president endorsed their project of a Lacey memorial "so that their sense of appreciation may be put in permanent form."

In such terms the Antiquities Act was discussed by the signer of it after he brought it into law, and by the author of it shortly after the earliest national monuments were created. Did they treat it as a law limited to cliff dwellings, etc., plus space for a dozen hitching posts and a horseless carriage? Theodore Roosevelt spoke of national monuments for preservation of forests and wildlife and "objects of natural and historic interest"; Lacey called it his bill for the preservation of "places of scenic and scientific interest."

The two largest monuments proclaimed by Theodore Roosevelt—Mount Olympus National Monument and Grand Canyon National Monument—had a combined area of exactly 1,440,000 acres. Each of them, I told Gillette, complied with the restrictive requirement of the Antiquities Act that they be confined "to the smallest area compatible with the proper care and management of the objects to be protected." In the test case challenging the larger of the two, the Supreme Court specifically held that its establishment was in conformity with the act.

Senator Gillette wrote to me on September 20 that the information on Lacey was "so pertinent and so helpful" that he had ordered it printed in the

Congressional Record.

Conrad Wirth, National Park Service chief of lands, made this comment: "Undoubtedly you have presented the most compelling declaration of historic facts that we could have to clear away the serious misunderstanding which for a long time has been clouding the truth as to the origin and use of that Act." He asked me to find out the cost of printing three thousand copies of the letter to be distributed under Senator Gillette's frank. He thought the money could be raised from various individuals, as was done with the statements by congressmen Peterson and Cochran. The reprints were made, from the *Congressional Record* of September 8, 1944, and Senator Gillette furnished the franked envelopes.

On December 11, the Barrett bill easily passed the House of Representatives, 187 to 107. I wrote at once (December 12) to Senator Carl Hatch of New Mexico, chairman of the Senate Committee on Public Lands, saying that it would be extremely unfortunate if this bill came up in the Senate, in the few remaining days of the session, "as a hangover from the Republican presidential campaign," in which the repeal movement was used "for outrageously false charges against President Roosevelt, and for the spread of a no less false impression regarding the history and original purpose of the law under which the monument was created." If the bill was to be considered, I requested that public hearings be held and that I be permitted to testify against it.

The Senate committee ordered hearings held, but allowed so little time that the only witnesses—in the order of their appearance—were Secretary Ickes, myself, NPS director Newton Drury, and Harlean James and Horace Albright of the American Planning and Civic Association. All spoke against the bill. I testified for the Emergency Conservation Committee, and broadened my statement with facts which I dug up from public records after writing to Senator Gillette. I have no record of my testimony, but the new disclosure was that Lacey's insertion of the words "objects of historical or scientific interest" in his Antiquities bill was intended to achieve the purposes of three other bills sponsored by him.

One Lacey bill was to create a Petrified Forest national park. A second was to create the Mount Olympic Range Elk Reserve. A third was to authorize the president, at his discretion, to establish national parks on the public domain by proclamation. All of these objectives were achieved, in substance, by giving the president power to create national monuments for the preservation of objects of "scientific interest." Would the bill have passed if such a multiple intent had been avowed? Certainly not, since a single objection would have killed it in the Senate. But the bill's author had the broader purpose in mind, the president had it in mind, and the Supreme Court held it to be within the ordinary meaning of the words employed.

At the hearing on the Barrett bill to abolish the monument, Albright made a fine exposition of the facts concerning John D. Rockefeller's acquisition of lands for the public and concerning the adverse machinations in Jackson Hole. The Senate committee, if free of outside pressure, would probably have sustained the president. However, I told Mrs. Edge on December 16, the committee "reported the Barrett bill favorably this afternoon, nine to four." They did this "partly to help [Senator] O'Mahoney politically," partly in support of stockmen. I overconfidently predicted that since Senator Hatch, chairman of the committee, was opposed and the bill could come up only by unanimous consent, there seemed no chance of its passage "unless a bad slip occurs." If the bill was beaten, there would probably be an attempt to work out a satisfactory solution to the county tax problem and to put a bill through Congress making the monument part of the Teton park.

Two days after that was written, the Senate passed the Barrett bill, not through some "bad slip" by its opponents, but by some very slippery work by its supporters. This occurred, I wrote to Mrs. Edge, "only fifteen minutes after one of the leading members of the Senate told me that it would not be allowed to come to a vote. The supporters of it made the false statement that Secretary Ickes had withdrawn his opposition to it and was willing to let it go to the President, to be vetoed by him."

"All that Ickes did," I said, "was release two Senators [Hatch and Gerald P. Nye of North Dakota] from a promise to object to it, because of the pressure to which they were being subjected from their home states." Both Ickes and Hatch asked me to get somebody else to object. I did so, obtaining the promise of Senator Guffey of Pennsylvania, while Demaray of the Park Service was given a similar promise by Senator Byrd of Virginia. However, "A garbled account of what Ickes said was used to prevent the objections from being made."

I had no doubt that Roosevelt would veto the bill. Ordinarily when legislation was sent him by Congress he had ten days to sign it, veto it, or let it become law without his signature. But since Congress had adjourned *sine die* a few minutes after passing the Barrett bill, a different course was open to him. He could kill the bill by a pocket veto, simply by not signing it within the time limit, but that would not prevent him from sending a rejection statement to the next Congress.

Having a decided preference about the method, I wrote a letter to FDR on December 22 and handed it to him at the close of that day's press conference, saying that I hoped he would reject the bill. He replied instantly, "I'm going to," and then, contrary to custom, read my letter at once. I recounted in it that the bill had passed because of an erroneous—even false—report that Ickes had withdrawn his opposition. I hoped, I said, that he would not only veto the bill but would issue a statement "to counteract the vicious propaganda that has been circulated over the country."

My letter then turned to the political bearing of the drive against the monument, which had been part of a "recklessly false and vicious political attack by western Republicans" on what they called the "dictatorial propensities" of FDR.

My final paragraph summarized the study I had made of the origin and purposes of the Antiquities Act. On reading this, Mr. Roosevelt asked me to prepare a statement on that subject for inclusion in his veto message, first talking it over with Judge Rosenman, his speech writer and legal adviser. This I did. When I delivered the paragraph to the White House on December 26, Steve Early told me that the president had that day received a three-page letter from Senator O'Mahoney, urging him to sign the bill. He said nothing about FDR's reaction to it. What I wrote became the second paragraph of Roosevelt's "veto memorandum" (called that because the bill was dead) of December 29, 1944. Following my draft, it recounted presidential precedents in establishing national monuments and the upholding by the Supreme Court of the Antiquities Act, and then stated the president's conviction that Jackson Hole was an "object of historic or scientific interest" within the meaning of that act. Therefore, he said, creation of the monument was lawful.

In other portions of his veto memorandum, presumably written by Judge Rosenman and Interior officials, President Roosevelt pointed out that private and state lands within the monument were not affected in any way by its creation: "The rights of the owners are the same as they were before the proclamation was issued." The private lands were still subject to taxation by the state and county. Grazing permits issued by the Forest Service would be honored during the lifetime of the present holders and the members of their immediate families.

The president recognized the seriousness of the tax problem in Teton County if lands "acquired by private interests for ultimate incorporation in the monument" were removed from the tax rolls before offsetting county revenues had been built up through development of the tourist industry. "I would be sympathetic to the enactment of legislation whereby revenues derived by the Federal Government from the national park and monument system could be used to offset, on an equitable basis, any loss of taxes due to the Federal acquisition." Also, he would like to see administrative policy for such things as grazing rights written into law.

On New Year's Day, 1945, at the request of Secretary Ickes, I drafted a letter from him to John D. Rockefeller, Jr., to assure him that, with conservation organizations alerted and the real facts known, no new bill like Barrett's would go through Congress in future. The letter cited the president's desire for legislation to relieve Teton County of tax losses caused by the transfer of private lands to government ownership—meaning, of course, "those acquired by you for the purpose of a gift to the nation." I went on, "I believe . . . an early transfer of your lands to the United States is the most certain method of securing the protection of the Teton County tax structure which all parties desire. It is the surest, indeed the only, way of preventing the delay that would be caused by resumption of bitter opposition." As long as these lands were privately owned, one faction would demand postponement of acceptance until the tax question was settled, another faction would try to delay a tax solution in order to block the gift completely.

With the monument established and the Barrett bill defeated, the Ickes letter concluded, "You can make a transfer of title without taking part in the later adjustments, and with a knowledge that they will be hastened and made easier. Indeed, it seems probable that if your planned gift is completed before the extremist opposition gets into organized action again, there will not only be prompt and satisfactory tax relief for Teton County, but . . . a systematic plan for sharing revenues will be adopted covering the entire national park and monument system." My draft closed "with deep appreciation of your public spirit and matchless patience."

Early in February, after being tied up writing a series of editorials for the New York newspaper *PM*, I had a long talk with House lands committee chairman Peterson about the situation in the new 79th Congress. Barrett had stirred considerable speculation by failing, so far, to re-introduce his Jackson Hole repeal bill. Peterson doubted that Barrett, at heart, was strongly against the monument. His bill would get decidedly less support in the House than it had in 1944, although it would pass the committee again if pushed.

Congressman James O'Connor of Montana had introduced a bill to repeal the Antiquities Act, but that hazard virtually disappeared when O'Connor suddenly died. And Peterson thought there was a good chance to get the Teton County tax-relief bill out of committee.

This information I passed along at once to Rockefeller, in a letter of February 12. I told him that everybody with whom I had talked about the abolition bill said there was "no possibility whatever of its being enacted into law, over a veto." There was also "no chance whatsoever of the President signing a bill to abolish [the monument]." I told of my talks with Roosevelt on that subject and added, "His feeling toward those who have combined political chicanery and selfishness in Jackson Hole is like that of the elephant who has been fed a quid of tobacco, and he won't forget. There seems no reason to question the permanence of the monument."

I quoted chairman Peterson's statement to me that the tax-relief bill for Teton County was certain to pass if the Wyoming delegation pushed for it and that all he feared was a long period of inaction in Congress, which might cause a resumption of heavy pressure from Wyoming upon the delegation from that state. Opponents would lose in a renewed fight, but it might cause a year or two of delay. Peterson had advised that if Rockefeller would accept the veto as final and transfer the lands immediately, perhaps including "a reversion clause, for your own protection," the Wyoming delegation would then press for passage of the tax-compensation bill. The Wyoming delegation, I wrote in conclusion, was in a difficult situation. Only Senator Robertson was opposed. Barrett was indifferent and O'Mahoney was for the monument at heart, but politically they were not free agents.

Rockefeller's conservation director, Kenneth Chorley, replied in a few days. My report was cheering, but Mr. Rockefeller still felt reluctant to transfer the lands as long as there was any possibility of their being diverted from national-monument status.

President Roosevelt's veto of the Barrett bill intensified the Wyoming activity on both sides, but in particular it led to a new move by the defending forces. The Izaak Walton League, at its last national convention, had strongly endorsed creation of the monument. On March 1, 1945, thirty-six Jackson Hole residents applied to the national body for a local charter. It was promptly granted.

The declared purpose of this Jackson Hole chapter of the league was "to help preserve the wilderness character of Teton National Forest, Teton National Park, and the Jackson Hole National Monument. . . . We are in accord with the resolution adopted by the national Izaak Walton League of America giving support to the presidential proclamation creating the Jackson Hole National Monument." All applicants who subscribed to those principles would be accepted as charter members.

State president C. M. Simpson of Cheyenne announced that the charter would be presented at a banquet in the Wort Hotel in Jackson on March 23. (James and John Wort were among the organizers.) Two days before the banquet, opponents of the monument made a drive to capture the chapter. The *Jackson Hole Courier* of March 22 published parallel statements by the two sides. Acting chapter secretary Olaus Murie, the famous naturalist and a personal friend, wrote me that on the preceding day, a man flourishing a fistful of five-dollar bills handed him a list of twenty-two applicants for membership. Others telephoned during the day. All were told of the requirement to support the monument. None joined.

The opposition statement, denouncing that requirement, bore four signatures "representing eighty local residents." If one took that figure at its face value, it obviously represented the full strength of the opposition in the Jackson Hole community. Against it could be placed the hundred and six signatures of those who signed or wrote endorsements of the letter to chairman Peterson—plus the unknown number who would have signed if they had dared to do so.

Here was fairly clear proof that majority sentiment in the Jackson Hole region favored protective administration of lands and wildlife, while heavy pressure was being exerted by the other side. The sources of that pressure were clear enough. Statewide, it came from stockmen's organizations; locally, from the dominating influence of the Jackson Hole office of the Forest Service and the president of the Jackson bank, a former Forest Service official.

Nationally, the issue had been taken up, magnified, and distorted as a presidential campaign issue, both through ignorance and through the malevolence of the anti-Roosevelt press.

There was room for dispute concerning the division of local opinion, but one political fact could be put down as an absolute: there would be no interference with the national monument as long as Franklin Roosevelt remained in the White House.

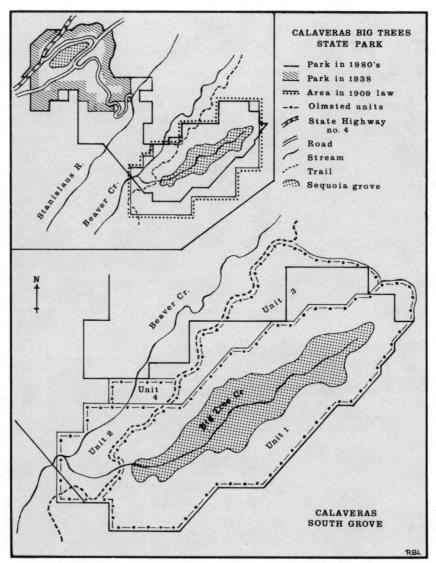

Calaveras Big Trees State Park

CHAPTER SIXTEEN

THE CALAVERAS GROVE
UNDER TWO PRESIDENTS

In May of 1941, with Kings Canyon National Park on the map and Porcupine Mountain on the tapis, I disregarded the old adage about too many irons in the fire and put another controversial project before the overloaded president and secretary of the interior. It was a California undertaking that needed federal support.

Calaveras County, in the Sierra Nevada above Stockton, contained two magnificent forests of giant sequoias, separated from each other by a deep rugged valley of indifferent-quality national forest. Congress in 1928 had passed an act authorizing the Forest Service, whenever California acquired either of these groves, to transfer twelve hundred acres of national-forest land to the state for a connecting highway. The Calaveras North Grove became a state park in 1931, but the transfer authorized in 1928 had not been made.

Adjoining the south Calaveras grove, along Beaver Creek, was the finest stand of sugar and ponderosa pines in the world. My proposal was that the United States should acquire the sugar pines by purchase or by exchange for national-forest stumpage, while the state of California should buy the south Calaveras sequoia grove, aided by the gift of the connecting federal corridor. Its value would help meet the requirement of California law that state-park purchase funds be matched from other sources.

Like virtually every project involving scenic forests, this one had been called to my attention by Dr. Van Name. I was able to write to him on May 12 that

President Roosevelt and Secretary Ickes both expressed keen interest in the proposal. He replied next day that my letter was the "best piece of news" he had had for a long time. Destruction of the grove would be a calamity, and if Ickes and the president would aid in its preservation, they would earn the gratitude of the people of today and of the future.

The south Calaveras sequoias and Beaver Creek pines were owned by the Pickering Lumber Company, which had been near bankruptcy at the depth of the Great Depression but was floating on a new tide of prosperity and zeal for profits. It was fighting hard against purchase by the state and was certain to be even more violently opposed to federal intervention, which would involve valuable sugar pines instead of sequoias almost worthless commercially. But the initiative lay with the state, and the state was slow to act.

The Pickering people told NPS director Newton Drury that their timber cutting was in a direction away from the scenic areas, which would remain untouched for four or five years. That allowed considerable time for effective planning and execution of plans. An effort by Dr. Van Name to enlist the support of the Save-the-Redwoods League brought a promise by its secretary, Aubrey Drury, in December 1941, to print a pamphlet Van Name had written, but the league dropped the project when war broke out. Van Name submitted the manuscript to me, for possible publication by the Emergency Conservation Committee. I suggested a rewriting of it to put emphasis on the 1928 act of Congress authorizing a gift of national-forest land to aid the state project. Then I rewrote the pamphlet at Van Name's request. Urging Mrs. Edge to bring the ECC into action, I said that I supposed the Forest Service would try to sabotage the program, "but if they do, it will reveal them to the people of California in a new light." Although the pamphlet was a joint product and Van Name furnished the fine illustrations, he insisted that I alone be named as author. Fourteen thousand copies of the twelve-page pamphlet, *Protect the South Calaveras Sequoia Grove*, came off the press in June 1942.

"Once more," I wrote, "it is necessary to call upon Americans to stop despoliation from within, even while we are battling the destroyer from without." This time it was the south Calaveras grove that was menaced, for the loggers were moving relentlessly toward it and the protected North Grove. Though but four miles apart, the two groves were connected only by a circuitous trail many times that long.

All of the lands desired for acquisition lay in the valleys or on the intervening ridges of three more-or-less parallel stream beds running southwest through the Stanislaus National Forest: the scenic gorge of the North Fork of the Stanislaus River; its large tributary Beaver Creek, with slopes of magnificent sugar and ponderosa pines; and, angling south of Beaver Creek, its tributary, little Big Tree Creek, site of the south Calaveras sequoia grove. Adjoining this area, the federal government owned thousands of acres of merchantable timber which could be exchanged for the scenic lands whose preservation was desired. The plan of acquisition was that a law be passed directing the

Forest Service to exchange standing national-forest timber for private lands needed for the park. When half of these lands were given by the federal government to the state, then California could legally use state-park funds to buy the other half. Quick action was required.

The pamphlet quoted a statistical survey of the South Grove sequoias made by the Forest Service in 1924:

DIAMETERS

Sequoias 16 feet or more in diameter 6 feet above the ground	37
12 feet or more but less than 16 feet	182
10 feet or more but less than 12 feet	133
less than 10 feet in diameter	595

HEIGHTS

Sequoias 300 to 320 feet tall	7
250 to 295 feet tall	263
200 to 248 feet tall	321
less than 200 feet tall	356
Total number of sequoias exclusive of young reproduction	947

Saving the South Grove, my pamphlet emphasized, was only part of the problem. Northward of the grove, the wild and picturesque gorge of the Stanislaus River, combined with the sugar pines and ponderosa pines of the Beaver Creek valley, slopes, and ridges, presented scenic views worthy of any national park. Here these species reached their finest development, with sugar pines 7 to 8 feet in diameter and 210 to 230 feet tall. Their massive cylindrical trunks stretched up into spreading crowns which bore immense elongated cones.

The only comparable stand of these two species of pine, lying forty miles to the south, had been lumbered and destroyed many years earlier, except for the small Carl Inn Grove preserved in Yosemite Park. Destruction of the wonderful Beaver Creek area might soon begin and would be "an irretrievable misfortune and disgrace to our present generation, and a just cause of indignation and reproach to all who come after us."

California, I repeated, had already done the larger part of its share by acquiring and preserving the north Calaveras grove. Congress had cooperated by authorizing a gift to California of twelve hundred acres of national-forest land whenever either of these groves should become a state park. California had fulfilled its obligation but the federal government had never completed the gift. The beautiful gorge of the Stanislaus was already in public ownership, as part of the national forest. The main problem was to buy the sequoia grove itself and the adjoining scenic stands of sugar and ponderosa pine needed to complete the proposed park. Congress and the state of California, acting together through the use of state funds and federal timber exchange, could save the trees.

In the late fall of 1942, after returning to Washington from three months of editorial work in Chicago, I arranged to meet with Forest Service officials to discuss the Calaveras situation. The office of chief forester was vacant. I met with L. F. Kneipp, head of land acquisition, and Edward Kotok, the FS liaison man on state parks. Kotok seemed friendly to the idea of state and federal cooperation, Kneipp not adamantly opposed to it. When I brought up the unfulfilled 1928 act of Congress, authorizing a gift of national-forest land to provide a connecting road between the two sequoia groves, Kneipp said that was out. The law contained a time limit and the limit had expired. Commenting on this some days later, I wondered whether the time limit actually had expired, but it never occurred to me that the whole statement might be false, as it ultimately turned out to be. There was no time limit whatsoever.

Kneipp did not utterly reject the idea of a timber exchange and gift but said there would be a difficult obstacle to it, namely (as I described the conversation to Mrs. Edge and Van Name) "that the timber available for exchange in California is committed to a program of trading to prevent clear-cutting of private stands." The lumber company would cut 50 percent of the stand on its holdings and trade the remainder of the timber and the land to the government in exchange for national-forest stumpage—which they would proceed to cut in the same way.

Kneipp said there was not enough national-forest timber available for more than a fifth of the laid-out program. "He seemed to think there was more chance of a straightout gift of national forest lands to the state, by act of Congress, to match the state's contribution for the purchase of the grove." He asked whether he should put the proposition up to the Forest Service, as coming from me, or whether California people should propose it first to Regional Forester Show. I preferred the latter method.

Van Name reacted to this information with a letter to Newton Drury, making so violent an attack on the Forest Service as a set of doublecrossers and stallers that the NPS director dared not answer it and thus force it into his files—a fact which I pointed out when Van Name sent me a copy with a complaint that Drury had made no reply. In that letter Van Name rightfully scoffed at the idea of a "commitment" that prevented cooperation through a timberland gift. Obviously, the Forest Service was committed only to its own desires. If that bureau blocked action, I thought, the alternative was to work for creation of a national monument.

When I mentioned this talk to Newton Drury, he told me that his brother Aubrey, secretary of the Save-the-Redwoods League, had planned to discuss Calaveras with Regional Forester Show. So I wrote to Aubrey, asking what Show's reaction was. I told him that I wanted to talk over various park matters with the new Forest Service chief, Lyle Watts, who had assumed that office on January 8, 1943.

In addition I described a talk with Congressman Englebright, whose district took in the two Calaveras groves. He was sympathetic toward preservation of the threatened areas but unwilling to introduce a bill on the subject unless it had Forest Service backing. My thought was that California people should urge the Forest Service to make a timber exchange. I felt sure that the California congressional delegation would get back of the proposal if it received strong support in that state.

Aubrey Drury wired me that Show was in Washington but he would talk with him on his return. Preservation of the South Grove, he said, had top priority in Save-the-Redwoods plans and he and the league "will aid all we can." Drury had his talk with Show and reported his reaction—a flat rejection of both proposals I had made: the first, that national-forest lands be used to make a timber trade to provide the outside contribution needed to match state funds in purchase of park lands; the second, that national-forest lands contiguous to the sequoia lands be used as a gift to the state for matching purposes. And, said Show, "I believe that this [refusal] is [according to] the policy of the present chief forester."

Although Secretary of Agriculture Wickard had many faults, it was to his credit that he made Lyle F. Watts head of the Forest Service. I had not met Watts at the time (March 31, 1943) when Regional Forester Show expressed belief that the new chief would oppose a Calaveras timber exchange. However, Watts's record as regional forester at Portland, after President Roosevelt forced Buck out of that office, indicated genuine friendliness toward the Olympic National Park and the park system in general. This did not mean, I commented to Mrs. Edge, that there would be an overnight change in Forest Service policies (the Silcox experience proved that), nor would it even ensure an ultimate change, but a friendly chief "is certainly better than an unfriendly one." It was my hope that the Calaveras project could be carried through "without necessitating a criticism of the F. S."

I had a long talk with Watts on April 24, 1943. He said that he had first heard of the Calaveras Grove question on the previous afternoon, as a preliminary to my visit. Watts said that as a matter of policy he was opposed to the use of national-forest stumpage for acquisition of land to be placed in either national- or state-park systems, because it was indirect financing of what should be financed directly. His attitude toward such use in the Calaveras area would depend on local conditions, which he would inquire into.

Watts told me that he did not share the antipathy felt by many Forest Service men for the national-park system; he had favored establishment of the Olympic National Park and wanted it to be a big one. He said that when the Jackson Hole National Monument was set up (five weeks before our talk) he had sent "airmail instructions to the Forest Service in Wyoming that it should do nothing to support protests against the action." As regional forester at Portland, he said, he had come to look upon lumbering devastation in the Northwest as a blot on the human race. In that office he had been engaged in making the timber trade that was designed to add the Bogachiel Valley private strip to the Olympic park, and had acquired more than half of its nine square miles for the government. I appraised Watts for Mrs. Edge, saying that I had formed a high opinion of the new chief forester. He was more friendly to parks than others in the FS, and I saw a chance for a far-reaching change in Forest Service policy since Watts did not have the commercial approach. He made the impression of a sensitive conservationist.

Summing up the situation for Aubrey Drury on May 3, 1943, I said it would be extremely helpful if Governor Warren of California, and Drury himself, would write to Watts and to Congressman Englebright asking what their attitude would be toward congressional enlargement of the federal grant of land authorized by the act of 1928, the new grant to be for matching purposes.

Or, I said, it might be possible to muster national support for a plan which I had submitted to Chief Forester Watts: introduce a bill in Congress to authorize a Calaveras National Monument, including the privately owned South Grove and an extensive national-forest area, all to be transferred to the state of California whenever the state should acquire the South Grove. Passage of such a law, I thought, would stimulate both state action and private gifts.

On May 11, 1943, I was surprised to receive the following May 10 "Memorandum for Irving Brant," signed FDR. "Since returning from my trip I have received a letter from the Secretary of the Interior, copy of which is herewith enclosed, in regard to the Calaveras Sequoi [sic] Grove. I hope you will take it up further with the Secretary."

The presidential papers reveal that this was the last of several memoranda on the subject. On April 10 the president had sent Ickes a copy of my unsigned pamphlet of June 1942, calling for protection of the south Calaveras sequoia grove and Beaver Creek sugar pines, with this accompanying note: "Are we doing anything about this Calaveras Sequoi Grove? If not, can we?" Ickes' April 30 reply told of a ten-year effort by the Park Service (which no doubt drafted the Ickes letter) to work out a protective system for the area. The North Grove of 1,951 acres had been made a state park and it was Ickes' judgment that the South Grove of 1,500 acres should be protected in the same manner. To help this along, the federal government could encourage the state to buy the lands, or the existing law which provided for a gift of certain lands to California could be amended, to make it "possible for the Federal Government to acquire the South Grove by exchange or purchase for transfer to the State when it is prepared to reimburse the Federal Government for the property."

Reporting these developments to Van Name, I said, "With the President taking an interest in the Calaveras Grove on his own initiative, I think we can assume that he will secure an affirmative attitude in the Washington office of the Forest Service." The key words were "on his own initiative"—this in the middle of a world war. Nothing could have more clearly demonstrated his personal involvement in the conservation cause.

I did spend fifteen minutes with FDR on May 11, but our talk was about foreign affairs and an interruption made it impossible to bring up the subject of Calaveras. Afterwards, pursuant to the president's written suggestion, I called on Ickes and outlined a plan for a bill authorizing creation of a national monument and also authorizing the transfer of public lands within the monument to the state of California, if it acquired the Calaveras South Grove for a state park. "Ickes thought it a good idea," I wrote to Van Name, "and likely to stimulate California action." But we agreed that it would be unwise to introduce such a bill while an attempt was being made to abolish the Jackson Hole National Monument.

A couple of days later the officers of the Woman's Conservation League of America, with headquarters in Milwaukee, wrote to ask how they could help to preserve the Calaveras big trees. But they could not approve a federal timber exchange. They spoke of being "anxious . . . to see this grove saved intact for posterity," but went on, "We feel that national timber should be maintained as a reservoir for future timber needs."

On that point I replied, "That is not the way it is administered in California. When I talked with Mr. Kneipp of the Forest Service about this timber exchange, his objection was that national forest timber in California is now being lumbered so extensively, and with such large future commitments, that it would be impossible to find any for exchange for the Calaveras Grove."

I described the system employed by the Forest Service in California: private loggers would buy and cut-over half of the government-owned timber in a national-forest area, then cut one-half of an equal stand on their own lands, after which the Forest Service would buy the half-cut private land and hold it for future cuttings. This meant that there was no preserving the forest uncut as a future reservoir. The choice as I saw it was between logging to acquire and preserve a scenic forest and logging to acquire a half-cut area that faced future logging. The desire of the women's group constituted, in fact, an argument for exchange.

Mrs. LaBudde, of the league, replied that my letter had "clarified the problem of the Calaveras Grove in California to some extent." But they still were opposed to timber exchange as a bad precedent, especially since "We have been told that this area is almost inaccessible and that it would be too expensive for the loggers to attempt to take out any trees for a long time to come." Told that by whom? Obviously by Jay H. Price, U. S. regional forester at Milwaukee, ousted by Roosevelt from California—the only person in Wisconsin who could put official position behind such a lulling misstatement.

My contact with the president and with the political situation in Washington was to be sporadic during the next year. Research material in the Library of Congress, concealed since war began, had been opened once more for public use. My wife and I could now resume intensive work on the Madison biography, but we decided to do so away from the city, relying on interlibrary loan for reference material. I resigned from the *Chicago Sun* on August 31, 1943, and we went to Gatlinburg, Tennessee, on the edge of

Great Smoky Mountains National Park.

During a short trip back to Washington to break in my successor on the *Sun*, I found activity stirring on the Calaveras front. Congressman Engle-bright of California, a Republican, had died in office. In a special election held August 28, Clair Engle, a Democrat, won a minority victory over Englebright's widow and another Republican who campaigned against federal land acquisitions. I had a talk with Engle, which I described to Secretary Ickes on December 15, after getting back to Gatlinburg. Avoiding the temptation to pun about Engle—"like Englebright but not so bright"—my description did not exclude that verdict. I had put the Calaveras timber exchange before him; he was not responsive. He would oppose such a move unless the people of Calaveras County favored it. Since the county was a center of hostility to public land ownership, federal or state, there was little likelihood of that.

Consequently, any pro-park leadership in California would have to come from other parts of the state, and that meant from the Save-the-Redwoods League. However, I thought there was "a possibility of doing a little missionary work" on Congressman Engle. "He is a man of intelligence and good intentions, but utterly uneducated in conservation matters." I told Ickes that if Engle did take a stand for federal land acquisition, then at the next election, where he would be facing just one opponent, he would meet sure defeat on that issue. However, "He does want to see the counties get some federal funds, but told me that he was uncertain which method ought to be employed"—whether through federal sharing of national-forest revenues with the counties, or sharing the revenues of national parks or monuments. I advised Ickes to invite Engle for a talk and let him see that he was friendly to the county governments. If Ickes could keep his temper, I said, while listening to anti-park statements, he might find Engle not a total liability, since he was not a Forest Service follower.

Ickes replied that, with Congress going into recess for three weeks, he would talk with Engle on the latter's return from California in January. In March, with the presidential campaign coming on, Paul A. Porter, director of public relations for the Democratic National Committee, asked me to come to Washington to consider spending some weeks marshaling ideas for President Roosevelt's fourth-term bid. We discussed it intermittently for two weeks. Nothing came of the project, possibly because a dearth of glittering ideas on my part coincided with a dearth of glittering gold in the Democratic coffers.

However there proved to be time and occasion for what turned out to be my last extended talk with President Roosevelt. He appeared to be in prime good health and spirits when we talked on March 21 or 28, 1944. Roosevelt was then under heavy pressure from southern racists to sign an emasculated bill on soldiers' voting rights, while liberals were urging a veto. The bill retained a 1942 ban on the poll tax for the military, but required cumbersome use of state ballots instead of a simple, and deliverable, federal form. Enough delays were legislated in to ensure that any state could reduce its soldier vote to a travesty. The president had said he would veto the bill if fewer soldiers could vote under it than under the 1942 act. I thought it was more important, politically, to accept even a nominal improvement in voting rights, and suggested that Roosevelt neither sign nor veto the bill but let it become law without his signature. He did just that, sending Congress a trenchant statement of the bill's inadequacies instead of a signature.

Later in the talk I urged that he keep Vice President Wallace on the ticket with him, saying that it was bad policy to break up a winning combination. To be sure, I admitted, "Anybody who would vote Democratic because of Wallace's liberalism would vote Democratic because of your liberalism." Roosevelt replied with a wicked grin: "That makes it look bad for Wallace . . ." Not wanting to hurt Wallace, I said nothing about this during the ensuing months of newspaper and congressional discussion of the choice of a vice-presidential running mate.

During this March trip to Washington I talked with Ickes and found that he felt, as I did, that nothing could be hoped for from Engle unless strong support for Calaveras protection was built up in California. In May the situation worsened. Van Name wrote that the Pickering Company had won a lawsuit whose outcome opened the way to construction of a logging railroad toward Beaver Creek and the South Grove.

I wrote to Aubrey Drury, hoping to bring the Save-the-Redwoods League into action. He forwarded my letter to Newton Drury, who wrote that hard work was going to be done in the next session of the California legislature. But relations with Engle were getting worse. He was belaboring Ickes to allow grazing in Lassen Volcanic National Park (in Engle's home county) and was teaming up with Congressman Elliott (the foe of Kings Canyon National Park) to open all national parks to grazing.

Six months later I saw the president again. Attending a White House press conference with a colleague from the *Chicago Sun*, Robert Lasch, I was shocked at the alteration in Roosevelt's appearance. He answered questions slowly, carefully, and with full command of his line of thought. But the old fire was gone, the exuberance had disappeared; he looked tired and wan. The sense of his being in command had vanished.

At the close of the conference, Lasch and I stopped at his desk. FDR said to me, "How did I do? Pretty well?" Never, in his prime, would he have asked such a question. I had intended to say something about the Calaveras situation. Instead, I introduced Lasch to him and we left—the president had enough to think about.

Immediately after the November elections my wife and I headed back from Gatlinburg to the capital to resume research at the Library of Congress. I hoped, but did not expect, that Roosevelt would serve his full fourth term. Now, with every press conference, my concern over the president's condition increased. I asked no questions at these meetings and, of course, made no effort to obtain a private conference. At every session with the press, however, I found myself looking for signs of a breakdown that never came.

The final vacation trip to Warm Springs in March took away the sense of crisis right at the moment it was about to climax. The president's death on April 12 came like a thunderclap even though I had been watching it approach. The world would never be the same again.

A week later I wrote to Mrs. Edge that the president had aged very rapidly. Even if he had not suffered the stroke I believed he soon would have been incapacitated for any but routine duties in office. I had always marvelled how he retained "his mental freshness" under the strains of the presidency.

So, on April 12, 1945, Vice President Harry S Truman was sworn in as president of the United States. I had known Harry Truman for twelve years and predicted immediately, in two articles in the *New Republic*, that he would make a strong, capable, and honest president.

Truman had no public record on conservation, and no private record except a promise to me (unfulfilled because of absence from Washington) to block a vote on the bill to abolish Jackson Hole National Monument. However, I was able to write to John D. Rockefeller, Jr., on June 15 that a half-hour conference with Truman revealed that he was generally familiar with Jackson Hole. "He told me that I could tell you" that he would not allow the Rockefeller land, when given to the nation, to be diverted from monument status. "Truman," I went on, "is as tough as they make them. . . . His remarks about Ickes ["I like the old bastard"] made it evident that no cabinet change is to be made" in Interior.

Chairman Peterson of the public lands committee, I told Rockefeller, had altered his tactics a little in regard to monument-foe Congressman Barrett. Instead of trying to bring out the tax-compensation bill as soon as he felt confident of having a committee majority for it, he would let Barrett do some sweating about the possibility that there would be no legislation. It was my opinion that as soon as gasoline restrictions were lifted, tourist travel would rebound and the Jackson Hole opposition would collapse. Kenneth Chorley replied, "Mr. Rockefeller was delighted that you had an opportunity to discuss this with President Truman and he is greatly pleased that the President feels as he does about this project."

Right at that moment an opportunity opened to find out what Chief Lyle Watts had done, if anything, about vandalism committed by his subordinates in the Jackson Hole National Monument while transferring Forest Service buildings to the Park Service. Mrs. Edge had written a few lines about it in an ECC publication. Opposition to the monument, she remarked, was "based on false fears and prejudice . . . largely stirred up by employees of the Jackson Hole office of the Forest Service"; then she said, "The temper of the Jackson Hole Forest Service group may be judged by the fact that, before they obeyed the Presidential order to turn national forest buildings and equipment over to the custodians of the new monument, every particle of plumbing and telephone equipment was ripped out of the buildings."

This understatement drew a long explanation and aggrieved protest from the chief forester on June 15. Through a "regrettable misunderstanding," some plumbing equipment had been removed from the buildings. The local forest officer had been instructed to remove Forest Service equipment, such as fire tools, but he had misunderstood and removed fixtures, which had been promptly replaced.

Because Mrs. Edge had received her information from me, she asked how Watts should be answered. My information had come from National Park Service personnel, but not wishing to embroil them, I suggested that a reply should be delayed until I could write to Wyoming and obtain a factual account from private sources, of both the vandalism and the role of Forest Service employees in stirring up opposition. Watts's letter, I remarked, was certainly naive, if not written with tongue in cheek: "I hope his Jackson Hole plumbing extractor is never asked to remove my hat. He would be sure to take the head with it."

I wrote to a friend in Jackson Hole (this correspondence has been lost but the only friends I had there were Olaus and Adolph Murie) and using the information received from that source, drafted a letter from Mrs. Edge to Forest Service chief Watts. What he thought of it I never learned.

This letter to Watts, written on July 5, 1945, opened with an explanation of the delay in replying—the need to inquire into the regional forester's denial of hostile activities by Forest Service personnel. I presented the report sent me from Wyoming, which told how the "organized opposition" had held nightly meetings in national-forest headquarters, until the forest supervisor was transferred in the fall of 1943. His transfer was seen in Jackson as a reward for this opposition, but my informant thought it was punishment for tearing up government buildings. The next forest supervisor had given no visible indication of hostility, but a prominent Jackson banker and former Forest Service employee was said to have "some kind of control" over grazing permits which he was using coercively against the monument.

My letter for Watts turned to the vandalism in the monument headquarters. Doors and wiring had been removed. The ripping out of toilets, sinks, and water pipes had caused structural damage. A hole four feet square had been sawed through the living room floor and floor joists. Out of that hole Forest Service personnel pulled up a hot-water heating system and the tubing from a well underneath the house. From the forest at large, as the National Park Service had told me, miles and miles of fire-lookout telephone wire were removed, leaving the trees exposed to destruction by fire. Watts, of course, was not personally responsible, but why, I asked, was the person who was responsible still in government employment?

Sending this draft to Mrs. Edge, to be used or modified as she might see fit, I took the occasion to scotch a rumor that was going around that I was to be White House press secretary. In fact for that position I had recommended

Roscoe Drummond of the *Christian Science Monitor*, a nonpartisan-minded Republican. President Truman made a fine choice—Charles Ross of the *St. Louis Post-Dispatch*—but several presidents would have been better off if they had gone to the "fairminded opposition" to fill that particular office.

By this time—July 1945—Congressman Barrett had three bills before the House Committee on the Public Lands—one to abolish the Jackson Hole National Monument, one to repeal the Antiquities Act of 1906, and one to turn the administration of the Jackson Hole monument lands over to the Forest Service. It was easy to account for the first two, but how could one explain the third, which ran directly contrary to the financial interests of Teton County? The only important effect of such a law would be to render it impossible to offset the county's tax loss from the Rockefeller gift by a federal-county sharing of national-park and monument revenues. My conclusion on this point was voiced in an article, "The Fight Over Jackson Hole," published in the *Nation* of July 7. I wrote that Barrett or his "banker-adviser" had lost his head, for it would be sounder politically to support a bill that would help Teton County.

That was written before I received a report of the Jackson banker's method of coercion, through his unexplained control of grazing permits—misuse of power was evident in the atmosphere of fear, but I had visualized only a conventional restriction or threatened restriction of bank credit. However, one thing was evident: while the managers of the opposition were going to foolish acts of desperation, the people of the community were moving in the other direction. The Izaak Walton League episode, combined with the signatures in the appeal to chairman Peterson, gave evidence of that.

Not long after these developments, the manager of Mr. Rockefeller's western lands wrote to me from Ogden, Utah, that if my plans for the summer should bring me out that way, he would like to discuss a new management project for the Teton holdings. That was to fence a part of them and surround it by a hidden roadway with occasional overlooks, so that the general public could observe animals in the wild (bison, elk, moose) without being observed. The plan was carried into effect and is still in operation.

Now, the ending of World War II had put America on wheels once more. Jackson, Wyoming, overflowed with tourists and the entire community rejoiced when the state's congressional delegation took the lead in merging the Jackson Hole National Monument into Grand Teton National Park, with the Rockefeller banner high in the forefront. Economic interests had triumphed, this time coinciding with the general welfare.

From California, during this period of White House transition, came two developments favorable to salvation of the Calaveras groves of sequoias and sugar pines. The state park commission, citing its own past actions and the support of the Save-the-Redwoods League, unanimously adopted a resolution calling for a new study of the south Calaveras grove and adjacent areas by the eminent landscape artist Frederick Law Olmsted, whose services were available without expense to the state. (Van Name had stimulated that generous offer.) This was to supplement the basic state-park survey made by Olmsted for the park commission in 1927-28.

A few weeks later the suggestion was made that a coastal redwood grove be dedicated as a memorial to President Roosevelt. The Save-the-Redwoods League expanded the idea to that of a Calaveras national monument, to be established by Congress in memory of Roosevelt. The proposal was put up to the Emergency Conservation Committee. I agreed to go with Fred Packard, a recently appointed ECC staff member, to talk with Ickes, and I commented that it would be good if Engle could be persuaded to sponsor the monument; but he would not if the local people were opposed.

Olmsted made a magnificent report to the state park commission, based on his study done jointly with Dan Hall, landscape architect of the California Division of Beaches and Parks. The area studied was the valley of Big Tree Creek, Tuolumne County, containing the Calaveras South Grove, and north-ward as far as the Calaveras North Grove State Park.

Logging operations, Olmsted found, had advanced to the immediate vicinity of the South Grove, and the Pickering Company was extending its logging railroad to give access to that grove in the coming year. The report recommended the acquisition and preservation of four units:

Unit 1, the valley of Big Tree Creek, including the entire South Grove of big trees (sequoias) and the enframing valley forest of sugar pines and ponderosa pines, roughly fourteen hundred acres. This should be held "as nearly as possible in its natural wilderness conditions."

Unit 2, federal lands already authorized to be given to the state of California for a road connecting with the North Grove State Park, plus a small amount of low-value Pickering land for the same purpose.

Unit 3, an area immediately north of Unit 1, containing sugar pines "of such extraordinary quality . . . as to make its permanent preservation in a virgin condition a close second in importance to the preservation of Unit 1."

Unit 4, an extension of Unit 3, "of high park quality," lying west of the projected logging railway.

Twelve pages of the fourteen-page report were devoted to detailed descriptions of the four units, with emphasis at all times on the magnificence of the forest and the need to preserve its wilderness qualities.

Disclosure of the report in mid-June 1945 led to immediate reactions in key places, two of which could have been taken for granted. The Pickering Lumber Company was bitterly opposed, the Forest Service hardly less strongly against it. Those two reactions upset the initial approval of the Save-the-Redwoods League, which was governed by two cardinal principles in acquiring park lands: 1. Never get into a fight with a lumber company; 2. Never antagonize the Forest Service. Gordon McDuffie, president of the league, wrote to the Emergency Conservation Committee, repeating his approval of the projected Calaveras National Monument. "I do not wish to shirk . . .

either responsibility or effort," he said—but a new redwoods project made it impossible to be active in the Calaveras campaign. Mrs. Edge in reply acknowledged "your letter of the 18th, shirking yours, and the Save-the-Redwoods League's responsibility." From that time onward, the Save-the-Redwoods League never lifted a finger during the fight to save the Calaveras big trees.

Late in 1945, newspapers repeatedly published rumors that Secretary Ickes was about to resign. He had gotten along well with President Truman, considering the vast difference between them in temperament and some divergence in views. There was no suggestion of a squeeze-out. Twice, when I telephoned to urge him not to resign, he replied: "I won't, if you will come in and help me run the department." His wording left it uncertain whether he wanted me to become his personal assistant or take the position of undersecretary. If the former, acceptance would be harmful to myself; if the latter, harmful both to me and to the government. I had neither the qualifications nor the willingness to assume administrative duties. On February 13, 1946, after thirteen years in office, Ickes resigned as secretary of the interior.

Not only did he hold that office for longer than any other man in history, but, in spite of numerous personal foibles, he surpassed all previous holders of it in quality of service to his country. On leaving office, he found an immediate outlet for pent-up energies by writing a newspaper column, "Man to Man."

I suggested to President Truman that he nominate Governor Monrad C. Wallgren of Washington as Ickes' successor. Wallgren, Truman replied, was needed where he was, for party reasons. His choice fell on Julius A. Krug, last chairman of the War Production Board, a man of recognized competence and good repute, but totally unfamiliar with the conservation problems which Ickes had handled so well.

Except for President Truman's promise to veto any revived bill to abolish the Jackson Hole National Monument, I had no opportunity to test him on conservation matters until August 1946. At that time I appealed to him to veto a bill abolishing the Parker River Wildlife Refuge in Massachusetts. This bill, I wrote to him, "passed Congress as the result of an incredibly false campaign of misrepresentation by a small group of sportsmen in Massachusetts whose blindness would destroy their own sport." Their false charge was that the Massachusetts government had not approved the establishment of the refuge. Their concealed motive was to increase the duck kill in that state.

I wrote that the chief benefit of any refuge was not to the state in which it was located, but to states farther north or farther south. Each of the refuges reduced the kill for local sportsmen, but together they built up the breeding stock. "With the breeding stock of ducks reduced 36 per cent this year, below last year, and last year's stock incalculably below the oldtime level, it would be both shocking and dangerous to make a break in the refuge system." Truman vetoed the bill, but signed one two years later reducing the refuge in size from 12,367 acres to 4,650 acres.

The Hoh rain forest. Timber interests many times demanded the elimination of rain forests from Olympic National Park, especially during the war years. The efforts of the American conservation movement helped prevent this (photograph by Marc Gaede, courtesy the photographer).

CHAPTER SEVENTEEN

AFTER FDR

In the fall of 1946, I completed a draft of the second volume of the Madison biography, which had then to be cut down drastically in size and loosened up in style. More than half a year's work on it lay ahead, but the revision could be done within reach of any historical library. Our urge to get out of Washington triumphed again, and my wife, daughter, and I went as far as possible, to a log cabin on a Vancouver Island fjord.

SECOND BATTLE OF THE BOGACHIEL

I was totally out of touch with conservation affairs until the arrival of a March 21, 1947, letter from Park Service director Newton Drury. Enclosed with it was a position statement dated three days earlier dealing with the boundaries of the Olympic park. Drury said that Congressman Norman of Grays Harbor had introduced a joint resolution to "throw the question of redefining the boundaries of the park into the hands of a commission that would be preponderantly local and commercial in its viewpoint." To block this, the NPS had induced Congressman Henry M. Jackson, whose district embraced most of the park, to sponsor a bill for boundary readjustments recommended by the Park Service and approved by Interior secretary Krug. Concerning these boundary measures, Drury wrote to me that he was enclosing "a statement of our position, which we believe is logical and can be defended."

Although local lumber interests would not be supportive, Drury hoped that conservation groups would be.

I wrote beside these remarks of Drury's "Good Lord!" Three similar bills to dismantle the park, offered by Norman and the two Washington senators (Magnuson and Cain), implemented the monstrosity. Drury's approved boundaries, supposed to displease the lumber interests, would take 56,396 acres out of the park, including 15,878 acres in the superlatively beautiful Bogachiel River valley. His plan also would prevent the addition of the nine square miles of formerly private Bogachiel lands, even then being acquired for inclusion by presidential proclamation. Thus the total loss would be more than 60,000 acres, one third of it consisting of the most magnificent rain forest in the world. And why was this monumental sacrifice to be made? Because of the timidity of national parks director Newton Drury, who was ready to run away from imaginary danger at the drop of a feather.

Likewise marked for elimination were 17,039 acres in the valley of the Calawah River, a branch of the Bogachiel. The Quinault area was to lose 18,185 acres of western rain forest; 4,270 acres were to be taken out in the Queets Valley and 1,024 acres in the Hoh. Some of the changes were minor, merely to follow ridges. But the major areas marked for elimination were all beautiful rain forests. They comprised more than half of the spectacular giant trees whose preservation furnished the principal reason for the enlargement authorized by Congress and consummated by President Roosevelt.

Mrs. Edge wrote that letters of protest were flooding in. At her request I wrote a circular for publication by the Emergency Conservation Committee calling for a nationwide rallying of forces against any sacrifice whatever. Twenty-two thousand copies were printed and distributed around the country. Harold Ickes wrote to me on April 1 that he had just learned that the NPS had "capitulated to the lumber interests." Ickes called on me to help, not knowing anyone who was "a better fighter." He was preparing a newspaper column on the subject. "If this letter will not bring you back in a hurry to to Washington," he wrote, "then we might as well prepare to run from the enemy and surrender all the gains that we have made during the Roosevelt years."

I replied that I was sure he would feel as he did about the cuts. Some of them did not seem objectionable and I had not seen the Calawah Valley, "but the Bogachiel portion is terrible." Moreover, "If this goes through it will open the floodgates for attacks on the [other] national parks"—Jackson Hole and Yellowstone. But there was no possibility of my going back to Washington at once; I was working twelve hours a day to finish the Madison volume by the end of April. Then on May 2 Irving Clark wrote asking for advice about procedures to get an "intensive campaign" started.

The need for such a campaign was speedily made manifest by an exchange of letters between Van Name and U.S. senator Harry P. Cain of Washington. Van Name appealed to him to help halt "the most disastrous attack on our wonderful National Park System that has been attempted for more than twenty years." The worst of it was, he said, that this attack had originated not with local commercial interests which would profit by it, but in the Interior Department and the National Park Service itself.

Senator Cain made an almost incredible reply. It was his understanding that the lands in question were transferred from the Forest Service to the National Park Service during Ickes' administration, even though "the Forest Service and the Interior Department were in opposition to the transfer at that time and, therefore, the Interior Department is consistent in supporting these bills at present to return them to the Forest Service." The Forest Service assured him, he said, that this stand of timber would not be destroyed, but that "selective cutting will create a healthier and more beautiful forest than being left as a part of the National Park."

The only fragment of truth in that fictional narrative was that the Forest Service, below the level of Chief Forester Silcox, had disliked President Roosevelt's enlargement of the park pursuant to law. Cain's story, unless he invented it, clearly revealed the role being played by that bureau under Chief Forester Watts and the old crowd.

Former secretary Ickes sent me two of his hard-hitting newspaper columns, the first published April 10. It opened with a statement that the timber interests "in reaching out to grab 56,000 acres of the Olympic National Park, cannot be charged with a statutory crime inasmuch as the Dept. of the Interior is well beyond the age of consent. And apparently Secretary Krug and Director Drury of the National Park Service were eager to consent."

The National Park Service, its former boss said, "does not seem to have thought that since this wonderful timber belonged to the people, they should have been consulted. . . . Of course, the timber interests had their private hearing before Interior officials. . . . They had Congressmen . . . opening the doors for them."

Secretary Krug, his predecessor said, "probably does not know anything about it"; but why did not Director Drury notify the men and women throughout the country who were always ready to do battle for the national parks, why did he not ask Krug to hold a public hearing?

Ickes' second column, of April 18, paid his compliments to the tree-butchers who were carrying on, in a new location, the destruction they had wrought earlier in Michigan and Wisconsin. He described the fight President Roosevelt put up to save the great scenic forests of the Olympic Peninsula. He recalled seeing Roosevelt when "in his own office . . . in the presence of the objecting Governor of Washington, he marked on a map with his own lead pencil an extension of the boundaries of the park." Said Ickes: "From my point of view, the Mount Olympic National Park [*sic*] is the greatest monument to the most conservation-minded President that we have. And now, lesser men would betray the ideals of the Department of the Interior as established under the great Roosevelt and be recreant to their trust."

At the end of April, the revised manuscript of my second Madison volume went to the publisher. We had reservations for a week's round trip in June to Prince Rupert, British Columbia, by steamship up the Inside Passage. In addition, I wanted to visit the Calaveras groves in California and hike into the yet-unvisited Calawah River valley in the Olympic National Park. So we set off on May 1 for an interim trip to the Calaveras big trees.

At Olympia I called at the office of Governor Wallgren to talk about the Olympic massacre, but he was out in the country, dusting his apple trees. A telephone call from Portland failed to catch him; so I wrote from California that I wanted to talk with him about the way the "Interior Department is capitulating to the lumber interests, in the emasculation of the Olympic National Park." Not only was Drury timid but he was unaware that he was surrendering. If President Truman were properly informed, the lumbering could be blocked again.

What seemed to be happening, I told the author of the Olympic Park Act, was that "to check the wholesale raid of the Grays Harbor sawmill interests," the Interior Department was sacrificing the Bogachiel Valley to the Port Angeles pulp industry, and Crown–Zellerbach was "going along with the latter out of neighborly solidarity. The thing should be stopped flat."

We reached the Calaveras region late in May. Mr. C. M. Goethe, head of a small but devoted conservation group, arranged a motor trip to the North Grove State Park, followed by a lengthy hike to the South Grove of sequoias and the Beaver Creek sugar pines. Taking part were the elderly Goethe himself, Edward F. Dolder of the California Department of Natural Resources, and the three Brants.

Dolder furnished me with an official status paper dated March 15, 1946, plus a postscript of March 22, 1947, which said there would be no cutting in the area of the proposed Calaveras park for at least a year. At the 1946 meeting, the state government had approved the acquisition of units 1 and 2 of the Olmsted report but had eliminated Unit 3 on account of prohibitive cost. This meant that the sequoia grove was marked for preservation, together with bordering sugar pines and ponderosas of Big Tree Creek, but the superlative Beaver Creek sugar pines were to be lumbered.

Our observation confirmed all that had ever been written about the magnificence of these groves, but turned up something disturbing. Every big sugar pine along a ridge between Big Tree Creek and Beaver Creek was marked for cutting. Were they marked by Pickering or the state? Mr. Dolder did not know. Under state regulations Dolder was forbidden to engage in propaganda for the park, but I seemed to detect a leaning when he constantly referred to unidentified persons concerned in the Calaveras business as "tree-butchers." Shortly after our trip, a memorandum from the head of the California park system to Governor Warren made it appear (as I wrote to Dolder) "that the trees which we observed, marked for cutting, are to be cut from a buffer strip" instead of being included in the park and thus preserved. This worsened the elimination of the Beaver Creek pines from the project. California was setting its sights entirely too low.

Back in Port Angeles at the end of May, ready for back-packing into the Calawah Valley, I was confronted with a publisher's letter saying that another thirty-five thousand words had to be cut out of Madison II. There was also a delayed letter from Newton Drury about the Olympic park. What to do? We were to sail up the Inside Passage on June 17. I recalled that in Moran State Park, on Orcas Island, there were large stone shelters with two fireplaces and lots of wood. We were there next day. In two weeks the work on Madison was finished.

In Vancouver, half a day before sailing, I wrote to Drury that the Interior Department was on the verge of making "an utterly needless and harmful surrender to timber interests" that had opposed the park and were fighting to emasculate it.

I said that I felt sure that he did not favor the boundary changes that he had endorsed, but I told him he was "making an abject surrender to the Port Angeles woodpulp and plywood interest." He was mistaken in the belief that he needed to do so in order to block the still more destructive aims of the Grays Harbor lumbermen. He had been led into a wrong position, I told him, by two errors in reckoning. First, the strength of park opponents had been exaggerated; second, he had "grossly underestimated" the support that could be rallied for national parks.

I asked whether the Interior Department had given thought to the embarrassment it would cause President Truman "if your so-called compromise passes Congress because of your support of it." If he vetoed it, he would have to do so without the aid of departmental backing. "If he signs it, he will be damned by conservationists from one end of the country to the other," with the condemnation continuing for generations as visitors drove through butchered valleys to enter an emasculated park. Truman would "never cave in to the commercial despoilers" unless he was misled by his advisers.

For the purpose of working off feelings, this would have been a good place to stop, but my hope was to get a reversal of policy, and I saw a way to that end. Congressman Norman, the instigator and only real driving force of the campaign, had just died. "With him gone," I said to Drury, "there is an excellent opening for the Interior Department to take the stand it should for protection of the park. You are not committed to the destructive compromise." I cited a similar situation, and the escape from it, a decade earlier when Secretary of Agriculture Wallace escaped serious embarrassment by failing to report on the Wallgren bill, even though his department had opposed it earlier.[1] By reporting against all of the present anti-park measures the Interior Department could save Truman a "terrific headache."

Returning to the States at the end of July, we made two Olympic excursions into the Calawah River valley. We went in first with Fred Overly of the Park Service, hiking from the end of a logging road on national-forest land that was being cut by the Rayonier Corporation. This was selective cutting by caterpillar tractor, the new method by which the Forest Service was going to achieve sustained yield without destroying scenic beauty. I described the visual effect in notes written for use before a congressional committee in case hearings were held on the Olympic Park boundary bills: "You would think you were on a World War battleground, with the forest as the beaten enemy." There were piles of earth and roots ten feet high and holes deep enough to hide an elephant. And this was called selective cutting. "I don't say that this national forest land had been mishandled, from the standpoint of land whose timber is to be cut and used. But let us not talk of preserving scenic beauty at the same time, unless we regard the head-on collision of two trains . . . as a preservation of beauty."

Crossing the park boundary from this scene of devastation, we came upon two hemlock forests in one. Prone on the floor of the Calawah Valley lay a forest of long-dead, moss-covered decaying logs, and above them a healthy, thrifty, growing hemlock forest on its way to a future climax. Taken by itself, I concluded, nobody would have regarded this little valley as of national-park caliber, but considered as part of a park of superlative beauty, it brought unique qualities of its own, highly valuable as a study in natural transition of forest types.

The day after our trip with Overly, we assailed the Calawah Valley from another direction. Starting from the Hoh River five miles below the Jackson Ranger Station, we made a two-day hike over two mountain ridges, following the Snyder-Jackson Trail from the Hoh to the Bogachiel, and then over the Indian Pass Trail to the Calawah, three miles upstream from the highest point reached with Overly.

Here the valley was entirely different. The Calawah River was a small, clear, beautiful stream, above which towered gigantic Sitka spruces. Water ouzels flitted along the shore. The main forest was of more mature hemlock. The valley sides were too narrow and steep for any but the most destructive lumbering. Owing to the war, the National Park Service had never explored this region, and was unaware of a sixty-five-foot waterfall a few rods from the Indian Pass Trail, where a small creek plunged down to the valley floor. I summed up in my notes for a hearing that never was held: "In the attempt to cut down the Olympic Park, the Calawah enters into the picture only as a talking point in the effort to get into the Bogachiel. Both valleys belong in the park, but it is the Bogachiel that stands out both for the magnificence of its scenery and as the coveted prize of those who would destroy it."

My notes for possible testimony assailed the proposed elimination of 18,185 acres in the Quinault River valley. Private ownership of land had been cited as the reason, but fewer than 900 acres were privately owned. If these few acres were lumbered, the cutover land could be bought by the government for almost nothing and the moist climate would soon provide a young forest covering, removing the eyesore. If the 17,000-plus acres of government land were taken out, a great scenic rain forest of gigantic trees would be destroyed, "utterly ruining the southwestern approach to the park and making Lake Quinault an isolated and ruined relic of what it is today."

When we emerged from the Calawah excursion, a sheaf of correspondence from Van Name was at hand. He had written a strong letter of protest to President Truman and received a discouraging reply from Undersecretary of the Interior Oscar L. Chapman that was a repetition of Newton Drury's apologia of the preceding March—eliminations to prevent worse eliminations—and an assurance "that there [would] be retained in the park nothing less than the finest samples of the forest for which the Olympic is notable."

Van Name commented to me, "How a high official of the Interior Department could sign his name to a letter so full of lies as this one is more than I can understand." I assured him that Drury wrote every line of Chapman's letter, and that the "lies" were not lies but "just the self-delusion of the timid man" seeking to justify his position. Krug and Chapman, in my opinion, should not be written off; the need was to get the truth to them.

Secretary Krug had made a sweeping and vigorous defense of the boundaries of the Olympic park at its war-delayed dedication in June 1946. Van Name, in a letter published in the *New York Herald Tribune* of June 8, 1947, quoted the secretary's words of a year earlier with telling effect. After a brief description of the park's magnificent forests, Krug had asked rhetorically whether "too much of this kind of beauty" could be preserved. Although some felt that the park was too large, Congress had settled that issue in 1938. It might be difficult, said Krug, to determine what future generations would judge to be adequate or excessive. "But certainly it would seem better to err slightly on the side of too much rather than too little. In the judgment of most conservationists there is not now more preserved here than the minimum to provide an adequate representation of this type of forest."

Van Name, rendered cynical by thirty years' experience, contrasted this fine speech with "secret conferences with representatives of the local lumber companies," held a few months later under this same secretary. He charged that the confidence that this and other national parks would be strictly protected, given the public by President Roosevelt and Secretary Ickes, "is being shamefully betrayed." That put the issue squarely up to Secretary Krug, who had not participated in those "secret conferences," which actually were between the lumbermen and the late Congressman Norman. Thus the only past position Krug had need to defend was his own strong championship of a large park. But that required deeds, not words.

September was at hand when, at my publisher's office in Indianapolis, I received Newton Drury's reply to my letter of June 17 pillorying him for his needless surrender to the timber butchers. He was in seemingly casual but full retreat. Employing the escape route that I had pointed out to him, he wrote on September 5 that the secretary would study the issue further. The Park Service did not "initiate the issue," nor was it "pressing any of the bills."

No, the National Park Service did not "initiate the issue," but it initiated the surrender on the issue. However, what counted was that, habituated to surrender, it was now surrendering to counter-pressure from above. The roar of opposition from conservationists had convinced Krug that he had been misled by the NPS. His reversal of policy, I believed, would hold.

Drury's letter was written just before he and Assistant Secretary of the Interior C. Girard Davidson left for Seattle to attend House committee hearings on the Olympic Park emasculation bills. At their conclusion Davidson and the subcommittee chairman flew over the affected areas and Davidson did some exploring on the ground. A few weeks after his return to Washington, he expressed surprise to Mrs. Edge that the department's opposition to the Olympic bills was not known in the East. At her request, he wrote her a lengthy statement of Interior's position. He gave her permission to do anything she liked with it: "Give it to the press, if you want to."

The result was a headline in the *New York Times* of November 27, 1947: "NEW FIGHT BEGUN TO SAVE FORESTS / Interior Department to Oppose / Bills to Take 56,000 Acres / From Olympic Park." After summarizing the legislative situation, the news story quoted a statement from Davidson's letter that "the department is opposed to any changes in the present boundaries of the Olympic National Park and will so report to the Congress at any future hearings which might be held on the bills now pending." The letter, as quoted, told of the Seattle hearings and park inspection and concluded with the statement that the Park Service had decided there should be no changes in the park boundaries. This meant, the ECC commented, that the Interior Department "will be leading the fight for the preservation of the Olympic forests . . . for integrity of the Olympic Park, and for the safety of the whole national park system, which is so ominously threatened."

Shortly afterward, I called on Secretary Krug and he emphatically confirmed Davidson's stand. Passing this information along to Ickes, I remarked, "I think the Interior reversal is genuine. Krug made it plain to me that he felt that he had been misled and given bad advice by the N. P. S."

During a brief interlude of research at the Library of Congress, I asked for an appointment with President Truman to talk about the Olympic bills. There was no time for that, but he suggested that I write to him on the subject. Shortly afterwards, Harold Ickes asked me to write a column for him, combining defense of the Olympic park with a plea for preservation of the Calaveras groves. I sent the manuscript to him after getting established in Kissimmee, Florida, drawn there by the affinity between our canoe and two big lakes.

Writing for Ickes on the Olympic theme, I expressed pleasure at the change of attitude by the Interior Department. Its announced decision was to oppose all of the bills aimed at "despoliation of this beautiful park." This seemed, I said, to mark "the end of weak-kneed compromise in the department, but it doesn't eliminate the danger." Every effort would be made by "lumber congressmen" to get one of the bills through, "by force, misrepresentation or stealth. Fortunately, a lot of people who believe that national parks belong to the people are telling their senators and representatives what they think of these Olympic bills. If enough do so, that will settle it."

It was my expectation to go back to Washington to testify against the emasculation bills, if further hearings were held. Thanks to the 1946 congressional election, the chairmanship of the House Committee on the Public Lands had passed from pro-park J. Hardin Peterson of Florida to anti-park Frank Barrett of Wyoming. If I testified for the Emergency Conservation Committee, that would exclude chairman Rosalie Edge, a very valuable witness. If I applied as an individual, Barrett might yet exclude me as an ECC member. So I wired Peterson and wrote to Karl LeCompte of Iowa, a member of the committee, asking them to intervene with Barrett. Both did so and Barrett readily agreed to invite me. Ickes urged me to testify, saying that he knew "of no one who can present the case for the park as you could." But Barrett kept postponing the hearings month after month.

My invited letter to Truman was put off until adjournment *sine die* late in December produced some letup in legislative pressures. I then sketched briefly for him the enlargement of the park by President Roosevelt, mentioned the advisory part I had in that proceeding, along with superintendents Tomlinson and Macy, and told of the assurance given Roosevelt by the Forest Service "that these transfers of public land would not interfere with maintenance of the Olympic Peninsula woodpulp industry on a sustained-yield basis."

The current fight, I said, had been stirred up by the Grays Harbor sawmill interests and a Port Angeles plywood factory, in the hope of postponing their inevitable early shutdown. The wood-pulp people joined in as a matter of community solidarity. Crown–Zellerbach reported adequate reserves except for the decade A.D. 2010-2020. "That hardly calls for taking a national park away from the American people." I told of my recent trip through the Bogachiel and Calawah valleys and said that the Bogachiel was what the lumbermen wanted most. Since it was the finest example of what the park had been created to preserve, it would be a "lasting, visible stigma" to let it be devastated.

Secretary Krug, I said, received misinformation and began with compromise, but had straightened out the department's stand and was receiving support from all over the country in his fight against the bills. "But the time may come when everything will depend on your backing. I am confident that he will get it." I closed with a suggestion that the president prod the Forest Service into completing the timber exchange designed to bring nine square miles into the park by presidential proclamation. Of the 5,700 acres involved, the Forest Service had acquired all except about 160. Incorporation of this corridor into the park would ease administration, stop elk poaching, discourage the congressional lobbying of the timber interests, and "notify conservationists throughout the country (many of whom are now badly shaken) that you are with them in the fight to preserve this national park from commercial assault."

President Truman replied on January 5, 1948, "I read your memorandum of December twenty-eighth with a lot of interest. I have taken the matter up with the Secretary of the Interior and I think things will work out all right." Considering Truman's make-up, that came close to suggesting a veto if necessary.

Shortly after the new Congress convened, Representative Jackson asked that his bill cutting down Olympic Park boundaries be withdrawn. It was the easier for him to do this because the bill had been introduced "by request"—he did not say by request of the deceived secretary of the interior. Since nearly all of the Olympic National Park lay within Jackson's congressional district, and Norman's successor in the Grays Harbor district had not yet gotten his bearings, this ended any possibility of the Norman bill being reported by the House public lands committee. The idea of holding further hearings was dropped. Still remaining was the resolution calling for a study of park boundaries by a mixed commission of congressmen and private citizens. Such a commission, I wrote to Mrs. Edge, "is so utterly improper that the appointment of it would be quite likely to react against its sponsors." The wonderful Bogachiel rain forest was not yet entirely secure, and would not be until its nine-mile private corridor was added to the park, but the second Battle of the Bogachiel had ended in victory for its defenders.

THE CALAVERAS BIGTREE ACT

Without having conservation in mind, the American people saved that movement from disaster in 1948. They did it on November 2, by the skin-of-the-teeth re-election of President Truman over New York's governor Thomas E. Dewey. Compared with Franklin Roosevelt, Truman fell far short of Galahadry, but measured against Tom Dewey, he was the Angel Gabriel over Lucifer. Dewey's record on environmental matters became a presidential issue only in his home state, but there it was sharp enough to measure the kind of conduct his election would have fastened on the whole country. I had spent the summer of 1948 in New York City, where I had a good look at Dewey. With private-power interests and the army engineers intent on wrecking part of the Adirondack Forest Reserve by damming Panther Creek, Dewey ignored every demand that he state his position. On July 28, under a four-column head, the *New York Star* (shortlived successor to *PM*) published an editorial by me entitled "Your Land and Mine: An Open Letter to Governor Dewey." In it I enlarged the subject to a series of questions on national conservation topics. After quoting Bernard De Voto's remark that Dewey disavowed anti-conservation views "in words that made conservationists shudder," I said that "any Republican can be as good a conservationist as Theodore Roosevelt," and what the people "need to know is where you [Dewey] stand."

The editorial was reprinted and widely circulated by the Emergency Conservation Committee and New York state organizations; but the American people never were told where Dewey stood on conservation and, fortunately, never had to learn.

Following a postelection Thanksgiving worthy of giving thanks came a Christmas that brought an unbelievable present. It was a letter written in Los Angeles by a man I had never heard of, on a letterhead that I read over and over in disbelief. The writer of it was a retired oil man, John B. Elliott, and the letterhead read "California War Memorial Park Association." The letter, written on December 22, 1948, began by explaining that a California group was trying to save the sequoia and sugar-pine forests of Tuolumne County. Recently, Ickes had written Elliott about me. The group was in "great haste," because of impending logging on Beaver Creek. Elliott had become acquainted with this situation through a late-fall trip into the area in company with Willard Van Name. Organization had followed quickly. Oil furnished the needed money, of which Elliott had plenty; his newspaper background gave him publicity "savvy," and his high position in the California Democratic hierarchy ensured easy communication with federal and state officials. In short, his entry into the field was manna falling from the Sierra heavens.

John Elliott enclosed the association's first news release, dated November 29, 1948; it said that "every effort will be made in the next few weeks to have Governor Warren and the California legislature include in the State's next financial budget funds to save the great Sugar Pine and Sequoia trees of Tuolumne and Calaveras Counties from logging by midwest lumber interests." (Pickering Lumber Company headquarters were in Kansas City, Missouri.) The release warned that "it is now or never," if the trees were to be saved.

Supporting organizations were listed: the Save-the-Redwoods League, the Sierra Club, the Federation of Western Outdoor Clubs, the Izaak Walton League, and the Calaveras Grove Association[2] all had joined with the California War Memorial Park Association "to get the facts before the people." (The Save-the-Redwoods League had been virtually clubbed in by Harold Ickes, who, after his first appeal to the league for leadership had gone unanswered, and a second letter drew a reply which, he said, "told me precisely nothing," published a blistering attack on the league for aiding the lumbermen "by its silence and secrecy.")

Among its earliest publications, the War Memorial Association put out a two-sheet, large-type broadside with a lead article (plus map) by Dr. Van Name, headed "An Impending FOREST DISASTER," followed on the next sheet by conspicuously headed articles by Irving Brant and John Elliott. My portion consisted of three descriptive paragraphs excerpted from my 1942 pamphlet about the Calaveras groves. Elliott described his visit to the forest in the previous fall; moved by the "tragedy of its imminent and unnecessary loss," he had proposed dedicating it as a memorial to war veterans. "The response has been magnificent."

Early in January 1949 a tall young man tapped on the door of my study room in the Library of Congress. He introduced himself: Gene Wilbur, personal assistant to Elliott. He had been sent to Washington to enlist the support of the California congressional delegation in the campaign to save the Calaveras groves. Wilbur was purposeful, confident, and intent on getting started. First, he wanted to read the 1928 act of Congress authorizing a gift of national-forest land to help in acquisition of the South Grove of sequoias—a law which I had never read. I directed him to the law division in the main library building.

Wilbur came back in the afternoon with far more than he or I had bargained for. To begin with, the act of 1928 was still in force—not a hint of that time limit which the Forest Service told me had expired. But that was swept out of mind by what Wilbur said next. Searching through the index to the U. S. Code he had come upon the entry: "Calaveras Bigtree Act." The reference carried him not to the 1928 authorization of an inter-grove corridor gift, but to a law enacted in 1909 for acquisition of an area to be known as the "Calaveras Bigtree National Forest." The stated purpose was "to secure and protect for all time the big trees scientifically known as Sequoia washingtoniana," but the area described for acquisition included the Beaver Creek sugar pines—the very region owned and marked for destruction by the Pickering Lumber Company.

For forty years the Forest Service had been sitting on this law, doing nothing to carry out its provisions, saying not a word about its existence. My thoughts went back to 1943, when President Roosevelt asked me if there was anything he could do to help in the Calaveras fight. Given knowledge of this 1909 act of Congress, FDR would have had it moving toward swift fulfillment in a week's time. Now it would depend, not on Roosevelt's successor, who let cabinet members run their own departments, but on Secretary of Agriculture Charles F. Brannan. The immediate question was how far he would be governed by the usually omnipotent Forest Service, whose opposition could be taken for granted wherever preservation of trees was concerned.

Wilbur left to sound out the California delegation while I turned to the legislative history of the act of 1909. I found that, introduced by Senator George C. Perkins of California, it was reported favorably in 1907 by the Senate Committee on Forest Reservations and the Protection of Game and was taken up for debate on March 3, 1908. Senator Perkins had emphasized that the bill "makes no appropriation whatever for the purchase of these trees or any land. It simply authorizes the Secretary of Agriculture, under certain conditions, to make exchanges." He explained that the Calaveras Big Tree Grove was in private hands and the owners were asking an "exorbitant" price. Exchange of adjacent federal timber was the solution.

California people, Perkins said, were prepared to raise money for part of the cost. He then read, from the 1907 committee report, a letter from

Secretary of Agriculture James Wilson ("Tama Jim" of Iowa) approving the exchange. After explaining the mechanics of it, worked out by the Forest Service, Wilson had gone into a panegyric of praise for the undertaking. These "wonders of creation" should become public property and be protected from destruction.

The bill had passed the Senate unanimously without further debate. It was taken up in the House on January 30, 1909, and ran into lengthy discussion on the terms of timber exchange. Every speaker approved the objective. When floor manager Sylvester Smith of California remarked to a questioner that "the trees are said to be the oldest living things on the face of the earth," Oscar Underwood of Alabama replied, "I understand that, and I am heartily in accordance with the gentleman's idea of preserving these trees if we can do so in a constitutional way," without robbing the government of its timber or money. He would, however, waive the constitutional issue (whether the government had power to buy private lands for park purposes) provided he could be sure of a fair exchange.

That, said Smith, brought it down to a question of who could be trusted. He thought that "these two secretaries [James Wilson and Interior secretary James R. Garfield] can be trusted to give the government a fair deal." Somebody, remarked Congressman J. L. Slayden of Texas, had asked which secretaries the bill referred to—"those that are coming in or those that are now in." Smith of California replied, "That depends upon how soon we get the bill passed." Those words were significant. The timber exchange was to be made "in the discretion" of the two secretaries; quick passage was looked upon as an assurance of early action by two trusted and trustworthy officials.

The bill lay over until more information could be secured about timber exchange, and the debate was resumed on February 13. Amendments were adopted to make sure that lumber values alone would be used to determine prices and that no money would be appropriated to purchase land or trees. The only comments about the merits of the bill came from Representative Swagar Sherley of Kentucky, who presented two letters from Secretary of the Interior Garfield. In one letter Garfield cited a dozen constitutional precedents for the proposed land acquisition, starting with the purchase of the Louisiana Territory. In the other letter the secretary wrote that it would be a "national calamity" if the Calaveras trees were lost.

The Interior secretary then described three methods of assuring their preservation under the current bill, all without appropriation from the Treasury: (1) by an exchange of national-forest land for private land; (2) by exchange of national-forest stumpage for the private land and trees; (3) by one of these exchanges plus private gifts by Californians. Assured by the floor manager that the bill "does not permit of any fancy valuation of the trees," the House passed it by unanimous consent.

In the entire two years of its consideration by Congress, not one word was spoken against the bill's objective or against the propriety of preserving the trees through an exchange of lands or timber of equal commercial value. Why, then, was the exchange never carried out? One may suspect that it was because the bill was passed so close to the transfer of the presidency from Theodore Roosevelt to Taft, and of the Interior Department from Garfield to Richard A. Ballinger.

After interviewing all the California congressmen, Wilbur reported to me that Chet Holifield of Los Angeles and Clyde Doyle of Long Beach were strongly in favor of action under the 1909 law. Clair Engle, whose district was practically the private property of the Pickering Lumber Company, was rampaging against the proposition. Nearly all of the other members had reacted favorably but were not aggressive in support of the measure.

Meanwhile, in mid-February, I had my first contact with Secretary of Agriculture Brannan. We talked for some time before he brought in Forest Service chief Lyle Watts and Howard Hopkins, assistant chief for lands acquisition and planning. My desire at this stage was to get a line on Brannan—his character and his thinking. Sending Mrs. Edge the draft of a letter to accompany a California pamphlet on the proposed park, I gave an appraisal of the secretary. He was full of Forest Service misinformation, but not inclined to trust that agency, though he felt that its misdeeds were in the past. Also, his heavy load of other responsibilities prevented him from spending the time necessary to control it.

A couple of days later, this meeting was overshadowed by a conference which congressmen Holifield and Doyle, accompanied by Wilbur and me, held with Brannan, Watts, and Hopkins. This two-hour meeting displayed one silently enlightening feature. During the entire discussion, as far as I could remember, Chief Watts spoke not a solitary word after the initial introductions. Every question asked by the congressmen was answered by Hopkins, every objection came from Hopkins. One thing was certain: Lyle Watts had succumbed to his environment, swallowed up by subordinates of stronger purpose than himself.

Regional Forester P. A. Thompson of San Francisco was in Washington at this time, and I had no doubt that he suggested some of the inquiries that came from Brannan. The secretary had been told that the move to enforce the act of 1909 "was being secretly engineered by the Pickering Lumber Company," with conservationists as its aides or dupes. Holifield replied that Pickering "twice sent a lobbyist to Washington" to work against favorable action by the California delegation. Next, Brannan said he had heard from the same (undisclosed) source that it was "a scheme to make the federal government donate a state park to California," which had ample funds with which to acquire it. Holifield replied that he had a telegram from chairman Joseph Knowland of the state park commission pledging half a million dollars for transfer of the park to the state, and expressing belief that it could be raised to $1 million if Olmsted's units 3 and 4 (the Beaver Creek sugar pines) were included. Brannan seemed satisfied.

Wilbur and I talked with Regional Forester Thompson after this meeting and found him to be the ideological twin brother of Hopkins. The two conferences with the Forest Service had produced so sharp and concise a conflict of views that I set them down in "objection and answer" form in a letter I sent to Brannan the next day. First I explained that the 1909 act had established a "declared policy of the United States to acquire and preserve these trees through action by the Secretary of Agriculture." For the next thirty years the trees had remained protected by their isolation, but now "the building of a logging railroad makes execution of this [1909] law the decisive factor in their preservation." The Forest Service was interposing ten objections to the law's enforcement. My detailed analysis of the points at issue may be summarized as follows:

OBJECTIONS	ANSWERS
Timber exchanges should be used for national-forest, not state, benefit.	Congress set a different policy.
The act of 1928 superseded that of 1909.	The U.S. district attorney for Southern California said the 1909 act was still in force: the U.S. attorney general agreed.
Only sequoias were mentioned in the 1909 act; only sequoias should be protected.	Sequoias grew on no more than eight hundred acres of the three thousand included under that act.
Pickering refused to sell or exchange the sugar pines; the act provided no power to condemn.	Congressman Holifield thought public opinion would force Pickering to agree.
The law was forty years old.	Enforcement had been neglected for forty years.
California should buy the land.	State law required state funds to be matched by private gifts, unobtainable at present.
California would resent federal interference.	Both legislature and citizens called for federal action; only Pickering and a few officials were opposed.
If timber was exchanged, five counties would lose their 25 percent of receipts from timber sales, or $60,000 a year for ten years.	The counties' combined annual income from all national-forest timber sales during the past ten years averaged $5,580.90 (a figure from FS sales records which Watts and Hopkins refused to verify or refute).

The final two objections concerned reduction of timber resources available for sale in Stanislaus National Forest. My reply gave these figures: the national forest contained 4.4 (actually 4.358) billion board feet of commercial timer, compared to 100 million board feet in the proposed scenic reserve (as estimated by Olmsted). Hopkins claimed the footage was closer to 200 million. If he was right, commercial timber would be reduced from 4.4 to 4.2 (4.158) billion board feet. Furthermore, during the last ten years, a total of 127 million board feet had been exchanged by Stanislaus National Forest, for its own purposes, with no damage to the counties.

There seemed to be one difference, and only one, I told Secretary Brannan, between the routine exchanges then being made by the Forest Service and "the one which Congress . . . specifically authorized you to make. One is for commercial purposes; the other to preserve a part of the vanishing American heritage of the beauty and wonders of nature."

A set of questions which I prepared for Congressman Holifield to present to the Forest Service through Secretary Brannan produced one minor change in my "answers." The ten-year average of annual receipts from national-forest timber sales, received by the five counties, was lifted from $5,580 to $8,587. Assistant Chief Hopkins had "estimated" this total annual average at $60,000.

Harold Ickes and I talked with President Truman on February 21, hoping to stimulate action by Brannan. I commented about this to Mrs. Edge, "His attitude was good, though he did not commit himself. The Forest Service is getting in dutch in congressional quarters." I had also a possibly decisive development to report. Congressman Engle had changed his position; he was joining in a request by California congressmen that the full state delegation ask the secretary of agriculture to go ahead with the Calaveras action. The congressmen felt Pickering officials had deceived them by cutting trees they had promised to hold back on.

The full California delegation unanimously adopted a resolution on March 4, urging the secretary of agriculture "to take immediate action under the authority granted him" by the act of 1909 to obtain complete title to the lands covered by that act, or such part of them as he "deems adaptable to park purposes." Substantially the same lands had been recommended in the Olmsted report.

On March 20, Frederick L. Olmsted wrote to Secretary Brannan, offering to give what help he could in clarifying the delegation's reference to lands "included in the Olmsted Report of 1945" and identifying those "adaptable for park purposes" as set forth unit by unit in that report. It was his carefully considered professional opinion that, with the possible exception of fifty to eighty defined acres, the entire area specified in the delegation's resolution was not only adaptable for park purposes "but is as a whole of quite extraordinary importance, from a National standpoint as well as from that of the State," for preservation as nearly as possible in its natural condition. Olmsted amplified his position in a note of March 23. Thus the country's foremost landscape architect put his full weight behind the project.

Late in April, Holifield, Doyle, Wilbur, and I had another meeting with Brannan, Watts, and Hopkins. During the conversation Secretary Brannan asked Wilbur for some information about the quality of lands in the proposed park. "The best statement on that point," Wilbur replied, "is in Olmsted's letter to you of March 20." "I have never seen any such letter," said Brannan, and turned to the Forest Service men. "Oh," said Hopkins, "he wrote to you about . . ."—and mentioned something totally irrelevant to the controversy.

The next day I took copies of Olmsted's letters of March 20 and 23 to Brannan's office and sent them in to him with a covering note. He replied with a "thank you" note on May 4, accompanied by a confidential copy of his reply of that day to Olmsted. His note to me committed his department the furthest it had yet gone in support of the Calaveras project. It was also notable for mentioning the sugar pines, which the Forest Service had always carefully excluded from discussions.

Brannan's reply to Olmsted opened with "my sincere apology for the delay in acknowledging and thanking you" for the letters with their helpful information. He had been informed by the Pickering board chairman that the area designated for a park by the California congressional delegation "will not be cut, or at least will not be further cut, this summer." This pledge if confirmed would leave ample time for a field examination for which "your letters will be helpful. . . . A copy of your two letters will be sent the Regional Forester in charge of Forest Service Activities in California for use when the field survey is made."

I took malicious pleasure in informing Olmsted (on May 29) of the reason that Brannan had waited so long before answering the two letters. Concerning the attempt to suppress them I wrote, "It is routine, of course, to send letters addressed to the Secretary directly to the bureau with whose affairs they are concerned, but hardly routine, I should say, to have that bureau fail to prepare a reply for the Secretary's signature." After that, I said, Olmsted should not be surprised to learn that Regional Forester Thompson had given the state park commission on May 20 a statement on the Calaveras acquisition that "carefully and cleverly sabotoged it in every respect." That statement, I added, "is giving Mr. Brannan something to think about this week-end."

Thompson's subversive action came at the precise moment when it would do the most damage. Two days earlier, John Elliott had telephoned to me about the state park commission's meeting. He read me a telegram from chairman Knowland saying that it was being called to consider an assertion by Governor Warren that the federal government expected more from the state than the five hundred thousand dollars already pledged by Knowland. How much more? they wanted to know, and they needed more definite information about what Secretary Brannan planned to do and what he expected California to do.

I wrote all of this to Wesley McCune, Brannan's (pro-park) chief personal assistant. That was on May 19, the day before the park commission meeting in Sacramento. Next day came a wire from Gene Wilbur, telling of Thompson's actions. A copy of Thompson's presentation to the commission followed, accompanied by a note from Wilbur, who wrote that the meeting with the park commission would have been very successful if Thompson's testimony had not been so negative. "We wonder here in California," he said, if Brannan could possibly know the harm caused by such statements.

I wrote at once to Edward Dolder of the California Department of Natural Resources, telling him that as soon as Thompson's statement reached me I showed it to congressmen Holifield and Doyle. "They both regarded it— as I did—as deliberate and clever sabotage of the policies set forth by Brannan in the presence of all three of us" (and of Wilbur, Watts, and Hopkins).

Holifield and Brannan were both tied up by hearings, but Doyle made an appointment for himself and me with Wesley McCune, whose reaction I described to Dolder. Clearly, Thompson's statement was not an accurate reflection of departmental attitude, and Brannan was not aware of the situation. The Forest Service had officially reported a "constructive" conference.

I told Dolder that the one truthful assertion in Thompson's remarks—that Brannan had made no commitment to acquire timberlands by exchange—was presented in a way that falsified its meaning. What Brannan had told Holifield and Doyle, in my presence, was that, to prevent the government from being "put over a barrel," he would do all he could in negotiation "without doing anything that could be construed as a declaration of taking, which would compel a conclusion of the purchase." On that account he had "refrained from any actual commitment or any public statement."

I furnished Secretary Brannan with an analysis of Thompson's statement, listing nine misrepresentations of the secretary's position. The net effect had been to confine Department of Agriculture aid to implementation of the unimportant act of 1928, allowing that gift of land to match state funds used to acquire the South Grove of sequoias. Not a word had Thompson said about the all-important act of 1909 which covered the Beaver Creek sugar pines. I told Brannan also that Wilbur had talked with Governor Warren, while John Elliott had done the same by phone. Warren "committed himself in favor of what we are doing . . . this is reflected, apparently, in the attitude of the Park Commission."

Elliott send Regional Forester Thompson's statement to Ickes, and with it a letter from me incorporating what I had written to Secretary Brannan about Thompson. Ickes replied to Elliott, "I have never known Mr. Brant to go astray in his facts, and my experience with the Forest Service has instilled in my mind a doubt either as to [FS] accuracy, or as to its desire to be accurate."

My letter to Brannan about Thompson, I learned from Wesley McCune on June 16, caused the secretary to send Assistant Chief C. M. Granger (a fair-minded and reliable man) out to the Pacific Coast to "tell Thompson to get on the ball." By that time I had a reply from Dolder. Writing that day to Brannan, to thank him for sending Granger, I quoted Dolder's remarks confirming my opinion of the effect of Thompson's statement on the park commission, and stating that the commission would be glad to meet with Brannan.

Governor Earl Warren wrote to Brannan on June 17, setting forth the state's position and wishes regarding the area desired by the California congressional delegation. Warren's letter was published in California on the twenty-third, and Gene Wilbur telephoned me that evening. The letter, he said, was being rushed to me by air mail. It contained two features that deeply disturbed him and Elliott and they were sure I would feel the same way.

Warren's letter began with an excellent general statement that in his opinion, the area would constitute an "unsurpassable Memorial Park." He pledged California's cooperation. The governor told of the allocation of five hundred thousand dollars of state-park funds toward land acquisition, besides which, money would be available to reimburse the counties for loss of national-forest revenues. Then came the two disturbing features. The state hoped for acquisition of all the properties described in the Olmsted report and the congressional resolution. However, if this could not be achieved, the state "would be happy to proceed with you [Brannan] on a partial basis in accordance with the priorities set up in the Olmsted Report and adopted by the State Park Commission by resolution on May 15, 1946."

The suggestion of proceeding "on a partial basis," Wilbur and Elliott thought (and I certainly agreed with them), was a wholly voluntary and needless concession. But to make matters worse, Wilbur said, the governor had made an incorrect listing of the "priorities" set forth in the Olmsted report, putting them in their numerical order instead of Olmsted's declared order of preference. And, Wilbur said, he had learned that the governor was led into this course of action by Republican state senator Mayo, whose district included the Pickering lands, and who was in bipartisan alliance with Democratic congressman Engle.

Describing the governor's action to Secretary Brannan two days later, I wrote that Warren no doubt was told, and believed, that in using the terms Unit 1, Unit 2, etc., he was following Olmsted's order of preference, but that was not the case. "Olmsted numbered them along a geographical curve, with the most important areas at the beginning and the end." I quoted what Olmsted wrote in 1945 about the superlative quality of units 1, 3, and 4—but in the Warren letter, "Mayo's maneuver drops Units 3 and 4 to the bottom, thus setting the stage for an effort to eliminate them in the later negotiations." I hoped that the secretary would intervene again to prevent the regional office of the Forest Service from seizing on this confusion to block the preservation of the sugar pines.

More than the Calaveras groves was in suspense at this time. Congressman Holifield on July 21 received a surprising telegram from John Elliott, a copy of which was sent to me. Elliott was in hospital, slowly recovering from cancer surgery. He told Holifield, "You're damn well right the fight to save the sugar pines and sequoias of Tuolumne will continue under leadership [of] Gene Wilbur." He urged immediate federal-state action before other park projects depleted state funds.

Wilbur wrote on my copy of the telegram, "JB is getting along fine [though] it will be a while before he is up." (The doctors' eventual verdict to Elliott: "You will die sometime, but not of cancer." They were right.) Saying nothing about his hospitalization, Elliott had let only a few days go by after surgery before he swung into the dictating of letters and telegrams, plus long-distance telephoning, in furtherance of his beloved project. Ickes, likewise informed of Elliott's illness by a copy of the Holifield telegram, replied to Wilbur, "It was just like him to keep up his interest in the South Calaveras Grove in spite of his operation. He is a real fighting man."

A fighting man himself, Ickes inclined to blame the White House for lack of progress. "I am about persuaded," he observed to Wilbur, "that President Truman never lifted so much as a finger in this whole matter, and if necessary, I am prepared to take his hide off." Applied to Truman, that method of securing cooperative action would have been about as successful as attempting to skin a rhinoceros. Something, however, was definitely going wrong. Granger's trip to San Francisco, to tell Regional Forester Thompson to "get on the ball," had produced nothing but a loss of yardage.

Thompson sent word to General Hannum, head of the state-park system, that on orders from Washington the Forest Service was going to survey the lands covered by the congressional act of 1928. Hannum was elated, supposing that this referred to the entire Olmsted area. He fell into utter confusion when Wilbur told him that the proposed action related to nothing except the proposed corridor between the north and south sequoia groves. But unless Thompson was lying, it meant that Brannan was backing down on the sugar pines.

Wilbur came back to Washington in August and he and I tried to figure things out. On every specific issue, the Forest Service arguments against implementation of the land-exchange law of 1909 had been refuted. Brannan recognized their invalidity but still avoided decisive action. In California, Elliott's War Memorial Association and the newspapers had built up a statewide support of the park unprecedented in vigor and unanimity. The entire California delegation in Congress, except Engle, was firmly committed to preservation of all four of the Olmsted units. Yet Brannan hung back, without giving any reason, and in conflict with his early cordial endorsement.

Congressman Holifield finally dug out the cause. Brannan had been told, and believed the story, that Gene Wilbur and Irving Brant were undercover agents of the Pickering Lumber Company, which was seeking to unload its Calaveras property on the state of California at a gigantic profit, with state and nation footing the bill. Brannan repeated this story to President Truman, and Truman related it to me in a chance encounter in the White House. "I don't believe it *about you*," he said, "but I guess there are shenanigans on both sides." In other words, Wilbur was a crook and I was his dupe.

Manifestly, this canard came from the San Francisco regional office of the Forest Service. There was no way by which such an accusation could be factually disproved; a person either believed it or he didn't. Brannan believed all of it, Truman believed only half of it; but, as far as results were concerned, a charge against one was a charge against both of us, as well as against our alleged employer, the Pickering Lumber Company. The movement to save the Calaveras big trees was stymied.

Gene Wilbur had the characteristics of an investigative reporter. Possessed of a hunting instinct, he had discovered the act of 1909, lost from sight for forty years. Something—perhaps it was this charge of being a Pickering secret agent—now caused him to enquire into the history of that lumber company. Searching in Standard and Poor's *Manual of Corporations*, he found that in 1936 the hard-pressed Pickering Lumber Company of Kansas City, Missouri, borrowed $2.5 million from the government's Reconstruction Finance Corporation. In 1941 (flush with profits in a revived economy) the Pickering Lumber Company had repaid the loan. The following trio were listed in 1948 as officers and directors of the Pickering Lumber Company: Ben Johnson, chairman of the board; James Madison Kemper, vice president; and A. A. Calkins.

Wilbur turned next to *Who's Who in America* and the *Official Register of the United States*. They revealed that in 1936, the year Pickering received its RFC loan, Ben Johnson was special assistant to the director of the Reconstruction Finance Corporation in Washington, D.C. In that same year J. M. Kemper was chairman of the advisory council of the RFC in Kansas City. And in that same year A. A. Calkins was manager of the San Francisco office of the RFC. The approval of these three officers, and of nobody else, had been necessary to the granting of that $2.5 million loan to Pickering. Shortly after the loan was granted, these three men resigned from the RFC and became directors and highest officers of the Pickering Lumber Company, for which they had obtained the government loan that saved it from bankruptcy.

Wilbur and I, accused by the Forest Service of being Pickering agents in a plot to swindle the federal and state governments, promptly put these facts before Secretary Brannan. We told him that we were going to ask Congressman Holifield to call for a congressional investigation of the whole affair.

Holifield did so on July 20, 1950, setting forth the complete record of Pickering's opposition to the park projects, the grant of the RFC loan, and the provision of offices to the RFC officers who put it through. He said that he was writing that day to Senator J. William Fulbright, chairman of an RFC oversight committee, asking him to investigate. He asked for immediate passage by the House of Fulbright's Senate-passed bill specifically outlawing such practices as this.

Holifield's action cleared Wilbur and me with Brannan, but in order to get the history of it into Agriculture Department records I described the whole affair once more in an August 11 letter to Brannan and turned from that to other adversaries of the parks. "You probably know," I wrote, "that the Calaveras Grove Association has called a field meeting for August 28"—a meeting, I told him, to inspect the sequoia and sugar-pine areas and to recommend park boundaries. I asked if he was aware that the association had been organized to support the Pickering Lumber Company's effort "to rob the State of California" of $1,750,000 as payment for a part of Unit 1 and that the main purpose of the August meeting was to prevent including units 3 and 4 in the park.

I failed to mention that the president of the Calaveras Grove Association, Mr. Gibbons, was the Pickering Lumber Company's fire-insurance broker. In the same letter I did pass along the information, derived from Wilbur, that the original draft of Governor Warren's published letter to Brannan called for preservation of the entire Olmsted area, saying nothing about the priority of certain units. Wilbur asked General Hannum, head of the state-park system, why the change was made. State senator Mayo forced it, Hannum replied. "Don't blame the governor. He wants to save the whole area, but he couldn't help himself. He *had* to do what he did." I commented to Brannan that even though he could not alter that situation, he could assure that his Forest Service subordinates would carry out his desires.

The kind of support they were to receive became manifest on September 1 when I met with Senator Sheridan Downey of California and Assistant Chief Hopkins, at Downey's request. The senator said that he was anxious to save the sugar pines, a course overwhelmingly supported in California. What was the Department of Agriculture's attitude? Following is the gist of the conversation, based on my notes.

Hopkins represented the Forest Service position as one of waiting for California to take the initiative. In response to Downey's questions, he brought up the old objections: their solicitor, he said, doubted whether the secretary of agriculture could act under the 1909 statute, since it was improper to exchange federal timber to aid a state park. I answered that Congress had established that policy by passing the act. According to Hopkins, the solicitor also doubted whether the 1909 act was still in force, the 1928 act having "provided a different policy." I countered that the solicitor had told the secretary that the act of 1909 remained in force. When pressed, Hopkins admitted that the only solicitor's opinion he actually had was a statement that the Forest Service could not use condemnation proceedings for the land.

Downey offered to present a resolution to allow condemnation and hold a hearing on it at once. When Hopkins remained silent, I spoke in favor of a hearing; we might learn something about the Calaveras Grove Association. I pointed out that the association was headed by a close friend of Ben Johnson and of Pickering interests, who had gone before the California State Park Commission to oppose preserving units 3 and 4. I added that Pickering was asking $1,500 per acre for land assessed at $28 per acre. Downey remarked that if that was the assessment, Pickering had better make an exchange quickly. He thought that the Forest Service was not being very helpful.

When Hopkins insisted that the Forest Service wanted to save as much as possible, I asked him whether he thought the agency had worked wholeheartedly to preserve the entire area. Hopkins said that it wasn't called upon to do so. How was it, I demanded, that Gibbons, the head of the Calaveras Grove Association, had said in writing that the federal government would not help in acquiring the entire area and that it was the Forest Service which would determine government policy? Hopkins answered that he did not know of such a statement. I told him I had the letter. Hopkins then said that under the 1928 law the state could pay Pickering five hundred thousand dollars if the federal government matched it with a gift of land. The joker, I replied, was that this would limit the acquisition to Unit 1. If the federal government acquired the sugar-pine area by exchange, under the 1909 act, and gave it, also, to California, the state's money would go twice as far.

The farcical one-day horseback ride of the Calaveras Grove Association, designed to revise the exhaustive Olmsted study, produced the expected result—a unanimous recommendation by the Pickering Company's fire-insurance broker and several misled conservationists that the sequoias (worthless as lumber) be saved and the sugar pines and ponderosas be left to their fate. Shortly afterwards, Secretary Brannan held a meeting with leading Californians headed by Assemblyman Sam Yorty. Gene Wilbur, who was present, wrote about this and later events to Ickes: "Secretary Brannan was most emphatic about his desire to save the trees." Brannan even admitted that the Forest Service was not trustworthy. Speaking to Senator Downey, the secretary had been just as emphatic. It was Wilbur's impression that "Secretary Brannan is willing to commit himself whenever he talks to our friends, but when it comes to actually doing something it seems that is a different matter."

Wilbur urged that Ickes speak once more with President Truman about the matter and added, "I am taking the liberty of sending [a] copy of this letter to Irving Brant, and suggesting that he talk to you about it."

Regional Forester Thompson, replying to Downey's request to be kept informed about all conferences between his bureau and Governor Warren's representatives, assured the senator on December 13 that both agencies were "investigating possible action in line with recommendations of the Calaveras [sic] War Memorial Association, Sierra Club, Calaveras Grove Association, and other interested groups and individuals, most of whom participated in a planned field trip over the area in question."

How could there be action in line with the contradictory positions of Elliott's War Memorial Association and Gibbons's Calaveras Grove Association, the one committed to the preservation of all four Olmsted units, the other committed to the destruction of units 3 and 4 (the Beaver Creek sugar pines and ponderosa pines)? Thompson's artful letter pointed to the real state of affairs. Brannan, though distrusting the Forest Service, still allowed it to be his spokesman and could not penetrate its skillful maneuvering against his declared policy. The Pickering officers, unable to fight openly now because of fear of a congressional investigation of their RFC loan, were entrusting their interests entirely to the Forest Service and the Calaveras Grove Association, headed by Pickering henchman Gibbons.

The movement for big-tree protection took a long jump ahead on January 16, 1950, when the California State Park Commission announced that it was doubling its five-hundred-thousand-dollar September allocation of park funds for that purpose. The state would provide $1 million in matching funds, on condition that the United States carry out the provisions of the act of 1928 for a gift of corridor lands to the state.

Coupled with this doubling of the allocation, though not made a condition of it, was the fact that the Bureau of Public Roads, with the approval of the secretary of commerce, had agreed to build a highway in the inter-park corridor to be transferred to the state under the act of 1928. Combined with the value of the national-forest lands thus given, this would produce an estimated $1,250,000 to match the state's $1,000,000, producing a total of $2,250,000. All of the state money could then be applied to purchase of Pickering lands for park purposes. Add a moderate timber exchange under the act of 1909, and the entire area recommended by the Olmsted report could be saved from destruction.

These successive California actions, instead of ending the covert opposition of the Forest Service to enforcement of the 1909 law, intensified it. This was manifest both in its own actions and in letters drafted for the secretary's signature, subtly conflicting with his declared policy. On February 15, 1950, I wrote at length to Brannan, pointing out instance after instance in which his letters, routinely drafted by the Forest Service, had given hope to park opponents. I closed my letter by saying that I realized it was difficult for the secretary to believe that the Forest Service was "sabotaging" his policies; it had been difficult for me to believe when I first encountered this spirit in 1929.

Former Interior secretary Ickes took up this theme in a March 6 letter to the president. Reminding Truman that on two occasions "[Irving Brant] and I have both called on you with reference to this matter," he said that after his last talk with the president, "I took the liberty of quoting to him [Brant] what you had said to me about it"—that Secretary Brannan could be counted on to save the trees. Brant, he continued, had apparently verified that although Forest Service officials knew that California had increased its offer from half a million to a million dollars, they had not told Brannan. Perhaps now that the secretary had been better informed, he might "be disposed to go ahead and conclude this matter in the public interest."

"It would be just like the Forest Service," Ickes added, "to try to pull the wool over the eyes of Secretary Brannan." He told about the "deliberate deceit" the Forest Service tried to practice on President Roosevelt during the Olympic Park campaign. Now the issue was the finest sugar and ponderosa pines in the world, but "as usual" it would take superior force to make the Forest Service behave as it should.

Two days later, congressmen Holifield and Doyle addressed a joint letter to Chief Watts on happenings of the previous few days. It showed wide divergence between Forest Service attitudes as described by Secretary Brannan to the two congressmen and as described by the Forest Service itself to the same two congressmen. Writing for both himself and Doyle, Holifield stated that on March 2 Brannan had told them that the Forest Service was "in complete agreement" with the California State Park Commission. Four days later, Brant, Doyle, and Gene Wilbur had met in Holifield's office to go over the situation, as gleaned from statements by Hopkins and Assistant Chief Granger and from park commission records.

Our summary showed agreement between the state park commission and conservation organizations "for the preservation of the entire area covered by the Olmsted Report, if possible." Satisfactory arrangements had been made, "approved by the Forest Service," for joint federal-state action under the 1928 law to acquire units 1 and 2 of the Olmsted report and build an inter-park highway on national-forest lands thus given to the state.

Hopkins had also "discussed favorably" the acquisition of Unit 4 and a small portion of Unit 3, to be purchased with the available $1,000,000 in matching funds. With these additions, the amount appropriated by California would be short $550,000 to $800,000 of the purchase price of the park. Hopkins suggested that this deficit could be made up by state-park funds "to be matched by private gifts raised by conservation organizations."

Holifield and Doyle told the chief forester that the Forest Service proposed no plan for acquiring approximately four hundred acres described by Olmsted as containing a sugar-pine stand so distinctive that its like "will probably never be seen again anywhere in the world, if it is not preserved here." In fact, Hopkins said the Forest Service "has no plan to acquire any of these scenic forests by exchange," as authorized by the 1909 act. That was to be left to private contributions, concerning which the two congressmen declared, "Past experience in California leaves no doubt that the project will come to a halt at the exact spot where reliance has to be placed on private gifts, instead of joint State and Federal action."

The congressmen said that they spoke for the entire California delegation in saying that "our primary desire is to save the trees for recreational use of the people." The reasonable way to that end was federal initiative under the act of 1909 to secure the balance of the area.

A week later (on March 16) John B. Elliott, writing jointly to Harold Ickes and me, sent copies of a February 24 letter from Chief Watts to U.S. senator William F. Knowland of California. Elliott had just received it "through a third party." Sent by Watts in response to Knowland's request to be brought up-to-date on "the proposed sequoia-sugar pine state park," it bore all the earmarks of a Hopkins creation. Following a request by Secretary Brannan for state initiative, wrote Watts, a field trip had been "held last summer under the sponsorship of the Calaveras Grove Association." It resulted in agreement "that the best method of acquiring the selected area was via application of the 1928 law" matching federal and state contributions, "further supplemented, if necessary, by public contributions." This was satisfactory, Watts understood, "to all major conservation groups in California except the California War Memorial Association," which still insisted that the 1909 provisions be applied.

Watts was too fair-minded and not clever enough to have composed that letter, whose real meaning came down to this: A business attache of the Pickering Lumber Company, by means of an "expenses paid" excursion, had trapped honest conservationists into approval of boundaries that would protect the South Grove sequoias and deliver the Beaver Creek sugar pines to the Pickering axe.

It was felt, the Watts letter concluded, that continuation of this cooperative action by state and federal authorities and the private landowner would expedite acquisition and preservation "of the most valuable and scenic groves of virgin sequoia and sugar pine trees." There was no indication in the letter that the entire controversy hinged on the sugar pines.

John Elliott wrote Knowland a five-page, single-spaced analysis of Watts's letter, a copy of which, he said, he had received from a California friend. Watts had said he wanted to give Knowland "a FEW pertinent background facts." Elliott offered to supply some pertinent facts that Watts had omitted; the most important omission concerned sugar-pine preservation.

Elliott quoted what Olmsted had written about "these marvelous Sugar Pines," irreplaceable if destroyed. He then cited the state park commission's resolution of September 16, 1949, for acquisition of "the entire Olmsted area." Not a hint of this had gone into the Watts letter, although, said Elliott, Regional Forester Thompson was in the room when the park commission acted.

Watts likewise had ignored the unanimous resolutions of the California congressional delegation and the California State Legislative Assembly calling for preservation of the entire "Sugar Pine Forest" and sequoia areas. To cap it all, Watts's utterances conflicted with three letters or public statements by Secretary Brannan, quoted by Elliott, all committed to saving the total stands of sugar pines and sequoias. And all the backing for Watts's position was a one-day horseback and foot "inspection" of three thousand acres "by a dozen or so specially invited individuals," which was designed to make them "do just what they did do"—advance proposals "too ridiculous for most people, but not too ridiculous, apparently, to be taken seriously by Mr. Watts, who bases his decision on this *one-day, pedestrian and horse survey!*"

Mr. Ickes' letter of March 6 to President Truman, sent by the president to

Secretary Brannan, drew a reply from the latter dated April 12, in which, wrote Brannan to Truman, "I regret having to advise you that Mr. Ickes' account of the situation is not accurate." Ickes sent both letters to me with a request that I draft an answer from him to the president.

It was easy to dispose of Brannan's statement that Ickes' letter was "not accurate." I wrote that between March 6 and April 12 the situation had changed radically. A series of conferences between California congressmen and the Forest Service had led to an important enlargement of the project. Brannan now proposed using the 1909 act to acquire by exchange the northerly sugar-pine area. It was the previous omission of the sugar pines that had caused Ickes and me to bring the matter to Truman. I pointed out that although the California administration was Republican, leading Democrats of the state were working to save the trees. Any benefits their party might derive must result from wholehearted participation of the national administration in the movement. The general situation was immensely improved and there now seemed harmony of purposes among the California congressional delega-. tion, the state park commission, the California War Memorial Association, and the Department of Agriculture. Brannan's attitude was always affirmative, I added, but he had to bring his subordinates into line. "All that remains is to press the project to completion. In this the continued evidence of your interest is bound to be helpful."

That was close to being the final observation on the long and hard campaign. Secretary Brannan moved slowly toward fulfillment of his promise to negotiate a timber exchange, under the 1909 Calaveras Bigtree Act, for preservation of the Beaver Creek sugar pines. However, there was continued uneasiness concerning his final attitude.

On December 8, 1950, Elliott wired Congressman Holifield about putting fresh pressure on the secretary to do what he had agreed to do. President Truman could not be bothered at the current stage of the Korean war, Elliott wired, "but Ickes and Brant talked twice with the president and from what he said to them he must have told Brannan to act." Elliott gave Holifield my telephone number and said, "He and Ickes can and will I am sure remind Brannan what [the] president said."

Sending me a copy of this telegram, Elliott asked me to contact Holifield immediately. Holifield held a series of meetings with Secretary Brannan. The upshot was that Brannan wrote a final and conclusive letter to Governor Warren on January 29, 1951. The regional forester at San Francisco was directed to "negotiate with Pickering for the acquisition of" the remaining 330-acre tract through an exchange for other national-forest stumpage. This was the first formal, official order that the tract be acquired and protected under the controversial act of 1909, which thus was being brought into operation forty-two long years after its enactment.

Not knowing of this definitive action, John B. Elliott addressed a letter jointly to Harold L. Ickes, Irving Brant, and Dr. Willard G. Van Name. Expressing fear (not unfounded) that there might be a final slip-up in application of the 1909 law, he said he wished that "some large, private cash donations" could be obtained to match state contributions. It would mean "the certain saving of the great Pines . . . as well as the remainder of the area covered by the Olmsted Report."

Transmitted apparently by telepathy, that same thought entered into the mind of Aubrey Drury, who for six years had held the Save-the-Redwoods League to a strict course of non-benevolent neutrality. On learning of Brannan's order for action, and Pickering's surrender, Drury jumped on a train for New York City and came back with a pledge of $1 million from John D. Rockefeller, Jr. The Save-the-Redwoods League put out a news release, announcing that the most magnificent sequoias, sugar pines, and ponderosa pines in the world had been saved from destruction through the cooperative efforts of the Save-the-Redwoods League, the state of California, and the United States government and through the generosity of Mr. Rockefeller. Not one word was said by them about John B. Elliott, whose money ($75,000, according to Gene Wilbur), determination, years of unremitting devotion—and almost his heart's blood—had wrought this miracle.[3]

The Rockefeller gift, overpaying Pickering, reduced the need for the Forest Service timber exchange directed by the law of 1909. However, considering the decisive role which that law played in the salvation of the Beaver Creek sugar pines, the final agreement could rightfully be called the culmination of the Calaveras Bigtree Act.

Split Mountain and Green River gorge, threatened with damming, was saved after the vocal and well-organized protests of conservationists (photograph by Marc Gaede, courtesy the photographer).

CHAPTER EIGHTEEN

FROM DINOSAUR
TO THE FUTURE

Late in the 1940s, two dangerous new assaults on the national-park system were launched. First, the Bureau of Reclamation developed a plan to build two hydroelectric-power dams in the Dinosaur National Monument on the Green River in Utah and Colorado. The chosen locations were Echo Park and Split Mountain, the most spectacular spots in a mighty gorge comparable in beauty to the Grand Canyon of the Colorado several hundred miles downstream. Conservation organizations rose in their defense, but pro-dam forces were powerful and the general public showed no concern.

Interior secretary Oscar Chapman wrote me on March 16, 1950, that "eager to have the fullest possible presentation of the 'pros and cons'" before deciding whether or not to approve the projects, he was going to hold a public hearing in Washington on April 3. Knowing of my interest in the matter, he wished me to testify.

My testimony took the form of a letter written to Chapman for the record at the close of the hearing. The proposal by Reclamation to build those two dams, I said, "is one more move in the incessant drive to break down the national park system by subordinating all values not measurable in dollars." This one was the more serious because it came from a bureau that bore no malice to the Park Service. It was easier to deal with a deliberate attempt at destruction than with lack of perspective. Moreover, since both of the involved bureaus were in the same department, the secretary was cast in the role of neutral arbiter rather than clearcut champion of conservation against outside assault. As to the specific issue: "The Dinosaur National Monument was enlarged in 1938 from 80 acres to 209,744 acres—from a dinosaur quarry into an awe-inspiring example of the making of river canyons and a cross-section of the earth's history before, during and after the age of dinosaurs." However, the advent of World War II and continuing tensions in the years since prevented opening the enlarged monument. If it had been accessible to the American people, I said, they would now be rallying to stop the proposed flooding.

I turned then to the argument made in the hearing that the dams would add to recreational values: "Artificial reservoirs between canyon walls cannot develop a natural shore line in a thousand years." Seasonal fluctuation of the water level would turn creek beds—the only landing places—into hideous mud flats. The unique and tremendous educational value of Dinosaur National Monument, I wrote, lay in the "visible presence of the world's greatest prehistoric animals. . . . But if these dams are built, the one *living element* in the story—the mighty force of stream erosion—will be buried under stagnant ponds."

Why, I asked, were these sites chosen, rather than other sites available nearby outside the monument? To escape slightly higher costs and a trivially higher rate of evaporation. What would become of that lost water vapor? "It will be precipitated as rain on the western slope of the Rockies and come right back into the river system."

To my intense surprise Secretary Chapman made favorable reports on the Echo Park and Split Mountain dam bills—an action hailed with loudly expressed joy by Democratic senator Elbert Thomas of Utah, then a candidate for re-election. Defense of the national monument, however, was steadily rising. In February of 1951, I wrote to President Truman, asking if he was aware that his administration was needlessly headed into trouble because of Chapman's support of bills to build dams in Dinosaur Monument.

The Dinosaur dams, I said, were practically certain to be defeated in Congress, where they faced an unnatural but inevitable coalition of opponents—a combination of conservationists and private-power interests. The only result of Chapman's actions would be a black eye for the Truman administration: "I have every confidence in the good intentions of Secretary Chapman, but he has made a huge mistake in yielding to the little bloc of intermountain congressmen and the combination of pressure and callous inertia in the Bureau of Reclamation. Politics being what it is, the punishment will be visited on you, not on him." Yet, I said, if no dam sites existed inside the monument, dams would be constructed elsewhere with no concern for the insignificant objection (higher rate of evaporation) now made to other locations. I said that I was aware of the president's "hearty support" of the national-park system. I hoped that he would talk to Chapman.

President Truman replied immediately that it was "an interesting subject for discussion and one in which I am very much interested." He went on: "Sometime or other I hope to take a look at the River which is affected by these dams and see just exactly what the controversy is about. It has always been my opinion that food for coming generations is much more important than bones of the Mesozoic period but I'll be glad to talk to you about it sometime."

This comment indicated that Mr. Truman shared the widespread misconception created by the word "dinosaur" in the name of the national monument. He thought that the choice was between a needed irrigation project and the preservation of dinosaur bones located well above the flood level of the projected reservoir. A misconception like Truman's was implicit in the attitude of Michael W. Straus, commissioner of reclamation. Straus wrote to a friend (Henry Collins, Jr.) that on his return "from a slight trip around the world" he had been surprised at the protestors who had joined each other in "factless emotion" over dams that were "not going to inundate a single dinosaur bone." All that really was involved, he asserted, was "the highest use of these resources of water and land."

I had no share in developments which could have been labeled (1) the awakening of Secretary Chapman, and (2) the awakening of President Truman.

A few minutes before the dam-sites hearing opened, on April 3, 1950, Commissioner Straus took a paper out of his pocket and asked permission of Secretary Chapman to offer it in evidence. It was an agreement signed by Straus's predecessor John C. Page and national parks director Newton Drury, in which Drury gave full approval to the Echo Park and Split Mountain dams. Chapman forbade Straus to present it and put the paper in his own pocket. Later, Chapman showed it to former secretary Ickes, who said he had never heard of it until that moment. This deception of two secretaries of the interior finished Drury with Chapman, but left a question unanswered. Why had the secretary approved the bills? Chapman gave me the answer after he left office. He approved them by order of President Truman, who had been told by Senator Thomas of Utah that he must have a victory on the Echo Park dam in order to win re-election.

Election day came and the dam victory failed to save Thomas from defeat. Eventually, Secretary Chapman told me what followed. Several months after the election he pointed out to the president that now the main political beneficiary of the dams was Republican senior senator Arthur Watkins of Utah, the new sponsor of the bills. "Do you want to help Watkins?" he asked. "No," replied Truman. So Chapman withdrew his approval of the bills and they died. When they were revived in the Eisenhower administration, Senator Watkins obtained White House support for them, but the bills got nowhere and the project shifted to sites outside the monument.

The facts about Drury and Page came to me from Harold Ickes.[1] When the former secretary revealed the story of Drury's long-concealed surrender to the Bureau of Reclamation, he added another item. At the time that Secretary Chapman took office, in January 1950, after Krug's resignation, most of his bureau chiefs offered to resign as was customary. Drury did not. Six months later, however, he had the brilliant thought of confronting the secretary with the possibility that his services might be lost. As Chapman described it to Ickes, Drury came to him and said that if there were any idea of relieving him of office, he would like to know it, since he had just been offered a fine position outside the government. Chapman told him there was no thought of a resignation. Then, deciding that Drury might walk out on the job at any time, he called him back and asked him to resign, advising him to accept the outside position. Drury admitted that he had no immediate prospects of another job. He resigned soon afterwards.

Shortly afterward, press dispatches reported that Earl Warren was about to make Drury (his college classmate) director of the California state-park system. Harold Ickes almost set his typewriter on fire in a four-page recital of Drury's incompetence and misdeeds. I wrote to Warren about my own experiences with Drury, and, with her permission, also sent the governor a telegram over the signature of Rosalie Edge, chairman of the ECC, saying that Drury "repeatedly jeopardized national park system by craven surrenders to lumbermen and other commercial interests." Old school ties won, and Drury did not do badly in his new position. A competent bureaucrat, he stirred up no controversies and luckily encountered none; so there was nobody to surrender to.

The end of the Truman presidency approached; war hero General Eisenhower defeated philosopher Adlai Stevenson for the presidency. In the field of conservation, one of the great works of Franklin D. Roosevelt still lacked consummation.

For fourteen years the U. S. Forest Service had been carrying out the command of the chief executive to acquire government title to nine square miles of private timberland in the Bogachiel River valley, to be added to the Olympic National Park by presidential proclamation. Still to be added to the park, also, were the Queets River corridor to the sea and the ocean-front strip running northward to Lake Ozette. A total of forty-six thousand acres were ready for inclusion.

The Bogachiel exchange had gone along steadily at first, with hard successful bargaining between the Forest Service and the principal landowners, Crown–Zellerbach and a Michigan-based lumber company. It inched along after those successful negotiations, and came to an abrupt stop with only eighty-two acres yet to be acquired. The Polson Lumber Company, owner of that isolated tract, could not reach it for lumbering, but Polson hated the Forest Service only a little less than he hated the National Park Service. He flatly refused to negotiate. Hope flared when Rayonnier Corporation absorbed the Polson Lumber Company, but alas, Polson's president became Rayonnier's vice-president for land management.

Eisenhower's election thrilled the Washington-state enemies of the Olympic National Park, and they fairly vibrated at the news that Governor Douglas McKay of Oregon was to be secretary of the interior. If presidential action could be staved off until after inauguration day, all of these lands would be saved FOR instead of FROM lumbering, and a new drive could be made in Congress to eliminate the entire Bogachiel Valley.

Conrad Wirth, successor to Drury as director of the National Park Service, was alert to the danger. Through Interior secretary Chapman, he secured White House authorization to draft a proclamation by President Truman placing the forty-six thousand acres in the park. Late in December 1952, Wirth asked me for an immediate conference. At it, he told me that secretary designate McKay was putting terrific pressure on him, through Oregon Republican senator Cordon, to delay completion of the presidential proclamation until after Eisenhower took office on January 20. Would I carry the matter to President Truman?

Knowing Truman, I phrased my letter of December 24 with two things in view—to stir him to anger and touch his pride. It began with this sentence: "Governor McKay seems to think he is already Secretary of the Interior." I then cited the pressure that McKay "is trying to exert through Senator Cordon, to keep you from enlarging the Olympic National Park by proclamation." I quoted from a newspaper interview with anti-park Congressman Mack of Grays Harbor. Mack had said that if the size of the park were to be increased before Eisenhower succeeded Truman, "it is doubtful that any congressional proposal to reduce the size . . . would stand chance of passage, as conservation groups fight such measures usually with much success."

In other words, I said, "They know that Eisenhower won't act, and that if you do, public opinion will sustain you. I have no doubt about your intentions, but am concerned lest the proclamation should accidentally be held up in the Bureau of the Budget or Department of Justice." Aside from the great merits of the addition, I said, the making of it "will link you . . . with the two Roosevelts in a half century of consistent work" for Olympic conservation.

I then warned Truman against what he was being told by Governor Arthur B. Langlie of Washington, that "modern methods of selective cutting will preserve the beauty of scenic forests." He should look at the cutting being done by the Rayonnier Corporation "under the best methods known," in the national forest at the very edge of Olympic National Park. Trees 250 feet tall, selectively cut, were being dragged out by bulldozers with virtually no difference visible to the eye between that and clear-cutting. Dirt piles were heaped up ten feet high.

The Grays Harbor sawmill interests, I said, wanted the private corridor left out of the park as an argument for eliminating the entire Bogachiel Valley. This scenic forest was not essential to the major wood-pulp interests, which operated on a sustained-yield basis, and lumbering it "would not save the dying sawmills which have doomed themselves by devastating their own lands." I concluded with hopes that he would take final action before the New Year.

In a brief conversation, Truman asked me to give his executive assistant, Charley Murphy, a thorough briefing on the Olympic situation. He followed that with a written "thank you" for my letter, closing with the words "That Executive Order will be issued very shortly." I talked with Murphy and found him thoroughly cooperative. Then, on January 5, the president wrote that I should be pleased to know that he was going to issue a public statement next day, saying that he had signed an executive order adding 47,753 acres to the Olympic park.

There was one thing Truman did not know, and I never told him—that, at the request of Charley Murphy, I had written the presidential statement on the subject. Truman's announcement said that the additions "bring to completion a great conservation undertaking sponsored by two former Presidents and authorized by the Congress. Theodore Roosevelt first gave it form on March 2, 1909, when he issued a proclamation establishing the Mt. Olympus National Monument. . . . The Olympic National Park, established for the benefit and enjoyment of the American people, now becomes the only park in the world to extend from snow-capped mountains to ocean beaches."

With the signing of the Truman proclamation, active hostility to the park dwindled to the opposition of two principal figures—Governor Langlie of Washington and William B. Greeley, general manager (retired) of the West Coast Lumbermen's Association. In May 1953, Governor Langlie appointed an "impartial" fourteen-person Olympic National Park Review Committee to consider park boundaries. Nine of its members could as well have been named Greeley. The committee invited comment, held hearings, and argued for eleven months, then made two reports. The nine Greeleys wrote one sentence: that the secretary of the interior should "designate two or more men of national standing in civic or land use planning to study all aspects of the Olympic National Park" and submit recommendations on boundaries or other aspects of management.

The governor refused to disclose the minority opinion signed by three women and two men, in this sequence: Mrs. Neil Haig, Karl Hartley, Jack Hollingsworth, Mrs. John A. Dyer, Rosamond P. Engle. The Washington state press began to clamor for disclosure; the governor remained obdurate. At last, on March 20, 1954, Langlie uttered one sentence: "Under the circumstances, I feel there is not sufficient crystallization of opinion among the committee members or among the public generally in this State, to warrant any further studies by a public agency of the State or Federal Government at this time." Still he refused to disclose the minority report. Three weeks later the *Port Angeles Evening News* got hold of both reports and published them on April 13.

The dissenters set forth their views in fourteen numbered paragraphs—championing the rain forests and other scenic wonders of the park, defending its territorial integrity, opposing timber cutting within it, and calling for reform of lumbering practices in forests under private ownership. It was not these arguments, however, that had caused Governor Langlie to suppress the minority report. The crowning blow was statistical. Of 307 persons who wrote to the committee during its year of activity, 300 were in favor of retaining present boundaries. That amounted to 98 percent. Langlie had dropped the study because there was "no crystallization of opinion" on it. There was in fact crystallization with a vengeance.

President Eisenhower looked upon conservation with total indifference rather than hostility. Secretary McKay displayed enough ineffective ill will to make all friends of conservation rejoice when he was supplanted by the better disposed Frederick C. Seaton in 1956. During the Eisenhower era conservation went through eight twilight years: no progress, no loss.

Every change of presidential administration has produced the same political phenomenon. Western henchmen of organized lumber, mining, and grazing interests have put public and private pressure on the president-elect to name a secretary of the interior who "understands the peculiar problems of the West"—that is, one who could be counted on to support lumber, mining, and grazing interests in their reckless exploitation of the country's natural resources.

I was living in Washington, D.C., when John F. Kennedy defeated Richard Nixon in 1960. Some days after the election, newspaper stories reported that two leading contenders for the Interior position were Congressman Clair Engle of California and Colorado governor Stephen L. R. McNichols. From the conservationist point of view, the only question was which was the frying pan, which the fire. But *Time* and *Newsweek* speculated about a cabinet post for Stewart Udall, the conservation-minded congressman from Arizona who had worked for Kennedy's nomination. The president-elect was then in Miami. I had no personal acquaintance with him. I telephoned to Meyer Feldman, head of Kennedy's personal staff, outlined the situation, and said that I wanted to write to JFK about it. Mr. Feldman told me to take one copy of my letter to Kennedy's office and have it put in a special mail sack to be sent to Miami that evening. He would carry another copy with him and deliver it personally.

My letter to Kennedy told about the chronic "problems of the West" syndrome and then described in detail the two-year campaign of Congressman Engle—in conflict with all the rest of the California delegation—to prevent the preservation of the Calaveras sugar pines and sequoias. If Engle should be chosen for secretary of the interior, I told Kennedy, millions of American conservationists would be thrown into a state of deep alarm. As for McNichols, naming him would cause despair.

It is a political truism that you can't beat somebody with nobody, but I did not want to weaken my case by plugging overtly for my preferred choice. So, without expressing a preference, I nominated five members of Congress, any one of whom, I said, would make a fine secretary of the interior. Of the five thus named, I knew that senators Jackson and Humphrey had other plans for the future, and George McGovern had said he would not leave the Senate. Chet Holifield would be "superlative" (but had little chance). I also filled out my list with three men of little or no political background. The fifth member of Congress that I named was Udall.

My letter was delivered to Kennedy, and I gave Udall a copy of it. Some days later, newspapers reported that the Arizona congressman had been summoned to the president-elect's home in Georgetown. I was in Udall's office when he came back from the conference and told me that he was to be secretary of the interior. His brother Morris Udall, who was elected to Stewart's seat in the House of Representatives, said to me at our first meeting, "You put me in Congress."[2]

My early talks with Secretary Udall were in line with a letter which I wrote to Secretary of Agriculture Orville Freeman on September 10, 1961. I had hoped, I told Freeman, to call on him before leaving the previous June for Eugene, Oregon, but pressures connected with completion of my final Madison volume had made that impossible. I said I had wanted to talk with him about the resistance of the Forest Service to the establishment of national parks and monuments. His "affinity of principle and purpose" with Udall should bring about effective cooperation.

"I am writing just now," I said to Freeman, "because of a situation that came forcefully to my attention during a motor trip this summer to the Pacific Coast." Shortly before leaving Washington, I had suggested to Secretary Udall "that he talk with you about . . . a joint request" for proclamation of a Mono Craters National Monument, to protect a twenty-mile chain of small volcanic mounts, craters, and lakes in the Inyo National Forest near Mammoth Lakes, California. Udall said this would need to have congressional backing from California. So I called on Representative Harold Johnson, in whose district the Mono Craters were located. "He did not commit himself, but his attitude sustained the good reports I have heard about him." Before coming out for such a plan, he said he would need support from his district, especially in and around Bishop, California.

So, I told Freeman, we had stopped at Mammoth Lakes on our way to Oregon. There I sought out John Haddaway, a manufacturer and leader of the pro-monument movement, who had introduced me to the subject in Washington. A tour of the area confirmed its national-monument caliber. It was as if all the great volcanic cones of the Cascades were brought into line in miniature, set in a beautiful forest of Jeffrey pines—parklike trees hundreds of years old but held to small size by low rainfall. Here was the situation as I retold it to the secretary of agriculture:

Mammoth Lakes was a small but fast-growing summer resort, with all homes and business buildings located on public land leased from the Forest Service. When the national-monument idea was broached, almost the entire community gave it enthusiastic support. So did businessmen at Bishop, fifty miles to the south. The supporters had three objectives: (1) to preserve the Mono Craters, (2) to halt the cutting and sale of Jeffrey pine (worthless as lumber) to a box factory at the giveaway price of $3.50 per thousand feet, (3) to stop in advance the impending ruinous mining of pumice blocks on the slopes of the little volcanoes. Haddaway told what happened after the Forest Service swung into action, and I relayed the story to Secretary Freeman. Resort owners on public land were notified that their establishments were substandard. When they discovered that "crippling expenditures" were needed to save their leases, they turned overnight into vociferous opponents of the national monument. Other pressures were exerted at Bishop. Most property owners in the region were now opposed.

What will happen, I asked, if Congressman Johnson consults businessmen in a community where fear is endemic? "He will find solid opposition among people who would be for the monument except for Forest Service coercion." (Needless to say, the monument project soon died, but it was not a natural death.)

I then described to Freeman the deliberate deceptions with which the Forest Service fought the establishment of the Olympic and Kings Canyon national parks and its similar campaign against preservation of the Calaveras sequoias and sugar pines. On my arrival in Eugene, I told him, I was hardly surprised to find the Forest Service fighting against its own system of wilderness protection. The supervisor of Willamette National Forest—the largest national forest in the United States—was addressing public meetings, telling people that the pending wilderness bill (which would become law in 1964) was a scheme to lock up timber resources and prepare the way for conversion of the entire wilderness system into national parks. That same forest supervisor, I reported, was working for a recreation plan that would open the beautiful Waldo Lake area to logging. Also, the Forest Service had in 1957 taken large forested areas out of the Three Sisters Wilderness and had begun bulldozing roads into the eliminated areas to frustrate any movement to restore their protection. I concluded with the hope that Freeman would tackle the difficult job of making the national forests serve the national benefit.

At the very moment this letter was written a fresh dispute over Olympic National Park was rising above the horizon. Most of the owners of 3,535 acres of private land in the North Quinault area (140 acres of which were cleared for pasture and homes) wanted their lands taken out of the park. Bills for that purpose were introduced in Congress. The Senate Committee on Interior and Insular Affairs (successor to the Committee on Public Lands) asked the secretary of the interior to appoint a group to study the problem and to submit its report to the committee.

Thus it came about that, in mid-July 1961, I was invited by Interior secretary Udall to become part of a three-man Quinault Study Committee. The two other members were Gordon D. Marckworth, dean of the College of Forestry of the University of Washington, and John Osseward of Seattle, president of Olympic Park Associates, Inc. The committee was appointed, Udall wrote, "for the specific purpose of studying and preparing recommendations on the desirability of excluding from Olympic National Park the privately owned land along Quinault Lake and in the Quinault Valley." Nothing was said about the public land intermingled with those private holdings.

At our organizational meeting in September (delayed by an Osseward business trip to Alaska), Osseward and Marckworth told me that their letters from Udall included the suggestion that I be made chairman. This was pleasing to my ego but conflicted with my judgment. John Osseward, I said, knew far more about the issues than I did, was acquainted with the people involved, and lived close at hand. He was elected chairman by two votes, with one abstention.

Disclosure of the committee's personnel brought cries of anguish from aggrieved landowners. Dean Marckworth was satisfactory to them, but Osseward and Brant were notoriously pro-park. There was some basis for their protests, because Osseward and I had long championed the park, but all three of us believed that the landowners had genuine grievances and we were determined to make a fair and thorough examination.

In truth, however, their demand for exclusion was made almost hopeless by the legal situation. The state of Washington in 1944 transferred exclusive jurisdiction over both public and private lands in the park to the federal government. That included a transfer of the state's police power. If only the private 3,535 acres were taken out, that would mean a change of governmental control every few hundred feet—an unworkable situation. So the actual question was whether 28,000 acres should be taken out to satisfy eleven resident and thirty-seven nonresident owners, and thirty-five year-round renters, or whether their legitimate complaints could be satisfied by improved administration.

The committee devoted four days—two in September, two in December—to lengthy meetings with the affected residents and the non-resident owners. Before leaving for a trip to Mexico, I sent my individual recommendation to Osseward for study by him and Dean Marckworth. It had become evident, I said, that all of the dissatisfied residents had important grievances but they were divided three ways about getting their lands out of the park. Some had an intense desire to get out, some a mild desire, and some were indifferent. My remarks would be based on an assumption that the desire to get out was strong and universal. In my view the private lands under study ought not be removed from the park. But the petitioners had real grievances, which I listed: (1) the North Shore Road was inadequate as to solidity and freedom from overflow, (2) road taxes paid by Quinault taxpayers were spent elsewhere, (3) enforcement of state laws against crime was inadequate, (4) possession of firearms was forbidden without a park permit, and (5) predators could not be killed without a permit.

The principal apprehension, we had found, was that through condemnation or negotiated purchases the government would ultimately destroy the Quinault farm community. School teacher Orlo Higley, president of the North Shore Association, made that the crux of the whole matter. "If we could be guaranteed keeping our private property," he said, "we would be satisfied."

To allay this apprehension I suggested that the use of condemnation power be limited to the prevention of nuisances or subdividing; that continued private ownership of farm houses be encouraged along with pasturage to open scenic vistas (already the principal use on the 140 cleared acres whose sandy soil was unsuited to agriculture); that purchase should be negotiated only for the unimproved lands along the heavily forested northern shoreline of Lake Quinault; that during the next half-century the government should purchase cutover lands for reversion to forest.

My recommendations were virtually identical with those drafted by Osseward and signed by the full committee. Marckworth, however, made a supplemental statement advising that "before final action is taken a committee of Congress hold an open hearing at Lake Quinault," so as to enable all property owners to "place their cause directly before members of Congress."

The 216-page report, crowded with pertinent pro-and-con factual material, represented chiefly the herculean labors of John Osseward, who also was responsible for establishing a friendly personal relationship between the committee and virtually every one of the dissatisfied property owners. The report was duly presented to chairman Henry M. Jackson of the Senate Committee on Interior and Insular Affairs. Several years went by, and I asked the clerk of the committee why the report had never been made public. "The chairman," the clerk replied, "thought it best to let sleeping dogs lie."

The report became public early in 1966 and stirred not an audible murmur of protest. Today the Quinault North Shore Road is paved and unfloodable. The private land is still privately owned. Further moves to take the inholdings out of the park have petered out for lack of support. Eventually, the same transformation may take place in public sentiment that has occurred in Jackson Hole, Wyoming. In 1943, at Jackson Hole, actor Wallace Beery and a young rancher named Clifford Hansen drove six hundred head of cattle across the protected land in symbolic protest against its inclusion in the national-park system. In 1974 this same Clifford Hansen, by then a United States senator from Wyoming, announced a vastly different project. Looking ahead to the twenty-fifth anniversary of the establishment of Grand Teton National Park, the senator asked, on September 5, 1974, that a presidential panel study the possibility of including more of Jackson Hole within park boundaries. The ranchers, Senator Hansen said, had found that their future lay with the park.

Although no such dramatic transformation has taken place in the Quinault Valley, people in Washington state are protective toward "their" parks now. Each threat to the Olympic National Park has been beaten back more decisively, with state support coming to be as strong as national.

The 1961 Quinault assignment nearly closed my national activities in conservation. That year also marked the beginning of the most harmonious relationship between the secretaries of the interior and agriculture that had been witnessed since March 3, 1909, the last day of Theodore Roosevelt's administration. Secretaries Freeman and Udall, after taking office, promptly formulated and signed a joint declaration of policy on relations between the departments, requiring close consultation between their bureaus in an effort to iron out differences. This bore rich fruit in 1968, when Congress passed a bill creating the North Cascades National Park, located east of 10,750-foot Mount Baker. The Forest Service had been fighting against its establishment for twenty years, with such success that organized support was long passed up as hopeless.

During regional Senate hearings on this bill in 1966, avaricious timber interests chose that occasion for a last desperate attempt to invade the Olympic National Park. They proposed a compromise, elimination of the Bogachiel River valley from the Olympic park, as the price for creation of a North Cascades park. Conservation organizations unitedly fought the scheme. My daughter Robin Lodewick testified and presented my testimony against this surrender, summarizing past struggles. The scheme was asphyxiated by lack of senatorial support.

Strangely enough, the greatest conservation struggle of the Kennedy-Johnson period involving the national forests was waged within the Forest Service itself between the Old Guard and the New Guardians. Within that bureau the Old Guard won at the outset, but the New Guardians teamed up with the forces of conservation, across the country and in Congress. That coalition produced the Wilderness Act of 1964, which not only was the greatest forward step of the decade in conservation, but came close to ending the long series of combats between the Forest Service and the National Park Service.

The Wilderness Act put the sanctity of law behind the pre-existing wilderness system, which had been set up in the national forests by successive secretaries of agriculture, but which could be abolished or reduced in size by departmental order. The Old Guard of the Forest Service, entrenched at the top and dominant all the way down, fought desperately to retain this unrestricted power to destroy its own handiwork, putting that above the immense gain that would accrue from undisputed sway over a consecrated wilderness system.

Congress overpowered the Forest Service and made it the unwilling guardian of its own wild places. The result: conservationists lost their feeling of need to turn outstanding wilderness areas into national parks for the sole purpose of making them secure against commercial exploitation. This almost wiped out the basis for the old antagonism between the Forest Service and the National Park Service, with benefit to both.

Yet controversies remain. In the seventies, two decades after the secretary of agriculture, at the behest of the Forest Service, took out close to a third of Oregon's Three Sisters Wilderness, this issue still festers. The purpose of the elimination (as I told Secretary Freeman in 1961) was to open the area—especially French Pete Creek valley—to roads and lumbering. In 1956 there were 175 such valleys in the Oregon Cascades—heavily forested, roadless valleys at a moderate altitude and ten miles or more in length. Twenty years later there are two—one on the slopes of Mount Hood, the other, French Pete, in the Willamette National Forest east of Eugene. In spite of growing sentiment to "Save French Pete," the Forest Service has been planning to log the valley. Preserving it, they said at protest meetings, would take away thirty-six future jobs. The Willamette National Forest has the largest commercial cut of any national forest in the United States; thirty-six future jobs mean nothing in the up-and-down swings of employment.

Several years ago French Pete received an apparent reprieve when the old saw-and-axe forest supervisor retired and one of the finest conservationists in the Forest Service took his place. But all that Zane Grey Smith could do was put French Pete as far into the future logging schedule as he was able to. Smith was afterwards promoted to a high position in the Forest Service's Washington, D.C., office—unfortunately, not one that determined policy.[3]

In the national-forest system as a whole there are dozens of similar conflicts between conservationists and the Forest Service over the establishment and management of wildernesses, and over roadless areas. The Old Guard is stubborn, but the New Guardians are growing in numbers and strength. Today in 1976, there are three high Forest Service officials, below chief forester, whose conservation principles are hard to distinguish from those of the Sierra Club. It is fair to say that if the best half dozen men in the Forest Service were placed in the top half dozen positions, it would work a miracle, bringing that all-important bureau into the final quarter of the twentieth century.

This improvement is due in part, I believe, to a slow growth of environmental sensibility in American schools of forestry. Years ago, Mrs. Harold Ickes asked me to recommend a conservation-oriented school of forestry, a subject in which her son was interested. I relayed the request to Interior forester Lee Muck—a man of knowledge and vision. He said that out of twenty-four schools of forestry in the United States, he could name only four that did not put paramount emphasis on the commercial aspect of forest management. In 1970, the Sierra Club and the Wilderness Society published a symposium grading forestry schools from the standpoint of ecology. Only the school at Cornell University received a passing mark. Nevertheless, the schools are sharing in the recent growth of national concern over the environment.

There can be no doubt about a vast upturn in both sentiment and organization for the defense of nature. Almost inconceivable developments have taken place in the forty-six years since Mrs. Edge and I organized the Emergency Conservation Committee—a committee without a constituent body behind it, as its enemies pointed out. In that day the only other aggressively active conservation organizations with national influence were the Sierra Club, Dr. Hornaday's Permanent Wildlife Protection Fund, and the American Society of Mammalogists. The new Wilderness Society was half free. Nearly all others were either comatose or wrapped in the hidden or open embrace of lumbermen, duck clubs, or gun and ammunition companies.

Today those shackles have been thrown off. The Emergency Conservation Committee broke the gunmakers' and duck clubs' control of the National Audubon Society. Time removed the remaining lumberman incubus, millionaire William P. Wharton, both from Audubon and from the National Parks Association. Irving Clark and fellow directors of the Wilderness Society smashed the tree-butchers' fingers that had grabbed its publication facilities. The Izaak Walton League no longer lets gun and ammunition companies pay its office rent. Of all the one-time "white slaves," only one remains a strumpet—the American Forestry Association. Organized, financed, and controlled by the timber industry as protective coloration, it still performs the same function to satisfy the same needs. Along with the regeneration of long-established conservation bodies came great increases in membership. New organizations proliferated; of more than thirty notably active conservation bodies, sixteen came into existence after 1950.

The Sierra Club, organized in 1892 for protection of the Sierra Nevada, remained so-localized for more than thirty years. It is now an international body approaching a membership of two hundred thousand. The Audubon Society, organized in 1905, corrupted in 1911, redeemed in 1935, now has an incorruptible membership of comparable size.

The National Parks Association, long after William Wharton's hold on it ended, changed its name to National Parks and Conservation Association and lived up to the two words newly inserted in its title. Women's clubs, garden clubs, and the League of Women Voters have enlarged their conservation work over the years.

New organizations gave promise in their names to what is being fulfilled in their deeds—Friends of the Earth; Friends of Animals; The Nature Conservancy; Resources for the Future; Trustees for Conservation; Defenders of Wild Life; League of Conservation Voters—the list is endless.

Environmental concern has become increasingly visible in federal and state courts, under the spurring of such bodies as the Sierra Club, the Wilderness Society, the Environmental Defense Fund, and the Natural Resources Defense Council. The courts gained immeasurably in power with passage by Congress in 1969 of the National Environmental Policy Act, which not only broadened their jurisdiction but made virtually all public works subject to an environmental impact study. Fortified by that act, courts have made decisions and victories have been won in cases that would have been tossed out for want of jurisdiction forty years ago.

The impress of environmental concern made itself felt upon Congress. In the face of alarm over a shortage of hydroelectric power, sixty-eight miles of Hells Canyon on the Snake River was saved from dams in 1975, its wild river and wilderness converted into a national recreation area. Outside pressure would have been exerted in vain had not the four congressional delegations most concerned—those of Idaho, Oregon, Washington, and Montana—united in championship of the protective legislation. Once these delegations were leaders on the other side.

Against this recital of gains must be placed a mindless aberration which temporarily dragged the National Park Service into the edge of the moral cesspool known as "Watergate." In December 1972, President Nixon forced George Harzog to resign as director of the National Park Service and replaced him with Ronald Walker, a White House aide who had been the president's number one advance man during the presidential campaign. The *New York Times* protested in vain against this political appointment.

Mr. Walker, ensconced in office, lost little time in formulating plans to "improve" the park system. In September 1973, the Yosemite Park and Curry Company (the Yosemite Park concessionaire) was purchased by MCA Recreation, Inc., a subsidiary of the Music Corporation of America. Following that, MCA Recreation asked the National Park Service for permission to tear out 150 low-rent cabin-tents at Camp Curry and replace them with luxury motel units. NPS professional planners protested, and Walker conceded that an environmental-impact statement must be submitted. Nevertheless he notified MCA that the decision had been made and they could proceed to build the new units.

When news of these happenings reached the environmental groups, the Sierra Club, the National Parks and Conservation Association, the Wilderness Society, and Friends of the Earth raised nationwide outcries. Congressional committees began an investigation, headed jointly by Henry S. Reuss, chairman of the Subcommittee on Conservation and Natural Resources of the Committee on Government Operations, and John D. Dingell of Michigan, chairman of the Subcommittee on Activities of Regulatory Agencies of the Permanent Select Committee on Small Business.

Reuss and Dingell had found out enough before the December 1974 hearings to suggest that "the concessioners, not the National Park Service, are running the national parks." New facts were piling up. The Walker plan included development of Yosemite Valley as a year-round convention center, with big hotels surrounded by a veritable amusement park and with the valley used as a scenic setting for commercial motion pictures to stimulate visitation (already too great).

The two subcommittees held joint hearings in December 1974, going into the whole subject of national-park administration of the concessionaire system. Walker's troubles flared higher with the filing of a $1.2 million damage suit against him and other Nixon "advance men" on the charge of violating civil rights and liberties by "dirty tricks" in the 1971-72 presidential campaign. Interior secretary Rogers Morton could not stand the heat and in October demanded Walker's resignation. He obtained it, effective December 31, 1974.

The resignation did not cancel the congressional investigation. Walker was ordered to appear before the two subcommittees on December 20, 1974. He consulted various assistant secretaries and was advised to fly out to Denver. The committees could be told that an important conference prevented his attendance, while his deputy director appeared instead. Walker went, and received an ultimatum: appear tomorrow or face a subpoena and possible charge of contempt of Congress. At 6 p.m. on the twentieth Walker took the stand before the fuming congressmen. He explained that to avoid flying all night and appearing unprepared, he had flown all day—and was still unprepared.

The hearing record filled more than three hundred pages given over to pillorying Walker and exposing the evils of the concessionaire system—evils that will never wholly disappear until Congress follows the advice of Secretary Ickes that the government provide all housing and camping facilities in the national parks. The physical and managerial scars left by the Walker-Nixon invasion of Yosemite have been wiped off, except for the damage to lichened rocks painted over by movie crews.

Looking ahead to future presidential administrations, we know that conservation will become an ever-more-central issue, both nationally and worldwide.

The broadened outlook of concerned Americans today finds expression in the growing use of the word "environment," which expands conservation of natural resources to preservation of the planet Earth as a place fit for human abode. The task of preservation is widening yearly as technology permeates industry and the human mind penetrates more deeply into the secrets of the universe. New problems sweep into view before old ones are solved.

Will human error dissolve the ozone layer of the atmosphere at the edge of space and bring down on us the destructive ultraviolet radiation of the sun? A six- or seven-degree change in the earth's climate, down or up, would produce a new ice age or melt the polar ice caps and flood great cities and lowlands. Will excessive burning of fossil fuels produce such a change of climate? Will a nuclear accident depopulate a city or state? Will nuclear warfare wipe out half of the world's population and its radioactivity exterminate the other half, along with animal and plant life? Such an all-consuming calamity is not a mere remote possibility. It is an actual likelihood as nuclear knowledge is recklessly disseminated for financial gain and nuclear weapons pass into less-and-less responsible hands, potentially including those of American, Soviet, or Chinese madmen. Compared with the hazards that lie ahead, the vast growth of environmental understanding during the last decades is no more than a child's—barely a beginning—and time is growing short. Let us bring the matter down from cosmic errors to more controllable but hardly less critical matters. The Mediterranean Sea, according to oceanographer Cousteau, is gradually turning into a dead body of water, soon to become devoid of all marine life, owing to excessive runoff of salinated water and to human pollution. How many years have we left before the three great oceans are similarly afflicted?

Closer at hand, and rushing inexorably toward us at terrific speed, is the catastrophe of over-population of the world by its dominant mammal, man. The time is close at hand when population must be controlled rationally, to avert control by some such means as the lemmings use—periodic wholesale plunges from Norwegian cliffs into the sea. With this problem clearly visible, how do we react to it? By debate in Congress, in the courts, and among the great branches of the Christian religion, over the exact moment when abortion of a human foetus becomes an act of murder.

If the choice of mankind is birth control by starvation, the method will be disastrously effective. First the poverty-stricken millions of the southern hemisphere will obliterate all birds and nonhuman mammals except the brown rat; then the process will creep northward, with the United States the last but not the least to suffer. By upsetting the balance of nature, we invite insects to take over croplands and spread disease. The attempt to wipe out supposedly useless forms of life, as former president James Madison told the Albemarle County Agricultural Society in 1818, can have disastrous effect upon the useful varieties. American government and society have not yet resurrected that truth.

Herein lies the great anomaly: while millions of Americans are joining forces to protect our heritage of forests, mountains, lakes, and rivers against destructive commercialism, while great national parks and wilderness areas are being set aside in America, worldwide conditions are being ignored—conditions that threaten to draw the entire human race into a vortex of destruction.

Looking ahead, I foresee a new assault on our protected areas. Wasteful overcutting of public and private forests and inadequate reforestation will produce attempts to raid both national forests and national parks. Such an attack can be coped with because it is easy to understand and the protectors are ready. But the leadership essential to that task must be dedicated to a greater chore—the salvation of the world from its greatest potential preserver and actual destroyer, Homo sapiens. The world needs a planetary leader comparable to Franklin Delano Roosevelt, and the human support needed to make that leadership effective.

NOTES

Initials at the end of each note identify its author. Some were included by Brant (I.N.B.) in his original manuscript; others were added later by editors Ruth Brant Davis (R.B.D.), Robin Brant Lodewick (R.B.L.), and Harold K. Steen (H.K.S.).

CHAPTER ONE

1. John M. Phillips is not to be confused with John C. Phillips, president of American Wild Fowlers. —I.N.B.

CHAPTER TWO

1. The *Star* had taken over and absorbed the *St. Louis Times*. —R.B.D.

2. Mrs. Edge's appearance on the program may have been a sign of change. Within the year, the American Game Association had been taken over by the broader-based American Wildlife Institute and the American Game Conference had been transmuted into a North American Wildlife Conference. Both changes were instigated by Darling and FDR. —R.B.L.

3. The Division of Grazing, established in 1934, supervised use of the public domain until 1946, when it was combined with the General Land Office and several smaller offices to form the Bureau of Land Management. —R.B.L.

CHAPTER FIVE

1. Congressman Cochran wrote Brant on Friday, August 13, 1937, that the Wallgren bill had been reported to the House, although Agriculture and Interior did not file reports on it "as they are still fighting among themselves."

Brant and Cochran did not know that Wallace had just prepared a three-thousand-word statement opposing the park bill. A ribbon transcript of this statement (dated August 13, 1937) is held by the Franklin D. Roosevelt Library at Hyde Park, where it is contained in a folder on the Olympic National Forest which was prepared by the Forest Service in 1937. See *Franklin D. Roosevelt and Conservation*, Edgar B. Nixon, ed. (Hyde Park, New York, Franklin D. Roosevelt Library, 1957. 2 vols.), item 700, footnote 2. —R.B.L.

2. The paragraphs which follow were checked, cursorily, against Clark's letter before the Brant papers were sent to the Library of Congress in 1977. When the manuscript quotations were fully checked against the papers at the Library of Congress in 1979, the Clark letter was missing. A paraphrase of it appears in a letter Brant wrote May 3, 1954, to Herman Kahn of the Hyde Park Library. The material in the present text to the best of my recollection is taken exactly from Clark's letter. Schulz's letters of October 27 and November 22, 1937, contain much of the same information. —R.B.L.

3. Official reports written by Tomlinson, Macy, and forest supervisor Bruckart give somewhat different accounts. Tomlinson wrote that neither National Park Service men nor people from groups favoring the park were invited to attend until the president said he wanted a representative of the Park Service. Regional Forester Buck phoned Tomlinson at 6 a.m. to say that the president wanted to see him at Lake Crescent that evening. Tomlinson met Macy (who had not been invited) at Port Angeles and took him along, though Buck doubted there would be room for Macy at the lodge. The Park Service men were finally assigned the last cabin.

Roosevelt asked both Tomlinson and Macy to confer with him; after a half-hour talk the senators, congressmen, and Forest Service representatives were brought in. Buck displayed a map of the peninsula which did not distinguish between small-growth and large-growth timber, using it to support his claim that good Douglas fir stands were found mainly along the Elwha River, near Port Angeles. Roosevelt understood the deception. The president pointed out that 80 percent of the land in the monument was barren mountain tops; he demanded more big trees in the park and said it should be three times the size of the area in the current bill.

Later Congressman Smith brought up the job-loss issue. FDR quoted figures to show that the timber in the proposed park amounted to 4 percent of what had already been cut on the peninsula and said that what remained was more valuable for recreation. The president also spoke about salvage cutting of dead trees in parks. —R.B.L.

4. Roosevelt learned that the sign had been moved, at Buck's orders, from an anonymous letter sent him by a Forest Service employee. (Carsten Lien, unpublished manuscript, *Olympic Battleground*) —R.B.L.

5. Total acreage in each of the three Wallgren bills varied slightly during their consideration by Congress. —R.B.L.

CHAPTER SIX

1. Arno Cammerer was the main speaker at the banquet. A news item in the *New York Times* on the following day (January 22) casts some doubt on Mrs. Edge's version of events, but does not disprove it. Under a Washington dateline of January 21, the *Times* refers to "tonight's dinner" and calls Ickes a "guest," who also spoke. Such evening events are sometimes written up in advance. —R.B.D.

2. I did not know until some years later that the larger of these closed-down mines was owned, through inheritance, by John Osseward of Seattle, one of the strongest advocates and stoutest defenders of the Olympic National Park. —I.N.B.

3. Wallace's approval of the second Wallgren bill in 1938 reversed his stand against both the first bill (H.R. 7086) in 1935 and the second bill (H.R. 4724) during the committee hearings in 1937. —R.B.L.

4. Brant gave Martin full credit for knowing what a "consultation" was. —R.B.D.

CHAPTER SEVEN

1. This refers to the fact that the sulfite process, which produces a strong paper that bleaches very white, requires wood pulp made from the lighter colored non-resinous softwoods like hemlock and spruce. Spruce was considered the standard material at the time; later, with less spruce available, hemlock and true fir were found to do as well. —R.B.L.

2. Copies of the printed Olympic report were also furnished to associate NPS director Demaray and park superintendents Macy and Tomlinson. I was given two copies, one of them for the rare book collection of the Library of Congress; two were retained by the NPS. President Roosevelt's copy never reached the Franklin D. Roosevelt Library at Hyde Park. Major Tomlinson's copy passed at his death to Irving Clark. After Clark's death it was catalogued at his house as a gift to the University of Washington, but disappeared before his books were transmitted to the university library. —I.N.B.

Both NPS copies were missing as of 1986. —R.B.L.

CHAPTER EIGHT

1. Ickes' practice of revising one sentence puzzled me until I discovered the reason for it in his published diary. He wrote that in the preparation of speeches he always furnished an outline of what he wanted to say; a subordinate then wrote a tentative draft, which he—Ickes—thoroughly revised. Not once, in the many speeches I wrote for him, did he give me more than the subject or the place and date. In the Roosevelt letter to Martin, Ickes altered the words "to express once more my conviction" to "to say once more that my conviction is." —I.N.B.

CHAPTER NINE

1. The explanation was in a letter to an enquirer, J.A. Cecil. —R.B.L.

2. In *The Secret Diary of Harold L. Ickes* (New York, Simon and Schuster, 1954. 2 vols. 2:486), Ickes says he had not expected to make a speech at the dedication, "but when called on did speak extemporaneously for about fifteen or twenty minutes." Raymond Clapper, in a column published October 11, quoted almost verbatim from the speech Brant wrote and attributed the words to Ickes. —R.B.D.

3. Ickes' speech was in part aimed at persuading Babler to contribute further to the cause of conservation, like Rockefeller. Asked for such help later by Conrad Wirth of the National Park Service, Babler said "no" but added, "Tell Secretary Ickes that if he runs for president, I'll put a hundred thousand dollars into his campaign." Ickes' desire to be president was known to everybody. I mentioned Babler's offer to Ickes, expecting a laugh. None came. At last he said, as if to himself, " I—wonder—if—he—would."

Sometime after that I learned firsthand how Ickes felt about the "Sixty Families" speech that had utterly ruined his presidential hopes. Tom Corcoran entered the secretary's office while Ickes and I were talking; during the conversation the "Sixty Families" speech came up. Ickes said to Corcoran, forcefully, "I didn't want to deliver the speech. YOU KNOW I didn't want to deliver it." —I.N.B.

CHAPTER TEN

1. The record for oldest known living tree has been held by bristlecone pines since the mid-1950s. First was Pine Alpha (4,300 years), discovered in the White Mountains of Inyo National Forest. The Methusaleh Tree, growing in the same area, took over in 1957, aged 4,600 years. During the 1960s a living 4,900-year-old bristlecone was found on Mount Wheeler in eastern Nevada. Since its discoverer established its age by felling it, Methusaleh remains the titleholder.

Certain live colonies of bog and desert plants are now thought to be far older than the bristlecones.—R.B.D.

CHAPTER ELEVEN

1. The *Congressional Record* for May 2, 1939, uses the spelling Dunwoodie, as do articles in the *Fresno Bee* at that period. All earlier references, including the record of the committee hearings on the Kings Canyon bill, use Dunwoody. —R.B.L.

CHAPTER TWELVE

1. Tehipite and Cedar Grove valleys were finally made part of Kings Canyon National Park by Congress in August 1965, while Stewart Udall was secretary of the interior. In 1984, the Sequoia-Kings Canyon Wilderness was established within the two national parks. —R.B.L.

CHAPTER THIRTEEN

1. William Schulz remained in the Northwest, working for the Interior Department. After an illness, he turned to freelance newspaper writing. When Mrs. Edge asked him in 1942 to work on the ECC Calaveras campaign, he declined because of writing commitments and the likelihood of being drafted. —R.B.L.

2. So-called "salvage" logging in Olympic National Park continued until 1956, when revelation by seasonal park naturalists and outraged protest by conservation organizations reduced the practice. (Carsten Lien, unpublished manuscript, *Olympic Battleground*) —R.B.L.

CHAPTER FOURTEEN

1. The Porcupine Mountains were commonly referred to in the singular, as Porcupine Mountain. —R.B.L.

CHAPTER SEVENTEEN

1. See chapter 5, footnote 1. Brant never knew of Wallace's statement of August 13, 1937. —R.B.L.

2. This Calaveras Grove Association took the same name as an earlier group which had worked for state purchase of the North Grove, then disbanded in 1932. —H.K.S.

3. Brant evidently relied on memory, rather than his records, in writing this paragraph. The actual purchase and land exchange took three more years. In April 1954 the *New York Times* reported purchase of the South Grove by the state of California, state money being matched by a donation of national-forest land (under the 1928 law), by small amounts contributed through the Save-the-Redwoods League and the Calaveras Grove Association, and by a million-dollar grant from John D. Rockefeller, Jr. A first exchange of sugar-

pine acreage (under the 1909 law) had taken place early in 1953; it was mentioned by John B. Oakes in his conservation column in the *Times*. On July 6, 1954, Oakes reported that the last of the Beaver Creek grove had been transferred to the Forest Service, which was to give it to the state for a "war memorial" park. In this column he gave credit to Elliott. —R.B.L.

CHAPTER EIGHTEEN

1. Most of the information on Drury is recorded in the letter that Ickes wrote to Governor Warren on April 2, 1951, opposing Drury's appointment. Ickes evidently sent a copy of his letter to John Elliott, who passed it on to Brant on April 5. But since Brant mentioned the contents of Ickes' letter in writing to Mrs. Edge on April 3, he probably heard the facts directly from Ickes. —R.B.L.

2. Another conservationist who promoted Udall's appointment was David Brower, executive director of the Sierra Club. —R.B.D.

3. In 1978 Congress passed bills sponsored by Oregon senator Bob Packwood and Congressman Jim Weaver of the Eugene area, restoring French Pete Creek and neighboring valleys to the Three Sisters Wilderness. —R.B.L.

FOR FURTHER RESEARCH

UNPUBLISHED SOURCES

The *Irving N. Brant* papers are held by the Library of Congress. In bulk, the papers occupy twenty-four feet of shelving and include approximately thirty-seven thousand items. They cover the years 1910 to 1977, with most of the material concentrated between 1926 and 1975. The collection includes correspondence, speeches, research notes and manuscripts. Seven of sixty-four containers are filled with Brant's Conservation Papers. The Franklin D. Roosevelt Library at Hyde Park holds a microfilm copy of the Conservation Papers, as does the University of Washington Library.

The *Irving M. Clark* papers are held by the University of Washington; they occupy about three feet of shelving. The material covers the years 1934 to 1960.

The *Rosalie Edge* papers are held by the Denver Public Library; they cover the years from 1925 to 1955. The most complete collection of Emergency Conservation Committee publications is included in the Edge papers; a similar collection is being acquired by the University of Washington Library.

The papers of *Harold Ickes* are held by the Library of Congress and consist of approximately 117,000 items for the years 1911 to 1946.

Material on the history of Olympic National Park appears in "Olympic Battleground," by Carsten Lien (manuscript in preparation).

The *Franklin D. Roosevelt* papers are held by the Franklin D. Roosevelt

Library, Hyde Park, New York. A calendar of Roosevelt's conservation documents is available on microfilm; approximately one-third of the total has been published in *Franklin D. Roosevelt and Conservation, 1911-1945*, compiled by Edgar B. Nixon (1957, 2 vols.)

The records of the U.S. Forest Service and National Park Service are held by the National Archives and its regional records centers. *North American Forest History: A Guide to Archives and Manuscripts in the United States and Canada*, compiled by Richard C. Davis, offers easy access to these enormous collections.

PUBLISHED SOURCES

Buchheister, Carl W., and Frank Graham, Jr. "From the Swamps and Back: A Concise and Candid History of the Audubon Movement." *Audubon* 75 (Jan. 1973), 4–45.

Engbeck, Joseph H., Jr. *The Enduring Giants: The Giant Sequoias, Their Place in Evolution and in the Sierra Nevada Forest Community.* Berkeley: University Extension, University of California, 1973. This contains a history of the Calaveras sequoia groves.

Farquhar, Francis P. *Yosemite, the Big Trees and the High Sierra: A Selective Bibliography.* Berkeley: University of California Press, 1948.

Fox, Stephen. *John Muir and His Legacy: The American Conservation Movement.* Boston: Little, Brown, 1981.

Ickes, Harold L. *The Autobiography of a Curmudgeon.* New York: Reynal and Hitchcock, 1943.

————. *The Secret Diary of Harold L. Ickes.* 3 vols. New York: Simon and Schuster, 1953–54.

Richardson, Elmo R. "Olympic National Park: Twenty Years of Controversy." *Forest History* 12 (April 1968): 6–15.

Saylor, David J. *Jackson Hole, Wyoming: In the Shadow of the Tetons.* Norman: University of Nebraska Press, 1970.

Strong, Douglas H. *Trees—or Timber? The Story of Sequoia and Kings Canyon National Parks.* Three Rivers, Cal.: Sequoia Natural History Association, 1968.

Twight Ben W. *Organizational Values and Political Power: The Forest Service Versus the Olympic National Park.* University Park: Pennsylvania State University Press, 1983.

INDEX

free-lance writing, 5
government work, 97, 116–17, 172, 211,
220, 221, 315–17
offered or rumored work, 115–16, 134,
268, 271, 273–74
pamphlets: on Calaveras, 262–63, 266
on Kings Canyon, 157, 159, 163,
166–68, 197
on Olympics, 71, 82, 91, 93, 98–99
on waterfowl, 18–19, 20, 25–27, 28,
41–43, 49, 51–52, 134
speech writing, etc.: for Ickes, 105–106,
124, 143, 154, 168–69, 171–72, 328
Ch.8 n1, Ch.9 n2
for Roosevelt, 143, 221, 256
for Truman, 312
testimony, 10, 12–13, 23, 39–40,
229–30, 307–308, 318
Brant-Tomlinson line, 132–33, 136
Brass hats, 233
British Columbia, 5, 86, 237, 277, 280
Brower, David, 330 Ch.18 n2
Bruckart, John R., 125, 326 Ch.5 n3
Bruette, William A., 2, 4, 8, 10–12, 13,
15, 17–18, 23, 43
Brundage, F. H., 235
Buck, Clarence J., 87, 88–89, 98, 109–10,
125, 126, 132, 139–40, 142, 265, 326
Ch.5 n3
Buckingham, Nash, 9
Buckman (of California Mountaineers), 157
Budget, Bureau of the, 57, 68, 102,
201–202, 206, 220, 228, 230, 238–41,
242, 246, 311
Bureau . . . *See* under next major word
Burlew, Ebert K., 103, 113, 140–41
Burnham, John, 2, 5, 6
Butler, Ovid, 24, 56, 170, 190, 191, 198,
199, 236

Cain, Harry P., 278–79
Calaveras Act of 1928, 261, 262, 264, 266,
288, 291, 294, 296, 298–99, 300,
301, 302
Calaveras Bigtree Act of 1909, 288–92,
294, 296, 297, 298, 300, 301–302,
303, 304
Calaveras County, 287
Calaveras Grove Association, 287,
298–300, 302, 329–30 Ch.17 nn2,3
Calaveras groves (including South Grove),
261–68, 269, 272–74, 280, 284,
287–96, 298–304, 329–30 Ch.17 n3.

See also Beaver Creek grove; Olmsted
report
income loss, 291–92
North Grove, 261, 262, 263, 266, 273,
280, 296
Calawah River and valley, 196, 235, 278,
280, 281–82, 285
California Mountaineers, 156, 158, 167,
214–15
California State Chamber of Commerce,
62, 158, 168, 170–71, 183, 184, 186,
214
its branches, 65, 152, 169–70
California State Legislature, 171–72, 269
Legislative Assembly, 302
Senate, 162, 181
California State Park Commission, 272,
293–94, 298, 300, 301, 302, 303
California State Senate, 162, 181
California War Memorial Park Association,
287, 296, 299, 302, 303
Calkins, A. A., 297
Camalier, Raoul, 213, 214
Cammerer, Arno B., 65, 89, 97, 98, 99,
100, 115–16, 30, 137, 139, 224
Campfire Club of America, 9, 13, 27
Carl Inn Grove, 55–68, 73, 75, 199, 234,
263
tax loss, 56, 63, 65, 66
Cary, Robert, 246
Case, Otto A., 236
Catton, Bruce, 238
Cedar Grove, 150, 151, 153–54, 155–56,
160, 162–63, 166, 169, 194, 199–200,
205, 208
Cedar Grove and Tehipite (dam sites), 148,
151, 153–55, 158, 160, 166–67, 170,
187, 189–90, 192, 195, 198, 199,
206–208, 210, 211, 212, 213, 214,
216, 329 Ch.12 n1
Central Valley Project, 181
Chapman, Frank M., 13, 21
Chapman, Oscar L., 282, 307–310, 311
Chicago Sun, 233, 243, 248, 267–68, 269
Chorley, Kenneth, 258, 270
Christian Science Monitor, 59, 78, 97, 158
Clark, Irving, 72, 77, 78, 87–88, 91, 97,
98, 107, 115, 125, 130–32, 135, 137,
141, 142, 171, 198, 235, 236–37, 278,
320, 326 Ch.5 n2, 327 Ch.7 n2
Clarke, John D., 10, 12
Clayton, Joshua, 27

Echo Park. *See* Dinosaur N.M., and dams
Ecological cycle, 77, 93, 96, 120, 282
Edge, Rosalie, 15–17, 41, 45, 52, 310,
   319–320, 327 Ch.6 n1
  and Audubon Society, 15, 19, 21–22
  and Calaveras, 262, 274, 290
  and Carl Inn, 56, 61, 66
  and Darling, 46
  and eagles, 49, 210–11
  and Ickes, 63–64, 191, 225, 236, 242
  and Jackson Hole, 270–71
  and Kings Canyon, 170, 179, 191, 195,
   197, 209, 213, 219, 224
  and Olympics, 72, 76, 77, 78, 82, 93,
   97, 103–104, 115, 130, 278, 284, 285
  and Porcupine Mtn., 229, 230
  and predators, 17, 28
  and Schulz, 58–60, 61, 329 Ch.13 n1
  and trumpeter swans, 232–33
  and Van Name, 15, 56, 59–60, 82, 158,
   241
Eicher, Edward C., 63, 106
Eisenhower, Dwight D., 311, 313
Electric power interests. *See* Private power
  interests
Elk. *See also* Olympic Range Elk Reserve
  in Yellowstone, 23, 245–46, 249–50,
   272
  Roosevelt elk, 71, 72, 75, 90, 99, 108,
   118, 121, 133
Elliott (of California Mountaineers), 157
Elliott, Alfred J., 159, 176–78, 179, 182,
   183, 184, 185, 186, 188–89, 193–94,
   198, 200, 201–202, 203–205, 211, 269
Elliott, John B., 287–88, 293, 294,
  295–96, 302, 303–304, 329–30 Ch.17 n3
Ellis, Clyde T., 207
Elwha River and valley, 123, 326 Ch.5 n3
Emergency Conservation Committee,
   15–17, 21–22, 27, 28, 39, 41, 46, 49,
   59, 60, 62, 71, 82, 91, 153, 157, 166,
   191, 195, 204–205, 208, 229, 230,
   233, 241, 254, 262, 273, 278, 284,
   285, 287, 319–20
Emerson, Frank C., 23
Engle, Clair, 268, 269, 273, 290, 292,
   295, 296, 313
Engle, Rosamond P., 312
Englebright, Harry L., 63, 65–66, 68,
   106, 177, 180, 181, 182, 184, 185, 195,
   198, 207, 211, 264–65, 266, 268
Ennes Creek valley, 231
Environmental Defense Fund, 320

Environmental Policy Act, National, 320
Everglades National Park, 30
Exchange of federal lands, 74, 80, 169,
   220
  in Calaveras, 262–63, 264–67, 285,
   288–90, 290–92, 294, 298–99, 300,
   301, 303–304, 329–30 Ch.17 n3
  in Carl Inn, 56
  in Olympics, 86, 120–21, 144, 237,
   265–66, 285, 310

Farley, James A., 33–34
Farr, Dexter, 247
Fauver, James, 171
Federal Bureau of Investigation, 204
Federal Power Commission, 24, 179,
   186–87, 200–203
Federation of Western Outdoor Clubs, 287
Federation of Women's Clubs (Seattle),
   105, 132
Feldman, Meyer, 313
Field (engineer), 200
Filberg, Robert, 237
Fish and Wildlife Service, 116, 134, 232,
   241. *See also* Biological Survey (before
   June, 1940)
Fishing: in Olympics, 121–122
  in Kings Canyon, 177, 220
Fishing, commercial, 18
Fletcher, John (California state senator) and
   Fletcher amendment, 161–62, 215
Fletcher, John (Olympics rancher), 221–22
Fletcher, Lena Huelsdonk (Mrs. Fred), 222
Foote, James A., 190–91, 199
Foran, Arthur, 38
Ford, Mrs. Bruce (Sophie), 97
Forest and Stream, 2, 15, 17, 23
Forest fires: in Glacier N.P., 176
  in Olympics, 119, 131
Forest Service, 8, 142, 154–55, 201, 205,
   220–21, 273, 318–19 *See also* Brannan,
   C.F.; Buck, C.J.; Exchange of federal
   land; Government reorganization;
   Price, J.H.; Roosevelt, F.D., and
   Forest Service; Silcox, Ferdinand;
   Thompson, P.A.; Wallace, H.A., and
   Forest Service; Watts, Lyle
  and Calaveras, 262–67, 273, 288,
   290–95, 296–97, 298–303, 329–30
   Ch.17 n3
  and Carl Inn, 56–57, 64–65
  and French Pete, 319
  and Jackson Hole, 245–46, 258, 270–71